Critical theory and demagogic populism

Manchester University Press

Critical theory and contemporary society

Series editors:
David M. Berry, Professor of Digital Humanities, University of Sussex

Darrow Schecter, Professor of Critical Theory and Modern European History, University of Sussex

The *Critical Theory and Contemporary Society* series aims to demonstrate the ongoing relevance of multi-disciplinary research in explaining the causes of pressing social problems today and in indicating the possible paths towards a libertarian transformation of twenty-first century society. It builds upon some of the main ideas of first generation critical theorists, including Horkheimer, Adorno, Benjamin, Marcuse and Fromm, but it does not aim to provide systematic guides to the work of those thinkers. Rather, each volume focuses on ways of thinking about the political dimensions of a particular topic, which include political economy, law, popular culture, globalization, feminism, theology and terrorism. Authors are encouraged to build on the legacy of first generation Frankfurt School theorists and their influences (Kant, Hegel, Kierkegaard, Marx, Nietzsche, Weber and Freud) in a manner that is distinct from, though not necessarily hostile to, the broad lines of second-generation critical theory. The series sets ambitious theoretical standards, aiming to engage and challenge an interdisciplinary readership of students and scholars across political theory, philosophy, sociology, history, media studies and literary studies.

Previously published by Bloomsbury

Critical theory in the twenty-first century Darrow Schecter
Critical theory and the critique of political economy Werner Bonefeld
Critical theory and contemporary Europe William Outhwaite
Critical theory of legal revolutions Hauke Brunkhorst
Critical theory of libertarian socialism Charles Masquelier
Critical theory and film Fabio Vighi
Critical theory and the digital David Berry
Critical theory and disability Teodor Mladenov
Critical theory and the crisis of contemporary capitalism Heiko Feldner and Fabio Vighi

Previously published by Manchester University Press

Critical theory and epistemology Anastasia Marinopoulou
Critical theory and feeling Simon Mussell
Critical theory and legal autopoiesis Gunther Teubner
Critical theory and sociological theory Darrow Schecter

Forthcoming from Manchester University Press

Critical theory and contemporary technology Ben Roberts

Critical theory and demagogic populism

PAUL K. JONES

Manchester University Press

Copyright © Paul K. Jones 2020

The right of Paul K. Jones to be identified as the author of this work has been asserted by him in accordance with the Copyright, Designs and Patents Act 1988.

Published by Manchester University Press
Oxford Road, Manchester M13 9PL
www.manchesteruniversitypress.co.uk

Introduction to Leo Lowenthal and Norbert Guterman: *Prophets of Deceit. A Study of the Techniques of the American Agitator* (Harper & Brothers, 1949) © Theodor-W. Adorno-Estate. Reprinted by kind permission of Suhrkamp Verlag Berlin.

British Library Cataloguing-in-Publication Data
A catalogue record for this book is available from the British Library

ISBN 978 1 5261 2343 5 hardback
ISBN 978 1 5261 6373 8 paperback

First published 2020
Paperback published 2022

The publisher has no responsibility for the persistence or accuracy of URLs for any external or third-party internet websites referred to in this book, and does not guarantee that any content on such websites is, or will remain, accurate or appropriate.

Typeset by
New Best-set Typesetters Ltd

In memory of
György Márkus (1934–2016)
and
Andrew Goodwin (1956–2013)

Figures and table

Figures

1. An initial distinction 35
2. Psychotechnics of modern demagogy 51
3. Some contingent pathways in populist politics and demagogic leadership 86
4. Freud's diagram of libidinal constitution of groups. Source: Freud, Sigmund. *Group Psychology and the Analysis of the Ego*. Translated by James Strachey (London: The International Psychoanalytical Press, 1922), 80. 123
5. First still from writers' room scene, *A Face in the Crowd* 183
6. Second still from writers' room scene, *A Face in the Crowd* 184

Table

1. Worsley's ideal-typical 'populist principles' drawn from Shils 12

8 Structural transformations of demagogic populism 205
   (a) Towards a conclusion: mediated physiognomics and demagogic populism 205
   (b) A disintegrating public sphere? 207
   (c) Structural transformation of 'social structures' and institutions of the public sphere 209
   (d) The dialectic of contradictory institutionalization and demagogic populism 213
   (e) The return of the repressed? 217

Appendix: Adorno, Theodor W. 'Introduction to *Prophets of Deceit*' (1949, previously unpublished) 231

Bibliography 245
Index 269

4 Gramscian analyses of fascism and populism: Poulantzas, Laclau, Hall 92
   (a) Gramsci's legacy: a brief sketch 93
   (b) Laclau and Poulantzas on fascism and populism 97
   (c) Laclau's formalist reading of Worsley 102
   (d) Hall's 'authoritarian populism' and other challenges to Laclauian hyperformalism 108
5 Towards a synthesis of critical perspectives 119
   (a) Adorno contra Laclau on Freud's *Group Psychology* 121
   (b) A Poulantzian mediation 128
   (c) Towards a social-formalist synthesis 132

Part II Populist contradictions of the culture industry

6 Cultural populisms and culture industry 145
   (a) From *Volk* to culture industry 145
   (b) 'Mass culture' and the attribution of 'cultural elitism' to the culture industry thesis 150
   (c) Cultural populism: deepening the concept 153
   (d) From cultural populism to 'popular arts' 159
   (e) Popular arts and 'contestation' 162
7 Counter-demagogic popular art: towards a selective tradition 175
   (a) *Below the Surface* 175
   (b) *A Face in the Crowd*: the paradigmatic case 178
   (c) Left-demagogy and counter-demagogic popular art 186
   (d) Successful liberal exposure: Murrow's 'slaying' of the McCarthyist dragon and its aesthetic legacy 191
Excursus: an outline of Trumpian psychotechnics 200

Contents

List of figures and tables   x
Acknowledgements   xi

Part I Critically theorizing demagogic populism

1 Introduction: from orthodox 'populism studies' to critical theory   3
  (a) An enduring orthodox dilemma: contesting 'populism' and 'radical right'   4
  (b) The Radical Right project: enter the demagogue   7
  (c) Towards modern demagogy and demagogic populism: plan of the book   16

2 The Institute's analysis of 'modern demagogy'   25
  (a) From 'authoritarian(ism)' to 'modern demagogy'   25
  (b) Demagogic devices, their social psychology, and populism   36
  (c) Psychotechnics: the modern demagogue as cultural producer   47

3 Expanding the reach of the Institute's analysis   62
  (a) The problem of 'modern' populism and demagogy   62
  (b) From 'Weberian Marxism' to ideal-typification   70
  (c) The state capitalism thesis as 'negative' ideal-type   73
  (d) Ideal-type and physiognomy   77
  (e) Towards a critical-theoretical comparativist typology   81

Acknowledgements

Research for this book was undertaken over some years. I received valuable collegial comment on papers based on draft material delivered at: The Institute of Communications Studies, University of Leeds; The Yale Center for Cultural Sociology; UNSW Sociology; ANU Sociology; Macquarie University Sociology and the memorial colloquium for György Márkus at the University of Sydney. My thanks too to the ANU Critical Theory Reading Group. Sections of Chapters 1 and 8 were previously published in articles in *The European Journal of Social Theory* and *The Australasian Journal of American Studies*.

Special thanks to Martin Jay for hosting and encouraging me at Berkeley at an early stage of the research. Jack Jacobs kindly and fulsomely confirmed the provenance of the unpublished Adorno text I came across in the Lowenthal archive (included as an appendix to this book).

Conversations with colleagues and friends over the years provided valuable assistance in the writing (apologies for oversights): Jeffrey Alexander, Georgina Born, Manuel Clemens, Melinda Cooper, John Corner, Laura Fisher, David Hesmondhalgh, David Inglis, Ron Jacobs, Oliver Kozlarek, Paolo Mancini, Chris Rojek, Larry Saha, Phil Smith, Nadia Urbinati, Johannes von Miltke and Judy Wajcman. Michael Symonds provided meticulous feedback on each chapter as it emerged and expert advice on Max Weber. Pauline Johnson was a regular dialogue partner as we each navigated the minefield that is 'populism studies'. Many of the ideas in this book were first ventilated in teaching, so my thanks to my students too. All errors of course are my own.

Everyone at Manchester was highly supportive throughout: Alun Richards, Caroline Wintersgill (who commissioned the book), Tom Dark and the academic series editors, Darrow Schecter and David Berry. My thanks too to the anonymous readers Manchester University Press organised, and to Beverley Winkler for indexing.

I cannot imagine having completed this project without the love and care of my partner, Catherine Waldby.

This book is dedicated to the memory of two departed colleagues: György Márkus, an exemplary critical theorist who introduced me to that tradition as an ongoing project, and Andrew Goodwin, an inspiring fellow traveller at the interface of critical theory and the critique of 'popular art'.

Canberra (obscured by apocalyptic smoke) PKJ
January 2020

Part I

Critically theorizing demagogic populism

1

Introduction: from orthodox 'populism studies' to critical theory

As I was completing the manuscript for this book a marketing email arrived from Verso Press. It was headed, 'Populism: how can we define it?' That the publisher of Laclau and Mouffe, among others, *still* considers this the central appeal of publications on populism is indicative of a wider problem in the field of 'populism studies'. Indeed, it was Laclau who pointed to the endlessly self-reproductive form of this intellectual dilemma of classification. Its broad contours are now well-known: populism can be 'left 'or 'right'; it lacks an articulated 'ideology'. In short, it is not a proper 'object' for orthodox political science.

There is little doubt that that self-reproducing dilemma is still alive and well. Populism studies as a field is usually traced to a 1968 conference at the London School of Economics. It led to the publication of an anthology of national/regional case studies and theoretical papers the following year. Less noted is the fact that sociologists played a prominent organizational role in this enterprise. The book's conclusion, 'The Concept of Populism', was written by another sociologist, Peter Worsley. While it is well-cited fifty years later, its critical dimensions are usually neglected.[1]

Worsley explicitly warned against the standard methodological approach of such nation-mapping anthologizations: attempts at post-hoc inductivist 'generalities' across these multiple studies which inevitably fail to achieve their goal. He might also have warned against the other inductivist tendency to which even his own essay became subject, the cherry-picking of fragments of conceptual argument for 'operationalization' in order to conduct ... nation by nation comparative surveys. Had Worsley's advice been heeded at the onset of the current populist surge, which is usually dated from the late 1980s, we might have seen fewer such anthologies.[2] Instead there has been a deluge and, equally predictably, all open with acknowledgements that the 'classification dilemma' concerning populism continues as if it were still 1969. Of course, this is not the only mode of published research in this field, but it is fair to say it is hegemonic.[3]

First, it is worth stressing the disciplinary dimension of this problem. Whereas sociologists were heavily involved in that foundational period of populism research, the recent wave is almost the exclusive domain of political scientists and political theorists. This is partly due to the form in which the 'new' populist surge first achieved recognition in the academy: the *electoral* success of populist political parties and presidential contenders in European 'established democracies'. Populism appeared to have 'spread' from the Third World, a term Worsley popularized, to what used to be called the First.[4] However, there are interdisciplinary rivalries within the field.

This introductory chapter briefly situates the 'classification dilemma' in orthodox populism studies and the recent tension over the status of 'radical right' within this literature. It then turns to the 'original' Radical Right project and its debts to the US-resident Frankfurt School. Finally, the structure of the rest of the book is outlined.

(a) An enduring orthodox dilemma: contesting 'populism' and 'radical right'

While the 'classification dilemma' in comparativist populism studies is vulnerable to Worsley's warnings, this does not mean that its focus on attempting adequate conceptualization is simply wrong. Similar concerns to Worsley's were raised almost simultaneously within political science by Giovanni Sartori. One of his key warnings concerns 'conceptual stretching'. By this he means the unwarranted overextension in application of a signifier to the point where it loses effective specificity. The result is not 'a more general concept' but 'its counterfeit, a mere generality'. Understandably, Sartori's principles of appropriate concept development have been invoked in the populism literature.[5]

For 'populism' is surely such a case of overextension. Social movements, parties and leaders from distinct nations, regions and historical periods can all fall within 'populism'. No wonder empirical researchers find themselves referring to quite distinct phenomena – for example electoral results in France

INTRODUCTION

and a social movement in Latin America – with the same 'generality'. This too was what Worsley had foretold as a risk for the field. Attempts to redress this problem with 'minimal definitions' have so emerged. These tend to be tied to the short-term goal of 'operationalization', i.e. formulations that can be plausibly measured, usually by analysis of electoral results.

Perhaps the most influential of these minimalist definitions was published by one of the most central figures in the field, Cas Mudde, in 2004: a ('thin') 'ideology that considers society to be ultimately separated into two homogeneous and antagonistic groups, "the pure people" versus "the corrupt elite", and which argues that politics should be an expression of the volonté générale (general will) of the people'.[6] As we shall see, a richer version of this same twofold configuration was developed by Worsley thirty-five years earlier.

Mudde has made clear in his subsequent prolific work that his focus has been the classification of the rising, predominantly European, political parties and 'party families' broadly identified as populist. Such taxonomies were certainly another of Sartori's interests.[7] Indeed, empirical 'party-centrism' is a core feature of the hegemonic political science literature on populism. Mudde's earliest work addressed 'extreme right' parties and he subsequently sought to distinguish his position from that of Hans-Georg Betz, one of the first to analyse the rise of parties associated with the populist surge.

Betz's analysis was also initially Europe-focused but used the category of 'radical right-wing' instead. Although quite party-centric, it was also more sociologically grounded, having developed from a recognition of parallels between emerging right-wing populists and the Green new social movement in West Germany. His work thus shares much with the rare sociological contributions to this literature that emphasize this social-movement-like 'mobilization' dimension.[8] Betz further located the rise of these parties within structural socio-political features of European nations and the European union: the decline of the welfare state and 'organized capitalism'; the decline of traditional (class-based) electoral loyalties; rising mistrust of 'the political class' and rising xenophobia. With especially the last of these features, it is the related 'mobilization of resentment' that Betz highlights as a key populist practice: 'their unscrupulous use and instrumentalization of diffuse public sentiments of anxiety and disenchantment'.[9]

Mudde advances 'populist radical right' as a classificatory category superior to Betz's 'radical right-wing populist'. At stake for him is the 'ideology' of these groups and, in particular, how to assess the relative weighting within these of positions such as neoliberalism, liberalism, nationalism, nativism and authoritarianism. Such assessment can then be checked against not only electoral results but attitudinal surveys of ideological affiliation.[10]

Further, he places Betz at the head of a tradition of recent analysts who subscribe to a 'normal pathology' thesis. By this Mudde means the defining of the radical right as 'outside' the bounds of 'normal' politics by social psychological explanation like Betz's use of *resentment*, and overarching accounts of structural change and/or crisis. In effect, Mudde accuses radical right theorists of conflating 'extremism' and 'radical right'. For Mudde, extremism is opposed to democracy *in toto* while 'radical' positions are anti-liberal but still accept a minimalist understanding of democracy as election-based procedure. Mudde's populist radical right here coincides with contemporary understandings of 'illiberal', often applied to figures like Viktor Orbán in Hungary.[11]

Mudde proposes instead a 'paradigm shift' to 'pathological normalcy' that would acknowledge that populist radical right parties are 'well connected to mainstream ideas and much in tune with broadly shared mass attitudes and policy positions', albeit via radicalization of this mainstream.[12] If there were any doubts that Mudde's paradigm shift is intended to purge populism studies of all social-theoretical and social psychological contamination, this 'profound consequence' is announced: 'First and foremost, it means that the populist radical right should be studied on the basis of concepts and theories of mainstream political science.'[13]

Mudde's positivist prioritization so misses a core feature of Betz's work: its attempt to capture the *dynamic* interplay between structural change, nation-specific developments, social movements, 'mobilization' and the 'instrumentalizing' strategies of these parties. Betz recognizes something that seems to elude Mudde's somewhat static taxonomization: that the 'ideologies' of these parties are better understood as shifting contradictory mixtures than the 'thin' ideology of Mudde's minimum definition above. Orbán's Fidesz party in Hungary, for example, started with a repertoire very different from its later illiberal antisemitism. As we shall see in later chapters, addressing this 'ideological content' issue conceptually requires neither the semiotic arbitrariness advocated by Laclau, nor the taxonomic purism attempted by Mudde.

Contra Mudde, a 'normal pathology' paradigm was already in place in populism studies but it was not a product of sociological contamination. Rather, as Urbinati pointed out in 1998, the USA's populist tradition appeared 'good' while Europe's appeared 'bad'. The USA still held the promise of a populist tradition that might function as a democratic corrective of social inequality, as had some nineteenth-century radical-populist movements in Europe. So, notwithstanding that empirical emphasis on Europe, it was rare for the proliferating anthologies to 'problematize' the US case even when Europe was not the sole focus. Mudde himself co-edited a collection in 2012 addressing 'Populism in Europe and the Americas' that did not include a chapter on the USA. The normalizing US case became present in its absence.[14]

It is not accidental, then, that Mudde traces the fault he sees in 'radical right' frameworks to the 'original' project that employed that term. For that project broke with the heroic view of the US populist tradition and sought to highlight its susceptibility to demagogic leadership.

(b) The Radical Right project: enter the demagogue

What I term 'the Radical Right project' began as a 1954 symposium analysing McCarthyism that was organized by Daniel Bell. It featured other prominent sociological figures within the New York Intellectuals such as Seymour Lipset and, most controversially, the historian, Richard Hofstadter. Most contributors regarded Senator Joseph McCarthy as a demagogue. A collection of essays, entitled *The New American Right* in its first edition and subsequently *The Radical Right*, was published the following year.[15]

Also in 1955, Hofstadter's *The Age of Reform: Bryan to FDR* had challenged an orthodoxy that regarded the USA's 'producerist' 1890s Populist movement as the heroic forerunner of twentieth-century Progressivism, so contributing to a 'Progressive faith in *the people*'.[16] Hofstadter sought to acknowledge US Populism's 'zany fringes' as well, including its tendencies towards conspiracy theorization and antisemitism in its portrayal of Eastern plutocrats. Critical response in the discipline of history was swift and hostile. As with Mudde's more recent critique of later radical right approaches, such criticism was in part directed at the importation of concepts from sociology and social psychology. 'The Hofstadter controversy' remains a continuing reference point in US historiography. *The Age of Reform* has recently been invoked in contemporary populism studies as an 'infamous' text.[17]

The anti-Hofstadter polemic and its insistence on the benign character of US Populism had initially 'crossed over' from the discipline of history into populism studies via Canovan's canonical 1981 overview of the field. She uncritically adopts the anti-Hofstadter historians' perspective and glosses the Radical Right project as 'these attempts to tar the Populists of the 1890s with the McCarthyite brush'. Her influential 1999 article at the beginning of the current phase of populism studies anticipates Mudde's disciplinary line-drawing by setting itself against approaches that view populist movements 'as pathological symptoms requiring sociological explanation'.[18]

The anti-Hofstadter polemic has been sustained through to the present by Michael Kazin, probably the best-known authority on domestic US populism, especially outside the USA. Both Mudde and Laclau defer to his expertise. Kazin's *The Populist Persuasion: An American History* is ostensibly 'firmly equivocal' about its subject. However, it makes an explicit case for US populism's non-extremist exceptionalism and thus its likely necessary role in achieving its author's progressive vision. Yet it launches an unequivocal attack on Hofstadter and his fellow researchers under the heading, 'The Great Liberal Fear'. On Kazin's own hyperbolic account, this fear was based in a false portrait of 'the initial Populists' as 'irrational bigots' which led to casting 'a disapproving glance over the whole enterprise of mobilization for anti-establishment ends, to brand as populist any prejudices held by large numbers of Americans'. Indeed, it seems almost impossible, even in the context of the 2016 presidential election, for Kazin to briefly discuss the contemporary legacy of US populism without rehearsing the terms of this 60-year-old controversy. Kazin insists that all *critical* invocations of the concepts of populism and demagogy should be rejected as they necessarily operate at the level of journalistic parlance and overlook legitimate popular grievances.[19]

The Radical Right project made no such claims. Hofstadter explicitly warns against exaggerating the intensity of Populist antisemitism and stresses 'it did not lead to exclusion laws, much less to riots or pogroms'. Rather, the legacy was 'a peculiarly persistent linkage between antisemitism and money and credit obsessions'. Here Hofstadter cites a 1944 essay by Bell in which he acknowledges the radical import of the 1890s Populists and then tracks in considerable detail a succession of subsequent demagogues. These 'terrible simplifiers', Bell states, practised 'a grotesque transformation of an originally progressive idea' based in the 1890s grievances with the result that '(t)he populist tradition ... has shrunk and become twisted into a reactionary form' with decidedly fascist potential.[20]

Two key figures here were Huey Long and Father Charles Coughlin, the 'radio priest'. Each has been classified as both populist and demagogue. Both rose to prominence in the late 1920s. Coughlin gathered a vast audience as his on-air addresses became increasingly political, treading a path between anti-capitalism, especially focusing on the role of international banking interests, and anti-communism. By 1930 he was networked by CBS and by the mid-1930s his regular radio audience was conservatively estimated at ten million and claimed to be the largest in the world. By 1938 he was overtly fascist and succeeded in fostering a Franco-like paramilitary 'Christian Front' organization, so meeting one of Mann's criteria for distinguishing fascist movements.[21]

Huey Long (1893–1935) was governor of Louisiana and a federal senator. He assembled a powerful coalition of social groups in one of the most economically polarized sections of the country during the Great Depression. His programme was a decidedly left-populist one, committed to educational expansion and public infrastructure while relentlessly attacking 'elite' interests such as Standard Oil. While Long was not known for employing xenophobia, one of his lieutenants who led his Share Our Wealth movement had such involvements. Long sought to 'over-win' once he had state power and used his corrupt networks to maintain de facto governorship of Louisiana while in the US Senate.[22] He established his own state-run newspaper by tithing state employees and requiring state police to distribute it. He too was an 'early adopter' of new means of communication, including radio, on which he considered himself the most effective orator.[23] Long was considering a presidential challenge in 1936, possibly as a third-party candidate. However, he was assassinated in 1935.

Like Long, Coughlin's ostensible political position, following initial support, was to the left of Roosevelt's New Deal. He had considered supporting Long's challenge to FDR. With Long assassinated, Coughlin supported a lacklustre presidential candidate in 1936 who performed well below Coughlin's predicted 10 per cent of the vote. Kazin advances the view that it is only at this point that Coughlin resorted to a virulent antisemitism as 'a more sensational issue on which to attempt to incite a rising of the people'. He assesses Coughlin's political trajectory in the same quasi-strategic terms such that 'Coughlin's antisemitism was a populism of fools'.[24] As Kazin partly acknowledges, Coughlin employed antisemitism in his speeches well before 1936. He rightly sources Coughlin's 'social justice' nomenclature and framework to papal encyclicals but is curiously reluctant to acknowledge Coughlin's debt to the 1890s Populists – most notably his campaign for 'free silver' – which was even more substantial according to most experts on Coughlin.[25]

None of this historical background led the Radical Right project to claim that there was a necessary connection between such demagogues and populist movements. Instead, they sought to theorize the determinants of such demagogic capture.

Hofstadter and his sociological colleagues engaged in a decade-long public development of a 'speculative hypothesis' concerning the social psychological dimensions of movements of the political right from 1955 to 1962, initially focused on McCarthyism. This body of work was not readily compatible with either the inductivist-empiricism of orthodox historiography or orthodox political science. *The New American Right* was a 'thesis book' that did not aim to present 'a total view'.[26] Any critical engagement that interpreted it through a narrower lens was likely to be, unwittingly or not, partial. Moreover, the whole project understood itself to be anti-orthodox. As Bell later put it in situating the project against two still-dominant orthodoxies, 'One thing soon became clear: ... the standard explanations of American political behaviour

– in terms of economic-interest-group conflict or the role of the electoral structure – were inadequate to the task.'[27] Indeed, much of the critical hostility towards the social psychological dimensions of this project relied on an understanding of political action as necessarily rationally motivated by economic interests.

The focus of the Radical Right project was on a shift in conservative politics to a 'pseudo-conservatism' that was argued to be qualitatively new. Pseudo-conservatives, inside and outside the Republican party, still saw themselves as conservatives, but were hostile to all or some democratic institutions and resentful towards targeted scapegoats. They sought to 'over-win'.

Initially, the organizing causal concept was 'status politics': forms of 'dissenting' political mobilization outside times of economic crisis that take a less overtly economic interest-based form. McCarthyism was plainly not a product of economic hard times and, as Bell emphasized, the elites McCarthy attacked were not the economic ones targeted by Huey Long but those composed of intellectuals and governmental figures.[28] Hofstadter's first theorization baldly announced itself as that 'speculative hypothesis': that 'pseudo-conservativism' was largely a product of the projection of status anxieties into the political realm. The USA's lack of a system of ascribed status, its social mobility and its increasing ethnic heterogeneity were regarded as preconditions here. Either rising or falling status could contingently contribute to members of certain social groups adopting pseudo-conservative positions. In the later edition Bell and Hofstadter shift towards replacing 'status politics' with 'cultural politics' where the latter becomes identified with 'moralism'.

While the provenance of 'status politics' was quasi-Weberian on Bell's later account, there is a further Weberian explanation in Bell for such moralism embedded within the status politics thesis. In his contribution to *The New American Right*, Bell briefly explores the exceptional features of US moralism. He cautiously adopts Ranulf's proposition that moral indignation is a product of repressed envy in middle-class psychology as a kind of fellow travelling variant of the status politics thesis. Bell rejects the view that the USA is best characterized as a case study of ascetic Puritanism whereby the regulation of conduct is a signal of piety. Rather, it is evangelicalism that takes a 'largely unique' US form. This is not merely because of the greater prominence of Methodism and Baptism. Bell refers here to what became known as the 'great awakenings' led by evangelical preachers in the Western frontiers from the early eighteenth century and which have recurred in different forms. Anticipating a fuller elaboration of an argument made by Hofstadter, Bell portrays these camp meetings as 'egalitarian and anti-intellectual' in their rejections of the formal liturgies of more orthodox churches. Again moving in parallel with

Hofstadter, he locates within this cultural context William Jennings Bryan, the leader of the 1890s Populists, as a 'religious as well as economic champion of the West'.[29]

Bell here stresses the historical contingency of a Bryan-like moralism's achieving such overtly political expression. Bell invokes US exceptionalism himself at this point: 'the United States has been able to escape the intense ideological fanaticism – the conflicts of clericalism and class – which has been so characteristic of Europe'.[30] However, he argues that a *reversal* is underway whereby '[w]hile we are becoming more relaxed in the area of traditional morals ... we are becoming moralistic and extreme in politics'. In *The Radical Right* it is Hofstadter, in his autocritique of 'status politics', who supplements the 'moral indignation' dimension of cultural politics with another 'projection': paranoia. Anticipating the fuller formulation of the 'paranoid style' thesis that was to become his most famous, Hofstadter argues that paranoia best characterizes the wilder conspiracies fostered by newer radical right groups like the John Birch Society. Employing a conception of the USA's 'populistically oriented political culture' (detailed below), he warns of the disproportionate effect such paranoid projections might achieve in the wider polity.[31]

The 'mature' schema of the New York Intellectuals' approach to populism can now be discerned. A paranoid radical right holds the capacity to exploit a 'populistic' political culture. That culture is losing its capacity for civility and compromise and is increasingly subject to the potentially fanatical moral indignation formerly confined to evangelical religious culture.

Of course, to suggest a connection between evangelicism and US conservatism hardly seems an innovation today; nor does the related conception of an emergent moralistic 'cultural politics'. Du Bois, for example, had pointed to the risk of demagogy for Baptist ministers as early as 1899.[32] But the Radical Right project had postulated a larger Weberian implication – that the evangelical tradition in the USA facilitates a *secular* form of moralistic fundamentalism.

Having made a case for a secularization of evangelical moral indignation, Bell leaves this figure of the 'secular evangelist' conceptually underdeveloped and the determinants of its expansion undertheorized. Only a few pages earlier he had commented of McCarthy: 'Calling him a demagogue explains little; the relevant questions are, to whom was he a demagogue, and about what.'[33] The Radical Right project became overly focused on the first of these questions. The statistically empirical dimensions, led by Lipset, were dedicated to a re-reading of electoral and polling data related to the constituencies of McCarthy and precursor figures like Coughlin, which in turn became the target of narrowed critiques by political scientists.[34]

As a consequence, the project tended not to distinguish between 'bottom-up' and 'top-down' movements. McCarthy's demagogic exploitation of populist thematics certainly garnered significant popular support – usually evidenced by poll results – but his was plainly a top-down demagogic mobilization that lacked even the clubs that formed around Long and Coughlin.

Likewise, there was no comparably detailed response to Bell's second 'relevant question' regarding demagogues. Nor was the concept of the demagogue sufficiently articulated with that of the secular evangelist. In the absence of such a formulation, the radical right project also risks a Sartorian 'overextension' of 'populism'. That term is often required to bear the conceptual burden of demagogy *as well as* referring to long-standing institutional features of the US 'democratic tradition'.

A more explicit account of US populism and demagogy came from the parallel work of Edward Shils, often considered a fellow traveller of the New York Intellectuals. He was also a translator of Weber and author of influential sociological works on charismatic leadership and tradition. Shils published his own monograph on McCarthyism in 1956, *The Torment of Secrecy*.[35] It is from this text that Worsley extracted his preferred ideal-typification of populism a decade later. This is presented as Table 1.

At first glance it appears identical to Mudde's twofold 'minimal definition' presented in section (a). However, on closer examination it can be seen to be richer. It is plainly not confined to a 'thin ideology'. Rather, it recognizes a 'cultural populist' dimension in its 'folkloric' framing of the particularity of the appeal to the supremacy of 'the will of the people'. Such cultural dimensions have also tended to be expunged in the recent political science orthodoxy. In the words of one much-cited primer on populism, such matters have 'little in common with more political uses of the term'.[36]

Table 1 Worsley's ideal-typical 'populist principles' drawn from Shils

Populist principle	Particular dimensions
(i) Supremacy of will of the people	– quasi-religious belief in virtues of uncorrupted, simple common folk – distrust of 'smart', 'over-educated', effete, supercilious, aristocratic, idle, wealthy, functionally unnecessary, degenerate and corrupt.
(ii) Desirability of unmediated direct relationship between people and leadership	– denial of autonomy to legislature or indeed any institution – resentment against order imposed by long-established ruling class which is believed to hold monopoly of power, property, breeding and culture.

Shils explicitly casts the relationship between populism and demagogy as one between a 'permeative tradition', the legacy of populism as popular movement, and charismatic leadership:

> Populism is not ... recalcitrant to leadership. Great spellbinders who would bring populists substantive justice are capable of moving them and bending them to their will. ...
>
> Populism acclaims the demagogue who, breaking through the formalistic barriers erected by lawyers, pedants and bureaucrats, renews the righteousness of government and society.[37]

This passage clearly alludes to the Weberian conception of charisma. For Weber, charismatic leadership is one of three modes of legitimate authority in which a 'charismatic bond' is formed between leader and follower, cast as a secularized form of religious charisma. More significantly, while charisma can be institutionalized via bureaucratic rationalization – as in the 'charisma of office' – charismatic leaders may also renew such institutions.[38] In Shils's re-rendering, the challenge to representative institutions and separation of powers is coexistent with charismatic renewal but it is the demagogue's populist claims to directness and substantive justice that renew 'righteousness'. Demagogic populism so becomes a threat rather than renewal. Consistent with the Radical Right research, Shils argues that the regions of strongest historical populist support have tended to produce charismatic leaders from 'spellbinders' like Bryan through to the demagogy of Coughlin and McCarthy.

Such a claimed tradition is, of course, exactly what infuriated Kazin. But Kazin's indignation relies on his own theoretically impoverished understanding of 'demagogue' as no more than a 'journalistic' synonym for racist agitator. If we instead understand it to mean a form of charismatic leadership, and an extreme form of Bell's secular evangelist, much changes. Where Kazin and Canovan see a retrospective besmirching of heroic populists as demagogues, the Radical Right project recognized, albeit falteringly, a change in leadership modes from charismatic moralism to demagogic secular evangelism.

Shils and Bell held to a somewhat Tocquevillian historical understanding of the USA's 'populistic culture' as having replaced its founding Madisonian precursors in the early nineteenth century. From that point, they argue, election campaigns increasingly resembled spectacles.[39] This perspective bears a striking resemblance to Weber's account – in his second vocation lecture – of the defeat of 'the notables' in leading political parties and the arrival of demagogic leadership. Weber discusses the rise in Britain of the '"grand" demagogy' of prime minister Gladstone and, earlier, that of Andrew

Jackson in the USA. In effect, Weber deployed this less pejorative conception of demagogue to examine matters that Shils and Bell termed a 'populistic culture'. Scholars have rightly also connected this dimension of Weber's work to his conception of charismatic authority, but is worth adding that his image of the demagogue in his other vocation lecture is closer to Bell's and Shils's pejorative usage.[40]

As we have seen, Worsley presciently warned that a coherent conceptual understanding of the populist phenomenon would not arise from inductive generalizations of perceived commonalities emerging from cross-national comparative studies. Only a 'higher level of abstraction' generating Weberian ideal-types could offer this perspective, which Worsley extracts from Shils.[41] This is not because the US case is seen as paradigmatic for Shils or Worsley, but rather because Shils decentres US populism as 'not just populism in its specific historical meaning, although that was an instance of the species'.[42]

While Worsley, a leading figure of the 'first' British New Left, saw no problem in employing the work of the more conservative Shils, the question of demagogy did lead Worsley to amend Shils's schema. For Worsley, the unmediated directness craved by populist discourse could be met by a 'genuine' popular social movement. Yet he concedes that 'pseudo-participation' achieved by demagogic leadership can also substitute for such 'genuineness'.

So, Worsley's own strategy becomes clearer if it is represented as a series of steps:

(i) The rejection of 'low-level' inductive generalization from cross-national comparative research of diversely understood 'populisms' as inadequate and the advocacy of ideal-typification instead
(ii) The adoption of Shils's account of populism as the basis of the advocated 'high-level' ideal-typification (Table 1)
(iii) The announcement of a *second* typology employing a distillation of the contents of Table 1 whereby:

> populism is better regarded as an emphasis, a dimension of political culture in general, not simply as a particular kind of overall ideological system or type of organization. Of course, as with all ideal-types, it may be closely approximated to [sic] by some political cultures and structures, such as those hitherto labelled 'populist'.

(iv) The decentring of Shils's role for demagogic leadership
(v) The sketching of that second typology as a 'continuum' of modes of populist practice in different political orders: 'from 'total non-involvement of the mass of the people at one end to the ideal self-regulating anarchist commune at the other'.[43]

INTRODUCTION

In many citations of Worsley, the quoted passage within his third step above tends to be hypostasized without acknowledging its immanent understanding of populism as the contents of Table 1 and/or acknowledging that it announces a second typologization. Laclau is perhaps the most prominent example here despite his own efforts at a fuller construction of a 'populist logic'.[44] Another would be recent tendencies to interpret populism as primarily a performative (mediated) 'political style'.[45] One likely reason for this cherry-picking is that Worsley's 'continuum' typology provides only the sketchiest indication of the 'variety of political cultures and structures' that align with his first ideal-typification.

Nonetheless, here at one of the foundational moments of populism studies was a programme of considerable social theoretical sophistication that prioritized the populism-demagogy connection. Yet there is little evidence of its ever being carried further. Unlike the party-centric orthodoxies within political science frameworks, its fuller typology aims to recognize the dynamic relationship between social movements, parties and demagogic leadership.

Remarkably, Worsley even schematizes a role for modern means of communication in creating 'pseudo-participation'. This factor was at most implicit in Bell's and Shils's accounts of a populistic US culture, although Shils later extended this thesis to argue that in comparable circumstances 'the availability of the media of mass communication is an invitation to their demagogic use'.[46] The shift in modes of charismatic leadership in the Radical Right project's accounts most commonly pivots on Coughlin, in part because his 'career' seems to straddle both the moral quasi-Populist 'spellbinder' and the overt antisemitic demagogue. Prior movements comparable to Coughlin's explicitly fascist phase – even the most extreme, such as the pogrom-like murders by the Ku Klux Klan – were regionally confined, as was Coughlin's strongest support.[47] What the Radical Right project did not address was nationwide broadcasting systems' capacity to transcend such regional limitation. As noted, both Coughlin and Long were communicative innovators. Indeed, Coughlin pioneered the broadcast commodification of such demagogy. *Coughlin is the prototypical modern demagogue* and the modern culture industry is central to the transformation of the USA's 'populistic culture' into one more susceptible to demagogy.

The fulfilment of Worsley's larger plan is beyond the scope of this book. However, it is informed by his prioritization of a social theorization of the populist phenomenon that recognizes a key role for demagogy, social movements and modern means of communication. Orthodox recognition of the last of these has been chiefly limited to 'political communication' understood as communication by, and reportage of, governments and parties.

The book's focus is thus on what I term 'demagogic populism', understood as that form of populism in which modern demagogic leadership has played a role. Necessarily, much of the discussion focuses on the USA but it is by no means confined to that case.

(c) Towards modern demagogy and demagogic populism: plan of the book

The Radical Right project was deeply indebted to the Frankfurt School's US-focused Studies in Prejudice Project, detailed in Chapter 2. Considerable interaction occurred between the Institute for Social Research – during its period of 'exile' in the USA (1934–50) – and the wider formation of New York Intellectuals. Despite being better known as a critic of the Institute, Shils (like Bell) even worked directly on aspects of the Prejudice project. McCarthyism arose just as the Institute formally returned to Frankfurt in 1950. The analysis of demagogues within Studies in Prejudice thus formed the Institute's most pertinent legacy for the Radical Right project.

Hofstadter displays this influence most openly. He acknowledges the Institute's main published demagogy study, *Prophets of Deceit*, in his critique of US Populism in *The Age of Reform*. 'Pseudo-conservative', a concept used heavily in the Radical Right project, was prominently acknowledged as a central analytic category developed by Adorno within *The Authoritarian Personality*.[48] Hofstadter likely borrowed two further psychoanalytic concepts that, as we shall see in subsequent chapters, Adorno regarded as pivotal to Studies in Prejudice: paranoia and projection.

Recent positive recognition of the relevance of the Radical Right project to contemporary analysis has been mainly limited to invocations of Hofstadter's 'paranoid style'. Only this later thesis seems to have escaped the dampening effect of 'the Hofstadter controversy'.[49] *The Authoritarian Personality* too courted controversy comparable to, if more civil than, that Hofstadter experienced which has delimited its potential influence.[50] Nonetheless, the Radical Right project provides a strong indication of the potential import of the Institute's work to the analysis of contemporary demagogic populism and, notably, the depth of its sociological relevance.

As stated, one purpose of this book is to reassert the relevance of such sociological approaches to populism, in contrast with the positivist orthodoxy just assessed. This issue is also related to how this book addresses critical theory. It follows the theme of the series within which it is published in emphasizing the work of 'first generation' Frankfurt School figures. For reasons that become clearer in later chapters, discussion is largely delimited to those Institute members involved in the Studies in Prejudice Project (although the final chapter extends to Habermas). The key figures so become Adorno, Lowenthal, Horkheimer and, via his earlier work's influence on that project, Fromm.

In dealing with the broader secondary literatures, the dominance of philosophers and political theorists soon became evident. With notable exceptions among historians of ideas and those in German Studies, much of the interpretative literature regards critical theory as a domain of philosophy. The sociological dimensions of an Institute committed to a titular 'Social Research' are frequently lost while the significance of the US context is often overlooked, even by some German critical theorists. So, this book aims to contribute to redressing such tendencies.[51]

Understanding the Institute's US 'exile' has been made easier by the archival work of recent scholars who have built upon Martin Jay's foundational publications in this area.[52] The Studies in Prejudice Project itself has also undergone significant reconstruction in recent years. Important works have focused on its core analyses of antisemitism and so speak to a disturbing aspect of our present. Some of this work has also begun to address recent populism.[53]

In remarkable contrast to these scholarly developments, over the same period the Institute's US-based work has received prominent attention in the conspiracist claims concerning a 'cultural Marxist' plot within and beyond the US academy. The ironies here, as Jay and Huyssen have each pointed out, are intense as it was precisely this form of organized irrationality that Studies in Prejudice analysed.[54] Indeed, the contours of this conspiracism bear a striking resemblance to both McCarthy's demagogy and that of the antisemitic demagogues of the generation before him. Needless to say, these developments only add to the contemporary pertinence of the Institute's work and its legacy in the Radical Right project.

This book aims to bring the Institute's analysis of 'modern demagogy' to bear directly on the lacunae in orthodox populism studies: the *integral* transformative role for demagogic populism of what Adorno calls the 'physiognomics' of modern media – notably 'time coincidence' and 'space ubiquity' – which render the culture industry pivotal; the related question of cultural populism and of course the social psychological dimensions of modern demagogy which Adorno regards as a form of 'psychotechnics'.

Chapters 2 and 3 provide an account of the Institute's full theorization of 'modern demagogy'. The reconstruction in this chapter and the following contest the common view that the Institute's work simply imposed European understandings of fascism onto the US case. Mudde, for example, sets the Institute's work aside along with the Radical Right project with a variant of this claim, adding that they overly focused on charismatic leadership to the exclusion of other dimensions.[55] It is understandable that the orthodox literature has sought to distinguish the 'new' populism from any simple continuity with the fascist period in Europe (i.e. as 'neo-fascism').[56] The net effect, however, is to bracket out consideration of a possible continuity with the fascist period *in the figure of the demagogue* as a mode of leadership. While the issue of 'charismatic leadership' and 'personalization' is frequently acknowledged in the political science orthodoxy, it nearly always plays a marginal role in the classification struggles.[57] Rather, the role of demagogic leadership is pivotal to understanding contemporary populism.

Chapters 4 and 5 open a dialogue between the Institute's work on demagogy and 'Gramscian' analyses of populism and fascism. A critique of Laclau's hyperformalist theory of populism is contained within this as it might be considered the 'de facto' contemporary critical theory of populism. Chapter 5 develops a synthesis of components of the two traditions. It so provides a wider situation of contemporary neoliberalism as well as a 'social formalist' synthesis of the Institute's analysis of demagogic 'devices' and the post-Gramscian understanding of 'elements' within populist discourse. So closes Part I of the book.

Part II examines 'populist contradictions of the culture industry'. The culture industry thesis is one element of the Institute's work in the 1940s that was not employed by the Radical Right project. Instead, as detailed in Chapter 6, it was picked up by other members of the New York Intellectuals who formed the fatefully determinist association of 'mass culture' and 'conformism' later attributed to the Institute by Shils. Rather, the culture industry is indeed pivotal to modern demagogy and modern populism but its transformative capacities are contradictory. Chapter 6 directly addresses the issue of cultural populism which is often bracketed out in the orthodox literature. The chapter moves this term beyond the confines of its recent critical application to the British cultural studies project, the latter being the source of many cultural populist charges of 'cultural elitism' against the Frankfurt School. Cultural populism's longer history and relevance to 'political populism' is examined, drawing on the final writings of Eugene Lunn. The little recognized role of 'popular art' within the Institute's culture industry writings is elaborated and deepened in order to move beyond the instrumental role of 'popular culture' in most Gramscian conceptions of the counter-hegemonic. Chapter 7 presents a counter-demagogic 'tradition' in popular art, including a contestation of 'left-demagogy'. The inclusion of left-demagogy was quite deliberate as another charge against the Institute's work, first enunciated by Shils, was that it neglected this phenomenon. Moreover, my critique of Laclau's work emphasizes its blindness to this risk in 'left-populist' strategies.

Following a brief excursus on Trumpian demagogy, the concluding chapter returns to the opening dialogue with orthodox approaches, this time focused on how 'political communication studies' has addressed the populist surge. The chapter moves from Habermas's recent revisitation of his early 'disintegration' thesis regarding the fate of the public sphere. This enables a socio-conceptual bridging of the Institute's demagogy research and recent developments in, and of, 'political communication'. It employs elements of Habermas's early work to examine the integral relationship between means of communication, the 'contradictory institutionalization' of the public sphere, the regulation of the culture industry and demagogic populism.

Notes

1 Ghita Ionescu and Ernest Gellner, eds, *Populism: Its Meanings and National Characteristics* (London: Weidenfeld & Nicolson, 1969); Peter Worsley, 'The Concept of Populism', in *Populism: Its Meanings and National Characteristics*, ed. Ghita Ionescu and Ernest Gellner (London: Weidenfeld & Nicolson, 1969).

2 Even such periodizations can be a matter of dispute. Here I adopt Betz's timeline. Hans-Georg Betz, 'The Two Faces of Radical Right-Wing Populism in Western Europe', *The Review of Politics* 55, no. 4 (1993). Most would agree that the electoral surge for Haider in Austria and Le Pen in France near the turn of the century were 'watershed' moments that triggered much increased academic interest. On timelines for populism studies itself, see Takis S. Pappas, 'Modern Populism: Research Advances, Conceptual and Methodological Pitfalls, and the Minimal Definition', in *Oxford Research Encyclopedia of Politics*, ed. William M. Thompson (Oxford: Oxford University Press, 2016); Paul K. Jones, 'Insights from the Infamous: Recovering the Social-Theoretical First Phase of Populism Studies', *European Journal of Social Theory* 22, no. 4 (2019).

3 Depending on selection criteria, at least ten such anthologies have published since the beginning of the this century. Examples: Yves Mény and Yves Surel, eds, *Democracies and the Populist Challenge* (New York: Palgrave, 2002); Daniele Albertazzi and Duncan McDonnell, eds, *Twenty-First Century Populism: The Spectre of Western European Democracy* (Basingstoke [England]: Palgrave Macmillan, 2008); Gianpietro Mazzoleni, J. Stewart and B. Horsfield, eds, *The Media and Neo-Populism: A Contemporary Comparative Analysis* (Westport, Connecticut: Praeger, 2003). Toril Aalberg et al., eds, *Populist Political Communication in Europe* (London: Routledge, 2016).

4 Peter Worsley, *The Third World* (Chicago: University of Chicago Press, 1964). Hans-Georg Betz and Stefan Immerfall, eds, *The New Politics of the Right: Neo-Populist Parties and Movements in Established Democracies* (New York: St Martin's Press, 1998).

5 Giovanni Sartori, 'Concept Misformation in Comparative Politics', *The American Political Science Review* 64, no. 4 (1970): 1041. The best invocation of Sartori I

have found is: Pappas, 'Modern Populism: Research Advances, Conceptual and Methodological Pitfalls, and the Minimal Definition'.

6   Cas Mudde, 'The Populist Zeitgeist', *Government and Opposition* 39, no. 4 (2004): 543. One measure of influence here is that this passage was directly adopted as 'the classic definition' by the UK's *Guardian* newspaper for its 'The New Populism' project in 2018; e.g. Mark Rice-Oxley and Ammar Kalia, 'How to Spot a Populist', *The Guardian* (2018).

7   Cas Mudde, *Populist Radical Right Parties in Europe* (Cambridge: Cambridge University Press, 2007); Giovanni Sartori, *Parties and Party Systems: A Framework for Analysis* (Cambridge: Cambridge University Press, 1976).

8   Hans-Georg Betz, 'Political Conflict in the Postmodern Age: Radical Right-Wing Populist Parties in Europe', *Current Politics and Economics of Europe* 1 (1990); Hans-Georg Betz, *Postmodern Politics in Germany: The Politics of Resentment* (Houndmills: Macmillan, 1991); Jens Rydgren, 'The Sociology of the Radical Right', *Annu. Rev. Sociol.* 33 (2007); Robert S. Jansen, 'Populist Mobilization: A New Theoretical Approach to Populism', *Sociological Theory* 29, no. 2 (2011). Betz recently adopted Jens's position explicitly in: Hans-Georg Betz, 'The Radical Right and Populism', in *The Oxford Handbook of the Radical Right*, ed. Jens Rydgren (Oxford: Oxford University Press, 2018).

9   Betz, *Postmodern Politics in Germany*; Hans-Georg Betz, *Radical Right-Wing Populism in Western Europe* (New York: St Martins Press, 1994), 4. This early period of Betz's work is also in dialogue with the contemporary work of Habermas. However, to my knowledge Betz does not draw on the work of first-generation critical theorists in such writing nor is there any substantial dialogue with the US Radical Right project discussed in the next section. Nonetheless, I am conscious I have positioned Betz as a more orthodox figure than these links with critical theory suggest, mainly because this is how Mudde positions him.

10 Mudde, *Populist Radical Right Parties in Europe*, 30.

11 Cas Mudde, 'The Populist Radical Right: A Pathological Normalcy', *West European Politics* 33, no. 6 (2010). This article forms the basis of the opening of: Cas Mudde, *On Extremism and Democracy in Europe* (London: Routledge, 2016). On 'illiberal': Fareed Zakaria, 'The Rise of Illiberal Democracy', *Foreign Affairs* 76, no. 6 (1997); Mabel Berezin, *Illiberal Politics in Neoliberal Times* (Cambridge: Cambridge University Press, 2009).

12 On republishing this essay in 2016 Mudde acknowledged that the 'transformed political context' led him to be 'increasingly on the side of those I have criticised for decades'. Yet he still saw exaggeration in 'much of the academic writing'. No wider theoretical rethinking seems to have followed. Mudde, *On Extremism and Democracy in Europe*, xxiii.

13 Mudde, 'The Populist Radical Right', 1178–1179. This echoes a similar disciplinary demarcation announced in Margaret Canovan's influential 1999 article on populism: Margaret Canovan, 'Trust the People! Populism and the Two Faces of Democracy', *Political Studies* 47, no. 1 (1999).

14 Nadia Urbinati, 'Democracy and Populism', *Constellations* 5, no. 1 (1998); Cas Mudde and Cristóbal Rovira Kaltwasser, eds, *Populism in Europe and the Americas: Threat or Corrective for Democracy?* (Cambridge: Cambridge University Press, 2012).

15 Daniel Bell, ed. *The New American Right* (New York: Criterion Books, 1955); Daniel Bell, ed. *The Radical Right: The New American Right Expanded and Updated* (Garden City, New York: Doubleday, 1963); Daniel Bell, ed. *The Radical Right*, 3rd edn (New Brunswick: Transaction Publishers, 2002).

16 David S. Brown, *Richard Hofstadter: An Intellectual Biography* (Chicago: University of Chicago Press, 2008), 151. Richard Hofstadter, *The Age of Reform: From Bryan to FDR* (New York: Knopf, 1955). The historical 'Populist' movement of 1890s is usually capitalized.
17 For a sampling of this debate: Theodore Saloutos ed., *Populism: Reaction or Reform?* (New York: Holt Rinehart & Winston, 1978). Hixon and Rogin provide more thorough critical assessments, with Hixson's being the more scholarly. Plotke's is the most sophisticated and measured overview. William B. Hixson, *Search for the American Right Wing: An Analysis of the Social Science Record, 1955–1987* (Princeton: Princeton University Press, 1992); and Michael Paul Rogin, *The Intellectuals and McCarthy: The Radical Specter* (Cambridge, Mass.: MIT Press, 1967); David Plotke, 'Introduction to the Transaction Edition', in *The Radical Right 3rd Edition*, ed. D. Bell (New Brunswick, NJ: Transaction Publishers, 2002). On the 'infamous' charge and my critique thereof: Yannis Stavrakakis and Anton Jäger, 'Accomplishments and Limitations of the "New" Mainstream in Contemporary Populism Studies', *European Journal of Social Theory* 21, no. 4 (2018). Jones, 'Insights from the Infamous'.
18 Margaret Canovan, *Populism* (New York: Harcourt Brace Jovanovich, 1981), 184–185; Canovan, 'Trust the People! Populism and the Two Faces of Democracy', 2.
19 Michael Kazin, *The Populist Persuasion: An American History (Revised)*, 2nd edn (Ithaca, New York: Cornell University Press, 1998), 190–193, 192; Michael Kazin, 'How Can Donald Trump and Bernie Sanders Both Be "Populist"?', *The New York Times Sunday Magazine*, 27 March (2016).
20 Hofstadter, *The Age of Reform*, 80–81; Daniel Bell, 'The Face of Tomorrow', *Jewish Frontier* 11 (1944): 16–17.
21 Alan Brinkley, *Voices of Protest: Huey Long, Father Coughlin, and the Great Depression* (New York: Knopf, 1982), 119; Donald I. Warren, *Radio Priest: Charles Coughlin, the Father of Hate Radio* (New York: Free Press, 1996), 188ff; Michael Mann, *Fascists* (Cambridge: Cambridge University Press, 2004).
22 See the discussion of Gerald L.K. Smith in Chapter 2 (a). To 'over-win' for Urbinati is characteristic of demagogic practice: 'the use of speaking abilities and political liberties in order not only to win a majority vote but to over-win and reduce the opposition to a meaningless entity with no role in the political game'. Nadia Urbinati, *Democracy Disfigured: Opinion, Truth, and the People* (Cambridge, Mass.: Harvard University Press, 2014), 138.
23 Reinhard H. Luthin, *American Demagogues: Twentieth Century* (Boston: Beacon Press, 1954); Richard C. Cortner, *The Kingfish and the Constitution: Huey Long, the First Amendment, and the Emergence of Modern Press Freedom in America* (Westport, CT: Greenwood Publishing Group, 1996); Ken Burns, *Huey Long* (Alexandria, VA: PBS Video, 2010), videorecording.
24 Kazin, *The Populist Persuasion: An American History* (revised), 127, 132.
25 See Brinkley, *Voices of Protest*, 163. and David Harry Bennett, *The Party of Fear: From Nativist Movements to the New Right in American History* (Chapel Hill: University of North Carolina Press 1988), 256.
26 Daniel Bell, 'Interpretations of American Politics', in *The New American Right*, ed. Daniel Bell (New York: Criterion Books, 1955), 4.
27 Daniel Bell, 'Preface', in *The Radical Right*, ed. Daniel Bell (New York: Anchor, 1964), ix.
28 Bell, 'Interpretations of American Politics', 14.
29 Bell, 'Interpretations of American Politics', 18–19. Richard Hofstadter, *Anti-Intellectualism in American Life* (New York: Vintage, 1963). Drawing on recent

historical research, Urbinati notes the significance of these meetings as a crucible of populism but does not track evangelicism specifically; *Democracy Disfigured*, 145–147.
30. Daniel Bell, 'Afterword: 1996', in *The Cultural Contradictions of Capitalism: 20th Anniversary Edn* (New York: Basic Books, 1996), 319; Bell, 'Interpretations of American Politics', 20.
31. Bell, 'Interpretations of American Politics', 20; Richard Hofstadter, 'Pseudo-Conservatism Revisited: A Postscript (1962)', in *The Radical Right*, ed. Daniel Bell (New York: Doubleday, 1963), 83.
32. W.E. Du Bois, *The Philadelphia Negro* (New York: Schocken Books, 1971), 20.
33. Bell, 'Interpretations of American Politics', 14.
34. See Seymour Martin Lipset, 'The Sources of the Radical Right', in *The New American Right* ed. Daniel Bell (New York: Criterion, 1955); Seymour Martin Lipset, 'Three Decades of the Radical Right: Coughlinites, McCarthyites, and Birchers', in *The Radical Right: The New American Right Expanded and Updated*, ed. Daniel Bell (Garden City, New York: Anchor, 1964). Cf. Hixson, *Search for the American Right Wing: An Analysis of the Social Science Record, 1955–1987*.
35. Edward A. Shils, 'Charisma, Order, and Status', *American Sociological Review* 30, no. 2 (1965). Edward Shils, *Tradition* (London: Faber, 1981); Edward A. Shils, *The Torment of Secrecy: The Background and Consequences of American Security Policies* (London: Heinemann, 1956).
36. Paul A. Taggart, *Populism* (Milton Keynes: Open University Press, 2000), n1, 9.
37. Shils, *The Torment of Secrecy: The Background and Consequences of American Security Policies*, 103–104.
38. Max Weber, *On Charisma and Institution Building: Selected Papers* (Chicago: University of Chicago Press, 1968).
39. Bell, 'Interpretations of American Politics', 6–7; Shils, *The Torment of Secrecy: The Background and Consequences of American Security Policies*, 143.
40. Max Weber, 'The Profession and Vocation of Politics', in *Weber: Political Writings*, ed. Peter Lassman and Ronald Speirs (Cambridge: Cambridge University Press, 1994), 342–344; Christopher Adair-Toteff, 'Max Weber's Charisma', *Journal of Classical Sociology* 5, no. 2 (2005); Stephen Turner, 'Charisma Reconsidered', *Journal of Classical Sociology* 3, no. 1 (2003).
41. Worsley, 'The Concept of Populism', 245–246.
42. Shils, *The Torment of Secrecy: The Background and Consequences of American Security Policies*, 102–103.
43. All citations in this listing from: Worsley, 'The Concept of Populism', 245.
44. See the discussions of Laclau in Chapters 4 and 5.
45. Benjamin Moffitt and Simon Tormey, 'Rethinking Populism: Politics, Mediatisation and Political Style', *Political Studies* 62, no. 2 (2014). For a rare instance of a fuller usage: Benjamin Arditi, 'Populism as a Spectre of Democracy: A Response to Canovan', *Political Studies* 52, no. 1 (2004).
46. Edward A. Shils, 'Demagogues and Cadres in the Political Development of the New States', in *Communications and Political Development*, ed. Lucian W. Pye (New Jersey: Princeton University Press, 1963), 67. See further discussion in Chapter 4(c).
47. Lipset, 'The Sources of the Radical Right'.
48. Hofstadter, *The Age of Reform*, 72n; Richard Hofstadter, 'The Pseudo-Conservative Revolt', in *The New American Right*, ed. Daniel Bell (New York: Criterion Books, 1955), 35. Leo Lowenthal and Norbert Guterman, *Prophets of Deceit: A Study*

of the Techniques of the American Agitator (New York: Harper, 1949). Theodor W. Adorno et al., *The Authoritarian Personality* (New York: Harper & Row, 1950).

49 One of the the most insightful of these is: Arlie Russell Hochschild, 'The Ecstatic Edge of Politics: Sociology and Donald Trump', *Contemporary Sociology* 45, no. 6 (2016).

50 For an historical account of this debate see Martin Roiser and Carla Willig, 'The Strange Death of the Authoritarian Personality: 50 Years of Psychological and Political Debate', *History of the Human Sciences* 15, no. 4 (2002).

51 On this sociological recovery, see also within this series: Darrow Schecter, *Critical Theory and Sociological Theory: On Late Modernity and Social Statehood* (Manchester: Manchester University Press, 2019).

52 Martin Jay, *The Dialectical Imagination: A History of the Frankfurt School and the Institute of Social Research, 1923–1950* (London: Heinemann, 1973); Martin Jay, 'Adorno in America', *New German Critique* 31 (1984); Anson Rabinbach, 'German-Jewish Connections: The New York Intellectuals and the Frankfurt School in Exile', *German Politics & Society* 13, no. 3 (36) (1995); David Jenemann, *Adorno in America* (Minneapolis: University of Minnesota Press, 2007); Thomas Wheatland, *The Frankfurt School in Exile* (Minneapolis: University of Minnesota Press, 2009).

53 Jack Jacobs, *The Frankfurt School, Jewish Lives, and Antisemitism* (New York: Cambridge University Press, 2015); Jack Jacobs, 'Antisemitism, Islamophobia, and Racism in the Era of Donald Trump: The Relevance of Critical Theory', *Berlin Journal of Critical Theory* 3, no. 1 (2019); Lars Rensmann, *The Politics of Unreason: The Frankfurt School and the Origins of Modern Antisemitism* (Albany: SUNY Press, 2017); Lars Rensmann, 'The Noisy Counter-Revolution: Understanding the Cultural Conditions and Dynamics of Populist Politics in Europe in the Digital Age', *Politics and Governance* 5, no. 4 (2017); Martin Jay, 'The Jews and the Frankfurt School: Critical Theory's Analysis of Anti-Semitism', *New German Critique* 19 (1980); Eva-Maria Ziege, *Antisemitismus Und Gesellschaftstheorie: Die Frankfurter Schule Im Amerikanischen Exil* (Frankfurt am Main: Suhrkamp, 2009).

54 I employ here Muirhead and Rosenblum's recent advocacy of 'conspiracism' over 'conspiracy theory' in analysing such phenomena to emphasize the relative poverty of the former's capacity for 'explanation'. This is consistent too with the 'recombinant' model of demagogic speech I build in this book. Likewise, Huyssen is surely correct when he points to the role of paranoid projection (a psychoanalytic conceptualization detailed in Chapter 2) in the 'cultural Marxist' conspiracism. Russell Muirhead and Nancy L. Rosenblum, *A Lot of People Are Saying: The New Conspiracism and the Assault on Democracy* (Princeton, NJ: Princeton University Press, 2019); Martin Jay, 'Dialectic of Counter-Enlightenment: The Frankfurt School as Scapegoat of the Lunatic Fringe', *Salmagundi* 168/9 (Fall/Winter 2011); Andreas Huyssen, 'Breitbart News and the Frankfurt School. A Strange Meeting of Minds', *Public Seminar* (2017), https://publicseminar.org/2017/09/breitbart-bannon-trump-and-the-frankfurt-school/.

55 Mudde, 'The Populist Radical Right', 1169.

56 Mudde even periodizes the field with this criterion while Betz's earlier work stressed these parties' own self-distancings from 'the backward looking, reactionary politics of the traditional extremist (i.e. neo-fascist and neo-nazi)' and their subtler understanding of modern political communication. Cas Mudde, ed. *The Populist Radical Right: A Reader* (London Routledge, 2017), 3; Betz, *Radical Right-Wing Populism in Western Europe*, 3.

57 A chapter is devoted to this issue in: Cas Mudde and Cristobal Rovira Kaltwasser, *Populism: A Very Short Introduction* (Oxford: Oxford University Press, 2017); Cf. also: Takis S. Pappas, 'Are Populist Leaders 'Charismatic'? The Evidence from Europe', *Constellations* 23, no. 3 (2016). The radical right framework has been more attentive to this issue but even Eatwell's valuable discussion tends to rely on electoral data as the deciding evidence: Roger Eatwell, 'Charisma and the Radical Right', in *The Oxford Handbook of the Radical Right*, ed. Jens Rydgren (Oxford: Oxford University Press, 2018).

2

The Institute's analysis of 'modern demagogy'

> ... it seems to be an intrinsic characteristic of the modern demagogue that he earns his living through his performance.
>
> Adorno, (Draft) Introduction to *Prophets of Deceit*

(a) From 'authoritarian(ism)' to 'modern demagogy'

As shown in the previous chapter, the figure of the demagogue is, at worst, completely neglected or, at best, highly contested terrain in populism studies. Even Hofstadter's modest importation of some of the Frankfurt School's work is still regarded as highly controversial.

The research on demagogy by The Institute for Social Research took place some years after its effective relocation from Europe to New York in 1934. It formed part of the broader Studies in Prejudice research programme. This was conducted with the financial and institutional support of the American Jewish Committee (AJC) which commissioned it. The project formally commenced in 1943 and ran until the Institute's closure of its New York office in 1950. It also overlapped considerably with the period Adorno and Horkheimer spent in California, where much of the empirical work for Studies in Prejudice, and the composition of *Dialectic of Enlightenment*, were undertaken.

Although always acknowledged in major works on the Frankfurt School within critical theory, the Studies in Prejudice research project has only recently received concentrated scholarly attention, with the publication of several valuable monographs.[1] These discussions of the project have focused on its analysis of antisemitism, which was certainly its primary purpose. However, the project expanded beyond this remit to examine broader 'prejudice'. Likewise, while the demagogues studied all professed antisemitic views, the model of 'modern demagogy' (as I will call it) that emerged covered a wider range of demagogic practices. Crucially, Adorno and Lowenthal also connected demagogy to the culture industry.[2] This latter dimension has received least attention to date.

Five monographs, all published in 1949–1950, and a considerable number of articles and essays, were produced from Studies in Prejudice. One of the monographs, *The Authoritarian Personality*, attributed to multiple authors led by Adorno, continues to overshadow the rest of the project.[3] Only one of those five published monographs focused on demagogy – Lowenthal and Guterman's *Prophets of Deceit: A Study of the Techniques of the American Agitator*.[4] As we saw, Hofstadter drew on this text as well.[5] Almost as much material went unpublished, most notably a study of antisemitism and American labour. The unpublished work also included 'pilot studies' of demagogues, including a monograph on Martin Luther Thomas by Adorno in 1943.[6]

This chapter focuses on Lowenthal's demagogy study and Adorno's considerable related work, including his unpublished draft introduction to Lowenthal's monograph. The demagogy studies provide the crucial link between the Institute's work and populism. The chapter argues that the figure of the demagogue is common to both fascist and *some* populist irruptions. Indeed, it is demagogic leadership that can 'capture' some, but not all, such irruptions. This means that the Institute's work on domestic 'fascist' demagogues is applicable to demagogic populism.[7]

First, the intellectual background to Studies in Prejudice and earlier related work by the Institute need to be traced. It emerges that the category of 'authoritarian' leadership is not as central as is usually supposed and that the core concept is in fact that of the demagogue.

The relationship between familial structure and authority had been advanced as a component of the Institute's earliest reflections on the German proletariat, initially in the context of revolutionary failure but also as a prescient recognition of potential support for authoritarianism.[8] The *Studien über Autorität und Familie* was the Institute's first major interdisciplinary project. It produced a vast multi-authored publication in 1936 which included theoretical elaborations by Horkheimer, Fromm and Marcuse, an empirical project overseen by Fromm and a final section overseen by Lowenthal.[9] (Adorno was not yet formally part of the Institute.)

Its overarching perspective is routinely referred to as the tying of authoritarianism to the 'decline of the patriarchal family' in secondary literatures – and by Lowenthal in *Prophets* – but the analysis is more nuanced and multi-perspectival than that summation suggests, even becoming explicitly national-comparative in later work.[10] Equally significant are the differing roles of the bourgeois and working-class family forms and, most significant of all for Horkheimer in 1936, the reduction of the bourgeois family from a production-embedded institution to a 'limited' consumerist one.[11]

Nonetheless, there is no question that the *Studien* confirmed the Institute's interest in psychoanalysis. The influence of Erich Fromm here was pivotal. While there was enormous intellectual resistance to this embrace of psychoanalytic elements outside the Institute, the socio-psychoanalytic approach Fromm developed in this period became extremely influential later, inside and outside the academy, most notably in *Escape from Freedom* (1941). However, by that time he had parted with the Institute.[12]

As early as a contribution to the first volume of the Institute's *Zeitschrift* (journal) in 1932, Fromm had sought a solution to the problem of reconciling Marxian social determination and the Freudian conception of the psyche by establishing a mediating role for characterology.[13] Freud's characterology had typified his patients according to dominant character traits deriving from the childhood focus on specific bodily functions. For Freud these were of libidinal origin in pre-genital sexuality. Fromm's development of a 'social character' typology relied on regarding 'the family as the psychological agency of society'. Given that Freud privileged individual psychic development – located within the family – and that for him the infant's experiences 'had scarcely anything to do with "society"', Fromm resolved the perceived sociological deficit in Freud, in another 1932 essay for the *Zeitschrift*, thus:

> There is no real problem here at all. Of course, the first critical influences on the growing child come from the family. But the family itself, all its typical internal emotional relationships and the educational ideals it embodies, are in turn conditioned by the social and class background of the family; in short they are conditioned by the social structure in which it is rooted. (For example: the emotional relationships between father and son are quite different in the family that is part of a bourgeois, patriarchal society than they are in a family that is part of a matriarchal society.) The family is the medium through which the society or the social class stamps its specific structure on the child, and hence on the adult. *The family is the psychological agency of society.*[14]

As he later put it, the social character was a 'nucleus' shared by members of a group which was distinct from those members' individual characters.[15]

Accordingly, Fromm's social characterology in the *Studien* developed an account of both the internal familial dynamics of psychic character formation and the relationship between these social characters and forms of social authority (i.e. the social character's 'function'). It was the sado-masochistic character that was tied by Fromm to authoritarianism. The 'social helplessness of the adult marks its stamp on the biological helplessness of the child and allows the superego and authority to take on such significance in a child's development'.[16] This character was suited to authoritarian regimes as its key features were submission to the stronger and contempt for the weaker.

In the reformulation consolidated in *Escape from Freedom*, Fromm shifted his overarching emphasis from helplessness to the 'aloneness and powerlessness' deriving socio-historically from the anxiety provoked by the project of an autonomous self announced by the Reformation. Sado-masochism was again tied to an authoritarian character together with two other neurotic forms: 'destructiveness' and 'automaton conformity'. While the sadism of the authoritarian character 'aims at incorporation of the object; destructiveness (aims) at its removal'.[17] The appeal of Nazism to the moral indignation of the German lower middle class is thus tied by Fromm to this destructive form, though the authoritarian character is also drawn on in his fuller analysis of Nazism.[18] Conformity, in contrast, is identified with the loss of critical thinking in the desire to identify with external societal norms in non-fascist 'modern society', a formulation later popularized as 'other-directed' by another of the New York Intellectual contributors to The Radical Right project, David Riesman.[19]

Horkheimer's theoretical essay for the *Studien*, 'Authority and the Family', plainly relies on Fromm's schema for the sado-masochistic character and ties it to the changing structure of the patriarchal family, which is usually referred to as 'a crisis of the family' (rather than the patriarchal as such). The patriarchal form of the family had always well-suited the preparation of male children who observe external social authority and this continued in the early bourgeois era.[20] The decline of the patriarch in both working-class and bourgeois families is tied principally by Horkheimer to the family's loss of productive power and the progressive concentration of such power outside the family. The affinity between the internal familial respect for the power of the father and his external authority within the production system is progressively broken, most obviously in the working-class family. This has not led, Horkheimer stresses, to a corresponding rise in matriarchal authority, despite the evident potentiality of women to play a progressive role at this point. The countervailing forces – from the regulation of monogamy to women's independent wage-employment being blocked by mass unemployment – are too potent (but noticeably contingent). Nonetheless, because women 'foster human relations ... the present-day family is a source of strength to resist the total dehumanization of the world and contains an element of anti-authoritarianism.'[21]

If the *Studien* left this sense of structural crisis somewhat open-ended, despite the obvious context of consolidating fascism in Europe, the Studies in Prejudice Project provided a more precisely targeted, if no less ambitious, research programme.[22] While wartime formation made the question of European fascism highly relevant, the overwhelming empirical focus was on the USA.

As Fromm had left in 1939, the monographs in this series were the first major publications in English with the Institute's imprimatur. *The Authoritarian Personality*'s aim to develop a means of identifying *potential fascists in the USA* fitted with the more assertive understanding of Jewish self-defence within the AJC. Accordingly, the famous 'F-scale' was developed from repeated testing of questionnaires and interviews with selected subjects. The 'F' stood for fascist personality type and the appeal to a characterological typology displayed a debt to Fromm while the larger project resembled the scale and division of labour of the *Studien*. The key difference was that the leading advocate of the informing psychoanalysis had become Adorno rather than Fromm.

Now, subsequent debate about *The Authoritarian Personality* focused on its methodological protocols, in much the same way that Hofstadter's work was to be challenged by repeated inductive historiographical arguments about mid-Western populists. This has meant that the identification of 'authoritarians' has remained the central focus of interpretation. Shils's 1954 critique remains the definitive 'unsympathetic' interpretation in charging that the research design is flawed by the assumption that there can be no left-authoritarians.[23] Sympathetic interpretations have comparably elevated the 'authoritarian' to the status of an enduring type, even a subfield of political and social psychology.[24]

The irony here, as Billig and others have noted, is that the titular use of 'authoritarian' was somewhat arbitrary, even an ad hoc afterthought at the end of the writing process.[25] Such usage was in keeping with the debt to the *Studien* and, despite theoretical differences about psychoanalysis, to Fromm. Variants of 'authority' had become available as a potential title following Fromm's own shift in preference to 'freedom' for the title of his 1941 bestseller.

Yet the text of *The Authoritarian Personality* is clearly focused on fascism and potential fascists. Here, however, another much overlooked aspect of this work comes to the fore. As Billig puts it, neither Fromm nor Adorno and his team paid specific attention to fascist 'leaders', focusing instead on 'followers' and at best assuming a congruence between them. Part of the ambiguity results again from the titling of the book – 'authoritarian' has since become more strongly associated with a mode of political leadership, partly in deference to that work.

The emphasis on *the potentially fascist individual* is certainly made plain in the opening pages but, crucially this is tied to the question of *antidemocratic propaganda*:

> individuals differ in their *susceptibility* to antidemocratic propaganda, in their readiness to exhibit antidemocratic tendencies. It seems necessary to study at this 'readiness level' in order to gauge the potential for fascism in this country.[26]

Propaganda is here understood as the work of demagogues, a category which certainly included Hitler but, as the focus of this research was the USA, its key exemplars were radio demagogues like Coughlin. The central role of such propaganda is rarely highlighted in discussions of *The Authoritarian Personality*. At most it is noted that the Institute's demagogy studies contributed important thematic material to the development of its questionnaires.

What even Billig misses, then, is that rather than leadership being neglected, there is, in effect, a division of labour within Studies in Prejudice between research on 'followers' and 'leaders'. *The Authoritarian Personality* is concerned with potential followers while the demagogy studies and related essays address the 'leaders' and their 'propaganda'. As is consistent with Billig's insight regarding the arbitrary status of 'authoritarian' in this literature, these leaders are not called 'authoritarian leaders' but 'demagogues' or 'agitators', two terms that are used synonymously by the Institute. Each is often, but not always, prefixed by 'fascist'. Significantly, these can refer to either those demagogues holding state power or those 'agitating' for it. That is, the discussions of such demagogic leadership can move easily, too easily perhaps, between European fascists in power and the most insignificant 'small-time' US agitators. Of the two terms, agitator and demagogue, I will consistently use the latter.

However, this categorical overlap does not mean that the Institute regarded the US demagogues merely as 'fifth columnists' operating on behalf of European fascists. Such influence did of course exist, but these figures were not usually mere copycats. Adorno repeatedly quoted the line attributed to Huey Long that any US fascism would be based in American democratic roots by those who declared themselves antifascist.[27]

It is in this context that this work by the Institute can be conceptually linked to populism. I discuss the rare but significant explicit references to US Populism in the demagogy studies in section (b). But it is at a conceptual level that the relevance of the Institute's conception of demagogy becomes clearer. For it is the demagogy-populism relationship that is critical here.

We saw in Chapter 1 that Nadia Urbinati identified the normative binarization of US populism as 'good' and European populism as 'bad'. More recently, she has provided a retheorization of populism within political theory. She is one of the few in her field to pursue a systemic role for demagogy and modern means of communication. Urbinati tends to see a complete identification of the demagogue and populism which occludes the prospect of populist movements that evade demagogic capture. Her conception of the demagogue is primarily Aristotelian and she acknowledges the former neutrality of the term in Athenian practice, consistent with its Greek derivation's literally meaning 'to speak in public assembly' (i.e. as in the agora). Thus, for Urbinati, '(d)emagoguery represents a form of political language that is consonant with assembly politics and thus democracy'. The demagogue who becomes a tyrant for Aristotle is a figure from within the wealthy class of notables who exploits the many to challenge the few in self-interested pursuit of office. Urbinati regards this definition as 'timeless'.[28]

One of Urbinati's key sources at this point is Melissa Lane's reconstruction – in the historical semantic mode of *Begriffsgeschichte* – of the transformation of 'demagogue' from this former neutral sense to a pejorative one. For Lane, what has tended to be timeless is the intellectual disposition – even 'mental laziness' – to invoke a pejorative sense of demagogue by contrasting it with Plato's positive pole, the statesman, one who, in contrast with the tyrant, supports rule by 'the laws'. In elitist formulations, the demagogic pole is equated with not merely self-interested disregard for the laws, but an alliance with 'the mob'.

Curiously, Lane does not address the work of Max Weber on this point, which was briefly sketched in Chapter 1. Famously, Weber also draws attention to the ambiguity of the term demagogue in his vocation essay on politics. The demagogue constitutes one form of charismatic leadership, which in turn is one of Weber's three types of legitimate authority. In discussing the relationship between 'officials' and modern elected political leaders while developing a typology of professional politicians, he turns to the same pivotal formative reference that informs Lane's discussion of statesman/demagogue: Thucydides' contrast between Pericles, who is treated as worthy, and Cleon, who is not. Weber comments:

> Ever since the advent of the constitutional state, and even more so since the advent of democracy, the typical political leader in the West is the 'demagogue'. The unpleasant overtones of the word should not make us forget that it was Pericles, not Cleon, who first bore this title … Actually, modern demagogy, too, employs the spoken word, and does so to an enormous extent, if one considers the electoral speeches a modern candidate has to make. But it makes even more sustained use of the printed word. The political writer, and above all, the *journalist* is the most important representative of the species today.[29]

Weber's key example of modern demagogy is Prime Minister William Gladstone, one of the first British leaders to navigate the consequences of the expanded (male) suffrage. His charismatic leadership skills entailed both 'the firm belief of the masses in the ethical content of his policies and above all their belief in the ethical character of his personality'.[30] Weber's allied views regarding charismatic 'leader democracy' and its possible influence on the Weimar constitution have been endlessly debated in the wake of the rise of Nazism shortly after his death. Yet the above attention to the *communicative* distinctiveness of 'modern demagogy' as compared with classical demagogy has tended to be overlooked. Plainly, for Weber, there is a complex relationship between modern demagogy, the means of political communication and related institutional forms, such as the profession of journalism.

Likewise, the less-cited reference to demagogy in Weber's other vocation lecture is remarkable for its clear rejection of 'the prophet and the demagogue' who exploit the monological *communicative monopoly* of the lectern for political gain. Instead, Weber advises they should 'go out in the street and speak to the public', a citation from the book of Jeremiah but also an allusion to the Greek etymological derivation of 'demagogue' mentioned here.[31] So while modern demagogy is not universally understood by Weber pejoratively, he does deploy the pejorative sense when the communicative and institutional circumstances require it. Adorno also regarded Weber's conception of charisma as being subject to transformations in available means of communication.[32]

For Lane, however, there appears to be no distinction between classical and modern demagogy. Thus, for her, Adorno's understanding of the demagogue is merely the most prominent twentieth-century example of the reproduction of the statesman/demagogue dichotomy:

> Adorno does not use the term 'statesman', but here we have a pure statement of the statesman-demagogue distinction which bulks up the bare popular bones of the ancient concept with a particular epistemological diagnosis: the statesman who communicates only in terms of rational truth and enlightenment, versus the demagogue who uses irrational means of persuasion to sway people against their own rational interests.[33]

The sole Adorno text Lane relies on here, 'Democratic Leadership and Mass Manipulation', appeared in an edited volume on leadership in 1950.[34] It was one among the significant group of essays Adorno wrote between the mid-1940s and early 1950s which not only publicized the Studies in Prejudice Project but, crucially, spoke across the intellectual division of labour between the demagogy studies and the other sections of the project.

Lane is right in thinking that for Adorno the demagogue is understood only in a pejorative sense. However, Adorno, like Weber, is portraying a set of 'modern' demagogic circumstances that are qualitatively different from the classical usage. Unlike Urbinati's formulation, Adorno's modern demagogy is not based, *pace* Urbinati, in 'a form of political language that is consonant with assembly politics and thus democracy'. Indeed, notwithstanding the presence of some fascist leaders in assemblies, in many ways it is its opposite. By this I refer to the implication in Urbinati's and much of the classical formulation that the demagogue – good or bad – succeeds by means of a chamber oratory which at least resembles that portrayed in the rules of classical rhetoric.

Such demagogues certainly existed in the twentieth century. The two most notable examples would be Oswald Mosley and Enoch Powell. Mosley was leader of the openly antisemitic British Union of Fascists in the 1930s which tried to employ Nazi stormtrooper tactics on London streets. Powell was the renegade Tory MP who prophesied 'rivers of blood' in Britain in 1968 as a consequence of immigration from the 'new commonwealth' nations. Each served in the British House of Commons and each changed party affiliation. Each held appropriate cultural capital including considerable skills of chamber oratory. Mosley had an impeccably 'notable' background in the British aristocracy. Powell's cultural capital was accumulated instead via education. He was even a former classics scholar and professor of Ancient Greek. The 'rivers of blood' image was a citation from Virgil's *Aeneid*.

The Institute's conception of the demagogue, based principally on their US case studies and the German experience of Nazism, is not such a figure. While modern demagogy for Adorno is indeed 'irrational', its content is almost incoherent compared to the usual understandings of chamber oratory. The demagogue's preferred locale is the rally, not the parliamentary chamber. The 'Mass Manipulation' essay attaches an appendix entitled, 'Illustrations of Manual', exemplifying the 'educational' plan for a 'popular manual' that publicized demagogic 'devices' (discussed in detail in section (b)). The plan's opening line commences: 'The Manual first describes the difference between the political orator and various kinds of agitators'.[35]

In the passage cited above, Lane attributes to Adorno the view that the statesman 'communicates only in terms of rational truth and enlightenment'.[36] In fact Adorno, warns against over-reliance on such a strategy of confronting 'modern' demagogic propaganda with an 'enlightened' opposite of orthodox reasoned argument, 'truth propaganda'. His core example is 'The Protocols of the Elders of Zion' document, which was 'exposed' as a fake yet was not only still being promoted in 1950 but still had its believers.[37] That text of course also endures today. I will call this 'truth propaganda' strategy 'liberal exposure'.

Lane's reading ignores or cannot grasp the immanent reworking of 'truth and enlightenment' Adorno here undertakes. Indeed, his premiss displays even greater disdain for the empty 'statesmanship' stance than Lane does: '(u)nless the truth principle is formulated more concretely, it will remain an unctuous phrase'.[38] Presumably as a requirement of contributors to a volume on leadership, Adorno makes some rare programmatic suggestions which he acknowledges 'may seem a hopeless endeavour'. His primary concern is to warn against democratic leaders' emulating the techniques of the demagogue – what both Shils and Žižek include within 'the populist temptation'.[39] So, as a first step, all instrumentalization of political communication should be avoided – a 'renunciation of propaganda'. Adorno eventually includes in this frame a prescient anticipation of what may lie ahead otherwise, what is currently called 'a crisis of trust':

> For the superficial observer the political sphere seems to be predestined to be monopolized by shrewd propagandists: politics are regarded by vast numbers of people as the realm of initiated politicians, if not of grafters and machine bosses. The less the people believe in political integrity, the more easily can they be taken in by politicians who rant against politics.[40]

Second, and most importantly, he expands the usual fact-centric conception of truth in discussions of political communication to include 'insight' in its psychoanalytic sense. For those susceptible to what he glosses as 'mass manipulation' will not be persuaded by mere facts and correctives – that is, 'truth propaganda':

> *The psychological phase of the communication no less than its content should respect the truth principle.* While the irrational element is to be fully considered, it is not to be taken for granted but has to be attacked by enlightenment. Objective, factual reliability should be combined with the effort to promote insight into the irrational dispositions which make it hard for people to judge rationally and autonomously. The truth to be spread by democratic leadership pertains to facts which are clouded by arbitrary distortions and in many cases by the very spirit of our culture. It seeks to foster self-reflection in those whom we want to emancipate from the grip of all-powerful conditioning. This double desideratum seems to be the more justified since there can hardly be any doubt about the existence of an intimate interaction between both factors, the delusions of antidemocratic ideology and the absence of introspection (the latter fact being largely due to defense mechanisms).[41]

Adorno here relies on an understanding of psychoanalytic insight as consistent with the Kantian characterization of the Enlightenment project of intellectual autonomy from servitude, to which he directly alludes in this essay. Crucially, the kind of epistemic model of political communication relied upon recently by Habermas is found to be necessary but insufficient.[42] Rather than the quarantining of irrationality attributed to him by Lane, Adorno wishes to redress the irrational dispositions of demagogy's followers with what he deems reason's appropriate reflective achievement, psychoanalysis. However, the logic of this approach leads him even further away from any 'statesman'-like remedy. Yet, Adorno's democratic leader does provide, in effect, a social-psychological re-rendering of Weber's 'ethical' portrait of 'positive' modern demagogy.

It may have been more useful if the Institute had employed the classical distinction between demagogue and tyrant – or even distinguished 'demagogue' from 'authoritarian leadership' – as this would have reduced some of the resultant ambiguity. However, there are advantages in its 'dual' usage of the pejorative sense of demagogue. First, it served the immediate purpose of recognizing the empirical continuities between European fascist demagogues in power – 'tyrants' – and the varyingly successful demagogues in the USA. This conceptual equation may 'overestimate' the significance of some US demagogues, but it also made it easier to stress the trajectory of these figures from their less powerful beginnings.

From the perspective of populism studies, the Institute's model of the demagogue makes plain *the contingent commonality of demagogic leadership for populist and fascist movements*. Figure 1 displays this contingency. A more elaborated version of this trajectory is provided in Chapter 3.

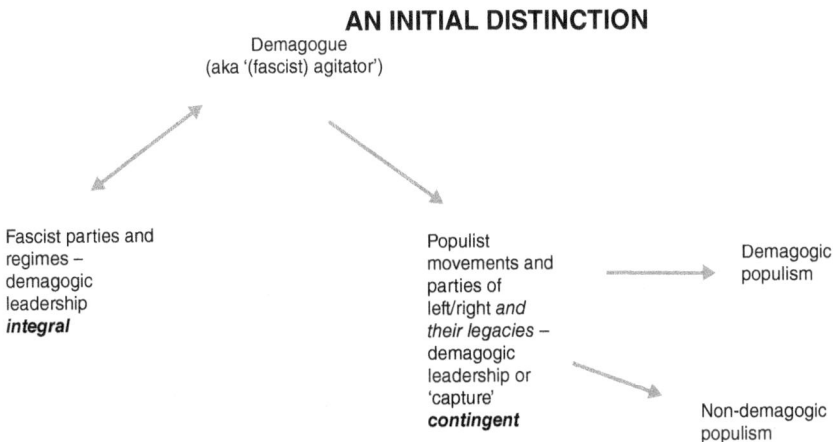

1 An initial distinction

(b) Demagogic devices, their social psychology, and populism

The Studies in Prejudice project, at least as initially conceived, was to have two chief lines of research: a more limited one to 'deal with specific problems facing educational agencies' and a more comprehensive one that was broader in scope. These goals did not, however, precisely correspond with the eventual output.[43] Adorno's and Horkheimer's explicit references to establishing an educational handbook to counter demagogical 'propaganda', consistent with that AJC remit, have seemed at best perplexing, not least because they went unfulfilled.[44] Yet the model for this idea and key elements of the critical approach to the demagogues is quite clearly declared: both of the monographs on demagogic techniques, and especially Adorno's body of work on this topic, acknowledge the influence of the 1939 'handbook' by Alfred and Elizabeth Lee, *The Fine Art of Propaganda*.[45] The Lees worked under the auspices of another institute, The Institute for Propaganda Analysis. Their intellectual influence went beyond that of 'educational' exemplar. In the 'mass manipulation' essay discussed in section (a) Adorno refers to the Lees' book as if it were a de facto publication of Studies in Prejudice.[46]

It is a measure of the inattention to the demagogy studies that no discussion of this influence appears to have occurred within critical theory.[47] Conversely, in propaganda studies, where the Lees' book has come to be regarded as a canonical example of 'progressive' propaganda analysis, Adorno and Lowenthal's expansion of that project has there gone un-noted.[48] This 'progressive' tradition of propaganda critique is not to be confused with the behaviourist 'media effects' models with which it and, in some literatures, Adorno's work on the culture industry, are often conflated. It was a 'muckraking' tradition that saw its task as one of critical popular education.[49]

Like Adorno's monograph, *The Fine Art of Propaganda* is focused on the oratory of a single radio demagogue. However, while Adorno's Martin Luther Thomas remains a remarkably obscure figure, the Lees' Father Charles Coughlin was the most famous and influential radio demagogue of all. Of particular pertinence to *Studies in Prejudice* too was the Lees' collection of their Coughlin material in a period in which the question of his antisemitism had come to the fore.[50] *Prophets of Deceit* draws on speeches, broadcasts and published writings of many demagogic figures, including a substantial body of material by Coughlin (yet not Thomas).

Published a year before the Studies in Prejudice demagogy studies commenced, *The Fine Art* bequeathed a methodological emphasis on 'the techniques' of the demagogue's oratory which the Lees termed 'devices'. Unlike Adorno and Lowenthal, the Lees chose 'Coughlin's radio talks because they represent a fairly typical borrowing of foreign anti-democratic propagandist methods by an American propagandist'.[51] They established seven devices, popular knowledge of which they thought would alleviate the effects of propaganda. Separating 'the device from the idea' enabled seeing 'what the idea amounts to on its own merits'.[52]

Of course, neither Adorno nor Lowenthal endorsed such a simple form/content distinction. As we shall see, Adorno would argue that there was very little if any 'idea' left once the devices were fully analysed. This is consistent with Adorno's discussions of immanent ideology critique whereby the 'truth content' redeemable by critique is dependent on the presence of such a potentiality within the aesthetic or ideological work in question. As Adorno later argued in *Aspects of Sociology*:

> Accordingly, the critique of ideology, as the confrontation of ideology with its own truth, is only possible insofar as the ideology contains a rational element with which the critique can deal. That applies to ideas such as those of liberalism, individualism ... But whoever would want to criticize, for instance, the so-called ideology of National Socialism would find himself victim of an impotent naiveté. Not only is the intellectual level of the authors Hitler and Rosenberg beneath all criticism. The lack of any such level, the triumph over which must be counted among the most modest of pleasures, is the symptom of a state, to which the concept of ideology, is no longer directly relevant ... rather it is a manipulative contrivance, a mere instrument of power, which actually no-one, not even those who used it themselves, expected to be taken seriously. With a sly wink they point to their power: try using your reason against that, and you will see where you end up ... Where ideologies are replaced by approved views decreed from above, the critique of ideology must be replaced by *cui bono* – in whose interest?[53]

Of course, in Studies in Prejudice the focus is on 'irredeemable' views from figures who are not 'above', i.e., holding state power. Each of the Institute's major demagogy studies so employed the exegetical/analytical mode of the Lees' device typology. Such instrumentalization suited their emphasis on rationalized standardization (discussed in the final section of this chapter). Although commonly renamed by Adorno and Lowenthal 'techniques' and even 'tricks', such 'devices' thus became their analytic alternative to the categories of classical rhetoric and especially its emphasis on rational argument, consistent with the irredeemability of this material. This set of methodological protocols also accounts for the paradox, as Crook sees it, that Adorno 'is not interested in "rhetoric" as such'.[54]

Adorno repeatedly compares Thomas to Coughlin and cites four of the Lees' devices in so doing. He adds many more devices but locates these in a set of socio-psychological dynamics completely absent from the Lees' work – hence the 'psychological technique' of his title and the 'techniques' in Lowenthal's subtitle.[55] As Adorno later put it: 'The devices pointed out in McClung Lee's book on Father Coughlin ... are only elements of a much farther-reaching pattern of behaviour.'[56] This 'psychotechnics', as he often called it, also went beyond the pursuit of 'interest' (*cui bono*) as the alternative to the critique of ideology portrayed in the citation from *Aspects of Sociology* above.

Indeed, Adorno even ties one of these 'farther-reaching patterns' to one of the Lees' devices in order to elucidate a key feature of modern demagogic techniques. Here the 'rhetorical' performative mode of the modern demagogue is made clearer: what Adorno calls (in a passage cited later in this chapter) a dissociational 'flight of ideas':

> Argumentation has been replaced by the device, termed in the book on Coughlin by the Institute of Propaganda Analysis the 'name-calling device.' This is grounded not only in the weakness of fascist reasoning itself, which, from the viewpoint of its profiteers, is reasonable enough. It is rather based upon a cynical contempt for the audience's capacity to think – a contempt overtly expressed by Hitler. Thomas reckons with an audience who cannot think, that is to say, who is too weak to maintain a continuous process of making deductions. They are supposed to live intellectually from moment to moment, as it were, and to react to isolated, logically unconnected statements, rather than to any consistent structure of thought. They know what they want and what they do not want, but they cannot detach themselves from their own immediate and atomistic reactions. It is one of the main tricks of Thomas to dignify this atomistic thinking as a kind of intellectual process. By reproducing in his speeches the vagueness of a thinking process confined to mere associations, a 'monologue interieure', Thomas provides a good intellectual conscience for those who cannot think. He cunningly substitutes a 'paranoic' [sic] scheme for a rational process.[57]

This is indicative of the reworking of the Lees' work Adorno undertakes. The Lees remain focused on a counter-demagogic strategy I categorized in the previous section as 'liberal exposure'. That is, they argued that the demagogue could be defeated by the exposure of demagogic/propagandist rhetorical devices and, to a lesser extent, the 'fact-checking' of such oratory's specific content. It is thus allied to the liberal norms of journalism and an implied 'informed citizen' discussed in Chapter 8.

Adorno respects the Lees' identification of devices, especially their role in qualitatively distinguishing demagogic propaganda from, and its displacement of, reasoned argument. Yet liberal exposure is insufficient. As we saw, his own term for this strategy is 'truth propaganda'. Nonetheless, in the above citation he characteristically positions his critique *against* the contempt the demagogue holds for the audience, rather than against that audience itself. This perspective privileges neither a hypostasized 'reason' nor 'emotion' but, rather, the use of reflective insight.

The demagogy studies also overlapped with the composition of *Dialectic of Enlightenment*, the leading 'basic research' element of Studies in Prejudice. Adorno later identified its 'Elements of Anti-Semitism' as theoretically 'determinative' of his participation in the wider project.[58] In its sixth subsection he and Horkheimer argued that the major socio-psychological mechanisms at work in antisemitic demagogy were paranoia and 'false projection'.[59] The key projection, the first stages of which are evident in the process described in the citation above from Adorno's demagogy study, lies in the demagogue's attribution of undesirable qualities to the othered which actually exist within himself.[60]

As Jay has observed, because it was only first translated into English much later (1972), *Dialectic*'s 'objective complement to the subjective approach of the *Studies* was lost to view' in the USA.[61] As we have just seen in the case of Lane's 2012 critique of Adorno, however, the interdependence of these disparate texts continues to facilitate misunderstandings many years after that translation was published. Jay's framing nonetheless helps us place Lane's accusation that Adorno merely adds an epistemological dimension to the traditional statesman-demagogue distinction in a different, again psychoanalytic, light. For Adorno and Horkheimer's account of the paranoia/projection dynamic distinguishes a *legitimate* epistemological role for projection which, they argue, is embedded in all perception. Consistent with Adorno's argument in the 'mass manipulation' essay, the redemptive warrant here is Kantian as Kant employed a role for projection in his discussions of perception in *The Critique of Pure Reason*.

Moreover, as in the 'mass manipulation' essay, the capacity for insightful reflection emerges as the enduring (but threatened) achievement of the Enlightenment, which is not reduced to, but includes, insight achieved via the practice of psychoanalysis. Reflective insight so functions both epistemologically and psychically. Epistemologically, it 'consciously' mediates and 'preserves the tension between' subject and object (in Jay's phrasing) such that neither subjectivism nor objectivism (especially positivism) dominates. Psychically, reflective insight regulates the relationship between the inner and outer world, between self and others. Psychic projection, essential to the very process of conceptual thinking, is disabled by paranoia, 'the shadow of cognition'.[62] Such paranoia is integral to 'false projection', of which antisemitism is a supreme example.

The 'healthy' epistemological alternative to paranoid projection thus does not rely on a contrast with 'emotionality' – as Lane's statesman-demagogue distinction would require – but with a paranoid pseudo-knowledge, the domain of projective conspiracy 'theorization':

> Paranoid forms of consciousness tend to give rise to leagues, factions, rackets. Their members are afraid to believe their madness on their own. Projecting it, they everywhere see proselytizing and conspiracy.[63]

Such paranoid pseudo-knowledge is indeed central to many of the 'devices' Adorno and Lowenthal map. Adorno and Horkheimer speculate that religions formerly provided a collective means of regulating projection. In contrast, 'bourgeois property, education and culture drove paranoia into the dark corners of society and the psyche'. However, in late capitalism, 'the present order of life allows the self no scope to draw intellectual or spiritual conclusions'. The fetishism of knowledge as facticity, for example, disables 'the self-reflection of the mind, which counteracts paranoia'.[64]

A third psychoanalytic mechanism was identified by Adorno in the last of his 'sidebar' essays: narcissism. Here too the titular focus was 'propaganda': 'Freudian Theory and the Pattern of Fascist Propaganda' (1951). While a role for narcissism was strongly implied in 'Elements of Anti-Semitism', it is this text that lays out the schema systematically. Indeed, the paper is explicitly presented as a necessary 'theoretical frame of reference' to supplement the demagogy studies and so prevent their analyses of devices remaining 'somewhat haphazard and arbitrary'.[65]

Adorno's solution to this need is a reading of Freud's *Group Psychology and the Analysis of the Ego* which, famously, is itself in part a reading of Le Bon's *The Crowd: A Study of the Popular Mind*. What distinguishes Freud from Le Bon, Adorno argues, is:

> the absence of the traditional contempt for the masses which is the *thema probandum* of most of the older psychologists. Instead of inferring from the usual descriptive findings that the masses are inferior per se and likely to remain so, he asks in the spirit of true enlightenment: what makes the masses into masses?[66]

So again, the project of psychoanalysis is tied to that of enlightenment. The appeal of the group psychology for Adorno is neatly summed up in this unusually fulsome footnote:

> The German title, under which the book was published in 1921, is *Massenpsychologie and Ichanalyse*. The translator, James Strachey, rightly stresses that the term group here means the equivalent of Le Bon's *foule* and the German *Masse*. It may be added that in this book the term ego does not denote the specific psychological agency as described in Freud's later writings in contrast to the id and the superego; it simply means the individual. It is one of the most important implications of Freud's *Group Psychology* that he does not recognize an independent, hypostatized 'mentality of the crowd,' but reduces the phenomena observed and described by writers such as Le Bon and McDougall to regressions which take place in each one of the individuals who form a crowd and fall under its spell.[67]

Accordingly, Freud so anticipated (for Adorno) the dynamics of the relationship between demagogue and follower by conceptualizing the libidinal bond between members of such a group. Thus, Adorno argues, 'it might be hypothesized that the bond in question is the very same the demagogue tries to produce synthetically; in fact it is the unifying principle behind his various devices'.[68]

For Freud, the libidinal bond of the group entails a release from repression of unconscious drives. He goes to some lengths to distinguish 'leaderless' groups from those with leaders and 'artificial' groups – such as the Catholic Church and the army – from primary groups. 'Artificial' groups have the capacity for enforcing membership and of course have leaders. They differ from Le Bon's 'rapidly formed and transient' groups (crowds) too. Having set aside Trotter's conception of 'herd instinct', Freud offers instead his famous informing historico-speculative conception of the archaic 'primal horde' led by a single dominant male who is slain by his sons. What is often overlooked, however, is that this conception of 'horde' is also used here to stress the different configuration of the groups which Freud highlights, so bringing the leader-group dynamic once again to the fore. Indeed, in facing the complexity of the modern situation of multiple points of identification for the ego, Freud uses the term 'prodigy' in its sense of supreme example, to suggest that the Le Bonian conception of the group as 'rapidly formed and transient' crowd is analogous to a 'pure type', in the Weberian sense, whereby the individual ego undergoes 'the complete, although temporary, disappearance'.[69]

Adorno seizes on Freud's key postulation of a shared 'ego ideal' by members of the group, for which Freud even provides a diagram.[70] The ego-ideal is understood by Freud at this point of his career as the imagined best self towards which the ego strives.

The import of this requires some psychoanalytic backgrounding. Commencing with the frustrated desire for a parent in the Oedipal phase, the ego commences on a process of inhibition and redirection of some sexual aims. With mature love the ego must differentiate 'sensual desire' from 'tender love' whereby the latter may involve the repression, sublimation or setting-aside of sexual aims. In the situation of an unachievable love object, *idealization* may result. Idealization 'falsifies judgement' so that the desired is viewed as perfect, incapable of doing wrong. Many forms of love relations contain a narcissistic dimension in that 'the object serves as substitute for some ego-ideal of our own'. The ego-ideal is thus a key feature of *identification* and *narcissism* in that 'narcissistic libido overflows on the love object' in its subject-object form.[71] In the group situation, however, the same love object – inhibited as an aim – is shared by all group members. This may be a leader or, in different circumstances, an 'idea'. The members of such a primary group take the leader as their ego-ideal and identify 'themselves with one another in their ego'.[72]

Perhaps the most significant connection for Adorno's conception of the demagogy-follower relationship occurs in this passage from Freud which follows directly from the 'prodigy' framing discussed above. Here Freud points to a scenario where the individual ego is not so completely subsumed:

> In many individuals the separation between the ego and the ego-ideal is not very far advanced; the two still coincide readily; the ego has often preserved its earlier self-complacency. The selection of the leader is very much facilitated by this circumstance. He need only possess the typical qualities of the individuals concerned in a particularly clearly marked and pure form, and need only give an impression of greater force and of more freedom of libido; and in that case the need for a strong chief will often meet him half-way and invest him with a predominance to which he would otherwise perhaps have had no claim. The other members of the group, whose ego-ideal would not, apart from this, have become embodied in his person without some correction, are then carried away with the rest by 'suggestion', that is to say, by means of identification.[73]

Much turns on this formulation for Adorno and indeed for 'modern demagogy'. It underlines the point that, psychologically if not socially, there is no need for a great gulf between follower and an 'elite' demagogic leadership. But, as a result, the demagogue must also employ the contradictory device of 'the great little man' to appear as both 'leader' and, in a sense, an 'enlargement' of the follower.[74] The demagogue's devices are thus characterized by ambivalence and, for Adorno, the sado-masochistic dynamic that first appeared in the *Studien*. The follower so wishes 'to submit to authority and to be the authority himself'.[75]

It is from this dynamic that Adorno employs Freud to reach an account of the central 'in-group versus out-group' features of demagogic practice. In a mode of argument not unlike Weber's, Freud postulates that the religious rejection and persecution of non-believers will not necessarily fade with the decline of religions but could be reconstituted in secular form. Adorno ties this to another of his devices, 'buck and sheep', which tracks such a secularizing redefinition of the out-group in Thomas's pseudo-religious technique. Likewise, a 'unity trick' refers to Thomas's inclusionary 'in-group' device: 'we're all in the same boat'.[76]

While it is indeed Adorno who follows through the psychoanalytic framing of the demagogy studies more explicitly in his supplementary writings, of the two monographs it is *Prophets of Deceit* which employs the paranoia/projection model more closely. It also gives a greater sense of the social contexts of the followers' group formation. Lowenthal states that he and Guterman 'have drawn freely' on Adorno's 'pilot study' but a key difference is their sourcing of demagogic techniques to multiple demagogues. By repeatedly establishing such consistency, *Prophets of Deceit* is able to demonstrate a process of rationalized standardization more readily, in orthodox social scientific evidentiary terms, than the typically speculative form the culture industry argument usually took.[77]

Notably, some of the material Lowenthal draws on predates Coughlin's most openly antisemitic period when, according to accounts like Kazin's discussed in Chapter 1, he was 'merely' a populist.[78] Another figure Lowenthal includes, Gerald L.K. Smith, had an even more remarkably 'transitional' career than Coughlin's: having started as 'a product of the mid-Western Protestant fundamentalist tradition', he progressed through clandestine membership of the Ku Klux Klan to being director of Long's Share Our Wealth movement. On Long's assassination, he failed to take over Long's legacy but then played a key leadership role in the coalition that supported Coughlin's candidate in the 1936 presidential election. Like Coughlin, his antisemitism became more intense later in his career but he 'flirted' with Pedley's fascist Silver Shirts even before his association with Long.[79]

While these 'career paths' seem at times bewildering, they ably demonstrate the significance of the commonality of demagogues to populist and 'self-declared' fascist movements and, of course, the contingency of left or right articulations of populist formations. *Prophets of Deceit* so provides evidence for the co-presence of modern demagogy in populist and fascistic formations, as I sketched in Figure 1.

Of course, a more prosaic description might refer to these figures as opportunists who attach themselves to whichever movement or quasi-movement arises. To some extent this dimension is included in Lowenthal's account and stated explicitly by Adorno in his unpublished introduction.[80] The demagogue thus differs from reformers and revolutionaries in that specific programmes of reform or specific proposals for wholesale structural transformation never emerge. Rather than finely tuning reformist policies or even promoting a dogmatic manifesto in response to changing circumstances, the demagogue instead opportunistically holds to consistently framed 'agitational themes'. Smith, for instance, readjusted the 'list of demands' for the Share of Wealth movement in part by monitoring those of Coughlin and other movements. The key demagogic 'constant' is the rendering of grievances as 'emotions or emotion complexes' (distrust, dependence, exclusion, anxiety, disillusionment). These rely on a subjectivization of the grievance such that it is understood as unmediated by social institutions. The experience of the grievance is thus presented as the result of actions by a personalized enemy who 'is presented as acting, so to speak, directly on his victims without the intermediary of a social form'.[81] The themes are, however, refined by improvisation and attunement with audiences in performance.

Consistent with Adorno's highlighting of paranoia/projection, Lowenthal's account of demagogic success turns on the demagogue's encouragement of 'a paranoiac relationship to the external world' in his audience. Accordingly, the thematic analyses focus on potentially paranoiac content in demagogic discourse: the hostility of the modern world, an escalating series of thematics relating to types of enemies (building to 'the enemy as Jew') and the construction of an endogamic community entailing 'housecleaning'.[82]

Adorno noted in 1968 that the discrete researches into 'fascist stimuli' (i.e. the demagogy studies) and socio-psychological 'susceptibility' (primarily *The Authoritarian Personality*) were never fully articulated within Studies in Prejudice, implying there was no 'audience research' as such.[83] Despite a similar disclaimer regarding audience reception, there is textual evidence within *Prophets of Deceit* that the 'skilled court stenographers' and 'trained reporters' who attended the demagogues' public meetings for its research kept records of audience reactions such as silent attentiveness and laughter.[84]

The fullest analytic integration in *Prophets of Deceit* of the thematic elements with such recorded audience reactions – and the paranoia/projection model – occurs in the treatment of the moment of transition to explicitly antisemitic rhetoric. In the key example, this move is achieved by the elicitation of laughter from the audience. This occurs when 'Goldstein' is revealed as the name of a figure (a psychiatrist, no less) in a complex conspiracy narrative. This narrative is also framed by what Adorno highlights in his book as the leading demagogic personalizing device: the 'lone wolf' self-description of the demagogue as 'persecuted innocent victim' (here, of the conspiracy in the narrative). The laughter punctures a period of silent attentiveness by the audience and signals a moment of recognition of what has previously been innuendo. It also marks a transition – via metaphors of 'cleansing' – into explicit antisemitic incitement whereby the 'persecuted' demagogue invites his audience to join with him in pursuing his 'persecutors'.[85] The laughter thus 'seems to foreshadow the pleasure of the anticipated hunt'. Lowenthal and Guterman go on from this point to give a precise conceptual elaboration of the same dynamic of paranoia and projection as that in 'Elements of Anti-Semitism'.[86]

The demagogue's performative role is pivotal to this process. Drawing on his own work and Lowenthal's in 1946, Adorno provided this account of how demagogic speech differed from traditional oratory and argument. It resembles the earlier citation of Adorno's psychoanalytic elaboration of the Lee's 'name-calling device':

> It does not employ discursive logic but is rather ... what might be called an organized flight of ideas. The relation between premises and inferences is replaced by a linking-up of ideas resting on mere similarity, often through association by employing the same characteristic word in two propositions which are logically quite unrelated. This method not only evades the control mechanism of rational examination, but also makes it psychologically easier for the listener to 'follow'.[87]

As we saw in Lowenthal's 'Goldstein' example above, such associational 'logic' can inform a suspenseful narrative dynamic too whereby the association is increasingly one of innuendo contained within a demagogic performance that enacts a mode of disinhibited hysteria. It is the performative removal of taboo/inhibition that consolidates the rapport with the followers/audience. For Adorno this capacity for disinhibited speech is the key distinction between the demagogue and his followers 'though they otherwise resemble their listeners in most respects'. This division of labour so includes risk-taking by the demagogues such that they 'are taken seriously because they risk making fools of themselves'.[88]

In 'Elements of Anti-Semitism' this performative liminality is elaborated in more detail. Its quasi-comic dimension is best known today via Chaplin's parody in *The Great Dictator* which also receives mention in *Dialectic of Enlightenment*.[89] Here it is illustrated via the devices of four canonical demagogic figures: Hitler, Mussolini, Goebbels ... and Coughlin. While Coughlin is here undoubtedly categorized as an antisemitic fascist rather than populist, it is important to note that Adorno elsewhere insists that such demagogic stereotypy, and especially the devices, are not confined to antisemitic usage.[90]

Moreover, the demagogy studies are replete with acknowledgements of the specificity of the US case and its populism in contrast to European fascism. Adorno's discussion of 'president-baiting' as a device, for example, points to opportunities provided by democracies in general 'and the American constitution in particular' in enabling a 'people vs the executive' polarizing discourse.[91] He also assesses the domestic resources on which a US fascist demagogue might draw when emulating the Nazi anti-statism which (at the time he was writing) had resulted in a conceptual/legal struggle between 'party' and 'state' whereby the Nazi regime was replacing 'state' with 'party', 'nation' or 'folk'. He sees considerable potential in Thomas's exploitation of US nonconformist religious traditions by employing a device that echoes the nonconformist call to the faithful to reject institutional doctrine for personal religious experience and revelation. A call to personal religious liberty is so turned towards its opposite, an anti-institutionalism that facilitates 'the fascist ideal'.[92] Indeed, Adorno found it necessary to establish a subset of dedicated religious devices. The parallel with Daniel Bell's later work on the secular evangelist discussed in Chapter 1 is here quite striking.

Lowenthal and Guterman's situations of US populism are less oblique and directly address the contingency of the demagogue in populist movements and proto-fascist formations. Indeed, this text regularly contrasts demagogic mobilization with other movements, whether reformist or 'revolutionary'. Now, the consensus that both Institute demagogy studies reach is that while the New Deal offered a viable target, a direct Nazi-like demagogic assault on democracy or 'established government' as such was not a viable option in the USA and thus other domestic traditions needed to be called on.[93] Lowenthal and Guterman recognize US Populism as one such resource 'whose tradition the agitator tries at many points to utilize'. 'Even the populist rebellion', they state, 'was mainly against various financial groupings rather than against the government as such'.[94] The implication here is that the US Populist movement of the 1890s is nonetheless regarded by demagogues as the most promising source from which to draw thematics.

In a 1948 essay Lowenthal and Guterman acknowledged that 'nobody is thinking of agitators right now' in the USA. Acknowledging Coughlin's and Smith's 'mass movements', they comment:

> Far more numerous are those less conspicuous agitators who are active locally and who, far from evoking the image of a leader worshipped by masses of followers, rather suggest quack medicine salesmen. Their

activity has many characteristics of a psychological racket: they play on vague fears or expectations of a radical change. Some of these agitators hardly seem to take their own ideas seriously, and it is likely that their aim is merely to make a living by publishing a paper or holding meetings. What they give their admission-paying audience is a kind of act – something between a tragic recital and a clownish pantomime – rather than a political speech. Discussion of political topics invariably serves them as an occasion for vague and violent vituperation and often seemingly irrelevant personal abuse. The line between the ambitious politician and the small-time peddler of discontent is hard to draw, for there are many intermediary types.[95]

All that US fascists are said to share with their Weimar counterparts of 1923–24 is that they are at 'a preliminary stage where movement and racket may blend'. However, they also refer to the recent successes of two such figures on a 'mass movement' scale during the New Deal, both of whom were analysed in *Prophets of Deceit*: Coughlin and Gerald K. Smith. As we have seen, these two did indeed have 'mass movements' and are commonly characterized as 'populists'. Lowenthal's implication of an ideal-typification of 'pure' and 'intermediary types' of modern demagogy was to go unfulfilled, however.

(c) Psychotechnics: the modern demagogue as cultural producer

Adorno provided this more explicit formulation of the specificity of the US demagogue in his unpublished introduction to Lowenthal's monograph:

> The relative accidentalness and emptiness of the content of agitation, its complete subordination to manipulative purposes, is obvious. There are profound reasons for this conspicuous lack of content, above all, the absence of a tradition of autocthinous [sic] and aggressive imperialist nationalism in America. Thus, American patterns of non-political manipulation – and especially certain marginal phenomena – had to be fused artificially with fascist notions of the Italian and German brand. One has to think of the barker who puts such high pressure behind advertising that it approaches violence. Much has also been borrowed from fanatic religious revivalism – promoting an ecstasy which is relished as such and unrelated to any concrete content, while rigid, dogmatic stereotypes, as e.g. the distinction between the damned and the saved ones, are ruthlessly plugged. The modern American agitator shrewdly feeds on

these old-fashioned methods. He warms them up for psychotechnical reasons and handles them quite consciously – as a political 'human relations expert'. Methods derived from industry and standardized mass culture are presented under a backward, obsolete 'character mask' and thus transferred to politics.[96]

'Psychotechnics', charismatic authority and culture industry are so linked for Adorno. This appears to be the only occasion in which he described this process as one of *transference* from culture industry to politics. Yet it is more consistent with his general argument about the specificity of modern demagogy than any other formulation – *culture-industrial demagogy so brings a qualitatively new dimension to the domain of politics*. Crucially, this psychotechnic mode of demagogy is not produced within the political sphere but transferred to it from its own space of 'synthetic' production. In effect the culture industry becomes a 'new' crucible for the production of modern demagogues. It is in the 'Culture Industry' fragment of *Dialectic* that he glosses psychotechnics as 'a procedure for manipulating human beings'.[97]

Adorno regularly uses the words 'artificial' or 'synthetic' to convey this form of demagogic leader–group bonding. But the whole process is regarded as a psychotechnics, a variant of the 'psychological techniques' (in English) of his demagogy monograph's title.[98] He seems to have first employed 'psychotechnics' in the *Martin Luther Thomas* draft in 1943. *Psychoteknik* attracted considerable interest in Weimar Germany as a modern 'rationalization movement' in its own right and as a mode of industrial psychology, including especially vocational aptitude testing, at times as a more humane rival to Taylorist methods.[99] Psychotechnics was widely adopted by German industries in the early 1920s and at least one advocate later adapted the technique to the needs of the Nazi regime.[100] Its leading proponent, Hugo Münsterberg, who also emigrated to the USA, wrote one of the first theoretical treatises on cinema and used cinematic techniques within his psychotechnics.[101] One of the main Weimar empirical psychotechnical studies conducted concerned The Tiller Girls dancing troupe. Any of these developments may have suggested to Adorno the relevance of psychotechnics to the culture industry and modern demagogy.[102] While he uses the term in an industrial sense to point to the intersection of wider industrial standardization/Taylorization and culture industry standardization, he also ties it to a complementary process in the sphere of cultural 'consumption'. Of course, unlike its early proponents, Adorno's usage relies on his core psychoanalytic dimensions for analysing demagogy, which are narcissism, paranoia and projection.

Both Lowenthal and Adorno point to the difference between the levels of explicitness achieved in the meeting/rally environment and the broadcast or printed transcript versions of demagogic performance. Innuendo plays this practical role but isn't entirely explained by it. For the disinhibited improvisational performance of the rally – its 'accidentalness' – is pivotal to the process of the production of demagogic speech. Adorno waivered here in different formulations concerning whether the demagogues employ their methods 'quite consciously', as he states in the passage above, or not. In his 'Freudian Theory' essay he portrays a more complex dynamic. At stake here is the related question of whether the demagogues had any psychoanalytic understanding of their own psychological role. Adorno sets this possibility aside but elaborates on the limits of the psychological resemblance of leader and follower, arguing that the leaders' disinhibited performances derive from their being 'oral character types' who speak compulsively. The related 'loss of ego control' adds to the ambivalent tension between projected strength and inner weakness. In practice, however, the agitator 'so to speak simply turns his own unconscious outward'.[103] Or, as Adorno put this more loosely, but starkly, five years earlier:

> Conditions prevailing in our society tend to transform neurosis and even mild lunacy into a commodity which the afflicted can easily sell, once he has discovered that many others have an affinity for his own illness. The fascist agitator is usually a masterly salesman of his own psychological defects.[104]

However, in the 'Freudian Theory' essay the analogue for this process of commodification shifts from Adorno's 'barker' and 'masterly salesman' and Lowenthal's 'quack medicine salesman' to 'creative' members of the culture industry: 'experience has taught him consciously to exploit this faculty, to make rational use of his irrationality, similar to the actor, or a certain type of journalist who know how to sell their innervations and sensitivity'.[105] This suggests a different level of 'conscious' procedure. For these examples imply practised performative improvisation and the contemporary analogue I would proffer is the stand-up comedian, not least because of the 'audience-testing' role of humour in demagogic performance. We might even consider the professional 'personality' as celebrity.

Such 'testing' leads Adorno to tie the 'surviving' tropes of demagogy more closely to culture industry practice:

> Through a process of 'freezing', which can be observed through the techniques of modern mass culture, the surviving appeals have been standardized, similarly to the advertising slogans which proved to be the most valuable in the promotion of business.[106]

This tension between 'creative' cultural-industrial production and advertising in these assessments of the commodification of demagogy strongly resembles that concerning popular music and broadcasting in Adorno's culture industry texts. Indeed, Adorno's repeated term for this intersection in *both* bodies of work is psychotechnics. Adorno regarded advertising too as a form of psychotechnics, but all cultural commodities risked being reduced to advertising.

The reference to 'freezing' above connotes the capacities afforded by recording processes, even though the demagogues' major means of 'reproduction' of demagogic propaganda did not include sold audio or visual recordings. Rather, in the 'Freudian Theory' essay 'freezing' refers to a comparable practice of standardization.

However, standardization for Adorno did not mean only formulaic production from a template, as important as that was for him in the case of popular song writing. In his 1941 essay, 'On Popular Music' (co-authored with George Simpson), and in the 'Culture Industry' fragment of *Dialectic*, he pinpointed specific procedures of standardized cultural production.[107] One of those became known in popular music studies as 'part-interchangeability', a term borrowed from Fordist production techniques. It is the principle that any comparable component of one hit song could take the place of another (as in Taylorized car manufacture). In the second subsection of the 'Culture Industry' fragment of *Dialectic*, the same argument is extended to Hollywood film, and in its conclusion he referred to this capacity by another name, 'the montage character of the culture industry'. That is, the formalist, component-like features of the aesthetic practice of montage lent themselves well to this 'industrial' process.[108]

Lowenthal's *Prophets of Deceit* opens with a three-page continuous citation of paranoid demagogic speech that reads as 'consistently' as any by Coughlin or his peers. Only in a footnote is it revealed that it is 'a composite of actual statements by American agitators', a montage from *different* demagogues. Lowenthal later called it an 'ideal-typical montage of an agitator's speech', so demonstrating what Adorno called the 'amazing stereotypy' of demagogic propaganda as well as its resemblance to the part-interchangeability of culture-industrial production.[109] I have summarized this process in Figure 2.

What then of the 'reception' of such culture-industrial demagogic propaganda? As detailed at the commencement of this chapter, identifying and predicting susceptibility to such propaganda had been the task of *The Authoritarian Personality*. As we saw, however, this production/consumption division of labour between that text and the demagogy studies was never resolved to Adorno's satisfaction. Yet, as we also saw, Lowenthal's demagogy study had included a modest reception dimension, albeit focused on the more explicit 'live' meetings held by demagogues.

Here it is important to distinguish the understanding of reception within the Studies in Prejudice Project from the connotations of the prefixed 'mass'

'a kind of psycho technics' (Adorno)

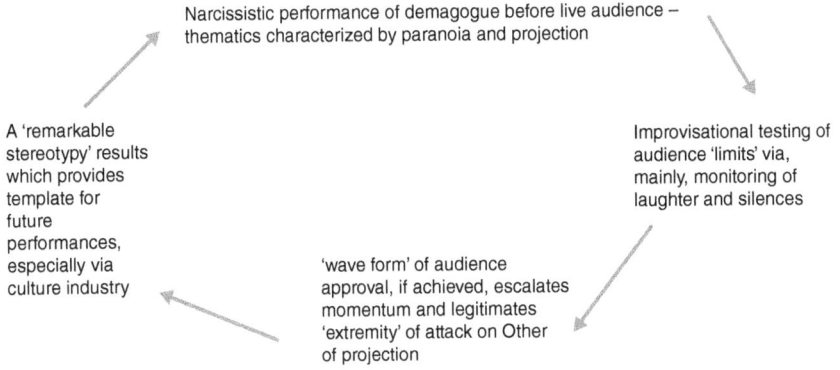

2 Psychotechnics of modern demagogy

often attributed to the Institute's work. Part of the confusion here certainly results from the Institute's incomplete – or inconsistent – practice of replacing 'mass culture' with 'culture industry' from the early 1940s, a dimension discussed in detail in Chapter 6. More typically, however, the Institute's work is simply incorrectly associated with variants of functionalist and even behaviourist approaches grouped under 'mass society' and 'mass communication'. The misreading of the Institute's *analogues* of 'mass culture' and (demagogic) 'propaganda' – and related associations with behaviourism – as an *equation* has only added to this confusion.[110]

Instead, the Institute's work was much more focused on the specificity of the demagogues' core addressees, who were never considered 'representative' of a societal 'mass'. The implicit group formation in, for example, Adorno's careful separation of Le Bon's 'contempt for the masses' from Freud's use of him, was the pogrom. Lowenthal's limited data on attendees at demagogues' meetings plainly worked from a similar assumption.

Indeed, *The Authoritarian Personality*'s initial identification of the reception of demagogic propaganda as a primary goal spells out a conception of a 'readiness level' in which those most susceptible to the propaganda could be expected to be the most inclined towards 'action'. However, the same text is at pains to point out the following:

> If there should be a marked increase in antidemocratic propaganda, we should expect some people to accept it and repeat it once, others when it seemed that 'everyone believed it', and still others not at all.[111]

This tripartite reception schema uncannily prefigures the very one that was subsequently pitched against a straw figure 'Frankfurt School determinism' in media and communications studies: Stuart Hall's model of dominant, negotiated and resistant decodings of a proffered media-message. Hall's model was linked with detailed, and somewhat inductive, 'ethnographic' audience research.[112] The Institute's schema, in contrast, sought primarily to delineate those most receptive to a specific form of communication.

If we return to the paranoia/projection dimension of demagogy in this context, it is significant that those interviewees in *The Authoritarian Personality* who had been 'typical high scorers' on the F-scale displayed ample evidence of paranoia and especially projection, making them likely candidates for the 'false projections' and paranoid thematics and devices offered by the demagogues. Moreover, these features also entail 'a tendency toward avoidance of introspection and of insight in general'.[113]

One can begin to see then the connections between *The Authoritarian Personality*'s findings and Adorno's guarded optimism that the provocation of 'insight' might be a more suitable line of contestation of demagogic propaganda than liberal exposure. He also sought to exploit another finding from *The Authoritarian Personality* interviews: the 'mobility in regard to the choice of their object of hatred'.[114] This refers to the capacity of the paranoid projection to shift from one 'scapegoat' to another in given circumstances (and thus a major reason why Studies in Prejudice could not be arbitrarily confined to antisemitism). Thus the remarkably named 'operation boomerang' moved from this premiss: 'It is our intention to use the mobility of prejudice for its own conquest.'[115]

That said, Adorno's confidence in 1950 still lay in the capacity of 'our manual' as the chief possible agent of such disruption.[116] Yet none of the texts that resulted were truly 'educational' in this sense. That is, they remained scholarly monographs and articles and were not targeted as educational texts in a manner comparable to the way the Lees' book was for 'every intelligent American'. In that sense a manual pitched at proto-fascists never appeared, nor was it clear how it might differ from the Lees' own manual.

The Lees themselves, however, had succeeded in tying analysis of the devices to contemporary popular song and film, as part of their programme of taking their educational project into schools. They even based a rhyme on the 'Heigh Ho' song in the then just-released Disney film, *Snow White and the Seven Dwarves*:

> Oh, we are the seven devices,
> We turn up in time of crisis;
> We play upon your feeling,

We set your brains a-reeling,
We are seven active contrabanders,
We are seven clever propaganders.[117]

Of course, this would have been anathema to Adorno and Lowenthal, even allowing for Adorno and Horkheimer's apparent preparedness to work on B-movie scripts for their Hollywood acquaintances while in Los Angeles. Yet the idea of a filmic project as part of Studies in Prejudice was very real, even if it too never saw realization. Nonetheless, I argue in Chapter 7 that this planned filmic intervention did reach a point in planning which strongly resembles Adorno's 'interrupted projection' strategy.

Indeed, one of the more famous formulations of what Adorno termed psychotechnics was Lowenthal's quip that both 'fascist agitation as well as culture industry' practised 'psychoanalysis in reverse'. Adorno later cited this in a discussion of television.[118] It is important to add that neither would have understood this as a 'universal' phenomenon across all elements of the culture industry. Nonetheless, it might be said that Adorno's planned but unfulfilled counter-measures towards the psychotechnics of modern demagogy were informed by this quip and were thus a kind of 'psychoanalysis in reverse, in reverse'.

Notes

1 For example, Jay devotes effectively a chapter and Wiggershaus a sub-chapter of similar length, to the project: *The Dialectical Imagination: A History of the Frankfurt School and the Institute of Social Research, 1923–1950*, 221–252; *The Frankfurt School: Its History, Theories, and Political Significance*, trans. Michael Robertson (Cambridge, Mass.: MIT Press, 1995), 350–380. See also Chapter 1 n53.
2 Here I commence using these two authors' names as shorthand for works that each co-authored with others. In the case of Adorno it is also because some sections of *Dialectic of Enlightenment* closely resemble his other writings, especially those concerning the culture industry. Cf.: Paul K. Jones, 'Márkus and the Retrieval of the Sociological Adorno', *Thesis Eleven* (2021).
3 Adorno et al., *The Authoritarian Personality*. The other four volumes were: Lowenthal and Guterman, *Prophets of Deceit: A Study of the Techniques of the American Agitator*; Paul W. Massing, *Rehearsal for Destruction: A Study of Political Anti-Semitism in Imperial Germany* (New York: Harper, 1949); Bruno Bettelheim and Morris Janowitz, *Dynamics of Prejudice: A Psychological and Sociological Study of Veterans* (New York: Harper, 1950); Nathan W. Ackerman and Marie Jahoda, *Anti-Semitism and Emotional Disorder: A Psychoanalytic Interpretation* (New York: Harper, 1950).
4 Lowenthal and Guterman, *Prophets of Deceit*.
5 See Chapter 1(c).

6 Theodor W. Adorno, *The Psychological Technique of Martin Luther Thomas' Radio Addresses* (Stanford: Stanford University Press, 2000). Adorno's volume was first published (in English, as it was written) within the German *Schriften* in 1975. Massing also conducted a pilot study and Bettelheim and Janowitz separately published a more quantitative study: Bruno Bettelheim and Morris Janowitz, 'Reactions to Fascist Propaganda: A Pilot Study', *Public Opinion Quarterly* 14, no. 1 (1950).
7 See Figure 1 in this chapter.
8 I refer here to the 1929 study of German workers' 'mentality' conducted by Fromm for the Institute but, controversially, never published by it. Cf. Jay, *The Dialectical Imagination*, 116–117; Erich Fromm, *The Working Class in Weimar Germany: A Psychological and Sociological Study* (Leamington Spa: Berg, 1984); Cf. Neil McLaughlin, 'Origin Myths in the Social Sciences: Fromm, the Frankfurt School and the Emergence of Critical Theory', *Canadian Journal of Sociology* (1999).
9 Max Horkheimer, ed. *Studien Über Autorität Und Familie*, Schriften Des Instituts Für Sozialforschung (Paris: Felix Alcan, 1936).
10 See the entry on 'The Family' in Frankfurt Institute for Social Research, *Aspects of Sociology*, trans. John Viertel (Boston: Beacon, 1972). There the German case is specified further in terms of the relationship between differing religious traditions in nation-states and their differing regulation of sexual mores. As in the *Studien*, there is an ongoing dialogue with sociological analysis, especially that of the USA. For a recent feminist recovery of the contemporary significance of the Institute's neglected conception of the family see: Barbara Umrath, 'A Feminist Reading of the Frankfurt School's Studies on Authoritarianism and Its Relevance for Understanding Authoritarian Tendencies in Germany Today', *South Atlantic Quarterly* 117, no. 4 (2018).
11 Max Horkheimer, 'Authority and the Family (1936)', in *Critical Theory: Selected Essays* (New York: Continuum, 1972).
12 Erich Fromm, *Escape from Freedom* (New York: Farrar & Rinehart, 1941). This book was published in London a year later with a different title: Erich Fromm, *The Fear of Freedom* (London: Routledge & Kegan Paul, 1942). Fromm and the Institute parted company in 1939.
13 Erich Fromm, 'Psychoanalytic Characterology and Its Relevance for Social Psychology (1932)', in *The Crisis of Psychoanalysis* (New York: Holt, Rinehart and Winston, 1976).
14 Fromm, 'The Method and Function of an Analytic Social Psychology: Notes on Psychoanalysis and Historical Materialism (1932)', 144–145. Italicization in original.
15 Erich Fromm, 'Psychoanalytic Characterology and Its Application to the Understanding of Culture', in *Culture and Personality*, ed. S.S. Sargent and M.W. Smith (New York: Viking, 1949), 4. By this point, however, Fromm had moved considerably from Freudian libido theory.
16 Erich Fromm, *Studien über Autorität und Familie*, cited in Rolf Wiggershaus, *The Frankfurt School: Its History, Theories, and Political Significance*, 152.
17 Fromm, *Escape from Freedom*, 179.
18 On the viability of this analysis, especially its class dimensions see: Neil McLaughlin, 'Nazism, Nationalism, and the Sociology of Emotions: *Escape from Freedom* Revisited', *Sociological Theory* (1996).
19 Cf. David Riesman, Nathan Glazer and Reuel Denney, *The Lonely Crowd: A Study in the Changing American Character* (New Haven: Yale University Press, 1950); Neil McLaughlin, 'Critical Theory Meets America: Riesman, Fromm, and *The Lonely Crowd*', *The American Sociologist* 32, no. 1 (2001).

20 As Held and Umrath each note, the inattention to the psychic development of daughters in these texts is the most systematic limitation of their conception of gender and power; David Held, *Introduction to Critical Theory: Horkheimer to Habermas* (Berkeley: University of California Press, 1980), 129. Umrath, 'A Feminist Reading of the Frankfurt School's Studies on Authoritarianism', 870.
21 Horkheimer, 'Authority and the Family (1936)', 118. Such framings in the *Studien* strongly influenced Habermas's 1962 account of the role of bourgeois familial intimacy in the emergence of the bourgeois public sphere. Jürgen Habermas, *The Structural Transformation of the Public Sphere: An Inquiry into a Category of Bourgeois Society*, trans. T. Burger (Cambridge, Mass.: MIT Press, 1989), 48; 260–261 n248. See Chapter 8.
22 As mentioned above, The Institute also conducted a study of antisemitism in American labour in liaison with the AJC. Its results were never published, partly at least because Horkheimer felt that publishing results that indicated extremely high rates of antisemitism might provoke the perception of 'a bunch of foreign-born intellectuals poking their noses into the private affairs of American workers' (Cited in Jay, *The Dialectical Imagination*, 225). Given the subsequent controversies for Hofstadter and *The Authoritarian Personality*, his caution may have been justified. See the recent work by Eva-Marie Ziege in reconstructing this project: 'Patterns within Prejudice: Antisemitism in the United States in the 1940s', *Patterns of Prejudice* 46, no. 2 (2012); 'The Irrationality of the Rational: The Frankfurt School and Its Theory of Society in the 1940s', in *Antisemitism and the Constitution of Sociology*, ed. Marcel Stoetzler (Lincoln: University of Nebraska Press, 2014).
23 Edward A. Shils, 'Authoritarianism: Right and Left', in *Studies in the Scope and Method of 'The Authoritarian Personality'*, ed. Richard Christie and Marie Jahoda (New York: Free Press, 1954).
24 Bob Altemeyer, *Right-Wing Authoritarianism* (Winnipeg: University of Manitoba Press, 1981); Bob Altemeyer, *The Authoritarian Specter* (Cambridge, Mass.: Harvard University Press, 1996); K. Stenner, *The Authoritarian Dynamic* (Cambridge: Cambridge University Press, 2005).
25 Michael Billig, *Fascists: A Social Psychological View of the National Front* (London: Academic Press, 1978), 49. Cf. Nevitt Sanford, 'Authoritarian Personality in Contemporary Perspective', *Handbook of Political Psychology* (1973). Indeed, the only chapter title in *The Authoritarian Personality* that alludes to the book title is by Sanford. Another measure of this arbitrariness is that a 1946 report on the project by two of its members refers to an 'Anti-Semitic Personality': Else Frenkel-Brunswik and R. Nevitt Sanford, 'The Anti-Semitic Personality: A Research Report', in *Anti-Semitism: A Social Disease*, ed. Ernst Simmel (New York: International Universities Press, 1946).
26 Adorno et al., *The Authoritarian Personality*, 4.
27 *The Psychological Technique of Martin Luther Thomas' Radio Addresses*, 3, 50. Apparently Long never actually said this.
28 Urbinati, *Democracy Disfigured*, 142.
29 Weber, 'The Profession and Vocation of Politics', 331.
30 Weber, 'The Profession and Vocation of Politics', 342.
31 Max Weber, 'Science as a Vocation', in *The Vocation Lectures/Max Weber*, ed. David S. Owen and Tracy B. Strong (Indianapolis: Hackett Publishing, 2004), 20–21.
32 See Chapter 3(e).
33 Melissa Lane, 'The Origins of the Statesman–Demagogue Distinction in and after Ancient Athens', *Journal of the History of Ideas* 73, no. 2 (2012): 199.

34 Theodor W. Adorno, 'Democratic Leadership and Mass Manipulation', in *Studies in Leadership: Leadership and Democratic Action*, ed. Alvin W. Gouldner (New York: Harper & Row, 1950).
35 Adorno, 'Democratic Leadership and Mass Manipulation', 436.
36 Of course, this very formulation reveals Lane is unaware of *The Dialectic of Enlightenment*.
37 Adorno, 'Democratic Leadership and Mass Manipulation', 428 n426.
38 Adorno, 'Democratic Leadership and Mass Manipulation', 423.
39 Shils, *The Torment of Secrecy: The Background and Consequences of American Security Policies*, 143–148; Slavoj Žižek, 'Against the Populist Temptation', *Critical Inquiry* 32, no. 3 (2006).
40 Adorno, 'Democratic Leadership and Mass Manipulation', 423.
41 Adorno, 'Democratic Leadership and Mass Manipulation', 423–424.
42 Jürgen Habermas, 'Political Communication in Media Society: Does Democracy Still Enjoy an Epistemic Dimension? The Impact of Normative Theory on Empirical Research', *Communication Theory* 16, no. 4 (2006).
43 Jay, *The Dialectical Imagination*, 234–235.
44 Horkheimer's co-authored foreword to the *Studies in Prejudice* series which prefaced each volume mentions this manual and Adorno even supplied an 'Illustrations of Manual' appendix to his 1950 article on demagogic leadership. The examples within the latter concern demagogic 'devices' and overlap with the content of his Martin Luther Thomas monograph. Adorno, 'Democratic Leadership and Mass Manipulation', 436–438.
45 Alfred McClung Lee and Elizabeth Briant Lee, *The Fine Art of Propaganda: A Study of Father Coughlin's Speeches* (New York: Harcourt Brace and Company, 1939). The Lees' book is the most cited academic source in the Adorno book and it is the first citation in *Prophets of Deceit* where it is lauded as a 'pioneering exception' to orthodox approaches. Lowenthal and Guterman, *Prophets of Deceit*, xv.
46 Adorno, 'Democratic Leadership and Mass Manipulation', 425 n424. Hadley Cantril, like Adorno, had worked on The Princeton Radio Research Project. He aided in the establishment of Studies in Prejudice, and had also served as president of the Institute for Propaganda Analysis. He was thus one likely source of Adorno's and Lowenthal's familiarity with the Lees' work.
47 Jacobs, however, does note Alfred Lee's review of *Prophets of Deceit: The Frankfurt School, Jewish Lives, and Antisemitism*, 100–101.
48 Garth Jowett and Victoria O'Donnell, *Propaganda & Persuasion*, sixth edn (Thousand Oaks, Calif.: Sage, 2015). Sproule's history of this subfield provides a role for the Frankfurt School, albeit based on the usual mischaracterizations, and notes that Alfred Lee advised him in 1985 that he had attended some of the Institute's Columbia seminars and was unimpressed. Yet Lee did publish an enthusiastic review of *Prophets of Deceit*. J. Michael Sproule, *Propaganda and Democracy: The American Experience of Media and Mass Persuasion* (Cambridge: Cambridge University Press, 1997), 254. Alfred McClung Lee, 'Prophets of Deceit: A Study of the Techniques of the American Agitator. (Book Review)', *Public Opinion Quarterly* 14 (1950).
49 Sproule, *Propaganda and Democracy*; J. Michael Sproule, 'Progressive Propaganda Critics and the Magic Bullet Myth', *Critical Studies in Media Communication* 6, no. 3 (1989).
50 Lee and Lee, *The Fine Art of Propaganda: A Study of Father Coughlin's Speeches*, 25.

51 'Introduction to the Octagon Edition', in *The Fine Art of Propaganda* (New York: Octagon Press), x.
52 Lee and Lee, *The Fine Art of Propaganda*, 24.
53 *Aspects of Sociology*, 190. I follow Márkus in regarding this text as Adorno's: György Márkus, *Culture, Science, Society: The Constitution of Cultural Modernity* (Leiden: Brill, 2011), 69.
54 Crook's is the best detailed discussion of the Martin Luther Thomas text I have found but his treatment of the *Studies in Prejudice* context is limited by his editorial need to compare it with 'The Stars Down to Earth', Adorno's study of *The Los Angeles Times* astrology column conducted ten years later. Stephen Crook, 'Introduction: Adorno and Authoritarian Irrationalism', in *Theodor W. Adorno: The Stars Down to Earth and Other Essays on the Irrational in Culture*, ed. Stephen Crook (London: Routledge, 1994), 25. Similarly, Apostolidis's (2000) treatment of Adorno's Martin Luther Thomas analysis as a failed exercise in immanent ideology-critique of the religious elements underestimates this Adornian distinction between redeemable and irredeemable materials. Coughlin receives no mention. Yet I am sympathetic to Apostolidis's similar arguments re the redemptive elements of 'mass culture', although Adorno's own work already displays such potential (see Chapters 6 and 7).
55 Cavelletto rightly notes the interpretive significance of Adorno's 1968 retrospective 'renaming' of the titular analytic focus as 'socio-psychological technique'. George Cavalletto, *Crossing the Psycho-Social Divide: Freud, Weber, Adorno and Elias* (Burlington, Vt.: Ashgate, 2007), 152. Theodor W. Adorno, 'Scientific Experiences of a European Scholar in America (1968)', in *Critical Models: Interventions and Catchwords* (New York: Columbia University Press, 1998), 237.
56 Theodor W. Adorno, 'Anti-Semitism and Fascist Propaganda', in *Anti-Semitism: A Social Disease*, ed. Ernst Simmel (Madison, Wis.: International Universities Press, 1946), 135.
57 Adorno, *The Psychological Technique of Martin Luther Thomas' Radio Addresses*, 33–34.
58 Adorno, 'Scientific Experiences of a European Scholar in America (1968)', 230.
59 This was the final, effectively concluding, subsection in the 1944 manuscript; a seventh was added after the the Second World War and appeared in the 1947 version.
60 The demagogues examined were all male. Lowenthal is credited as a co-author of the first three sections of 'Elements of Anti-Semitism'. Max Horkheimer and Theodor W. Adorno, *Dialectic of Enlightenment: Philosophical Fragments*, trans. Edmund Jephcott (Stanford: Stanford University Press, 2002), 137–172, xix. Lowenthal later stated that he was present for much of the writing of *Dialectic*: 'Scholarly Biography: A Conversation with Helmut Dubiel, 1979', in *An Unmastered Past: The Autobiographical Reflections of Leo Lowenthal*, ed. Martin Jay (Berkeley: University of California Press, 1987). See also Jay's exemplary exegesis of these psychoanalytic elements: Jay, 'The Jews and the Frankfurt School: Critical Theory's Analysis of Anti-Semitism'.
61 Jay, 'The Jews and the Frankfurt School', 143.
62 Horkheimer and Adorno, *Dialectic of Enlightenment*, 161. In most references to this work I refer to the author as 'Adorno' for ease of exposition and because I am usually tracing links between it and a separate Adorno text.
63 Horkheimer and Adorno, *Dialectic of Enlightenment*, 163.
64 Horkheimer and Adorno, *Dialectic of Enlightenment*, 163. Jay interprets this account as far more pessimistic than the English-language section of the Studies 'with its

call for increased education for tolerance' ('The Jews and the Frankfurt School', 147). While such counteractions are not mentioned in this text, the theoretical framework would otherwise appear identical, as the parallels I have drawn with the 'mass manipulation' essay suggest. The exception would be the understanding of 'late capitalism' which in this version does seem more 'totalizing'. This matter is linked to the Institute's debate over the 'state capitalism' thesis discussed in Chapter 3.

65 Theodor W. Adorno, 'Freudian Theory and the Pattern of Fascist Propaganda', *Psychoanalysis and the Social Sciences* 3 (1951): 280. This paper also appears to fulfil the requirements of a fuller account of what Adorno had called the 'ritual' dimensions of demagogic performance in 1946, viz., 'A comprehensive theory of fascist propaganda would be tantamount to a psychoanalytic deciphering of the more or less rigid ritual performed in each and every fascist address' ('Anti-Semitism and Fascist Propaganda', 133).

66 Adorno, 'Freudian Theory and the Pattern of Fascist Propaganda', 282.
67 Adorno, 'Freudian Theory and the Pattern of Fascist Propaganda', 281 n284.
68 Adorno, 'Freudian Theory and the Pattern of Fascist Propaganda', 283.
69 Sigmund Freud, *Group Psychology and the Analysis of the Ego*, trans. James Strachey (London: The International Psychoanalytical Press, 1922), 102. I rely here on Strachey's translation of the German 'Wunder' which has the more everyday meaning of 'marvel'. In either case, Freud's intention is clearly that Le Bon's conception of the crowd is not universally applicable but represents an 'extreme' case of the complete realization of the dynamic Freud has portrayed. Cf. Sigmund Freud, *Massenpsychologie Und Ich-Analyse* (Leipzig: Internationaler Psychoanalytischer Verlag GMBH, 1921), 113.
70 Freud, *Group Psychology and the Analysis of the Ego*, 80; Cf. 'Freudian Theory and the Pattern of Fascist Propaganda', 288–290. This diagram is reproduced in the further discussion of this text in Chapter 5(a).
71 Freud, *Group Psychology and the Analysis of the Ego*, 74.
72 Freud, *Group Psychology and the Analysis of the Ego*, 80.
73 Freud, *Group Psychology and the Analysis of the Ego*, 102.
74 Adorno, 'Freudian Theory and the Pattern of Fascist Propaganda', 290. Cf. Adorno, *The Psychological Technique of Martin Luther Thomas' Radio Addresses*, 18–23.
75 Adorno, 'Freudian Theory and the Pattern of Fascist Propaganda', 290–291. Adorno's elaboration of an addended comment by Freud regarding homosexuality has become, unsurprisingly, a matter of some controversy in contemporary queer theory. Randall Halle's is the most detailed such critique I have found. Halle also reviews Reich's and Fromm's positions but reserves his strongest criticism for Adorno. He nonetheless assumes that all three 'could speak of a mass psychology only by positing universally shared natural drives … A society that fosters full development of these drives, will guarantee the harmonious coexistence and satisfaction of those members' (*Queer Social Philosophy: Critical Readings from Kant to Adorno* [Urbana: University of Illinois Press], 139). Such 'naturalism' was certainly Reich's view and, in a different form, was also one towards which Fromm moved. However, it was just this 'naturalism' that led to Fromm's expulsion from the Institute in a move led by Adorno. Halle further asserts that all three regarded 'heterosexual desire' as 'the only one form that was admitted as healthy'. Confining my comments here to Adorno, I can see no evidence for this in such texts. Freud's comment is that: 'It seems certain that homosexual love is far more compatible with group ties, even when it takes the shape of uninhibited sexual tendencies.'

Halle seems to acknowledge that the role of *repressed* homosexuality, the sado-masochistic group psychology formulation (which is consistent with Freud's linkage of 'cultural suppression' and masochism elsewhere) is defensible as such but then seeks to prove that Adorno held a similar view of *overt* homosexuality. His chief evidence for this is Adorno's footnoted comment that follows on Freud's: 'This was certainly borne out under German Fascism where the borderline between overt and repressed homosexuality, just as that between overt and repressed sadism, was much more fluent than in liberal middle-class society' (Adorno, 'Freudian Theory and the Pattern of Fascist Propaganda', 283 n287). Halle interprets this passage as disregard for the Nazi persecution of homosexuals, so missing the implications of the dialectical use of 'overt sadism' in Adorno's formulation. For it is plain Adorno is referring to the followers of demagogues throughout the entire essay and in this comment (i.e. the homosexuality reference is to that within the Nazi party and, perhaps, its core followers). All such critiques I've found seem to overlook the much more prominent role for homosexuality in Studies in Prejudice which was no matter of footnoted speculations but quite central to the core research, viz., one of the most enduring questions in the F-scale was testing for what would now be termed homophobia, i.e., the Institute posited that proto-fascists could be detected, in part, by their hostility towards homosexuality (e.g. Adorno et al., *The Authoritarian Personality*, 15).

76 Adorno, 'Freudian Theory and the Pattern of Fascist Propaganda', 291; *The Psychological Technique of Martin Luther Thomas' Radio Addresses*, 85–87; 47–50.
77 There is thus a strong echo of Lowenthal's highly regarded work on popular biographies, especially his US study: Leo Lowenthal, 'Biographies in Popular Magazines', in *Radio Research 1942–1943*, ed. Paul Lazarsfeld and Frank Stanton (New York: Duell, Sloan and Pearce, 1944). Cf. Jay, *The Dialectical Imagination*, 237.
78 The key inclusion from the earlier period is Coughlin's published 'discourses' of 1931–32. Charles E. Coughlin, *Father Coughlin's Radio Discourses 1931–1932* (Royal Oak, Mich.: The Radio League of the Little Flower/Wildside Press, undated).
79 David H. Bennett, *Demagogues in the Depression: American Radicals and the Union Party, 1932–1936* (New Brunswick, NJ: Rutgers University Press, 1969), 113–144.
80 Theodor W. Adorno, 'Introduction to *Prophets of Deceit* (Unpublished)', (Leo Lowenthal Archive; Houghton Library, Harvard University, 1949). This text is appendixed to this book. I cite the relevant passage below.
81 Lowenthal and Guterman, *Prophets of Deceit*, 7.
82 Lowenthal and Guterman, *Prophets of Deceit*, 18, 20ff.
83 Adorno, 'Scientific Experiences of a European Scholar in America (1968)', 237.
84 Lowenthal and Guterman, *Prophets of Deceit*, xvi, 150, 128, 163, 178. Wiggershaus too states that Adorno's suggestion to Horkheimer that such audience reactions be recorded by field workers 'was not acted on' but these passages suggest otherwise. Wiggershaus, *The Frankfurt School: Its History, Theories, and Political Significance*, 358.
85 Lowenthal and Guterman locate this analysis within a theme entitled 'Call to the Hunt' and also include 'persecuted innocence' as a device elsewhere, Lowenthal and Guterman, *Prophets of Deceit*, 58–63, 126–127; Adorno, *The Psychological Technique of Martin Luther Thomas' Radio Addresses*, 1–12.
86 Lowenthal and Guterman, *Prophets of Deceit*, 64–65. Freud's 'Psychoanalytic Notes upon an Autobiographical Account of a Case of Paranoia' is cited in support.

87 Adorno, 'Anti-Semitism and Fascist Propaganda', 129–130. Cf. Adorno, *The Psychological Technique of Martin Luther Thomas' Radio Addresses*, 29.
88 Adorno, 'Anti-Semitism and Fascist Propaganda', 131–132.
89 Horkheimer and Adorno, *Dialectic of Enlightenment*, 119, 197. Adorno also knew Chaplin socially. Jenemann, *Adorno in America*, 112, 209.
90 Horkheimer and Adorno, *Dialectic of Enlightenment*, 151–152. Adorno, 'Anti-Semitism and Fascist Propaganda', 133–134. Adorno also reported that this 'mobility of the object of hatred' was confirmed in the interviews for *The Authoritarian Personality*. This in turn informed his envisaged 'vaccine against authoritarianism' discussed at end of this chapter. Adorno, 'Democratic Leadership and Mass Manipulation', 433–434.
91 Adorno, *The Psychological Technique of Martin Luther Thomas' Radio Addresses*, 116.
92 Adorno, *The Psychological Technique of Martin Luther Thomas' Radio Addresses*, 87–91.
93 Adorno is the more explicit on this point. Adorno, *The Psychological Technique of Martin Luther Thomas' Radio Addresses*, 3.
94 Lowenthal and Guterman, *Prophets of Deceit*, 47.
95 Leo Lowenthal and Norbert Guterman, 'Portrait of the American Agitator', *Public Opinion Quarterly* 12, no. 3 (1948): 417.
96 Adorno, 'Introduction to *Prophets of Deceit* (Unpublished)', 4. Available as an appendix to this book. All references to this document are to original pagination.
97 Horkheimer and Adorno, *Dialectic of Enlightenment*, 133.
98 A similar English rendition of Psychoteknik as 'psychotechnique', in the singular, is used in the Jephcott translation of *Dialectic of Enlightenment*. Outside the title of the Martin Luther Thomas text, Adorno appears otherwise to have preferred the 'psychotechnics' in his own English publications.
99 Andreas Killen, 'Weimar Psychotechnics between Americanism and Fascism', *Osiris* 22, no. 1 (2007).
100 Anson Rabinbach, *The Human Motor: Energy, Fatigue, and the Origins of Modernity* (Berkeley: University of California Press, 1990), 275–280.
101 Hugo Münsterberg, *The Photoplay: A Psychological Study* (New York: Appleton, 1916); Jeremy Blatter, 'Screening the Psychological Laboratory: Hugo Münsterberg, Psychotechnics, and the Cinema, 1892–1916', *Science in Context* 28, no. 1 (2015).
102 However, as Ligensa et al. note, Adorno's usage, unlike Münsterberg's, is consistently negative. Annemone Ligensa, Klaus Kreimeier and Järg Schweinitz, 'The Aesthetic Idealist as Efficiency Engineer: Hugo Münsterberg's Theories of Perception, Psychotechnics and Cinema.', in *Film 1900: Technology, Perception, Culture*, ed. Annemone Ligensa and Klaus Kreimeier (New Barnet, Herts, UK: John Libbey, 2009).
103 Adorno, 'Freudian Theory and the Pattern of Fascist Propaganda', 296.
104 Adorno, 'Anti-Semitism and Fascist Propaganda', 130.
105 Adorno, 'Freudian Theory and the Pattern of Fascist Propaganda', 296. In his 1946 essay Adorno says modern demagogy is a kind of 'performance reminiscent of the theater, of sport, and of so-called religious revivals'. Adorno, 'Anti-Semitism and Fascist Propaganda', 131.
106 Adorno, 'Freudian Theory and the Pattern of Fascist Propaganda', 296.
107 Theodor W. Adorno and George Simpson, 'On Popular Music', *Zeitschrift für Sozialforschung* 9, no. 1 (1941).
108 For further discussion of this interpretation see: Jones, 'Márkus and the Retrieval of the Sociological Adorno'.

109 Lowenthal and Guterman, *Prophets of Deceit*, 1–4, 4n; Adorno, 'Anti-Semitism and Fascist Propaganda', 133. Lowenthal, 'Scholarly Biography: A Conversation with Helmut Dubiel, 1979', 134. Lowenthal reveals in the same interview that the montage was assembled, under instruction, by Irving Howe.
110 One indicative example from a book that seeks to correct some of the worst misrepresentations of the Frankfurt School: 'the intellectuals of the émigré Frankfurt School were arguing from the later 1930s that American mass culture was indistinguishable from propaganda'. David Goodman, *Radio's Civic Ambition: American Broadcasting and Democracy in the 1930s* (New York: Oxford University Press, 2011), 85.
111 Adorno et al., *The Authoritarian Personality*, 4.
112 Stuart Hall, 'Encoding and Decoding in the Television Discourse', *CCCS Stencilled Occasional Paper* 7 (1973). See also my detailed reconstruction of the career of this model in: Paul K. Jones and David Holmes, *Key Concepts in Media and Communications* (London: Sage, 2011), 73–80. Hall drew the contrast with a straw figure Frankfurt School himself in an introduction to the most-cited version of the 'Encoding/Decoding' essay: Stuart Hall, 'Introduction to Media Studies at the Centre', in *Culture, Media, Language*, ed. S. Hall et al. (London: Hutchinson, 1980).
113 Adorno et al., *The Authoritarian Personality*, 474–475.
114 Adorno, 'Democratic Leadership and Mass Manipulation', 433. Cf. Adorno et al., *The Authoritarian Personality*, 609ff. Adorno even suggests that the popular manual might provoke such insight.
115 Adorno, 'Democratic Leadership and Mass Manipulation', 434.
116 Adorno, 'Democratic Leadership and Mass Manipulation', 434.
117 Lee and Lee, 'Introduction to the Octagon Edition', x.
118 Leo Lowenthal, *An Unmastered Past: The Autobiographical Reflections of Leo Lowenthal* (Berkeley: University of California Press, 1987), 186; Theodor W. Adorno, 'How to Look at Television', *The Quarterly of Film Radio and Television* 8, no. 3 (1954).

3

Expanding the reach of the Institute's analysis

(a) The problem of 'modern' populism and demagogy

As we have seen, the Institute's demagogy studies were under-utilized at the time of their publication and their main intellectual influence, via the Radical Right project, was heavily contested within the US academy. While the broader Studies in Prejudice project, and especially *The Authoritarian Personality*, continues to exert influence in social psychological and political psychological studies of authoritarianism, it has rarely featured in the contemporary literature on populism.[1]

There is of course the related problem that this component of the Institute's work was US-focused and, as shown in Chapter 1, the intellectual resistance to 'pathologizing' the US case in populism studies remains considerable. This blind spot has also significantly disabled what is ostensibly one of the main methodological features of the field of populism studies: its comparativism. The tendency Urbinati identified to value-mark US populism 'good' and all others 'bad' diminished the capacity to recognize common features of populist insurgencies and the modern form of demagogy in particular.

Part of Urbinati's 1998 argument was that the good/bad contrast derived from the association of European populisms with the legacy of the fascist regimes. Most recently, Urbinati has joined her conception of populism as democratic disfigurement with that of historian Federico Finchelstein.[2] This has entailed a more elaborate historicization of the relationship between fascism and populism (and of course democracy) on a global scale. On this account, populism only emerges as 'a new form of government' following the demise of European fascism. Peronism in Argentina – 'the first populist regime in history'[3] – and other similar Latin American regimes mark the advent of this 'modern' form of 'post-fascist rejection of the fascist legacy':

> This marked a turning point and actually a foundational moment in the history of populism because it was then for the first time that populism became a power regime. We might thus say that populism was contextually created for a world order where fascism was no longer a viable anti-liberal option. But as a form of popular government preoccupied with reconstructing authority at the state level, populism nonetheless retained some key fascist features as it aimed to be a mass consented-regime ready to contest political tolerance and pluralism and limit the indeterminate character of the democratic people.[4]

This approach, centred on a conception of 'modern populism', has the distinct advantage of acknowledging the historical continuities and discontinuities between fascism and post-Second World War populism, a perspective almost impossible from orthodox political science approaches that bracket out the fascist period as anomalous. Indeed, Finchelstein and Urbinati's article is designed as a corrective to the tendency to similarly regard populism within democracies as anomalous. Their global comparative figuring of this corrective insight also moves in parallel with the Worsley-Shils typology discussed in Chapter 1.

To this extent one can also see a parallel between this framing of the fascism/populism relationship and the Institute's recognition of the historical legacy of US populism for fascistic demagogy. Indeed, Finchelstein has indicated his broad agreement with the situation of fascism in *Dialectic of Enlightenment* but regards it as 'limited to European developments and the '"continental" frame of reference'.[5] As we shall see, this is a not uncommon mode of overlooking the significance of the specificity of the US case for the Institute's work. Indeed, the US case presents some problems for the Finchelstein schema of a 'modern' populism emerging only after the defeat of European fascism. While the Trump presidency is acknowledged as a comparable contemporary populist 'power regime', the focus on national administrations overlooks populist 'regimes' like that of Huey Long in Louisiana. If such are considered, the fascism/populism nexus in the USA so emerges as being closer to that indicated in the Institute's work, and indeed in Urbinati's earlier challenge to the US revisionist historians. The case for the US populism of the 1930s as a 'foundational moment' for modern populism becomes stronger when one adds a dimension not addressed by Finchelstein: the crucial modern innovation of the culture-industrial commodification of demagogic speech and its legacy for the global mediation of such forms today. The specificity of this issue is developed in following chapters and dealt with at length in the final chapter.

As indicated in Chapter 2, the Institute's key innovation in this context was not so much a full theorization of modern fascism or modern populism – or indeed modern 'authoritarianism' – but of 'modern demagogy'. In that sense there is no need to problematize the Finchelstein/Urbinati schema any further as its broad emphases share far more with the Institute's work.

Moreover, the Institute's own attempts to extend its analysis beyond the 'fascist threat' context of Studies in Prejudice into the post-war period were far from unproblematic. Billig's careful critique of *The Authoritarian Personality* is pertinent here as he highlights a potential tension between those aspects of Studies in Prejudice conducted during the Second World War and those afterwards.[6] The demagogy studies' thematics and devices, for example, were based in empirical studies mostly pre-dating 1945. These were then used to inform questionnaires and interviews in *The Authoritarian Personality* that were administered towards the end of the war and afterwards. Billig so queries the relationship between the potentiality of the key figure of the 'potential fascist' and socio-historical circumstances. He highlights a later commentary by one of the book's co-authors, Else Frankel-Brunswick, in which she declares: 'We have always stressed that the validity of our results is limited to relatively stable circumstances in which there is a choice between alternative ideologies ...'.[7]

Billig concludes that the whole approach lacks a role for the kind of crisis in which potential fascists might become actual fascists and a fascist movement might flourish.[8] Although framed entirely within social psychological parameters, Billig's critique points to a real issue for the Studies in Prejudice project. However, Frankel-Brunswick makes plain that she is deferring to Fromm's *Escape from Freedom*. While this work likely provided the post-hoc titling of *The Authoritarian Personality*, its approach was not systematically employed, nor was the concept of 'authoritarianism'.

Variants of this critique arise in much commentary on the legacy of Studies in Prejudice or, taken in isolation, *Dialectic of Enlightenment*. The broader charge is not only that of conflating wartime and peacetime conditions, but of failing to theoretically account for historical contingency of any kind in a pessimistic understanding of modernity. Frankel-Brunswick's Frommian defence of *The Authoritarian Personality* might be considered an exercise in intellectual damage control: containing the problem of the significance of socio-historical context under a self-limitation to 'relatively stable circumstances'.

Billig's concern might thus be reformulated as one concerning the circumstances in which 'modern demagogy' flourishes, whether in the form of demagogic populism or fascism. As we saw in Chapter 2, Lowenthal plainly distinguished between the crisis of the war period and the period in which he published his work on demagogy. In part this schema relied on an underdeveloped typology of demagogues which included various kinds of opportunistic 'performers' as well as those of a dominantly political focus. Lowenthal had chosen to stay in the USA when the Institute relocated to Frankfurt in 1950. With the onset of McCarthyism, he was convinced of the relevance of his demagogy study and later claimed he *wanted* to be subpoenaed to testify before McCarthy's Senate committee:

> At that time, I used to keep my writings stacked on the desk in my office. On top of the pile I had placed an offprint of an essay with the title 'Portrait of the American Agitator.' That was an advance copy of my later book *Prophets of Deceit*. If I had been summoned to testify in Washington, I would have taken that stack with me and placed it so that the committee and the television crew could have read the title. Then if some senator, outraged at the unambiguous allusion, had asked me to explain myself, I would have calmly said that I brought the books along for the sole purpose of demonstrating my scientific qualifications to the honorable senators. Unfortunately, I was never given that chance.[9]

Lowenthal's anticipation of being subpoenaed was not fanciful as he had held a senior post at the Voice of America, the USA's state-run external broadcasting service, and one of McCarthy's targets. Aside from a somewhat prescient awareness of 'media management', these comments indicate that Lowenthal recognized in McCarthy a demagogue comparable to those examined in *Prophets of Deceit*. He makes no reference to fascism or populism, but this is clearly a proposed expansion of the Institute's analysis to include demagogic elected figures within the state. As we saw in Chapter 1, the critical analysis of McCarthyism in the 1950s fell to certain, dominantly sociological, New York Intellectuals and their Radical Right project. They tied the study of charismatic demagogues to tendencies in US populism.

Where Billig's concern about 'crisis' remains relevant is in the Institute's underdevelopment of a comparable theorization of the relationship between socio-historical circumstances and demagogic success. Much of the Studies in Prejudice Project is vague on this point. Lowenthal, most obviously, works with a conception of 'social malaise' that is a kind of sociological catch-all:

> The agitator does not spring his grumblings out of thin air. The modern individual's sense of isolation, his so-called spiritual homelessness, his bewilderment in the face of the seemingly impersonal forces of which he feels himself a helpless victim, his weakening sense of values – all these motifs often recur in modern sociological writings. The malaise reflects the stresses imposed on the individual by the profound transformations taking place in our economic and social structure – the replacement of the class of small independent producers by gigantic industrial bureaucracies, the decay of the patriarchal family, the breakdown of primary personal ties between individuals in an increasingly mechanized world, the compartmentalization and atomization of group life, and the substitution of mass culture for traditional patterns.[10]

Lowenthal's ambivalence towards some of these motifs is evident in his use of 'so-called' but this remains one of the few statements that is suggestive of the links between this research and two theses commonly attributed to the Institute: 'mass society' and 'mass culture'. However, I interpret this statement as less an affiliation with most of these positions than evidence of the lack of a wider framework as a core component of the analysis of demagogy.[11] On the first, as Jay has pointed out, it is plain that the more consistent position of the Frankfurt School, and Adorno particularly, was not compatible with the mass society thesis as they held to the necessity of a class analysis of contemporary capitalism rather than the theoretical rendering of it as a society of 'atomized individuals', as the mass society thesis entailed.[12] Indeed the 'profound transformations' Lowenthal cites are more consistent with the terminology of the Institute's internal debate over 'state capitalism' addressed in the next section. The question of mass culture is more complex and is dealt with in depth in Chapter 6; but it is important to stress here that Adorno's work more consistently employed the distinctly different culture industry thesis and that the later Lowenthal endorsed this position, even if he rarely used the term himself. 'The decay of the patriarchal family' was a core informing element of the Studies in Prejudice Project.

Perhaps more revealing is Lowenthal's immediately following comment that '(t)hese objective causes' are 'ubiquitous and apparently permanent' which he later associates with a vulgarized form of the Romantic conception of *Weltschmerz*, here *Weltschmerz in perpetuum*, an enduring or perpetual world-weariness or melancholy. The contrast with Frankel-Brunswick's 'stable circumstances' could not be greater. Lowenthal's claim relates more to the 'psychic crisis' that results for the individual but nonetheless such formulations leave little room for a role for – or theorization of – contingent circumstances. Finally, citing Horkheimer's *Eclipse of Reason*, Lowenthal adds to this list the Weberian conception of disenchantment.[13]

This theoretical lacuna implied by this catch-all tendency can be related most obviously to the Institute's rejection of orthodox Marxist understandings of economic crisis and their potentially revolutionary consequences.[14] The interpretative challenges of the ostensibly primary focus of *Studies in Prejudice* on antisemitism was a key factor here. Jay has charted the Institute's shift from openly economistic and class-reductivist understandings of antisemitism to its most complex rendering in 'Elements of Anti-Semitism'. On this reading, the Institute's final position was a 'decentred constellation of factors juxtaposed in unmediated fashion'; that is, it lacked an account of the relationship between these elements. This decentring partly results from that text's placement within the arc of the larger work: the dialectic of enlightenment and the domination of nature. Fascism's irrationalism marks a rebellion of (repressed) nature against its domination and its Jewish victims serve as both objects of false projection and the means of achieving fascism's own complete domination.[15]

This shift to a historical scale longer than even Marx's 'epochal' measure of the mode of production could certainly account for a corresponding diminution of attention to conjunctural socio-historical circumstances. Yet Jay also notes that Adorno declares another theoretical ambition in this contemporaneous statement in the opening of the 150-page series of qualitative analyses of interview material in *The Authoritarian Personality* attributed solely to him:

> The problem of the 'uniqueness' of the Jewish phenomenon could be approached only by a recourse to a theory which is beyond the scope of this study. Such a theory would neither enumerate a diversity of factors nor single out a specific one as a 'cause' but rather develop a unified framework in which all the 'elements' are linked together consistently. This would amount to nothing less than a theory of modern society as a whole.[16]

The recurrence of the term 'elements' here seems hardly coincidental. Nonetheless, in 1968 Adorno acknowledged a problem with this ambition that confirms Jay's observation that such statements 'tended to be lost in the work's more subjective approach'. Yet Adorno remained equally insistent that such an 'objective' dimension was always pivotal to the whole project. Indeed, while Jay rightly points immediately to the contrast between the social theoretical ambition of the passage above and the 'constellation' form of 'Elements of Anti-Semitism', Adorno instead considered the latter text as having 'theoretically shifted racial prejudice into the context of an objectively oriented critical theory of society'.[17] Of course a 'context' is not necessarily an achieved critical social theory.

It is fruitful to return here to the related but more specific problem posed above of the contingent determinants of modern demagogic success. Unlike Lowenthal's demagogy study, Adorno's Martin Luther Thomas monograph makes no extended attempt at a social theoretical contextualization. There are such gestures, however, in his unpublished introduction to *Prophets of Deceit*. We saw in Chapter 2 that for Adorno the appeal of the Lees' 'devices' framework for analysing demagogy correlated with a critical theoretical conception of 'proper' ideologies as necessarily containing a redemptive dimension while fascist discourse failed this test. In such instances, '[w]here ideologies are replaced by approved views from above, the critique of ideology must be replaced by the analysis of *cui bono* – in whose interest?'[18] This might well return us to an economically reductivist account and there certainly is a tendency for Adorno to use such 'interest' formulations in his unpublished introduction, viz.:

> Historically, demagoguery makes its appearance regularly at times when societies tilt over into dictatorship. Demagoguery has always been the means to guide masses, with whose potential impact one has to reckon, towards ends which run counter to their own true interests. This contradiction, inherent in all agitation, is the objective reason of its irrationality, in the last analysis of the role which it applies to psychological techniques.[19]

For Jay the challenge the Institute overcame was to move beyond such accounts which often failed to recognize the specificity of antisemitism and its irrationality. One can see here – in somewhat unpolished English expression – a transitional attempt to reconcile this tension in accounting 'rationally' (interest) for irrationality (persuasion by demagogy). As indicated above, Jay contrasted Adorno's ambition of a critical social theoretical account in *The Authoritarian Personality* with the lack of 'mediations' evident in 'Elements of Anti-Semitism'. Yet if we turn to the passage immediately following that statement of social theoretical 'ambition', we find a sketch of such a mediated formulation in the form of the synoptic prospectus Adorno provides of the sections of the book that follow. Here Adorno renders a subtly different version of both 'device' and *cui bono*:

> We shall first give some evidence of the 'functional' character of anti-Semitism, that is to say, its relative independence of the object. Then we shall point to the problem of *cui bono*: anti-Semitism as a device for effortless 'orientation' in a cold, alienated and largely ununderstable

world. As a parallel to our analysis of political and economic ideologies, it will be shown that this 'orientation' is achieved by stereotypy. The gap between this stereotypy on the one hand and real experience and the still-accepted standards of democracy on the other, leads to a *conflict* situation ... We then take up what appears to be the resolution of this conflict: the underlying anti-Semitism of our cultural climate, keyed to the prejudiced person's own unconscious or preconscious wishes, proves in the more extreme cases to be stronger than either conscience or official democratic values.[20]

In effect, *cui bono* is expanded beyond an economic interest to include a psychological interest and 'device' now also refers to the means of achieving this psychological interest. The problem of *cui bono* is reposed by Adorno thus: 'What good does accrue to the actual adjustment of otherwise "sensible" persons when they subscribe to ideas which have no basis in reality and which we ordinarily associate with maladjustment?' *Cui bono* here is not addressed to 'decreed views from above' but the form of psychological needs fulfilled 'below'. Thus '(i)t is these psychological instruments on which fascist agitators play incessantly'.[21]

I read this framework also as a set of mediations as it bears a striking resemblance to Adorno's concluding chapter entitled 'Mediations' in his 1962 work, *Introduction to the Sociology of Music*. While the material under discussion – music – is completely different, Adorno similarly identifies a 'functional' dimension which he then locates in a set of sociological mediations, most notably the primacy of production over consumption in the culture industry and the specification of distinct 'cultural productive forces' therein. This enables him to explicitly overturn orthodox Marxism's reductivist understanding of a determining base of forces, and relations, of production and a determined 'cultural' superstructure. Indeed, in his 1968 lecture series on sociology, he drew these two domains together himself.[22]

Yet, despite the greater subtlety of this 'mediated' position, it would still struggle to identify the relationship between demagogic success in times of economic hardship and demagogy that appeared disconnected from such circumstances. One reason for this is undoubtedly the dominant Institute characterization of the demagogue as one who changes the content of their actions only marginally in reaction to changing circumstances and instead reiterates basic devices and 'awaits their time'. A second reason is the analytic tendency to employ far longer historical arcs than the conjuncture of 'recent events'. It is the latter point that became of a matter of controversy in later interpretations of this body of work within critical theory in Germany. I will address these concerns next.

(b) From 'Weberian Marxism' to ideal-typification

It has become a mainstay of exegetical work on the Frankfurt School to categorize their project as, in Buck-Morss's apt phrasing for Adorno's position, a kind of 'Marx minus the proletariat'.[23] This meant not only a distancing from the Leninist model of the vanguard party, but also from the hopes in the proletariat as theorized by György Lukács by 1923 in his *History and Class Consciousness*.[24] What was adopted from the latter text, however, was its core concept of reification: by this term Lukács had 'anticipated' Marx's account of alienation in the yet-to-be published 1844 manuscripts. Both terms referred to the 'inversion' of subject–object relations under capitalist production relations. For Marx in 1844 this phenomenon was most typified by the loss of the object of labour by the wage-labourer. For Lukács, the archetypal case was that of the commodity form, its 'fetishistic' capacity to occlude the conditions and relations of its production as examined by the later Marx in the opening chapter of *Capital*. This process so subsumes qualitative empirical distinctions into an abstract quantitative ratio of exchange. Lukács saw reification as primarily a phenomenon besetting the consciousness of the bourgeoisie. The proletariat not only escaped reification but had the potential to challenge it. In contrast, *Dialectic of Enlightenment* applies the concept of reification universally. The incorporation of social psychological and psychoanalytic approaches to subjectivity was thus consistent with this reformulation.[25]

It is worth noting here, however, that this expanded scope for reification is still understood dialectically. Adorno articulated this position in 1968 as in part a reformulation of the Marxian metaphorical distinction between a 'base' composed of forces and relations of production and a superstructure of 'ideological forms'. Increasing 'integration' of the objective and subjective means that metaphor 'is losing its old clarity'. Thus:

> the motif of social psychology as we understand it, as an instrument or moment of the relations of production, has not only a rightful but necessary place in critical theory. It might be said that under present conditions the subject is both: on the one hand, ideology, because in reality the subject does not matter, and because there is something illusory about even believing oneself a subject in this society; on the other, however, the subject is also the potential, the only potential, by which this society can change, and in which is stored up not only the negativity of the system but also that which points beyond the system as it is now. I have said that, despite this, one needs to hold fast to the primacy of

objectivity, but it should be added that the recognition of the reification of society should not itself be so reified that no thought is permitted which goes outside the sphere of reification – that would lead to mechanistic thinking.[26]

This potentiality can also be understood as the capacity for reflective insight, now understood social psychologically as well philosophically, a key phenomenon in Adorno's 'vaccine' against authoritarianism that we met in the previous chapter. This effectively replaces Lukács's conception of 'potential' class-specific consciousness.[27] Partly as a result of this orientation, the Institute's early work, as Jay has argued, contained no 'discrete political theory' as such. Moreover, its early position on authority – chiefly framed by Horkheimer as we saw in the previous chapter – can be counterposed to that of Max Weber.[28] Yet, in contrast, Löwy has argued that the Frankfurt School's overall achievements should be included within the category of 'Weberian Marxism' schematized by Merleau-Ponty.[29]

What these two perspectives share is an understanding that the particular form taken by the Institute's theoretical work was not directed towards the kind of minutiae of liberal-democratic orders that US political sociology drew from Weber, underpinned by a positivistic reading of his conception of value-neutrality. 'Society' so emerges as a more central concept than 'polity' in critical theory.[30] For Löwy, the influence of Weber's conception of rationalization on Lukács's reification builds to the overarching 'pessimistic *diagnostic* of modern society' in *Dialectic of Enlightenment*.[31] For Jay, rationalization was not fully embraced by the early Frankfurt School because of Weber's neglect of the redemptive dimension of rationality that they then prioritized in a prospective socialist order. Indeed, as late as *Eclipse of Reason* (1947), it is Horkheimer who charges the Weber of 'Science as a Vocation' with 'pessimism with regard to the possibility of rational insight and action'.[32] It is in that text that Weber most explicitly identifies the price of Enlightenment as the 'disenchantment of the world' and maps the rise of various forms of rationality in a decidedly unheroic narrative.

Weber's typology of rationality in *Economy and Society* included as a subtype a form of instrumental (or practical) rationality defined by the use of reason for expedient and efficient means to achieve a certain end.[33] It was this formal separation of means and ends that Horkheimer regarded as his 'pessimism'. It certainly informs the core of Weber's famous metaphor of unending rationalization as an iron cage at the end of *The Protestant Ethic and The Spirit of Capitalism*.[34]

The curiosity, as Löwy notes, is that Weber's name is not mentioned in *Dialectic*. Yet the overarching framework of demythologization and instrumental rationalization of Enlightenment goals in that work and *Eclipse of Reason* strongly resonates with Weberian themes.

It is precisely the Weberian dimension of rationalization that is central to Habermas's critiques of *Dialectic of Enlightenment* and related works by Adorno and Horkheimer: '[t]hey solved the problem of connecting Marx and Weber by leaning all the more heavily on Weber'. However, Habermas continues, in so doing they provided a 'totalizing' account that overextended Weber's systemic role for instrumental rationalization but 'did not take seriously enough Weber's studies on the rationalization of worldviews, or the independent logic of cultural modernization'.[35] By the latter Habermas means Weber's provision for the formation of autonomous value spheres of science and knowledge, morality and art populated by 'expert cultures' (corresponding to Kant's three critiques). These are the 'moments into which reason has become differentiated'.[36] By the same logic Habermas's public sphere thesis opened up a space for formal and informal politics – the domain of opinion formation – that seemed to Habermas closed by Adorno and Horkheimer. Habermas also concludes that Adorno and Horkheimer 'were unable to appropriate the systematic content of Weber's diagnosis of the times and to make it fruitful for social-scientific inquiry'.[37]

Initially, a very similar position was advanced by Axel Honnneth. Opening his 1985 *The Critique of Power* with a chapter entitled 'The Incapacity for Social Analysis: Aporias of Critical Theory', Honneth argued therein that Horkheimer's initial characterization of critical theory suffered from a 'sociological deficit' that culminated in Adorno's 'theory of society' as 'the definitive repression of the social'. Honneth had drawn conclusions similar to Habermas's even before the latter's critiques of Adorno cited above were published.[38] Honneth's critiques shared with Habermas's mode of criticism what is now a familiar trope: the apparent relentlessness of Adorno's (and, at points, Horkheimer's) employment of 'universalizing' concepts like rationalization and reification left no space for social contestation of this new order.

As Honneth has put it more recently, Adorno's 'sociological papers':

> seem to lack any attention to the internal logics of spheres of social action, any trace of the innovative power of values, and any sensitivity to the resistance of subcultural interpretative models.[39]

However, on this occasion (2007) Honneth shifts to a decidedly more sympathetic reading of Adorno while claiming to hold to the core elements of his earlier critique(s). Honneth nonetheless implies an auto-critique when he argues that to focus on the 'the sociological part of his work as a specialized part of an explanatory analysis' (as Honneth once did) is no longer considered viable.

Within *both* Adorno's nominally philosophical and non-philosophical writings can be found not an explanatory schema but a hermeneutic that seeks 'to reveal the second, reified nature of historical reality using sociological analysis to expose the determining features of action and consciousness'.[40]

Honneth next provides a very impressive piece of scholarly 'detection' designed to demonstrate his new approach to Adorno's work. He mounts a convincing case that Adorno's 1931 inaugural lecture to the Institute, 'The Actuality of Philosophy', was strongly informed by a reading of Weber's essay on '"Objectivity" in Social Science and Social Policy'. In particular, Honneth argues that Adorno's advocated position is one that calls for, in effect, the production of *Weberian ideal-types* (using the term 'figure' in its place).[41]

I have reconstructed Honneth's 'journey' in some detail because, first, its auto-critique could apply to other too-ready dismissals of the 'sociological' capacity of 'first generation' critical theory. These tend to be highly selective in the texts chosen to demonstrate such failings and Honneth's in-principle recognition of this 'selectivity' issue is an important interpretative gain. However, I would argue this problem persists in the relative neglect of the Institute's 'empirical' US work undertaken within and beyond Studies in Prejudice.

Second, the question of the role of ideal-typification in the Institute's US work can be seen to be 'in play' in the other interpretative 'obstacle' to extending the demagogy studies' analyses to the present, 'the state capitalism debate'. This issue also speaks directly to the model of fascism that the Institute developed.

(c) The state capitalism thesis as 'negative' ideal-type

One of the most powerful interpretative conventions in approaching *Dialectic of Enlightenment* and the Institute's work of the 1940s concerns a perceived adherence to Frederick Pollock's state capitalism thesis. Crudely, it is this thesis that appears to confirm an alleged tendency to 'equate' European fascism and the USA, most notably via the latter's culture industry.[42]

Pollock's work grew out of a core commitment to political economy in the early work of the Institute.[43] Pollock had developed a theory that capitalism had mutated into a new form whereby, following the rise of Nazism, politics should supersede the former role of economy in Marxist theory. The state now organized and planned production with only distribution left to private corporations. All economies tended in this direction and democratic societies like the USA provided merely one variant of this state capitalist form. The role of the liberal entrepreneur was so held to be obsolete and the period of dominance by monopolies was itself only a point of transition to state capitalism. Moreover, the state capitalism thesis, if correct, demonstrated that capitalism had achieved a stabilized form, albeit a contingent one, so challenging the relevance of Marxist crisis theories that anticipated capitalism's imminent collapse.[44]

Although Pollock discussed the Soviet Union and the USA extensively in his main article advancing this thesis, debate within the Institute centred on its viability in accounting for the case of Nazi Germany, on which Pollock also contributed a dedicated article. Pollock's chief critic was Franz Neumann, whose *Behemoth* was a major study of the Nazi administration. He had insisted instead that the (private) monopoly form of capitalism was alive and well in Nazi Germany and, by implication, in the western democracies.[45]

This debate has been revived to some extent in recent years, in part as a discussion of the relevance of Adorno's work to contemporary analysis.[46] To a considerable extent this debate turns on whether Adorno and Horkheimer abandoned a model of 'monopoly capitalism' for 'state capitalism' as their informing economic framework. The Jephcott translation of *Dialectic of Enlightenment* even includes an appendixed interpretative essay by van Reijen and Brensen that makes the case that Horkheimer and Adorno, in deference to Pollock, systematically eliminated all references to monopoly and class relations from the 1947 edition and replaced those with terms such as 'rackets' and 'combines'. These changes, they argue, demonstrate that:

> in the mid-1940s Horkheimer and Adorno, in keeping with Pollock's analyses, had distanced themselves definitively from a form of Marxism which assumed the primacy of economics. Instead, the importance of control through politics and the culture industry moves into the foreground.[47]

This formulation, while immediately qualified by its authors, is especially revealing as it consolidates a tendency by commentators to conflate the debate within the Institute about Nazi Germany with the status of Pollock's broader intended applicability of his state capitalism thesis. Most accounts seek to apportion members of the Institute either to Pollock's or to Neumann's 'side'. In van Reijen and Brensen's case, the culture industry thesis is also understood as an entirely non-economic matter. As Schmidt has demonstrated, this argument overlooks the many references to monopoly that remain in the 1947 text, especially in the culture industry section.[48] I pursue the implications of this issue for the culture industry thesis in Chapter 6.

Van Reijen and Brensen's reading of the culture industry as a non-economic means of neutralizing class contradictions follows from Pollock's emphases on the supremacy of politics and state administration of the economy. This framing tends to dominate such discussions. Yet Pollock's thesis can also be criticized for its 'bracketing' of production as a site of non-contradiction and its 'one-sided' focus on an 'historical critique of the mode of distribution'.[49] This 'distributionist' approach echoes Adorno's oft-cited retrospective 1967 comment on the culture industry thesis that:

> the expression 'industry' is not to be taken literally. It refers to the standardization of the thing itself and to the rationalization of distribution techniques, but not strictly to the production process.[50]

Now, cultural *production* for Adorno was a much more complex matter and, crucially, was not at all lacking in contradictions, especially in what might be called cultural relations of production. From this perspective, although the state capitalism thesis or something like it is intermittently referenced in *Dialectic of Enlightenment*, and cultural standardization and distribution is its major industrial focus, the result is not 'Pollockian'. For it does not result, on any account, in what might be expected from a Pollockian understanding of these processes: a 'state culture industry' thesis. Instead, Horkheimer and Adorno follow the immanent contradictions of the culture industry, primarily *via differing socio-technical configurations* of enabling cultural productive forces, i.e., the new 'technologies' of audio recording, cinema and broadcasting. The contingency of contemporary capitalism thus becomes heavily entwined with this newly colonized, but internally contradictory, domain.[51] What this implies is quite different from an emphasis on 'control through politics and the culture industry' to the recognition of *a qualitative shift in capitalism* whereby distinctively new forces of cultural production enable the production of newly standardized cultural commodities – a whole new domain of capitalist expansion.

Also missing from such commentary is any acknowledgement of the mode in which Pollock presented his state capitalism thesis: as a 'model' where, Pollock states, that term 'is used here in the sense of Max Weber's "ideal type"'.[52] Indeed, Pollock's account not only invokes Weber's method but follows it by elaborating a Weber-like typology of subtypes of state capitalism: totalitarian and democratic (with an implication at points that 'Soviet Russia' demonstrates a third subtype due to its greater achievement of state capitalist distribution).

This ideal-typical framing of Pollock's model informed the internal debate in the Institute. Neumann challenged this method directly in *Behemoth* and in correspondence with Horkheimer whereby the use of ideal-typification was evidence of a 'departure from Marxism'. Horkheimer responded by defending the technique as he understood Pollock had deployed it:

> Ideal types should, in my opinion, fulfil precisely the function they accomplish in the essay. In truth, they are constituted by means of the abstraction and enhancement of certain elements of reality; but they are also a reply to reality. They are utopias, beautiful and ugly, against which reality is measured.[53]

Horkheimer attributes a normative dimension to Weber's ideal-typification to which Weber did not consistently adhere.[54] While the full scale of this debate is beyond the scope of this discussion, I should indicate my preference for David Held's more measured assessment of it. He argues that Horkheimer and Adorno were 'ambivalent' about the Pollock-Neumann controversy and saw failings and attractions in each position. This is more consistent with their mixed and even conflicting usage of Pollock's work in their texts of this period.[55]

One further implication of the state capitalism thesis is worth noting. Even if Horkheimer and Adorno had embraced Pollock's entire state capitalism thesis, then this should not have led to the alleged 'equation' of European fascist political control and the US culture industry. Rather the two would need to have been kept quite discrete, consistent with Pollock's two main subtypes. I would argue their 'ambivalence' nonetheless enables a similar recognition of such specificity and that this is particularly the case with their discussion of the US culture industry.

In his correspondence with Horkheimer, Adorno articulated his distance from Pollock by arguing that his 'pessimism' was correct but his approach 'undialectical'.[56] In his 1941 prefatory note to the issue of the *Zeitschrift* that includes Pollock's 'State Capitalism', Horkheimer discusses that article at length and, employing Pollock's second subtype, explicitly refers to the central role of planning in the US New Deal:

> The unprecedented governmental power necessarily associated with state capitalism is now in the hands of a democratic and humanitarian administration. It will be the goal of fascist groups within and without to wrest it away, and it is not too much to expect that the coming years will be marked by such attempts. However, the present war may end, men will have to choose between a new world era of consummate democracy or the hell of an authoritarian world order.[57]

It is not difficult to see the figure of Coughlin, and the other US demagogues, behind these comments. Coughlin, still broadcasting at this time, had maintained his 'left' position against the New Deal even as he moved into a more openly fascistic antisemitism.

Horkheimer's comment reminds us that, for all its emphasis on the consequences of Nazism, the Pollock-Neumann controversy was not pitched at a level that estimated the internal risks of fascism within the surviving democracies, beyond a putative economic foundation. To this extent the ideal-typical form of Pollock's proposition did not receive suitable elaboration and contrast with 'reality', as Weber's understanding of ideal-typification required.[58] It did, however, confirm that the Institute's thinking had moved decidedly beyond an orthodox Marxian model of economic crisis and the question of ideal-typification was now as much on the intellectual agenda as the better known Weberian-Lukácsian influences on the Institute. Moreover, the future of democratic institutions was also indexed, given the diagnosed threat of the fascist states during the Second World War *and* the threat of internal fascist demagogy even after the defeat of those fascist states. If any further evidence of the growing influence of ideal-typification at the Institute were required, the prospectus in the *Zeitschrift* for the Studies in Prejudice Project is prefaced by Horkheimer's presentation of a set of 'methodological viewpoints' heavily influenced by Weber's principles of sociological concept-formation. The prospectus itself then attempts an initial ideal-typification of modes of antisemitism.[59]

I continue this point in the next section's discussion of an instance where Adorno explicitly confirms Honneth's identification of the influence of ideal-typification on his own work. As in Horkheimer's comment above, it occurs within the context of the Studies in Prejudice programme.

(d) Ideal-type and physiognomy

For Honneth, Adorno's latent embrace of Weberian ideal-typification initiated a '"physiognomy" of social reality' which Honneth glosses as 'interpreting social reality's determining figures of action such that they can be understood as bodily or gestural expressions of the capitalist form of life'. Honneth notes that 'physiognomy' recurs as a kind of leitmotif throughout Adorno's work, suturing his musicological, sociological and philosophical writings.[60]

As we have seen, Honneth developed this interpretation of Adorno from a reading of his 1931 inaugural lecture, 'The Actuality of Philosophy', notably its discussion of the figure and its resemblance to one of Weber's elaborations of the practice of ideal-typification. Perhaps because Adorno's prime example of such a 'figure' therein is the commodity-form, and because twenty years earlier Honneth had argued that Adorno's entire project was defined by 'the universality of reification' and by 'the social reification of late capitalism', Honneth assumes that it is 'the capitalist form of life' that entirely corresponds with Adorno's understanding of the 'figures' analysed in a physiognomy of social reality.[61]

As with Habermas's critique of *Dialectic*, Honneth's critiques of Adorno pay little attention to his contemporaneous US work that was drafted in English. In 1939, while still in New York, Adorno completed his primary draft of a monograph on radio music. This text remained unpublished in his lifetime. It was called 'Radio Physiognomics'. Unlike some other invocations of 'physiognomics' by Adorno, here he outlined precisely why he thought it valid to invoke a method associated with a discredited form of early psychology based in facial analyses of character types.[62] As he puts it:

> The question is not merely terminological. It involves the relation between this study and the individual sciences of psychology, technology and sociology. Roughly speaking, we insist upon the physiognomic approach because the phenomena we are studying constitute a unity comparable to that of a human face. Here we are more concerned with analyzing the conditions of this unity, no matter what they may be, than with analyzing the divergent psychological, sociological and technological elements bound up with it.[63]

Adorno so isolates what communications theorists would later call 'the medium' from the content of any broadcast (or what he calls 'the how' from 'the what'). Indeed, the two primary 'how-elements' Adorno prioritizes completely anticipate the core concepts of what became known as 'medium theory': 'time coincidence' and 'space ubiquity'.[64] By these Adorno respectively means the capacity for broadcasting to achieve simultaneous reception and its related capacity to 'compress' vast distances. Both instances rely on what Adorno calls a 'descriptive' or 'phenomenological' method within the physiognomy in that the phenomenal forms of reception are central to the 'unity' he seeks to examine.

Now, compared with Honneth's understanding of the role of physiognomy for Adorno, this mode of analysis does not prioritize the commodity forms of capitalism nor does it assume a 'universal reification', though the former is not entirely absent from this text. However, consistent with Honneth's insight regarding ideal-typification, Adorno's five 'categories of radio physiognomics' (which include time coincidence and space-ubiquity) are indeed presented in a mode strongly resembling Weberian ideal-typing, i.e., as a set of subtypes forming an ideal typification of radio physiognomy.

In the 1949 draft of the planned introduction to *Prophets of Deceit* Adorno states:

> This book is not as much devoted to the agitators' social physiognomics as to the psychological contents of their standard devices, that is to say, to the elucidation of those inner and largely unconscious mechanisms at which agitation is directed. However, the psychological emphasis of the technique has to be understood sociologically.[65]

As shown in Chapter 2, such sociological understanding of 'the technique' included the socio-cultural sourcing of the forms of demagogic speech and their thematics and, for Adorno, the identification of standardization of these constituent elements. In his closure to the introduction Adorno takes the sociological dimension further by arguing for the ongoing relevance of the demagogy research:

> [*Prophets of Deceit*] ... does not pretend to give a photographic picture of today's political reality, and it does not overrate the immediate and literal importance of contemporary American demagoguery. Rather, it takes certain phenomena, which appear <u>prima facie</u> as negligible, under a microscope in order to gain pertinent diagnostic insight into the latent threat against democracy through the enlargement of its most extreme and apparently unrealistic manifestations. It is hoped that the microscopic diagnosis of remote and inconsiderable social deformations*, undertaken free from the pressure of any immediate political or economic crisis, will contribute to the evolution of planned and* effective long-term defence measures against the danger of terror that has survived Hitler's defeat.[66]

Here we can see a version of the hermeneutics of the 'figure' emphasized by Honneth – a 'prima facie negligible' element is taken as emblematic. Its 'enlargement' is located within a gestured political project of defence of a democratic order with remarkably strong echoes of Horkheimer's 1941 introduction to Pollock's essay and Adorno's own 'vaccine against authoritarianism'. Further, we also see the Institute directly addressing Billig's particular methodological concerns regarding the relationship between wartime and peacetime research. There is also a palpable sense of anticipation – confirmed only months later when McCarthy's demagogy achieved spectacular prominence.

The methodological implications do not stop at the characterization of demagogy as a microscopic enlargement of the extreme and 'prima facie negligible'. The 'ongoing relevance' motif is set up at the beginning of Adorno's draft in this way:

> Inasmuch as the main emphasis is placed on the meaning of the phenomena, the latter should be viewed in the light of their potential implications within the totality of present-day society and its dynamics, rather than their immediate effectiveness. Even when the direct impact of fascist agitation is at an ebb, the nature of its content and technique remains important as an example of *modern* mass manipulation *in its purest and most sinister form*.[67]

Now 'pure type' is a common alternative English translation to 'ideal type' (*idealtypus*). It may be that the conjunction of 'modern' and 'pure form' here is merely fortuitous and, as with the previous citation, a justification of the post-war publication of this study. However, the structure of this paragraph's argument is decidedly methodological and alludes to an earlier reference in the same text that stresses the need to evaluate the devices not 'in isolation' as 'each one may equally occur in an entirely different political and social context'. Thus:

> Their specific significance as means of fascist mass manipulation is obtained only within the structural unity of meaning evolved by the authors, and emphasis should be laid on this unity rather than any particular manifestation of demagoguery.[68]

The appeal to a 'structural unity of meaning' corresponds almost exactly with that in the passage above from the 'Radio Physiognomy'. Now, if we take these last two cited passages together, it is difficult not to read them as a case for the Institute's analysis of demagogy as a mode of ideal-typification. As we saw in Chapter 2, Lowenthal gestured towards such a typology too but did not elaborate one. 'Constituent elements' can be read as sub-typical components of demagogy. While the social physiognomics of the agitators is not a component of *Prophets of Deceit*, Adorno provides us with a sociological means of achieving such a physiognomy in any future situation.

It is this physiognomics that Adorno draws on to postulate in *Dialectic of Enlightenment*, albeit in a characteristically ironic form, that the metaphysical dimension of Weber's charisma – the elusive extraordinary qualities of the leader that forge the charismatic bond – is being replaced by radio's space ubiquity. He so 'updates' Weber's own tying of modern demagogy to the configuration of means of communication.[69]

(e) Towards a critical-theoretical comparativist typology

When Horkheimer announced Studies in Prejudice in the *Zeitschrift* its 'methodological viewpoints' were constituted as four protocols:

(i)   Concepts are historically formed
(ii) Concepts are critically formed
(iii) Social Concepts are 'inductively' formed
(iv) Social Concepts are integrative.[70]

Their fully articulated versions announced, in effect, a critical Weberian enterprise. Where these protocols differed from Weber's own methodological accounts was of course in the emphasis on 'critical' and its implications for the 'content' of Studies of Prejudice. We can see this shift in Horkheimer's attempt (discussed in [c] above) to extend Weber's 'ideal type' into a kind of normative utopianism. One can also see what Horkheimer was seeking to highlight: a means ('ugly utopia') of typologizing the irrational within modernity or what is currently called 'modernity's dark side'.[71]

Indeed, the irrational notably eludes the discussion of the second protocol as Horkheimer reproduces a case for immanent critique as an alternative to positivism and 'value freedom'. Horkheimer argues that given the imposition of political values on intellectual activity in 'the totalitarian states', pragmatic scepticism towards 'freedom of science' has arisen in democratic societies. A return to metaphysical norms has developed in response. Horkheimer offers another solution, a kind of third way:

> Social theory may be able to circumvent a skeptical spurning of value judgements without succumbing to normative dogmatism. This may be accomplished by relating social institutions and activities to the values they themselves set as their standards and ideals ... If subjected to such an analysis, the social agencies most representative of the present pattern of society will disclose a pervasive discrepancy between what they actually are and the values they accept.[72]

This is a clear restatement of the practice of immanent critique as a critical social theoretical method. As we saw, however, it is dependent on the existence of a redeemable norm. The irrationality of fascism and demagogy escapes this. We have already seen Adorno's reconstruction of *cui bono* as a means of redressing this critical methodological lack. Adorno's own later critical methodological comments on Weber move in a similar mode towards a 'third way'. In the section addressing 'Constellation in Science' in his *Negative Dialectics* (1966), Adorno makes plain his interest in Weberian ideal-typification as 'a third possibility beyond the alternative(s) of positivism and idealism'. The heuristic dimension of ideal-typification for Adorno 'circles the object' in a manner comparable to the construction of a constellation. Citing the heuristic form of concept-construction elaborated in the second chapter of *The Protestant Ethic and the Spirit of Capitalism*, Adorno so acknowledges Weber's reference to a compositional dimension, in the literary sense, of ideal-typification. Such a compositional practice enables Adorno to recognize the significance of Weber's habit of drawing parallels with aesthetic works in his social theoretical constructions. Thus: '[t]he subjectively created context – the "constellation" – becomes readable as a sign of objectivity'.[73]

However, this too is not a straightforward adherence to Weberian ideal-typification. When Adorno returned to the same point in his 1968 sociology lectures, he conducted an immanent critique of Weber using the example of charismatic authority. Here Adorno employs the immanent-critical principle relating to theoretical works that critique can draw out immanent consequences of an elaborated argument that were not evident to their author. As with Horkheimer's cruder reworking of ideal-type, the purpose here is to highlight the ideal-typification of the irrational. Adorno targets Weber's core ideal-typification of legitimate authority in *Economy and Society*.[74] He acknowledges that:

> of course, Weber was not an irrationalist, in the sense that he regarded charisma as a positive category. He understood it purely descriptively as an opportunity: if people attribute such charisma to another, the recipient has an opportunity to have his orders obeyed. Whether he really has charisma or not is a matter of indifference to this science which, as we know, makes much show of being value-free.[75]

However, according to Adorno, Weber breaks his own methodological protocols regarding ideal-types in his treatment of charismatic authority. This is not so much a matter of value-freedom but a reference to the 'compositional' procedure for ideal-typical concept development Adorno largely endorsed in *Negative Dialectics* and which is faithfully followed in Horkheimer's methodological protocols for Studies in Prejudice in the *Zeitschrift*. Adorno argues that a self-contradiction occurs when Weber states that charismatic authority can 'pass over into "traditional authority"'.[76] This 'substantiates', renders objective, what should be a 'purely abstract, arbitrary and ephemeral conceptual instrument' for Weber. Charisma ceases to be a concept acknowledging a belief-based mode of authority and becomes a kind of social force in its own right that exists independently of social belief systems.

It is likely the position is a misattribution. While Adorno separately acknowledges Weber's 'modern' relationship between the routinization of charisma and bureaucracy, he may have mistaken his account of the traditional routinization of charisma for a declaration of charisma's capacity to 'transcend itself and pass over into another ideal type'.[77]

The more significant point is that Adorno's immanent critique seeks to redress Weber's inattention, in his view, to the relationship between charismatic authority/leadership and 'what in critical theory is referred to as the objective laws of motion'. If we associate charisma with demagogic leadership in the mode the Radical Right project did, then this also addresses the social theoretical lacuna that this chapter has interrogated: the 'determinacy' of modern demagogic success. While Adorno goes no further in establishing such a relationship in this text, it is significant that he recognized the need for one. Moreover, his framing moves towards far greater conceptual specificity than did Lowenthal's 'catch-all'.

As we have seen, Adorno tends to offer two 'solutions' to this issue. One is the reconfiguration of 'interest' – *cui bono* – as a set of psychosocial interests finding their fullest articulation in the typology of social characters in *The Authoritarian Personality*. It is in this sense that he later recognized the need for 'the motif of social psychology' as a key component of critical theory. The second takes the less elaborated, somewhat 'meta-epochal' form of a conception of modernity in which reification plays a far greater role than that envisaged by Lukács. However, this is not a view that the 'objective laws of motion' have reached a terminal 'end of history' situation. Rather, the balance of forces has shifted such that 'the objective, institutional side of society has detached itself from and solidified in relation to the people of whom society is made up'.[78]

This might seem to legitimate Habermas's stringent critique of Horkheimer and Adorno in *The Theory of Communicative Action*. Yet the 1968 lecture from which the last citation was taken develops from an *endorsement* of Habermas's work on the public sphere. Adorno provided a similarly extended endorsement in 1964, including an agreement with Habermas's 'disintegration' thesis regarding the fate of the public sphere.[79] He also endorsed the strategy of immanent ideology critique on which the entirety of Habermas's *Structural Transformation* was based, on Habermas's own account.[80] We might then use as a criterion of the dubiousness of Adorno's alleged 'pessimism' the fact that he considered immanent analysis still possible. That is, that unreified, redeemable norms still existed. Indeed, such an emphasis on immanent analysis provided him with his very definition of sociology in the 1968 lecture series.[81] As Habermas has himself recently reinvoked the disintegration thesis, I will employ this intersection of Habermas and Adorno in my final chapter.

A more recent critique of Adorno within German critical theory came from Claus Offe in 2005. Unlike the Habermas and (initial) Honneth critiques, Offe focuses explicitly on Adorno's US residency period and his later references to the USA. Yet he makes similarly sweeping statements to Habermas's regarding the overarching argument of *Dialectic of Enlightenment* and *The Authoritarian Personality*. For Adorno, Offe claims, the USA provides no more than 'the object of an *exemplary* critique, which refers to developed capitalist societies as a whole' but which is based on neither sufficient empirical evidence gathering nor even engagement with parallel US critical intellectuals.[82] The result is the now familiar charge of a 'totalizing theory of the culture industry and the post-liberal society of total marketization'. Offe so finds almost inexplicable the evidence from the 1950s and 1960s of Adorno's positive views of aspects of the USA. The possibility that perhaps this is because his view of the culture industry and 'post-liberal society' in the 1940s was not 'totalizing' but dialectical, does not arise. Instead, Offe charges, 'Adorno the dialectician here forgoes the intellectual effort that might have clarified why both these positions are valid'.[83] While *The Authoritarian Personality* receives passing mention in Offe's critique, Studies in Prejudice does not. Yet even in *The Authoritarian Personality* the immanent appeal to liberal values and even 'genuine Conservatism' is pervasive. If there is a tension in Adorno's commentary, it is not one that arose after his return to Germany, as Offe insists.

One of Offe's final summative critical charges is extended beyond Adorno:

> the critical theorists of the 1940s, in their diagnosis of the times, clearly did not tackle the obvious question of why a fascist movement had far less chance than a socialist movement of capturing shares of state power in the United States.[84]

Offe is of course correct in that this particular question is not explicitly 'tackled'. Yet the central premiss of his 'obvious' question is highly contestable, so making its 'tackling' an odd task. Many would argue there had indeed been a fascist with state power in the USA in the 1930s: Huey Long of Louisiana. As mentioned in Chapter 2, Adorno was fond of quoting the apocryphal but somewhat dialectical line attributed to Long that any US fascism would be based in American democratic roots by those who declared themselves antifascist.

The broader retort to Offe would be that the 'totalizing' perspective he, Habermas and the early Honneth attributed to 'critical theorists of the 1940s' was never as 'totalizing' as they charged. Offe's critique only adds to the bizarreness of such hostility from this succession of later Frankfurt critical theorists about the work of the 'first generation' conducted in the USA. For even Offe doesn't demonstrate evidence of sufficient familiarity with their US circumstances nor of the political context in which they wrote. This is not to suggest that these interpretative issues are clear-cut. Much turns, as Offe rightly indicates, on the role of the culture industry thesis, which is examined further in Chapter 6.

Instead, it is Offe's attempt to situate Adorno's US work as 'an exemplary critique' of contemporary capitalism that is nonetheless insightful. For, if corrected for its own empirical failings, Offe's comment instead suggests a latent *comparativism* exists in Adorno's work and the critical theory project.[85] Such a comparativism is equally attributable to the influence of Weber's sociology: most markedly the repeated invocation – albeit with reservations – of ideal-typification, even in the state capitalism thesis, and Adorno's methodological reflections on ideal-typification as physiognomy and the sociology of charisma. However, this comparativism is by no means a fully fledged historico-comparativist enterprise, even if the bases for one could be argued to exist in the larger critical theory project.[86] Rather, the particular features on which the Institute focused – notably modern demagogy and the culture industry – provide a means of *empirically* complementing and correcting existing modes of orthodox comparativism. As shown in Chapter 1, the orthodox tradition of (comparative) populism studies tends to neglect such 'modern' dimensions of populism. Moreover, such a latent comparativism has particular pertinence to developing further the Worsley-Shils typological alternative.

Such comparativism provides one way of establishing mediations between the 'meta-epochal' tendencies of many of the socio-historical formulations of Studies in Prejudice and more specific conjunctures. This chapter opened with a consideration of the Urbinati-Finchelstein comparativist thesis that 'modern populism' arose in Argentina. Finchelstein's conception of 'the modern', however, was found to be too limited as the further 'modern' features Finchelstein neglected are those pioneered in the USA and its 'modern demagogy'. However, Finchelstein also importantly placed the question of 'modern populism' in the context of the fascist legacy. In a sense this provides a reverse form of the argument I have made for the relevance of the Institute's work for understanding populism: that the role of 'modern demagogy' renders their work ostensibly concerning fascism highly relevant to the analysis of contemporary populism. (cf. Figure 1 in Chapter 2).

Accordingly, Figure 3 maps contingent pathways in the mode of the Shils/Worsley ideal-typification typology and my emphasis on the contingency of demagogic capture of populist formations in Chapter 1. It thus can be considered an 'expansion' of Figure 1. It also situates the culture industry as an alternative

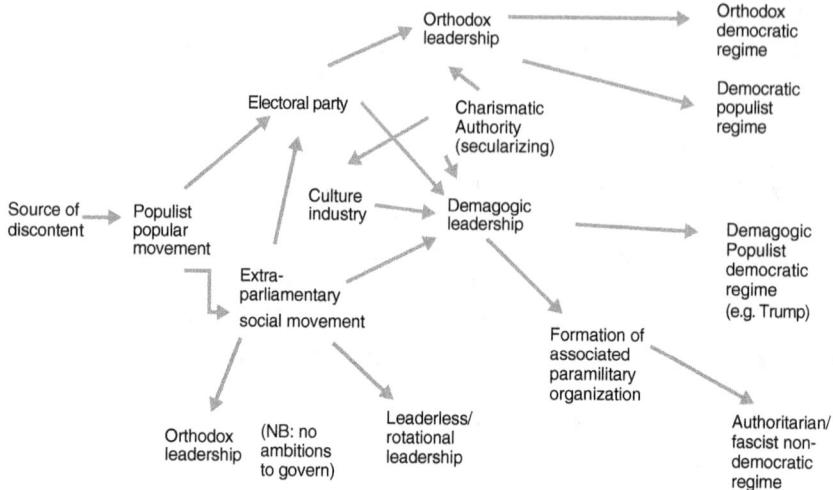

3 Some contingent pathways in populist politics and demagogic leadership

incubator of demagogues. Figure 2 could thus be considered an expanded elaboration of this component of Figure 3. I have employed in Figure 3 Michael Mann's further criterion for distinguishing fascist formations: the adoption of paramilitary activity.[87]

However, while we now have a means to 'ideal-typify' contingent pathways for modern demagogy, the relationship between the determinants of what I have called 'discontent' in Figure 3, demagogic success and related contingent circumstances still remain somewhat elusive. For that reason, it is important to assess next the Gramscian tradition of the analysis of populism, not least because this tradition has also produced what might be considered a 'de facto critical theory of populism' in the work of Ernesto Laclau.

Notes

1 An important exception here is the field of critical discourse analysis, most notably the body of work associated with Ruth Wodak. This field shares much with the 'social formalist' approach I advocate in later chapters. It has also at times directly associated itself with the project of critical theory (although I think this association requires more elaborate theorization). Wodak and her colleagues have addressed rising 'rightwing populism' in Europe in numerous works. Space limitations required abandoning a planned role for this field as the most impressive contemporary counterpoint to the political scientific 'enduring orthodoxies' in Chapter 1's overview of orthodox populism studies. In *The Politics of Fear*, for example, Wodak draws on *The Authoritarian Personality*'s categories of pseudo-masculinity and pseudo-femininity

to examine the under-researched role of gender in contemporary populism, notably the apparently paradoxical phenomenon of prominent charismatic female leaders of 'regressive' populist parties. Ruth Wodak, *The Politics of Fear: What Right-Wing Populist Discourses Mean* (Sage, 2015), 179ff; Theodor W Adorno et al., *The Authoritarian Personality* (New York: Harper & Row, 1950), 428–429.

2 Federico Finchelstein and Nadia Urbinati, 'On Populism and Democracy', *Populism* 1 (2018); Federico Finchelstein, *From Fascism to Populism in History* (Oakland: University of California Press, 2017); Urbinati, 'Democracy and Populism'.
3 Finchelstein, *From Fascism to Populism in History*, 18.
4 Finchelstein and Urbinati, 'On Populism and Democracy', 16–17.
5 Federico Finchelstein, *Transatlantic Fascism: Ideology, Violence, and the Sacred in Argentina and Italy, 1919–1945* (Durham: Duke University Press, 2010), 18; Cf. Finchelstein, *From Fascism to Populism in History*, 38.
6 Billig, *Fascists: A Social Psychological View of the National Front*, 35ff.
7 Else Frenkel-Brunswick, 'Further Explorations by a Contributor to "The Authoritarian Personality"', in *Studies in the Scope and Method of 'The Authoritarian Personality*, ed. Richard Christie and Marie Jahoda (Glencoe, Ill.: Free Press, 1954), 228.
8 However, Billig's own historicization is flawed by his view that: '(I)n the main the radio agitators failed to harness their support to organized political movements.' He seems here to slip into a narrowed view of 'organized movements' as electoral parties rather than social movements like those of Long and Coughlin. He also charges that reliance on the demagogy studies meant that the Institute assumed that 'a future fascist movement would replicate in detail the propaganda of the radio agitators', so conflating the distinction between themes/devices and 'content'. Billig, *Fascists: A Social Psychological View of the National Front*, 42–43.
9 Lowenthal, *An Unmastered Past*, 87. The title Lowenthal cites appeared as that of his book's first chapter and a 1948 journal article: Lowenthal and Guterman, 'Portrait of the American Agitator'.
10 Lowenthal and Guterman, *Prophets of Deceit*, 15.
11 Here my analysis parts company with Rensmann's recent discussion of the same passage in *The Politics of Unreason: The Frankfurt School and the Origins of Modern Antisemitism*, 257ff.
12 Martin Jay, *Adorno* (London: Fontana, 1984), 94–95.
13 Lowenthal and Guterman, *Prophets of Deceit*, 15, 17, 18.
14 The 'state capitalism debate' within the Institute discussed below is another measure of this shift.
15 Jay, 'The Jews and the Frankfurt School', 144–147.
16 Adorno et al., *The Authoritarian Personality*, 608. Cf. Jay, 'The Jews and the Frankfurt School', 143.
17 Jay, 'The Jews and the Frankfurt School', 143. Cf. Adorno, 'Scientific Experiences of a European Scholar in America (1968)', 230.
18 Frankfurt Institute for Social Research, *Aspects of Sociology*, 190.
19 Adorno, 'Introduction to *Prophets of Deceit* (Unpublished)', 3.
20 Adorno et al., *The Authoritarian Personality*, 608.
21 Adorno et al., *The Authoritarian Personality*, 618–619.
22 Theodor W. Adorno, *Introduction to the Sociology of Music* (New York: Continuum, 1976), 194–218. Theodor W. Adorno, *Introduction to Sociology*, trans. E.F.N. Jephcott (Stanford: Stanford University Press, 2000), 151–153.
23 Susan Buck-Morss, *The Origin of Negative Dialectics: Theodor W. Adorno, Walter Benjamin and the Frankfurt Institute* (New York: Free Press, 1977), 24–42.

24 György Lukács, *History and Class Consciousness: Studies in Marxist Dialectics* (London: Merlin Press, 1971).
25 Andrew Feenberg, *The Philosophy of Praxis: Marx, Lukács, and the Frankfurt School* (London: Verso, 2014), 150–155.
26 Adorno, *Introduction to Sociology*, 152.
27 Feenberg, *The Philosophy of Praxis*, 154. Indeed. Adorno's social psychological rethinking of 'class interest' in *The Authoritarian Personality* discussed above could also be read as a reworking of Lukács's 'potential consciousness'.
28 Jay, *The Dialectical Imagination*, 117–121, 155.
29 Michael Löwy, 'Figures of Weberian Marxism', *Theory and Society* 25, no. 3 (1996); Maurice Merleau-Ponty, *Adventures of the Dialectic* (Evanston Ill.: Northwestern University Press, 1973).
30 Equally significantly for Jay's estimate of the role of social theory in critical theory, there was nonetheless an implicit theory of political authority 'ultimately grounded in its philosophical assumptions'. *The Dialectical Imagination: A History of the Frankfurt School and the Institute of Social Research, 1923–1950*, 133.
31 Löwy, 'Figures of Weberian Marxism', 436.
32 Jay, *The Dialectical Imagination*, 120–121. Max Horkheimer, *Eclipse of Reason* (New York: Oxford University Press, 1947), 6 fn1.
33 For an elaboration see Stephen Kalberg, 'Max Weber's Types of Rationality: Cornerstones for the Analysis of Rationalization Processes in History', *American Journal of Sociology* 85, no. 5 (1980).
34 Weber, 'Science as a Vocation'. Max Weber, *Economy and Society* (Berkeley: University of California Press, 1978). Max Weber, *The Protestant Ethic and the Spirit of Capitalism*, trans. Talcott Parsons (London: Allen & Unwin, 1930).
35 Jürgen Habermas, *The Theory of Communicative Action Volume Two*, trans. Thomas McCarthy (Boston: Beacon Press, 1987), 332–333. Cf. discussion in Pauline Johnson, *Habermas: Rescuing the Public Sphere* (London: Routledge, 2006), 35ff.
36 Jürgen Habermas, *The Theory of Communicative Action Volume One*, trans. Thomas McCarthy (Boston: Beacon Press, 1984), 159–164. The final phrase is cited from Jürgen Habermas, 'Modernity: An Unfinished Project', in *Habermas and the Unfinished Project of Modernity: Critical Essays on the Philosophical Discourse of Modernity*, ed. Maurizio Passerin d'Entrèves and Seyla Benhabib (Boston, Mass.: MIT Press, 1997), 46. For a fuller elaboration of the value spheres: Michael J. Symonds, *Max Weber's Theory of Modernity: The Endless Pursuit of Meaning* (Farnham, Surrey: Ashgate, 2015).
37 Habermas, *The Theory of Communicative Action Volume One*, 333.
38 Axel Honneth, *The Critique of Power: Reflective Stages in a Critical Social Theory*, trans. Kenneth Baynes (Cambridge, Mass: MIT Press, 1991), Ch 1. Cf. Axel Honneth, *The Fragmented World of the Social: Essays in Social and Political Philosophy*, trans. Charles W. Wright (Albany: State University of New York Press, 1995).
39 Axel Honneth, *Pathologies of Reason: On the Legacy of Critical Theory*, trans. James Ingram (New York: Columbia University Press, 2009), 54.
40 Honneth, *Pathologies of Reason: On the Legacy of Critical Theory*, 54–55. Two years prior Honneth had argued for a critical revival of the concept of reification itself in the Berkeley Tanner Lectures: Axel Honneth et al., *Reification: A New Look at an Old Idea* (Oxford: Oxford University Press, 2008).
41 Honneth, *Pathologies of Reason: On the Legacy of Critical Theory*, 58–59. Theodor W. Adorno, 'The Actuality of Philosophy', *Telos* 1977, no. 31 (1977). Max Weber, '"Objectivity" in Social Science and Social Policy', in *On the Methodology of the Social Sciences* (New York: Free Press, 1949).

42 Eugene Lunn has put this view most explicitly: 'the failure to distinguish liberal capitalism from fascism often weakened the Institute's work and Adorno's analysis of modern society and "mass culture"'. *Marxism and Modernism: An Historical Study of Lukács, Brecht, Benjamin, and Adorno* (Berkeley: University of California Press, 1982), 161. However, Lunn's later work discussed in Chapter 6 develops a more subtle view.
43 Harry F. Dahms, 'The Early Frankfurt School Critique of Capitalism: Critical Theory between Pollock's "State Capitalism" and the Critique of Instrumental Reason', in *The Theory of Capitalism in the German Economic Tradition*, ed. Peter Koslowski (New York: Springer, 2000). Harry F. Dahms, 'Critical Theory as Radical Comparative–Historical Research', in *The Palgrave Handbook of Critical Theory* (New York: Springer, 2017).
44 Frederick Pollock, 'State Capitalism: Its Possibilities and Limitations', *Zeitschrift für Sozialforschung* 9, no. 2 (1941). See Jessop's broader account of the development of the theory of state capitalism: Bob Jessop, *The Capitalist State* (New York: New York University Press 1982), 32–77. Jessop tends to sideline or exclude the Frankfurt School's work in such accounts but he provides a more detailed discussion of their contribution in: 'The Future of Capitalism', in *Classic Disputes in Sociology*, ed. R.J. Anderson, J.A. Hughes and W.W. Sharrock (London: Allen & Unwin, 1987).
45 Frederick Pollock, 'Is National Socialism a New Order?', *Zeitschrift für Sozialforschung* 9, no. 3 (1941); Franz L. Neumann, *Behemoth: The Structure and Practice of National Socialism* (London: V. Gollancz, 1942).
46 Deborah Cook's case for Adorno's independence from Pollock reviews the major advocates of the view that Horkheimer and Adorno entirely supported Pollock's theory (although somewhat mischaracterizing David Held in the process). She has recently been criticized by Gangl. Deborah Cook, 'Adorno on Late Capitalism', *Radical Philosophy* 89 (1998); Manfred Gangl, 'The Controversy over Friedrich Pollock's State Capitalism', *History of the Human Sciences* 29, no. 2 (2016).
47 Willem Van Reijen and Jan Bransen, 'The Disappearance of Class History in "Dialectic of Enlightenment": A Commentary on the Textual Variants (1947 and 1944)', in *Dialectic of Enlightenment* (Stanford: Stanford University Press, 2002), 252.
48 James Schmidt, '"Racket", "Monopoly', and the *Dialectic of Enlightenment*', Nonsite. org (January 2016).
49 Moishe Postone and Barbara Brick, 'Critical Theory and Political Economy', in *On Max Horkheimer: New Perspectives*, ed. Seyla Benhabib, Wolfgang Bonss, and John McCole (Cambridge, Mass.: MIT Press, 1993), 227–229.
50 Theodor W. Adorno, 'Culture Industry Reconsidered (1967)' (translated by Anson G. Rabinbach). *New German Critique*, no. 6 (1975): 14.
51 Jones, 'Márkus and the Retrieval of the Sociological Adorno'.
52 Pollock, 'State Capitalism: Its Possibilities and Limitations', 200, 201n.
53 Max Horkheimer, *Briefwechsel 1941–1948 (Correspondence 1941–1948)*, vol. 17, Gesammelte Schriften (Complete Writings) (Frankfurt am Main: S. Fischer, 1996), 115ff. As cited in Gangl, 'The Controversy over Friedrich Pollock's State Capitalism', 29. Translated by Laura Radosh.
54 My thanks to Michael Symonds for this clarification.
55 Held, *Introduction to Critical Theory: Horkheimer to Habermas*, 63.
56 Cited in Gangl, 'The Controversy over Friedrich Pollock's State Capitalism', 28.
57 Max Horkheimer, 'Preface', *Zeitschrift für Sozialforschung* 9, no. 2 (1941). This comment stands in stark contrast to Habermas's view that Horkheimer's 'The Authoritarian State' (drafted 1940, and also influenced by Pollock) provides an explanation for why Horkheimer and Adorno 'view it as a simple fact that humanity

will sink into a new barbarism'. I would regard this as a further example of the one-sided emphasis on Pollock's totalitarian subtype and of the textually selective assessment of these works mentioned above. Cf. Jürgen Habermas, 'Notes on the Developmental History of Horkheimer's Work', *Theory, Culture & Society* 10, no. 2 (1993).

58 See for instance the account in Richard Swedberg, 'How to Use Max Weber's Ideal Type in Sociological Analysis', *Journal of Classical Sociology* 18, no. 3 (2018).
59 Max Horkheimer, 'Notes on Institute Activities', *Zeitschrift für Sozialforschung* 9, no. 1 (1941).
60 Honneth, *Pathologies of Reason: On the Legacy of Critical Theory*, 55.
61 Axel Honneth, 'Communication and Reconciliation: Habermas' Critique of Adorno', *Telos*, no. 39 (1979): 47. This text is ambiguous at points regarding Honneth's own views given its main task is a reconstruction of Habermas's 'implicit' critique of Adorno. But part of the block of text from which I've drawn the two references to reification reappears in Honneth's own later critique of Adorno. So, I take these phrases to be his own position in 1979 too.
62 Theodor W. Adorno, 'Radio Physiognomics', in *Current of Music: Elements of a Radio Theory*, ed. Robert Hullot-Kentor (Cambridge: Polity, 2009). Adorno's study of Mahler, for example, in which 'physiognomy' appears in the title, contains no comparable definition. Theodor W. Adorno, *Mahler: A Musical Physiognomy*, trans. Edmund Jephcott (Chicago: University of Chicago Press, 1992). It is likely not coincidental that Lukács employed the term in his socio-aesthetic analyses as well: György Lukács, 'The Intellectual Physiognomy of Literary Characters (1936)', in *Radical Perspectives in the Arts*, ed. Lee Baxandall (Harmondsworth: Penguin, 1972).
63 Adorno, 'Radio Physiognomics', 44. Note that philosophy is conspicuously absent from Adorno's listed disciplines. For this reason I would disagree with Hullot-Kentor, at least for the case of this primary draft, in his characterization of the larger set of texts as an aesthetics coexisting with 'a sociological critique of radio broadcast music'. Robert Hullot-Kentor, 'Editor's Introduction', in *Adorno, Theodor W. Current of Music: Elements of a Radio Theory*, ed. Robert Hullot-Kentor (Cambridge: Polity, 2009), 24ff.
64 John B. Thompson, *The Media and Modernity: A Social Theory of the Media* (Stanford: Stanford University Press, 1995).
65 Adorno, 'Introduction to *Prophets of Deceit* (Unpublished)', 6.
66 Adorno, 'Introduction to *Prophets of Deceit* (Unpublished)', 6–7. Asterisks indicate words that are corrected or added by insertion marks.
67 Adorno, 'Introduction to *Prophets of Deceit* (Unpublished)', 2 (emphases added).
68 Adorno, 'Introduction to *Prophets of Deceit* (Unpublished)', 1–2.
69 Horkheimer and Adorno, *Dialectic of Enlightenment*, 129. Cf. Chapter 2(a).
70 Horkheimer, 'Notes on Institute Activities'.
71 Cf. Dahms's recent critical theoretical adoption of this term from the work of Jeffrey C. Alexander: Dahms, 'Critical Theory as Radical Comparative–Historical Research'. Cf. Jeffrey C. Alexander, *The Dark Side of Modernity* (Cambridge: Polity, 2013).
72 Horkheimer, 'Notes on Institute Activities', 122.
73 Theodor W. Adorno, *Negative Dialectics* (London: Routledge & Kegan Paul, 1973), 164–166. Adorno seizes on Weber's italicization of 'komponiert' (composes). Regrettably, the word was translated into English by Talcott Parsons as 'put together' without italicization. Weber, *The Protestant Ethic and the Spirit of Capitalism*, 47. Adorno makes a similar aesthetic excursus in constructing his character typology in

The Authoritarian Personality which is itself a deliberate expansion of the typology of antisemitic character types in the *Zeitschrift*: Adorno et al., *The Authoritarian Personality*, 750.

74 Adorno, *Introduction to Sociology*, 120–124; Weber, *Economy and Society*, 212–301.
75 Adorno, *Introduction to Sociology*, 122.
76 Adorno, *Introduction to Sociology*, 122. Adorno says no more than that this occurs in *Economy and Society*. I have been unable to locate such a passage.
77 Adorno, *Introduction to Sociology*, 122–123.
78 Adorno, *Introduction to Sociology*, 151.
79 Adorno, *Introduction to Sociology*, 147. Theodor W. Adorno, 'Opinion Research and Publicness (Meinungsforschung Und Öffentlichkeit 1964)', in *Group Experiment and Other Writings: The Frankfurt School on Public Opinion in Postwar Germany*, ed. Andrew J. Perrin and Lars Jarkko (Cambridge, Mass.: Harvard University Press, 2011).
80 Jürgen Habermas, 'Concluding Remarks', in *Habermas and the Public Sphere*, ed. Craig J. Calhoun (Cambridge, Mass.: MIT Press, 1992), 463.
81 Adorno, *Introduction to Sociology*, 15.
82 Claus Offe, *Reflections on America: Tocqueville, Weber and Adorno in the United States* (Cambridge: Polity, 2005), 80. Curiously, on the question of Adorno's neglect of US critical intellectuals, Offe even names Veblen, on whom Adorno wrote considerably. Cf. Theodor W. Adorno, 'Veblen's Attack on Culture: Remarks Occasioned by *The Theory of the Leisure Class*', *Zeitschrift für Sozialforschung* 9, no. 3 (1941).
83 Offe, *Reflections on America*, 91.
84 Offe, *Reflections on America*, 91.
85 Indeed the passage on which Offe relies here, from Adorno's 1968 reflections on his US stay, provides another example of the empirically existent 'pure type' argumentative form Adorno employed: 'The country displays capitalism, as it were, in its complete purity, without any precapitalist remnants'. Adorno, 'Scientific Experiences of a European Scholar in America (1968)', 241.
86 For such a proposal, see: Dahms, 'Critical Theory as Radical Comparative–Historical Research'.
87 Mann, *Fascists*.

4

Gramscian analyses of fascism and populism: Poulantzas, Laclau, Hall

This chapter examines what I will call 'the Gramscian tradition'. The work of Ernesto Laclau and Stuart Hall are the best known self-styled Gramscians in non-orthodox populism studies and their work on populism constitutes a kind of 'de facto' critical theory of populism. Laclau's more elaborated theory of populism was long ignored in orthodox populism studies but has recently begun to inform it.[1] Hall's conception of 'authoritarian populism' represents only a brief component of his work but, at least as a signifier of current developments, it has seen a revival in recent years. Indeed, it is his term, 'authoritarian populism', that has been used recently to link the Institute's work and contemporary populism.[2]

Whereas orthodox analysis of fascism and its relationship with populism suffers from similar problems to those in orthodox populism studies, the Gramscian tradition has been remarkably productive and insightful. This is partly because it also constitutes a corrective to orthodox Marxism-Leninism and indeed Stalinism. To this extent, some parallels exist between the perspective of the Institute and that of Gramsci. Moreover, this Gramscian legacy has played a role in discussions of earlier waves of twentieth century populism i.e. those outside the current focus on Europe and the USA. Such contextualization deepens the potential for linking 'demagogic populism' with the broader populist phenomenon.

What both traditions share most, however, is the analysis of populism in tandem with a theorization of fascism. This chapter and the next thus seek to critically develop a framework that combines the most productive elements of each of these traditions. Necessarily, such an account requires an initial introduction to Gramsci's own relevant work.

(a) Gramsci's legacy: a brief sketch

Antonio Gramsci's work proved remarkably enduring in the eddies of 'post-Marxist' critical fashion that followed the collapse of Eastern European communism in the early 1990s. In the short period since its adoption by some intellectual leaders of the British New Left in the late 1960s, it had grown into a respected 'Western Marxist' framework that complemented the rise of the Eurocommunist 'democratic road' to socialism in the political sphere, chiefly in Italy and France.[3] This was remarkable because, unlike most other prominent figures usually categorized as 'Western Marxist', Gramsci remained a key organizational, and later inspirational but imprisoned, figure in a Leninist communist party during his lifetime. In many ways he was constituted as the Frankfurt School's 'activist' opposite.

His appeal lay in part in this very combination of orthodox revolutionary and anti-orthodox reflective thinker, the latter role becoming his major preoccupation, owing to his long imprisonment. Like the Institute's early work, his project was informed by a failed left uprising and the rise of fascism in his nation of origin (Italy). But, unlike the Institute's apparent political caution, there seemed to emerge from his prison writings a coherent, if ambiguous, strategy for transforming Western capitalism into socialism. Not long afterwards, a similar interest in his work emerged among intellectuals and activists in the 'new' nation-states, Worsley's 'Third World'.[4]

Indeed, it is not difficult to see how Gramsci's strategy of alliance-building beyond the proletariat intersected with the cross-class national 'populist' struggles that were a major focus of attention in the first wave of comparative populism studies. His interest in the relative underdevelopment of his *region* of origin, 'The Southern Question', spoke directly to contemporary concerns of uneven development of what he identified as 'peripheral' states. Indeed, it was in his 1926 essay on that topic that his conception of hegemony first appeared in an elaborated, if not yet fully realized, form.[5]

In the West – or what is now called the global North – however, his work appealed theoretically as a way forward from an increasingly discredited economic reductivism associated with communist party orthodoxies. In this sense he appealed to the dominant 'aesthetic' interests characteristic of contemporary Western Marxists who were seeking a non-reductivist relationship between social determination and aesthetic autonomy.[6] The same anti-reductivism spoke to the obsolescence of related political strategies centred on the proletariat as the sole 'subject of history', Marx's related 'immiseration' thesis and overconfidence in the 'inevitability' of capitalist economic crisis and collapse. Equally significantly, for an ostensible Leninist, Gramsci was unusually attentive to 'bourgeois' democratic forms. Following the Second World War, Western consumer capitalism seemed ripe for Gramscian analysis.

At the centre of these interests was the concept of hegemony. Gramsci's Marx here was that of the historico-journalistic writings, especially *The Eighteenth Brumaire of Louis Bonaparte*, Marx's sophisticated socio-historical analysis of the rise of the dictatorial Louis Napoleon in the wake of the defeat of the 1848 revolution in France.[7] Like Marx, Gramsci was interested in forensically assessing the social and political forces that had led to an unanticipated defeat. Gramsci borrowed from Marx the principle that the analysis of any given situation – what the Althusserians later called a 'conjuncture' – required finely tuned 'micro-level' concepts to assess 'the balance of forces'. It was by such means that 'infantile' economic reductivism could be avoided.

Marx's project is often introduced via his brief summation of his approach in 'The 1859 Preface' with the much misunderstood 'base and superstructure' metaphor, which was discussed in Chapter 3.[8] The 1859 usage of the metaphor refers to the constituents of an 'epochal' mode of production as the base: forces and relations of production as distinct from an 'ideological superstructure'. In *The Brumaire*, however, the metaphor is used in both that sense *and* a localized micropolitical sense in discussing the relationship between social classes and the 'political superstructure' which is also repeatedly metaphorized as a theatrical stage.

Marx's refinements meant that social class, for example, was subdivided into the smaller scale 'class fraction'. Likewise, Marx and Gramsci recognized the corresponding form of the 'bloc'. In Marx this term primarily referred to alliances of factions within the parliamentary sphere. In Gramsci the *historical bloc* was an amalgam of economic and political forces constituted by ever-vulnerable 'unstable equilibria'. Crucially, the historical bloc required an 'organic' ideology to hold its constituent forces together and it was this ideology, or a variant of it, that the historical bloc proffered as a form of intellectual leadership, so enabling the 'organization of consent', so central to hegemonic rule. Intellectuals provided the key mediating role within the historical bloc and the societal organization of consent, the latter being the core of Gramsci's redefinition of 'intellectual'. As Adamson comments, this is 'roughly what Weber meant by legitimation, though with a greater sensitivity to the interweaving of consent and culture'.[9]

The Eighteenth Brumaire later became a common reference point for the Marxist analysis of fascism. However, unlike some such usages, Gramsci avoided directly equating fascism with 'Bonapartism' (understood as a reference to, and direct modelling from, Louis Napoleon's counter-revolutionary precedent). He likewise avoided the related argument that fascism was 'the last resort' of the bourgeoisie when all other political forms had been exhausted.[10]

Rather, with the concept of Caesarism, Gramsci placed Louis Bonaparte within a wider typology of forms of resolution of 'organic' crises where there is a 'static balance of forces' – that is, where neither a ruling bloc nor its rival has the capacity to win decisively. Thus 'the content of the crisis is the ruling class's hegemony'.[11] Gramsci notes that this phenomenon appears as a 'crisis of authority'. As he states in his opening reflections on such crises:

> the immediate situation becomes delicate and dangerous, because the field is open for violent solutions, for the activities of unknown forces, represented by charismatic 'men of destiny'.[12]

Fascism, although not named as such, was thus one form of outcome – if not resolution – of such an organic crisis whereby coercion outweighed consent. In that sense fascism was not a hegemonic form of regime but one that dominated primarily through coercion. Gramsci's proposed typology suggests a continuum from military coup d'états through to progressive forms of Caesarism (Napoleon I).[13] However, Gramsci also makes explicit that 'in the modern world' the preconditions for either 'Napoleon I' or Napoleon III (Caesarism) have changed, most notably in the decline of the military's political role and the rise of 'modern political techniques' related to the 'expansion of parliamentarism and the associative systems of union and party' as well as 'the transformation which took place in the forces of order in the wider sense'. These are precisely the forces that Gramsci famously formulated as 'State = political society + civil society, in other words hegemony protected by an armour of coercion'.[14]

The counter-strategy towards fascism Gramsci conceived in prison involved the building of a (counter-)hegemonic project led by the proletariat but necessarily including an alliance with the peasantry and sections of the petty bourgeoisie. It thus entailed the construction of a historical bloc that would counter that constructed by the fascists (Northern industrial + Southern landowner bourgeoisie + sections of petty bourgeoisie). Crucially, the obstacles to this project were cultural-historical as well as political and economic. Italy, on Gramsci's analysis, had never produced a 'national culture', what he routinely called a 'national-popular'. The Risorgimento had failed because of its inability to render its project hegemonic through intellectual and cultural leadership. The key factor here was the isolation of Italian intellectuals as a caste disconnected from the subaltern classes, especially the peasantry. As a consequence, Italy, unlike other nations such as France, had 'neither a popular artistic literature nor a local production of "popular" literature'.[15] Gramsci's conception of '(t)he entire national-popular culture', was 'not restricted to narrative fiction' and included newspapers and popular knowledge of the natural sciences. The dominance of dialectic forms of the Italian language in many parts of Italy was paradigmatic of this crisis of the national-popular. This conception of the intellectual, especially the emphasis Gramsci places on the class origin and allegiance of intellectuals, strongly echoes his conception of the organic intellectual who elaborates 'embedded' specific qualities of a class and challenges the 'traditional' caste-like intellectual.[16]

Gramsci, who had studied linguistics, states in reference to the national-popular:

> One should note that in many languages, 'national' and 'popular' are either synonymous or nearly so (they are in Russian, in German, where *völkisch* has an even more intimate meaning of race, and in the Slavonic languages in general; in France the meaning of 'national' already includes a more politically elaborated notion of 'popular' because it is related to the concept of 'sovereignty': national sovereignty and popular sovereignty have, or had, the same value).[17]

Now, much follows regarding populism from this acute observation in comparative historical semantics, especially when one considers that a 'variant' of 'national-popular' in Gramsci's usage is 'nation-people'. Forgacs has supplied evidence that the informing model of 'national-popular' in the cultural writings is the Russian example – *narod* and *narodnyi* – acquired during Gramsci's time in Moscow. Forgacs treats this as a link to the term's circulation by early nineteenth-century Russian Romantics. However, in early comparative populism studies the case of the Russian *narodnik* of the 1870s was the significant outrider precisely because it was a form of 'intellectual populism'. Gramsci would undoubtedly have been familiar with this meaning because of the conflict between these populists and Marxists in Russia and especially because of Lenin's critiques thereof.[18]

Indeed, Gramsci makes clear elsewhere that he regarded such forms of 'intellectual populism' – in attempting to 'move towards the people' – as contradictory, i.e., they may or may not lead to his desired 'indirect education of the people' that would contribute to a counter-hegemony.[19] Of course, his highlighting of 'the intimate meaning of race' in the German *völkisch* variant above makes this contradictory dimension even more explicit. This legacy becomes critical for my linkage of the Gramscian project with that of the Institute in the next chapter.

(b) Laclau and Poulantzas on fascism and populism

Laclau's writings on populism and hegemony, including especially his co-authored work with Chantal Mouffe, became associated with a 'post-Marxist' framework following the controversy surrounding their 1985 book, *Hegemony and Socialist Strategy*.[20] However, what is most noticeable about that work in hindsight is its attempt to mark out a 'post-authoritarian' understanding of hegemony. The authoritarianism Laclau wishes to confront is principally that of the Leninist vanguard party and its correlates. The source of this authoritarianism, in Laclau's view, lay in transferring Marxism's 'ontological privileging' of the working class to 'the political leadership of the mass movement'.[21]

I highlight this anti-authoritarian dimension at the outset because what is most remarkable about the later Laclauian project is that it signally fails to anticipate that authoritarianism is not confined to such a vanguard party model. Rather, it is a contingent prospect in populist formations due to their susceptibility to demagogic leadership. Laclau assumes that once the Marxian 'ontological privileging' of the proletariat – and, eventually, 'the economic' – is jettisoned, the risk of authoritarian leadership disappears.

This is especially noteworthy as Laclau's earlier work included an analysis of the role of populism within European fascism which was in turn based in a sympathetic critique of Nicos Poulantzas's work on this subject. Indeed, notwithstanding its vulnerability to his own later 'post-Marxist' distancings, Laclau's first book remains one of the most elaborated theorizations to date of the relationship between populism and fascism.[22] Both Poulantzas's and Laclau's projects had sought to extend Gramsci's insights, most notably by developing his 'anti-reductionist' understanding of the relationship between the conceptual elements of the Marxian base and superstructure metaphor. In the case of fascism this also meant developing further his model of organic crisis within a historical bloc.

Laclau credits Poulantzas with having broken qualitatively new theoretical ground in the analysis of fascism. In a striking parallel with his later critique of the literature on populism, Laclau points out that while the period since the end of the Second World War had witnessed an increase in empirical historical research on fascism, there had been little comparable theoretical progress. Laclau characterizes the existent theoretical failing generically as the reduction of fascism to a 'simple contradiction'. Two such forms of this reductivism he identifies are: (i) the liberal and 'bourgeois social science' tendency to treat fascism as 'a parenthesis in normal historical development' and (ii) 'subjectivist' approaches that rely on 'psychologization' and/or a model of the vulnerable isolated individual in a mass society. Poulantzas, in contrast, builds on the Gramscian analysis of fascism which, for Laclau, focuses instead on the complex accumulation of multiple class contradictions.[23] It is here that Gramsci's 'organic crisis' becomes pertinent.

Poulantzas's reworking of Gramsci acknowledges that his model of organic crisis does not blindly follow Marxian 'Bonapartism'.[24] While he does not adopt Gramsci's own proposed typology of forms of Caesarism, he wishes to distinguish fascism from both Bonapartism and military dictatorship. He employs Gramsci's 'historical bloc' but renames it 'power bloc'.[25] He provides a more detailed configuration of the fractional participants in this bloc, notably adding 'monopoly capital' as the leading emergent class fraction seeking hegemony. As with Marx's analysis in *The Brumaire*, the petty bourgeoisie play a pivotal role in the rhythm and outcome of the crisis. The success of the fascist movement in Italy, for example, turns heavily on the role of the petty bourgeoisie as fascism transforms itself into a mass party while seeking alliances with different fractions of 'big capital'. Once this new bloc achieves hegemony it develops a new form of 'exceptional state' in which the petty bourgeoisie is set aside and overt moves against the proletariat commence.[26]

For Laclau, Poulantzas achieves his required analytic standard of 'multiple contradictions' by placing the petty bourgeoisie in this pivotal role. It provides the 'new' ideological content of the emergent organic ideology of the new historical bloc, partly by 'borrowing' 'elements' of 'proletarian ideology'.[27] However, Laclau's critique of Poulantzas focuses on these very gains. He questions the status of these 'elements' as ideological fragments, their mode of 'transformation' into new composites and Poulantzas's tendency to regard each 'element' as having a necessary 'class belonging'.

Now, this model of the 'ideological sub-ensemble', as Poulantzas also tends to call it, owes much to the influence of Lévi-Straussian structuralism on the project of Louis Althusser, with whom Poulantzas's work was often in dialogue. Althusser had employed the structuralist legacy to elucidate his re-readings of Marx's own texts, frequently with the goal of recovering Marx's theoretical innovations from orthodox 'vulgar' reductivist economism.

Lévi-Strauss had brought Jakobson's innovations in formalist literary analysis and Saussurean linguistics to bear on the study of 'primitive' myths.[28] The combination of 'elements', he argued, was one of the most fundamental procedures of mythic classification systems by which humans were understood to interpret their existence. This combinatory process was often called 'bricolage'. In his 1962 work, *The Savage Mind*, he claimed this approach could make a contribution to the Marxian 'theory of the superstructures' which had been 'scarcely touched on by Marx'. Ideologies were so understood as formally constituted in the same way as myths. In his 1963 *Structural*

Anthropology he argued that formalism 'converges with certain aspects of Marx's thought'.[29]

The highpoint of this structuralist influence, as Althusser later conceded in his 'Elements of Self-Criticism', came in *Reading Capital* (co-authored with Etienne Balibar). There formulations reliant on 'elements' constituting a structure are pervasive and *Structural Anthropology* is cited in support.[30] However, as critics of Lévi-Strauss pointed out at the time, there was a high theoretical risk in extending a process that was modelled on Saussure's conception of the 'unconscious' adoption of the rules of language beyond such myths. Most notably, there was no space for modern conceptions of intellectual autonomy in aesthetic and intellectual composition.[31] Accordingly, the Althusserian project also drifted into a mechanistic functionalism that was especially brutal in its reading of Gramsci in developing its conception of 'ideology'.[32] Gramsci's own subtle, if at times ambiguous, practice of setting up narrow and expansive senses of the same category/signifier – notably 'intellectuals' and 'state' – was completely lost. Althusser instead promoted the reductivist notion of 'ideological state apparatuses' to cover social domains such as religion and media. Here an earlier self-criticism did little to redeem the situation.[33]

While Poulantzas certainly adopted many Althusserian terms, even his earliest appropriations were, as Jessop notes, 'strangely ambivalent' towards this source. As in the legacy of critical theory, a key factor here is the role of sociology, the discipline with which Poulantzas identified. He also distanced himself from the Althusserian project's over-reliance on Lévi-Straussian structuralism and its tendencies towards functionalism.[34] Laclau's critique of Poulantzas is, in this context, remarkably uneven. He charges Poulantzas with succumbing to the Althusserian tendency towards formalism where that term refers to what Althusser called theoreticism in his self-criticism. Formalism for Laclau at this stage of his career refers to the consequences of employing conceptual schema 'set at a level of abstraction so high' that their elaboration becomes a purely formal concept-to-concept process whereby 'all contact with the original meaning [of these concepts] is lost'.[35] Confusingly, this usage of 'formalism' does not refer to the Jakobsonian literary formalism that inspired Lévi-Straussian structuralism and which the later Laclau adopts.

Yet Laclau's critique of *Fascism and Dictatorship* also builds to a charge that Poulantzas *underemploys* Althusser's conception of ideology.[36] By the latter Laclau means Althusser's appropriation of the concept of interpellation from Lacanian psychoanalysis whereby 'ideology in general' achieves the 'interpellation' of individuals as subordinated subjects by its modes of address. He even cites a long passage from Althusser deferentially.[37]

Interpellation, as Stuart Hall later pointed out, has a more evident structuralist than psychoanalytic heritage in that it relied on the removal of any suggestion of 'authorship' of any structure. Rather, like the Saussurean conception of language, the deep structure (*langue*), 'speaks us, as the myth speaks the myth-maker'. Thus, if all ideology is structured like a language – 'a process without a subject' for the Althusserians – and individuals are no more than 'bearers of structures', a position Laclau explicitly adopts, then its 'speaking' as interpellation constitutes 'us' as its subjects.[38] These minutiae of intellectual development are significant because Laclau rolls out his theorizations of populism over the following decades from a position based in these critical reworkings of the Poulantzian and Althusserian schema.

The theorization that Laclau develops from his critique of Poulantzas's *Fascism and Dictatorship*, then, relies primarily on interpreting fascism and populism as different forms of interpellation. This model replaces both of the limitations Laclau identified in Poulantzas: the 'class belonging' of ideological 'elements' and their reconstitution as an organic ideological ensemble. Without making this explicit, Laclau significantly revises the Althusserian conception of interpellation by arguing that:

(i) Multiple, often competing, forms of interpellation exist in practice. They can accordingly trigger an 'identity crisis' in the subject.
(ii) Interpellation, not a structuralist sub-ensemble, is the means of 'fusion' of what Poulantzas calls 'elements' of an organic ideology. Laclau nonetheless names this process with another structuralist term, 'articulation'.
(iii) Two generic interpellative mechanisms, condensation and displacement (ultimately sourced to Freud's *The Interpretation of Dreams*), apply to 'different situations'. He borrows these psychoanalytic metaphors and their roles from another Althusser essay.[39]
(iv) Displacement refers to the processes of 'neutralization' of ideological contradictions by a power bloc. Condensation is the process by which interpellations can symbolically stand for each other. In a crisis one mode of interpellation can condense others and become the chief means of challenging the hegemony of a power bloc.

In apparent emulation of Althusser's example of Christian religious interpellation (which was dominantly Catholic in its specificities), Laclau offers a speculative example that echoes Weber's analysis of the Protestant ethic. Because ascetic religious interpellations can 'coexist' with the consumption of worldly goods, a potential contradiction in capitalism is 'displaced'. However, in a crisis situation, the following 'condensation' scenario may ensue:

> There arises ... a religious reformer who blames all the evils on corruption and the abandonment of strict ascetic observance and who, through

his interpellation, gives his followers a new subjectivity. The religious interpellation thus comes to be a chief reorganizer of all familial, economic, and other aspects. The coexistence of various relatively consistent interpellations in an ideological discourse has given way to an ideological structure in which *one* interpellation becomes the main organizer of all the others.[40]

This counter-hegemonic 'condensation' scenario underwent many reformulations by Laclau in later years, but it shapes the core of his understanding of the 'constitutive' mechanism of populist practice. What is remarkable here is that he needs to introduce an 'agent' into his scenario, the religious reformer, *for whom there is no conceptual place in his structuralist model*. This might have been, for example, an ideal opportunity to 'reconnect' with Gramsci's analysis of the charismatic individual who 'arises' in a moment of organic crisis and from which he proposes his typology of Caesarism. *The under-preparedness for demagogy of the Laclauian schema is thus present in its first elaboration.* We might add that, at this stage at least, the model is quite unsubtle in its reliance on this untheorized component. The follower's subjectivity appears entirely malleable by the reformer's interpellation into a 'new' one; yet no details of this process are here provided.

At this stage of his project Laclau still holds to the Althusserian rendering of the Marxian view that the mode of production (forces + relations of production), the 'epochal' understanding of the metaphorical base, 'overdetermines' the play of political forces, especially in a crisis. It is the site of 'class struggle'. This was also Marx's view in *The Brumaire*. The complementary Althusserian concept is 'social formation', which approximates the 'concrete' existence of the nation-state. Accordingly, when Laclau brings his model of interpellation to bear on fascism, 'monopoly capitalism' plays a central role as the (over-)determining mode of production. However, in what is effectively a variant of Marx's 'in itself/for itself' distinction regarding classes, Laclau argues that not all antagonistic relations with the power bloc are constituted as 'class interpellations'. The latter are only readily available to those 'close' to the primary relations of production (bourgeois/proletariat). Those that are not class interpellations – indeed those that are distinctive of the (relatively) autonomous political sphere – may take the form of 'popular-democratic' interpellations generically addressed to 'the people'. 'Ideological transformation' is thus 'carried out through the production of subjects and the articulation and disarticulation of discourses'.[41] The 'people/power bloc' contradiction so becomes a constant invocation in Laclau's writings.

Fascism is thus marked by a crisis in the power bloc, consistent with Gramsci. But the weakness of the proletariat is redefined as an inability to fuse its class ideology with a popular-democratic one. The power bloc is no longer able to practise 'transformism' (Gramsci's term), the neutralization of contradictions by practices such as the 'co-option' of 'political parties' and clientelism. The latter term refers to the unequal transactional provision of 'favours'. Here a 'rupture' occurs whereby Jacobinism emerges, notably within the petty bourgeoisie, so tipping the people/power bloc dynamic into an anti-systemic form. Popular-democratic interpellation ceases to have a legitimating 'liberal' role and 'comes to acquire maximum possible autonomy compatible with class society'. This constitutes 'the moment when popular-democratic interpellation presents itself … in virtually pure form'.[42]

But this Jacobinist dimension is also crucial as it can take a fascist or socialist form. The failure of the proletariat to recognize the prospect of a condensation of this Jacobinism and 'its' class ideology – or 'socialist political discourse' – left open a role for monopoly capital to exploit this opening, along different paths in Italy and Germany, each traceable to what Gramsci regarded as an incomplete constitution of a 'national-popular'.[43] But their common feature was, for Laclau, to 'disarticulate this Jacobinism from any class discourse'. In the German case, Laclau explicitly states, Nazism 'interpellated the petty bourgeoisie' *as* a race.[44] Again, however, this advocated method of 'reconstruct(ing) the interpellative structures which constitute' the 'ideological level of determinate social formation' stops short at the provision of the details of interpellative success.

(c) Laclau's formalist reading of Worsley

If we turn to Laclau's first extended theorization of populism in the same monograph as the fascism essay, we soon find a likely reason for the absence of a theoretical discussion of 'agents' of populist interpellation. Of the existent approaches to populism he reviews, he spends most time challenging functionalist variants of sociological modernization theory as applied to Latin America. In the functionalist texts Laclau samples, populism is regarded as a phenomenon of the transition from traditional to industrial societies where the latter are based, descriptively in Laclau's view, on the trajectories of the nation-states in what is now called the global North. The likelihood of populism thus increases in inverse relation to the 'progress' towards 'modern industrial society' that has been achieved. Quite correctly, Laclau points out that the populist phenomenon has not been confined to 'transitional' societies but has existed in cases like Poujadisme in France. However, he reserves his harshest comments for the role attributed to 'élite manipulation' of 'poorly integrated' masses where that élite challenges a status quo in part by utilization of 'mass media'.[45]

Here Laclau sets aside uses of the category of demagogy (coupled for him with 'deceit') as 'moralism'. Characteristically, he does not address the 'media' dimension any further. Such a 'moralistic' charge was also used by Kazin in his rejection of the term 'demagogy' discussed in Chapter 1. Laclau's pejorative use of 'moralistic' is more likely related to the Althusserian theoreticist view that held that all moralistic discourse was 'unscientific' because it was incapable of adequate construction of a 'theoretical object' (i.e. conceptualization of the problem under investigation). Similarly, Laclau argues that such invocations of demagogy and manipulation reveal a theoretical inadequacy characterized by a conception of populism 'that is never defined in itself but in counter-position to another paradigm'.[46]

This is not the place to weigh up the complex history of modernization theory. Yet is worth briefly considering Shils's views here as a counterpoint. He is often portrayed as the paradigmatic modernization theorist and even more so in critiques of functionalism. Yet he had a quite different view from that Laclau criticizes. This emerges in his contribution to the most famous modernization and development text in communication studies, *Communications and Political Development*.[47]

Arguing against the 'populist shortcut', Shils portrays demagogy as the great risk facing 'the new states'. Rather than acting as guarantors of Westernizing virtue, 'the media of mass communication' add to this risk. The modernizing diffusion of broadcasting increases the risk of demagogy within populist movements of national independence and is visible in some demagogues already in power in those nations. Broadcasting's capacities for space-compression and unchallenged monologue are two key features identified by Shils. Notwithstanding his own immanent use of the term, Shils's warnings anticipate elements of later critiques of the 'modernization' agenda. For Shils the best bulwark against demagogic leadership is 'a civil sphere' underpinned by autonomous professional institutions with ties to media institutions. Accordingly, he regards 'the Indian case' as 'instructive' of the capacity for civil sphere building – partly because of its long-established newspapers – while the polity of contemporary Indonesia (then a military dictatorship) is for him a strong example of demagogic authoritarianism. Far from advocating wholesale Westernization while deeming demagogy a problem of the global South, Shils's paper makes plain that demagogy is 'a constant presence' in the Western democracies and 'all the stronger where there is a strong populistic element in the culture of the political profession'. For *all* nation-states then, 'the availability of the media of mass communication is an invitation to their demagogic use'. The 'advanced' democracies' relevant advantages – such as high levels of literacy – are not ascribed a quasi-natural superiority but delineated as part of a repertoire of necessary elements of a counterveiling civil sphere.

The more complex position Shils presents here is hardly one that Laclau might have preferred. But it nonetheless largely escapes the major tropes of his critique and addresses the question of 'mass media' at a level of sophistication that completely eluded Laclau.

I have included this sociological detour because *Laclau's critique fundamentally breaks with all sociological theorization at this point and from here he develops his theory of populism 'in itself'*.

In 1977, this theorization took a similar form to his theorization of fascism in the same volume, on which he explicitly draws: i.e. it is conceived in tandem with a role for a non-reductivist Marxian conception of social class, framed strategically as a project of 'articulation'. Thus, for example: '[t]he struggle of the working class for its hegemony is an effort to achieve a maximum possible fusion between popular-democratic ideology and socialist ideology.'[48] Its theoretical correlate is the following: *'populism consists in the presentation of popular-democratic interpellations in a synthetic-antagonistic complex with respect to the dominant ideology'*.[49]

In his 1985 book with Mouffe, the Marxian dimensions of such formulations are largely removed but 'socialist strategy' is still very much to the fore. Laclau had foreshadowed at the end of his 1977 fascism essay that the full 'implications' of Gramsci's concept of hegemony were yet to be worked out by Mouffe and himself.[50] As indicated above, Gramsci's project is 'de-Leninized' as an anti-authoritarian manoeuvre. Ironically, 'manipulation' – a term indicative of the 'moralistic' failings of modernization theory for Laclau in 1977 – now becomes an acceptable pejorative term as 'vanguardist manipulation'.[51] Crucially, the Gramscian 'leadership' role of the proletariat is abandoned. Moreover, the very category of 'the economic' is jettisoned as well, whereas in 1977 the concept of mode of production – which Laclau had gone to such lengths to advocate – still framed the overall analysis, as per Marx's *Brumaire*. In 1985 it and the base and superstructure metaphor are effectively replaced by 'articulation'. Here, however, Laclau also parts company with Althusser, without marking this as the autocritique it effectively is.

Core Gramscian concepts – or at least their signifiers – are nonetheless maintained within what is effectively a new epistemological and ontological position. The ontological status of populism is insisted on in an approach that he later self-labelled 'strictly formal'.[52] By this Laclau sought to break definitively with any content-based ('ontic') conception of populism. This 'content problem' corresponds with the orthodox 'classification dilemma' outlined in Chapter 1. Accordingly, his major 2005 work, *On Populist Reason*, sets out from a critique of such inductivism.

Most significantly, Laclau regarded his 2005 solution to the problem of nomenclature, prefigured in earlier writings, as a resumption of Peter Worsley's

1969 proposal for a social theoretical rethinking of the orthodox dilemma. As we saw in Chapter 1, only by addressing populism at 'a much higher level of abstraction', Worsley had argued, could that dilemma be overcome. For him this preferably meant following Weberian methodological prescriptions.[53]

It is quite remarkable that Laclau appears to have been the first in almost forty years to have seriously resumed Worsley's call for such a social theorization of populism. Like Worsley, he finds the classification dilemma a false problem in that generalities have been claimed from a mixture of empirical examples often arbitrarily labelled.

Laclau thus found the theorization of populism in much the same state Saussure is said to have found linguistics – a field rife with empirical studies generating arbitrary inductivist abstractions. Appropriately then, one of Laclau's papers on this problem is called 'Populism: What's in a Name' (2005) and undertakes, as its first step, a very elementary Saussurean separation of populism as signifier from populism as signified/referent. Where Worsley advocated a Weberian ideal typification, Laclau's retheorization relies instead on what we shall see is his self-declared theoretical formalism.

Laclau is especially taken with Worsley's concluding formulation that populism is a *dimension* of political practice in many varieties of political regime rather than an isolatable discrete phenomenon, as empiricist-inductivist approaches assume. Although it was partly cited in Chapter 1, it is worth reproducing the passage from Worsley that so impresses Laclau that he comments on it: 'this move is crucial':

> The populist syndrome ... is much wider than its particular manifestation in the form of or context of any particular policy, or of any particular kind of overall ideological system or type of polity: democracy, totalitarianism, etc. This suggests that populism is better regarded as an emphasis, a dimension of political culture in general, not simply as a particular kind of overall ideological system or type of organization. Of course, as with all ideal types, it may be very closely approximated to by some political cultures and structures, such as those hitherto labelled 'populist'.[54]

Laclau's immediate comment on this passage is also worth quoting in full:

> This move is crucial. For if Worsley is correct – and I think he is – then the inanity of the whole exercise of trying to identify the universal contents of populism becomes evident: as we have seen, it has repeatedly led to attempts to identify the social base of populism – only to find out a moment later that one cannot continue calling 'populist' movements with entirely different social bases. But of course, if one tries to avoid

this pitfall by identifying populism with a *dimension* that cuts across ideological and social differences, one is burdened with the task of specifying what that dimension is – something Worsley does not really do, at least in a sufficient and convincing way.[55]

Laclau so mistakes the middle of Worsley's argument for its beginning. For this comment comes in the middle of Worsley's five-step process which builds to his advocacy of a continuum of ideal-typification. Laclau even selectively cites from Worsley's 'alteration' of Shils's role for demagogy in his informing ideal-typification without acknowledging the methodological implications of Worsley's usage of the Weberian term. His reason? To make yet another charge against 'any easy reductionist attempt at seeing a spurious dimension of manipulation as necessarily constitutive of populism'.[56]

Given its significance for him, it is reasonable to query how Laclau was able to ignore Worsley's framing of this insight as an advocacy of ideal-typification that placed Shils's position as one component of a typology. If we look again at Worsley's 'syndrome' statement above, a 'Laclauian' way of reading the passage, entirely at odds with Worsley's actual practice, can be reconstructed. A 'dimension'-like quality distributed throughout multiple practices had been postulated as a central plank of Russian and Prague Formalism. The 'aesthetic function' was that dimension.[57] This decentring anti-essentialist manoeuvre was designed to bypass most existent forms of aestheticism which privileged certain aesthetic practices or works or resorted to a subjectivist psychologism. 'Literariness' and 'the aesthetic' so became a component of many practices, not only those ranked canonically as aesthetic 'works'. Jakobson so combined this conception of a distributed signifying function (the literary/aesthetic) with components of Saussurean structural linguistics. It was this composite that Lévi-Strauss adopted and developed into his structuralist project.

Now, it is important to emphasize here that Laclau remained committed in his later project to theorizing populist practice via the conception of an ensemble of 'elements' he had derived from Poulantzas's work. However, he lacked his desired non-reductivist means of theorizing this process. He would have found in Jakobson a figure who shared his impatience with arbitrary 'taxonomies', a charge he frequently levelled at Poulantzas.[58] To his credit, Laclau openly acknowledged the influence of the aesthetic formalist 'breakthrough' in a later section of *On Populist Reason* where he legitimates his expansion of his conception of discourse beyond reference to 'speech and writing' as:

> any complex of elements in which *relations* play the constitutive role. This means that elements do not pre-exist the relational complex but are constituted through it. Thus 'relation' and 'objectivity' are synonymous.

Saussure asserted that there are no positive terms in language, only differences – something is what it is only through its differential relations with something else. And what is true of language conceived in its strict sense is also true of any signifying (i.e. objective) element: an action is what it is only through its differences from other possible actions and from other signifying elements – words or actions – which can be successive or simultaneous. Only two types of relation can possibly exist between these signifying elements: combination and substitution. Once the schools of Copenhagen and Prague radicalized linguistic formalism, it was possible to go beyond the Saussurean enthralment to the phonic and conceptual substances, and to develop the full ontological implications of this fundamental breakthrough: all purely regional linguistic reference was, to a large extent, abandoned.[59]

The aesthetic has no explicit place here but the role of 'signifying element' in the above is identical to that of the literary/aesthetic in Jakobson's schema. However, Jakobson also had a means of 'ordering' this distributed aesthetic dimension, the declaration of 'the dominant' from his typology of linguistic functions.[60] This model found its way via structuralism to the Althusserian conception of 'dominant ideology' which partly framed the Althusser-Poulantzas understanding of 'ensemble of elements' discussed here. However, this later adoption by Laclau does not even incorporate this limited 'ordering' role for his 'relational complex' of elements. Contingency becomes paramount. All social practice is subsumed within this 'formalist projection'.[61] However, because his formalism abandons even Jakobson's self-limitations, I will call it a *hyperformalism*.

Although this position is routinely referred to by commentators as post-structuralist as well as post-Marxist, it remains primarily structuralist in the Saussurean sense as reworked by linguistic and literary formalism. I will return to this critique in the next section but first it is important to outline Laclau's 'mature' hyperformalist depiction of populism. This summary account plainly echoes the Worsley passage above:

> My attempt has not been to find the true referent of populism, but to do the opposite: to show that populism has no referential unity because it is ascribed not to a delimitable phenomenon but to a social logic whose effects cut across many phenomena. Populism is, quite simply, a way of constructing the political.[62]

Now such social logics, of which populist logic is one, are hereon understood by Laclau entirely in (post-)structuralist terms as discursively constituted.[63]

Their key mechanisms, accordingly, are structured on the model of language and, especially, on the Saussurean signifying principle of signifier self-differentiation. It follows for Laclau that 'differential and equivalential logics' lie at the core of populist practice.

Populism, Laclau states, thus has two chief preconditions:

(1) the formation of an internal antagonistic frontier separating the 'people' from power; and
(2) an equivalential articulation of demands making the emergence of the 'people' possible.[64]

These are each a socio-semiotic abstraction which seeks to render the 'social logic' of populism without reducing it to an epiphenomenon of something else, such as social class. Even when Laclau elaborates this position at monograph length, discussions of empirical cases are usually limited to very short illustrations of the formal property of the particular social logic under discussion.

The first precondition in the above citation refers to the historically common phenomenon of the populist embrace of a conception of 'the people' defined against an elite who hold, or are deemed to hold, significant power over 'the people'. This is the differential logic at work. The second precondition is more complex and, true to his formalist influences, Laclau only ever supplies self-referential technicist-formalist accounts of it (with those rare empirical flourishes). Its key features are: (i) an assertion that the core unit of analysis (corresponding to the Saussurean phoneme) should be the 'demand' by a particular social group; (ii) that when such demands escalate to a challenge to existing institutions, they form the prospect of a social alliance's development between different groups and the socio-semiotic formation (via an 'equivalential chain' of semiosis) of a unifying category of 'the people' becomes possible. It is here that the logic of difference is replaced by a logic of equivalence and a populist logic unfolds.

However, the specific content of this unifying category and the articulation of its demands cannot be predicted. Accordingly, to account for such contingency, its semiotic space is designated theoretically as a signifier that is not only unfixed, and thus 'floating' without a signified, but also 'empty'.

(d) Hall's 'authoritarian populism' and other challenges to Laclauian hyperformalism

Russian literary formalism was in part designed to confront the 'reflectionist' reductivism within orthodox Russian (party) Marxist approaches to art. In that sense there is an affinity between the critical orientation of Russian Formalism and its legacy and Laclau's anti-Leninism and anti-economism. However, even by the time of Laclau's earliest writings on populism it had become well known that the Russian debates had been more complex than a formalism–economism divide.[65] Bakhtin, Medvedev and Vološinov, members of the 'Vitebsk' group, challenged both economism and the ahistorical technicism of the Formalists. The ahistorical dimension of the Formalist project followed from its understanding of a self-reproducing literary system, analogous to Saussure's conception of linguistic system. Bakhtin and Medvedev proposed a new 'sociological poetics' while Vološinov provided a Marxian sociological critique of Saussure's structural linguistics itself. Raymond Williams dubbed this alternative tradition 'social formalism'.[66]

Laclau's hyperformalism did not go unchallenged, even among those who were influenced by him. Stuart Hall was one of the first to mark out key differences with the Laclau-Mouffe project, even though he remained indebted to Laclau's early work in his own discussions of 'Thatcherism' as an 'authoritarian populism' during the early 1980s.[67] Hall endorsed some of Laclau's reformulations of the Althusser-Poulantzas schema, especially those concerning ideological articulation, so much so that the latter term has become more associated with Hall than Laclau. Even at this stage, however, Hall considered Laclau's model too dependent on counter-hegemonic Latin American 'popular' politics. It thus neglected successful hegemonic articulations of 'the people' like that in Thatcherism.[68] Indeed, for Hall at this point, 'populist' signified an interpellative practice 'from above' while movements from below were 'popular'. Hall later distanced himself completely from what he understood as Laclau's and Mouffe's 'notion of society as a totally open discursive field' in which 'there is no reason why anything is or isn't potentially articulable with anything'.[69] Yet Hall struggled to make this disagreement sufficiently distinct theoretically.

However, Hall's own route through this theoretical terrain relied at times on the work of Raymond Williams, whom he frequently acknowledged as an influence, and on the work of Vološinov, one of Williams's 'social formalists'. After forty years, Vološinov's *Marxism and The Philosophy of Language* had recently been translated into English. It challenged the 'abstract objectivism' of the famous Saussurean *langue/parole* distinction, whereby *langue* represented the 'deep structure' of linguistic rules and *parole* the utterances of the individual speaker. Its de facto society-individual binarization rested, Vološinov argued, on a merely gestural sociality framed as an homogenous 'linguistic community' or 'community of speakers' (*masse parlante*).[70] The linguistic sign was thus not constituted, as Saussure presented it, as a signifier/signified (i.e. formal bearer vs 'meaning'). Rather, because the linguistic 'community' was not homogenous but riven by social division, it could be differently *accented*.[71]

Hall deploys this conception of the 'multiaccentuality of the sign' in an important 1977 essay.[72] The broader implication of the Vološinovian critique for the Laclauian schema, which Hall does not draw out, is that its formalist categories are built on asociological foundations. To project a form of 'social theory' or 'theory of the social' from such foundations is thus a very fraught exercise. Hall also independently developed his own critique of the Althusserian project in the same period as Laclau's *Politics and Ideology in Marxist Theory*.[73]

Now, both critics and supporters of the Laclauian schema tend to accept the argumentative terrain of its own claims to 'post-Marxist' innovation. Controversy has centred on the ostensible 'ontological' plausibility of this project. As with contemporary debates in other fields following the rise of structuralism and semiotics, such arguments tend to collapse into a polarization of realism/reductivism versus idealism/anti-reductivism. It is in such terms that Laclau rejects any 'regional' theories, another term borrowed from Althusser, such as accounts of the political field, in its 'relatively autonomous' specificity. Yet, with the possible exception of Laclau's rejection of the 'ontological privileging of the proletariat', such discussions 'ontologize' what are, in effect (a)sociological assumptions. As we saw in the previous section, Laclau's move beyond even a role for a Jakobsonian 'dominant' constitutes a *hyperformalism* that claims to reject all such conceptual ordering. It so marks not a 'post-structuralist' development but a retreat into a somewhat mechanical usage of Saussure that is forced to resort to a quasi-Saussurean 'community' repeatedly. Laclau's usage of 'ontic' and 'ontological' to categorize his adoption of formalist methods marks a turning point where an asociological methodological choice by him is misrepresented as 'the full ontological implications' of others' theoretical innovations. As we have seen, he claims this on behalf of both Gramsci and Jakobsonian formalism. This methodological choice takes the form of a categorical rejection of any role for mediating sociological categories (whether Marxian or not). This is the lacuna that social formalist approaches like Hall's can correct. It follows that it is possible to recognize Laclau's earlier formalist innovations without resorting to his hyperformalism.

Hall was so able to recognize the 'struggle over signification' as one involving modern means of communication and modern traditions of ostensibly 'autonomous' interpretation, notably journalism.[74] For Hall, then, not only news media but the entire terrain of popular culture becomes such a site of hegemonic and counter-hegemonic struggle. Like Laclau, he adopts the Poulantzian conception of power bloc and opposes it to a putative 'people', understood as a possible counter-hegemonic social alliance. However, consistent with his more modest critique of the early Laclau, he focuses on the susceptibility of 'the field of popular conceptions' – which he usually equates with a Gramscian conception of 'common sense' – to effective hegemonic interpellation/articulation. Margaret

Thatcher's capacity to employ the language of 'popular morality', concerning most notably race and crime, was his most prominent example. Thus: 'Under the right conditions, "the people" in their traditionalist representation can be condensed as a set of interpellations in discourse which systematically displace political issues into conventional moral absolutes.'[75] However, Thatcher's success was contingent on such factors as news reportage of crime that deferred to the racist stereotypes of criminals accepted by journalists who relied on the authoritative sourcing of their stories by police.

For all the sociological specificity Hall retrieved from Laclau's hyperformalism, a problem emerged in his approach that still haunts contemporary 'left' theorizations of populism. Having detailed Thatcher's successful practice of articulation with popular belief systems and its homological forms within media institutions, Hall's own strategic conclusion for counter-hegemonic practice was one of *emulation*. Only a comparable counter-practice of articulation and disarticulation could contest such a hegemonic achievement as Thatcherist authoritarian populism. Hall explicitly rejected the suggestion that his approach relied on a 'zero-sum game' strategy as he regarded that term as embedded in a monolithic conception of contending 'class ideologies', the position that both he and Laclau had rejected.[76]

Yet even if we accept his definition of 'zero-sum', Hall's 'emulative' strategy is highly vulnerable to a charge of *instrumentalization*. While he maintains a distinct role for social institutions, he interprets them instrumentally. Formal autonomy is acknowledged but is never demonstrated to be critically productive. For example, there is little room in his model for a non-partisan autonomous journalism that might play a socially critical role by means of the 'liberal' norms of transparency and accountability. Journalistic autonomy is recognized but only in order to demonstrate its non-conspiratorial, non-subjectivist (i.e. non-'bias'-like) articulation and reproduction of hegemonic elements of the political field.[77] Hall notably expanded this analysis to cast the institution of the BBC as 'an instrument of the national culture' at the very moment critical media scholars began to draw on Habermas's public sphere thesis to defend its autonomy. For Hall, however, its primary significance was that it 'served, at one and the same time, to maintain the cultural standards and values of the dominant class-cultures by organizing them into a single "voice", while incorporating the other class and regional voices into its organic and corporate framework'.[78] Most famously of all, he concluded his much-cited 1980 address on 'the popular' by declaring that, apart from popular culture's constitutive role in a socialist constitution of 'the people', 'I don't give a damn about it.'[79]

This instrumentalist tendency in Hall can be traced to Gramsci's lack of clarity about what kind of social order might result from a successful counter-hegemonic strategy. There is no academic consensus in interpreting Gramsci on this point. We can find gestures towards a possible anti-authoritarian conception of a new social order in Gramsci. The key lies in the educative leadership dimension of his concept of hegemony and 'national-popular' whereby the 'economic-corporate' does not constitute the sum total of Gramsci's strategic anticipations, especially in the West. His position thus significantly revises that of Lenin.

It is fair to say, however, that 'Caesarism' – in any of its forms typologized by Gramsci – is not a component of his vision of a socialist future. Plainly it is an obstacle or at best an indicator of a crisis of authority that may or may not offer the prospect of 'epochal' change.[80] Neither Laclau nor Hall, however, acknowledge this limitation in the Gramscian schema. Hall is almost silent on the question of such future leadership while Laclau's position becomes decidedly problematic on this point. Urbinati, for example, has charged that Laclau relocates Gramsci's understanding of Caesarism *within* his own conception of hegemony in his discussion of Juan Peron's role in Argentina. Slavoj Žižek's critique of Laclau comes closer to the mark in suggesting that charismatic leadership and its risks are effectively overlooked in the Laclauian conceptualization of populism. As I have already indicated at points in this chapter, this could be put more strongly as a rejection of all concerns about populist demagogy as 'moralistic'.[81]

It is not insignificant that the section of *On Populist Reason* that Urbinati and Žižek target in their critiques is the most extended 'application' of Laclau's schema to cases. His purpose is to examine historical scenarios whereby 'the construction of a "people" can easily misfire'. Each case involves the role of charismatic leadership but Laclau does not recognize this as such. Instead he treats Argentina's 'Peron', for example, as a formal point of condensation of his signifying practices. He concludes the discussion, remarkably, by calling for 'a wider typological description' that 'should be the aim of a fully developed theory of populism'. However, rather than invoke Worsley again to fully embrace his Weberian anticipation of this view, Laclau returns to an insistence on his hyperformalist premises for any such typology.[82] This self-contradiction is never resolved in his work.

Urbinati's and Žižek's critiques of Laclau propose similar cautionary conceptions of populism, despite their quite different normative premises. Urbinati holds that all populist movements – which for her includes all social movements – necessarily risk a demagogic disfiguration of democracy. Žižek makes a distinction between 'popular' and 'populist' movements which echoes the popular-democratic/authoritarian populist dichotomy employed by Stuart Hall. However, unlike Hall, Žižek emphasizes the significance of democracies' institutionalization of agonistic difference. Populist movements, for Žižek, fail to constitute their opponent as a social system and instead focus on 'the external enemy' configured as scapegoat. This practice, he points out, also follows the logic of Laclau's equivalential chain but not in the socially progressive manner Laclau assumes. In a passage Urbinati cites approvingly, Žižek states:

> for a populist, the cause of the troubles is ultimately never the system as such but the intruder who corrupted it (financial manipulators, not necessarily capitalists, and so on); not a fatal flaw inscribed into the structure as such but an element that doesn't play its role within the structure properly.[83]

Žižek so moves to his own theorization of the relationship between populism and fascism. Antisemitism emerges as the paradigmatic case of this populist failing to address the 'abstract' source of the inequity and replace it with the 'pseudo-concrete' figure imagined by antisemitism. Thus:

> As such, populism by definition contains a minimum, an elementary form, of ideological mystification, which is why, although it is effectively a formal frame or matrix of political logic that can be given different political twists (reactionary-nationalist, progressive-nationalist), nonetheless, insofar as, in its very notion, it displaces the immanent social antagonism into the antagonism between the unified people and its external enemy, it harbors in the last instance a long-term protofascist tendency.[84]

Here we can see the Gramscian tradition coming closest to the perspective adopted by the Institute's Studies in Prejudice Project. I will next examine the prospect of further points of potential productive critical synthesis between these traditions, developing further the social formalist corrective introduced in this chapter.

Notes

1 For example, Cas Mudde and Cristóbal Rovira Kaltwasser, 'Populism and (Liberal) Democracy: A Framework for Analysis', in *Populism in Europe and the Americas: Threat or Corrective for Democracy*, ed. Cas Mudde and Cristóbal Rovira Kaltwasser (2012).
2 Jeremiah Morelock, ed. *Critical Theory and Authoritarian Populism* (London: University of Westminster Press, 2018).
3 Perry Anderson, *The H-Word: The Peripeteia of Hegemony* (London: Verso, 2017); Fernando Claudin, *Eurocommunism and Socialism* (London: NLB, 1978).
4 Anderson, *The H-Word: The Peripeteia of Hegemony*, 79ff.

5 Antonio Gramsci, 'Some Aspects of the Southern Question (1926)', in *Selections from Political Writings 1921–1926* (London: Lawrence & Wishart, 1978); Walter L. Adamson, 'Gramsci's Interpretation of Fascism', *Journal of the History of Ideas* 41, no. 4 (1980): 626.
6 Raymond Williams, who had a significant influence on Stuart Hall (discussed below), is the most prominent example. See my *Raymond Williams's Sociology of Culture: A Critical Reconstruction* (Basingstoke: Palgrave Macmillan, 2004). The classic Williams text in this context is: Raymond Williams, 'Base and Superstructure in Marxist Cultural Theory', *New Left Review*, no. 82 (1973). The common 'aesthetic' orientation of Western Marxist intellectuals was identified by Perry Anderson in his *Considerations on Western Marxism* (London: NLB, 1976).
7 Karl Marx, '*The Eighteenth Brumaire of Louis Bonaparte* (1852)', in *Marx: Later Political Writings*, ed. Terrell Carver (Cambridge: Cambridge University Press, 2009), 407; Antonio Gramsci, *Selections from the Prison Notebooks of Antonio Gramsci*, trans. Quintin Hoare and Geoffrey Nowell-Smith (London: Lawrence & Wishart, 1971).
8 Marx, 'Preface' to *A Contribution to the Critique of Political Economy* (1859).
9 Adamson, 'Gramsci's Interpretation of Fascism', 627.
10 Donald Reid, 'Inciting Readings and Reading Cites: Visits to Marx's *The Eighteenth Brumaire of Louis Bonaparte*', *Modern Intellectual History* 4, no. 3 (2007): 550ff. Adamson, 'Gramsci's Interpretation of Fascism', 621.
11 Gramsci, *Selections from the Prison Notebooks of Antonio Gramsci*, 210.
12 Gramsci, *Selections from the Prison Notebooks of Antonio Gramsci*, 210. Of course, informing this was Gramsci's assessment of the balance of forces he faced in Italy, most notably his view of the 'immaturity' of the proletarian forces and, as he saw it, his own leadership's overdependence on a Bolshevik model in the occupation of the factories he had led in Turin.
13 Gramsci, *Selections from the Prison Notebooks of Antonio Gramsci*, 219–223.
14 *Selections from the Prison Notebooks of Antonio Gramsci*, 220–222; cf. 263.
15 Antonio Gramsci, *Selections from Cultural Writings* (London: Lawrence & Wishart, 1985), 206. Forgacs's usually reliable scholarship in this area appears to miss this 'modern' dimension of Gramsci's reworking of the Bonapartist thesis in his important (but early) overview of left approaches to fascism: David Forgacs, 'The Left and Fascism: Problems of Definition and Strategy', in *Rethinking Italian Fascism: Capitalism, Populism and Culture*, ed. David Forgacs (London: Lawrence & Wishart, 1986), 48 n45.
16 *Selections from the Prison Notebooks of Antonio Gramsci*, 1–23.
17 Gramsci, *Selections from Cultural Writings*, 208.
18 Forgacs relies here on an apparently unpublished paper by Maria Bianca Luporini. See his David Forgacs, 'Gramsci's Notion of the "Popular" in Italy and Britain: A Tale of Two Cultures', in *Performing National Identity*, ed. M. Pfister and R. Hertel (Amsterdam: Rodopi, 2008), 185. On discussions of Russian populism in early populism studies see: Andrzej Walicki, 'Russia', in *Populism: Its Meaning and National Characteristics*, ed. Ghiţa Ionescu and Ernest Gellner (London: Weidenfeld & Nicolson, 1969); Canovan, *Populism*, 59–97. Lenin devoted much of his first major publication, *The Development of Capitalism in Russia (1899)*, to criticism of the narodniki.
19 Gramsci, *Selections from Cultural Writings*, 363–364.
20 Ernesto Laclau and Chantal Mouffe, *Hegemony and Socialist Strategy: Towards a Radical Democratic Politics* (London: Verso, 1985). I refer to 'Laclau' in main text

as author of his solo and co-authored texts for ease of exposition. The subsequent debate with Norman Geras elaborated the 'post-Marxist' terrain: Norman Geras, 'Post-Marxism?', *New Left Review*, no. 163 (1987); Ernesto Laclau and Chantal Mouffe, 'Post-Marxism without Apologies', *New Left Review* no. 166 (1987); Norman Geras, 'Ex-Marxism without Substance: Being a Real Reply to Laclau and Mouffe', *New Left Review*, no. 169 (1988).

21 Laclau and Mouffe, *Hegemony and Socialist Strategy: Towards a Radical Democratic Politics*, 56.
22 Ernesto Laclau, *Politics and Ideology in Marxist Theory: Capitalism, Fascism, Populism* (London: NLB, 1977); Nicos Poulantzas, *Fascism and Dictatorship: The Third International and the Problem of Fascism*, trans. Judith White (London: NLB, 1974). While the essays on fascism and populism originated in this book, two chapters had previously been published. It is worth noting that the first of these was a stringent defence of the necessity of the concept of mode of production to any theoretical position claiming to be Marxist: Ernesto Laclau, 'Feudalism and Capitalism in Latin America', *New Left Review*, no. 1/67 (1971).
23 Laclau, *Politics and Ideology in Marxist Theory: Capitalism, Fascism, Populism*, 81–92. Cf. his critiques of orthodox populism studies: *Politics and Ideology in Marxist Theory: Capitalism, Fascism, Populism*, 143–158. Ernesto Laclau, *On Populist Reason* (London: Verso, 2005), 3–21.
24 Poulantzas, *Fascism and Dictatorship*, 58–59.
25 Curiously on introducing the term in an earlier book he claims this conceptualization 'is not actually pointed out by Gramsci'. Nicos Poulantzas, *Political Power and Social Classes*, trans. Timothy O'Hagan (London: NLB), 141. There is an earlier usage in: 'Preliminaries to the Study of Hegemony in the State (1965)', in *The Poulantzas Reader* ed. James Martin (London: Verso, 2008).
26 My account here is much abbreviated. Laclau provides a step-by-step summary while Jessop provides a much more detailed exegesis as well as his own critique: Laclau, *Politics and Ideology in Marxist Theory: Capitalism, Fascism, Populism*, 89–92. Cf. Bob Jessop, *Nicos Poulantzas: Marxist Theory and Political Strategy* (London: Macmillan, 1985), 231–262.
27 Poulantzas, *Fascism and Dictatorship*, 240–244.
28 Literary formalism is discussed in more detail in the final section of this chapter.
29 Claude Lévi-Strauss, *The Savage Mind* (London: Weidenfeld & Nicolson, 1966), 130; Claude Lévi-Strauss, *Structural Anthropology* (New York: Basic Books, 1963), 298.
30 Louis Althusser and Etienne Balibar, *Reading Capital*, trans. B. Brewster (London: NLB, 1970); Louis Althusser, 'Elements of Self-Criticism (1974)', in *Essays in Self-Criticism* (London: NLB, 1976), 125–131.
31 Paul Ricœur, 'Structure and Hermeneutics (1963)', in *The Conflict of Interpretations: Essays in Hermeneutics* (Evanston: Northwestern University Press, 1974).
32 This was also due to the charge of 'historicism' made against Gramsci based in turn in the structuralist conception of ideology as a 'process without a subject' (discussed below).
33 Louis Althusser, 'Ideology and Ideological State Apparatuses (Notes Towards an Investigation) (1969–1970)', in *Lenin and Philosophy and Other Essays* (London: NLB, 1977).
34 Jessop, *Nicos Poulantzas: Marxist Theory and Political Strategy*, 57–58; 72–74.
35 Laclau, *Politics and Ideology in Marxist Theory: Capitalism, Fascism, Populism*, 70.
36 Laclau, *Politics and Ideology in Marxist Theory: Capitalism, Fascism, Populism*, 100ff.

37 Althusser, 'Ideology and Ideological State Apparatuses (Notes Towards an Investigation) (1969–1970)'. On the psychoanalytic genealogy of interpellation as a concept see Veronica Beechey and James Donald, 'Introduction', in *Subjectivity and Social Relations: A Reader* (Milton Keynes: Open University Press, 1985).
38 Stuart Hall, 'Signification, Representation, Ideology: Althusser and the Post-Structuralist Debates', *Critical Studies in Mass Communication* 2, no. 2 (1985): 101; Laclau, *Politics and Ideology in Marxist Theory: Capitalism, Fascism, Populism*, 100; Cf. also Stuart Hall, 'Some Problems with the Ideology/Subject Couplet', *Ideology and Consciousness* 3 (1978).
39 Louis Althusser, 'Contradiction and Overdetermination (1962)', in *For Marx* (London: NLB, 1977). Laclau sources this directly to Brewster's glossary entry for these terms in the English translation: B. Brewster, 'Glossary', in *Louis Althusser: For Marx* (London: NLB, 1977), 250; Cf. Laclau, *Politics and Ideology in Marxist Theory: Capitalism, Fascism, Populism*, 102 n133. Sigmund Freud, *The Interpretation of Dreams*, trans. A.A. Brill (London: Macmillan, 1915).
40 Laclau, *Politics and Ideology in Marxist Theory: Capitalism, Fascism, Populism*, 103–104.
41 Laclau, *Politics and Ideology in Marxist Theory: Capitalism, Fascism, Populism*, 109.
42 Laclau, *Politics and Ideology in Marxist Theory: Capitalism, Fascism, Populism*, 115–116.
43 Laclau, *Politics and Ideology in Marxist Theory: Capitalism, Fascism, Populism*, 135.
44 Laclau, *Politics and Ideology in Marxist Theory: Capitalism, Fascism, Populism*, 119, 120.
45 Laclau, *Politics and Ideology in Marxist Theory: Capitalism, Fascism, Populism*, 147–158. The two theorists Laclau cites here are Gino Germani and Torcauto di Tella.
46 Laclau, *Politics and Ideology in Marxist Theory: Capitalism, Fascism, Populism*, 152–154.
47 Shils, 'Demagogues and Cadres in the Political Development of the New States', 67.
48 Laclau, *Politics and Ideology in Marxist Theory: Capitalism, Fascism, Populism*, 174.
49 Laclau, *Politics and Ideology in Marxist Theory: Capitalism, Fascism, Populism*, 172–173 (in italics in original).
50 Laclau, *Politics and Ideology in Marxist Theory: Capitalism, Fascism, Populism*, 141 n156.
51 Laclau and Mouffe, *Hegemony and Socialist Strategy: Towards a Radical Democratic Politics*, 58.
52 Ernesto Laclau, 'Populism: What's in a Name?', in *Populism and the Mirror of Democracy*, ed. Francisco Panizza (London: Verso, 2005), 44.
53 Worsley, 'The Concept of Populism', 244.
54 Worsley, 'The Concept of Populism', 245. Cf. Laclau, *On Populist Reason*, 14–15.
55 Laclau, *On Populist Reason*, 15.
56 Laclau, *On Populist Reason*, 15.
57 The Russian Formalists' initial focus was 'literariness' but this position expanded to a full aesthetic formalism, especially in the Prague School, notably in the work of Mukařovský. Roman Jakobson's work was a key link between these two groups. Jan Mukařovský, *Aesthetic Function, Norm and Value as Social Facts*, trans. Mark E. Suino (Ann Arbor: Department of Slavic Languages and Literature, University of Michigan, 1970).

58 E.g. R. Jakobson and J. Tynyanov, 'Problems of Literary and Linguistic Studies (1928)', *New Left Review*, no. 1/37 (1966).
59 Laclau, *On Populist Reason*, 68.
60 R. Jakobson, 'The Dominant (1935)', in *Readings in Russian Poetics: Formalist and Structuralist Views* ed. Ladislav Matejka and Krystyna Pomorska (Cambridge, Mass.: MIT Press, 1971). Linda R. Waugh, 'The Poetic Function in the Theory of Roman Jakobson', *Poetics Today* 2, no. 1a (1980).
61 I borrow this term from Jameson's critical coinage which was also developed further by Raymond Williams. Fredric Jameson, *The Prison-House of Language: A Critical Account of Structuralism and Russian Formalism* (Princeton, NJ: Princeton University Press, 1972); Jones, *Raymond Williams's Sociology of Culture: A Critical Reconstruction*.
62 Laclau, *On Populist Reason*, xi.
63 This replacement of Worsley's 'dimension' with 'logic' follows from Laclau's critique of 'mere rhetoric' accounts of populism. He thus adopts rhetoric's opposite in classical thought, logic, for his rethinking of Worsley's 'dimension'.
64 Laclau, *On Populist Reason*, 74. I have separated the two numbered paragraphs for clarity.
65 It would seem Laclau bypassed this sociological alternative by only addressing the legacy of the later but related Prague School. I have not found any reference to Russian Formalism per se in Laclau's declarations.
66 M.M. Bakhtin and P.N. Medvedev, *The Formal Method in Literary Scholarship: A Critical Introduction to Sociological Poetics* trans. A.J. Wehrle (Baltimore: Johns Hopkins University Press, 1978); Valentin N. Vološinov, *Marxism and the Philosophy of Language*, trans. Ladislav Matejka and I.R. Titunik (New York: Seminar Press, 1973). Raymond Williams, *Keywords: A Vocabulary of Culture and Society*, 2nd edn (London: Fontana, 1983), 139. Cf. Raymond Williams, *The Politics of Modernism: Against the New Conformists* (London: Verso, 1989), 166–167.
67 The key text here is: Stuart Hall, 'Popular Democratic vs. Authoritarian Populism: Two Ways of Taking Democracy Seriously', in *Marxism and Democracy*, ed. Alan Hunt (London: Lawrence & Wishart, 1980).
68 Hall, 'Popular Democratic vs. Authoritarian Populism: Two Ways of Taking Democracy Seriously', 176.
69 Stuart Hall, 'On Postmodernism and Articulation: An Interview with Stuart Hall', *Journal of Communication Inquiry* 10, no. 2 (1986): 56.
70 Ferdinand de Saussure, *Course in General Linguistics*, trans. Wade Baskin (New York: Philosophical Library, 1959), 77 (for translation note) and passim.
71 Vološinov, *Marxism and the Philosophy of Language*, 79–82.
72 Vološinov, *Marxism and the Philosophy of Language*. Stuart Hall, 'Culture, the Media and the "Ideological Effect"', in *Mass Communication and Society*, ed. James Curran, Michael Gurevitch and Janet Woollacott (London: Arnold, 1977).
73 For his later assessment of the Althusserian project see his Hall, 'Signification, Representation, Ideology: Althusser and the Post-Structuralist Debates'.
74 Hall, 'Culture, the Media and the "Ideological Effect"', 341–344. 'Laclauians' read this distinction as entirely an 'ontological' choice rather than a social theoretical failing in the foundational Saussurean moment of such (formalist) 'discourse theory'. See, for example, the guarded comments regarding Hall in: David Howarth and Yannis Stavrakakis, 'Introducing Discourse Theory and Political Analysis', in *Discourse Theory and Political Analysis*, ed. David Howarth, Aletta Norval and Yannis Stavrakakis (Manchester: Manchester University Press, 2000).

75 Hall, 'Popular Democratic vs. Authoritarian Populism: Two Ways of Taking Democracy Seriously', 181.
76 Stuart Hall, 'The Toad in the Garden: Thatcherism among the Theorists', in *Marxism and the Interpretation of Culture*, ed. C. Nelson and L. Grossberg (Urbana: University of Illinois Press, 1988), 58.
77 See the sophisticated analysis of a BBC current affairs programme which employs Bourdieuian field theory to establish a homology between the journalistic and political fields: Stuart Hall, Ian Connell and Lidia Curti, 'The "Unity" of Current Affairs Television', *Working Papers In Cultural Studies* 9 (1976).
78 Stuart Hall, 'Popular Culture and the State', in *Popular Culture and Social Relations*, ed. T. Bennett, C. Mercer and J. Woollacott (Milton Keynes: Open University Press, 1986), 43–44. Cf. Nicholas Garnham, 'The Media and the Public Sphere', in *Communicating Politics: Mass Communications and the Political Process*, ed. P. Golding, G. Murdock and P. Schlesinger (Leicester: Leicester University Press, 1986), 37–54.
79 Stuart Hall, 'Notes on Deconstructing "the Popular"', in *People's History and Socialist Theory* ed. Raphael Samuel (London: Routledge & Kegan Paul, 1981), 239. This instrumentalist tendency led to Williams's distancing himself from elements of Hall's work: Raymond Williams, 'The Paths and Pitfalls of Ideology as an Ideology', *Times Higher Education Supplement* (1977). This issue is revisited in Chapter 6(e).
80 Cf. Cohen and Arato's more critical reading which argues Gramsci revealingly contradicts himself in comments concerning a 'socialist civil society': Jean L. Cohen and Andrew Arato, *Civil Society and Political Theory* (Cambridge, Mass.: MIT Press, 1994), 142–159.
81 Urbinati, *Democracy Disfigured*, 155; Žižek, 'Against the Populist Temptation'.
82 Perhaps more remarkably he adds to this discussion an endorsement of Canovan's influential 1999 essay which works from entirely different theoretically premisses closer to the orthodox inductivism Laclau elsewhere rejects. Laclau, *On Populist Reason*, 221–222; Canovan, 'Trust the People! Populism and the Two Faces of Democracy'.
83 Žižek, 'Against the Populist Temptation', 555; Cf. Urbinati, *Democracy Disfigured*, 282–283 n281.
84 Žižek, 'Against the Populist Temptation', 557.

5

Towards a synthesis of critical perspectives

In Chapter 4 we saw how the Gramscian tradition developed its interpretations of populism from its analyses of fascism. While Gramsci himself came close to such an understanding in his conception of the national-popular, it was the sociological variant of 'structuralist Gramscianism', developed from the late 1960s by Poulantzas, that established the theoretical terrain for Laclau's first innovations in theorizing populism. However, whereas Gramsci and Poulantzas recognized the risks of quasi-demagogic leadership, most obviously so for fascism, Laclau actively avoided including such a dimension in his theorizations of populism. The more recent advocacy of 'a left populism' by Chantal Mouffe is vulnerable to the same criticism.[1]

The Institute's work provides an analysis of modern demagogy that speaks to this absence while the Gramscian tradition offers the prospect of a theoretical elaboration of the contingency of populist movements and their potential demagogic capture. In short, both speak to this book's focus on demagogic populism. Still, to propose any kind of substantial common ground between this Gramscian tradition and the Institute's work requires bridging a considerable gulf. This is certainly the case if we start with Laclau's project as the 'de facto' critical theory of populism today. He never seriously engaged with the work of the Frankfurt School and the Althusserian project, out of which his early work grew, was openly hostile to Lukács's legacy, including its influence at the Institute.[2]

In 1990, in the wake of the growing 'change of system' developments in eastern Europe, Laclau reiterated the stance taken in *Hegemony and Socialist Strategy* five years earlier. In a series of briefly staged skirmishes, he pitted his hyperformalist position against a number of intellectual projects, mainly Marxian, that might address the theme of 'dislocation' with which he chose to interpret 'the revolution of our time'.[3] Among these is a consideration of 'commodification' as a model of 'complete' domination by capitalism. Laclau here rejects 'the pessimism of an Adorno' understood as:

> human beings produced by this growing expansion of the market would be completely dominated by capitalism. Their very needs would be created by the market through the manipulation of public opinion by the mass media controlled by capital. ...
>
> ...
>
> The pessimism of the Frankfurt School stems from the fact that in its approach two central assumptions of Marxist theory remain unchanged: a) that the capitalist system constitutes a self-regulating totality and b) that the transformation of the system, as in any self-regulating totality, can only take place as a result of the development of the internal logic of the system itself.[4]

As we saw in Chapter 3, such extrapolation from a claimed summation of the culture industry thesis is a common mischaracterization, although Laclau's is unusually abbreviated and completely bereft of an immanent dimension.[5] To this Laclau adds his now familiar critical refrain concerning 'manipulation'. The result is quite inadequate. The Institute's discussions of the state capitalism thesis, for example, demonstrate a more complex, if unresolved, consideration of these issues.

A more serious comparison of the two projects would instead recognize that many of Laclau's own key insights, most notably the principle of the establishment of an 'internal frontier' in populist discourse, were anticipated by the Institute's work on demagogic devices. Adorno reached a very similar understanding of such a discursive process in his Martin Luther Thomas text. However, he never succumbed to a Laclau-like hyperformalism.[6] Nonetheless, as we saw, Adorno and Lowenthal struggled to join these studies with a compatible social theory.

Laclau offers no viable solution here. His critical comments on the Frankfurt School cited above are part of his less than clear 'break' with Marxian problematics, as he understands them, into his so-called post-Marxism. He states that he wishes to maintain a role for the Marxian conception of capitalism.

His price for this continued usage is the removal of all immanent 'ontological privileging' of an oppositional agent. However, he is unable to achieve this goal without also jettisoning all prospects of 'economic' determination. As the passage above indicates, this frequently takes the form of rejecting an attributed view of capitalism as a 'self-regulating totality', a variant of the old Althusserian critique of Lukács. This must be rejected in order to acknowledge forms of social movement that are not theoretically privileged, but contingent in their plurality and potential alliance-like construction as 'the people'. Ironically, this means Laclau can only offer to replace one allegedly determinist system with another: the discursive 'system' of his hyperformalism which he calls 'the general field of objectivity'. Worse still, this entails a level of structural determinacy of 'subject positions' in this field at least as reductive as any proposed in the period of 'high structuralism', a framework that even Althusser eventually had recanted.[7]

I have instead sought points of common contact or even prospective contact between the Gramscian and Institute projects.[8] The guiding principle here is my focus on a critical sociological approach to demagogic populism. The first of these is based on the pivotal role Freud's *Group Psychology* plays for both Adorno and Laclau. The next section discusses their readings of Freud's text in some detail. This analysis thus also develops further, indeed relies on, the introduction of Adorno's reading of the *Group Psychology* presented in Chapter 2.

The second section moves from Poulantzas's tangential comments in his final work, *State Power, Socialism*. For his use of the term 'authoritarian', in his conception of 'authoritarian statism', is derived from the Institute's writings. Poulantzas's work is thus revisited in the light of Jessop's recent 'updating' of the Poulantzian schema. The ground is so laid for building on Hall's related social formalist conception of 'authoritarian populism' and so moving toward a critical retrieval of Laclau's formalist insights regarding populism from his hyperformalism. This social formalist position so aids the missing social-theoretical framing of the Institute's demagogy studies.

(a) Adorno contra Laclau on Freud's *Group Psychology*

While both the Institute's Studies in Prejudice project and Laclau claim a psychoanalytic warrant for their work, Laclau's nearest acknowledgement of the Institute's precedent is a brief consideration of Fromm's *Fear of Freedom* in his first book.[9] Yet a more compelling demonstration of this conflicted proximity of the two projects can be found in a comparison of Adorno's and Laclau's readings of Freud's *Group Psychology and the Analysis of the Ego*.

As shown in Chapter 2, Adorno employed Freud's text to consolidate the theoretical framework of the demagogy studies. The narcissistic identificatory bond between leader and followers is understood by Adorno to be the key to demagogic success.

Adorno and Laclau certainly put Freud's *Group Psychology* to different uses: respectively, the examination of demagogic propaganda and the theorization of populism. Adorno repeatedly interrupts his reading of Freud with examples from demagogic practice in both Germany and the USA. Laclau's reading seems at least in part a response to criticisms of the implicit reductivism of his prior account of 'subject positions'.[10]

Within the context of the argument of *On Populist Reason*, however, Laclau seeks to draw out, chiefly from the margins of Freud's text, an elaboration of modes of group formation that are *not* authoritarian, either via a non-authoritarian model of leadership or 'leaderlessness'. Indeed, his line of argument partially resembles Worsley's qualification, in 'The Concept of Populism', of Shils's demagogic focus in his definition of populism. As we saw in Chapter 4, Laclau draws on Worsley's argument selectively in *On Populist Reason*. However, unlike the respective positions of Shils and Worsley, Adorno's and Laclau's are not merely 'complementary' but in important respects at odds with each other.

Laclau's reading of the Freud text comes at the end of his first three chapters which are collectively grouped under the heading, 'The Denigration of the Masses'. So Laclau first spends considerable time tracing the history of precursor texts in 'mass psychology', most notably Le Bon's *The Crowd*, but also works of Tarde and McDougall. All but Tarde are also discussed at length in Freud's text.[11] McDougall's 1920 work, *The Group Mind*, becomes especially significant in the discussion below as it establishes a distinction between ephemeral groups – such as Le Bon's crowds – and 'highly organized groups'.[12]

Laclau interprets these three figures via his hyperformalist framework. Accordingly, he argues that all these precursors strive towards, but fail to achieve, a common goal: 'to make homogenizing or equivalential logics compatible with the actual working of a viable social body'.[13] Instead, dualisms result such as Tarde's between the disorderly crowd and the orderly public. Only Freud, in Laclau's view, provides the means of eliminating such dualistic framings.

Like Adorno, Laclau reconstructs the psychoanalytic premisses of Freud's argument and then focuses on pivotal passages, some of which are identical to those highlighted by Adorno. For Laclau, 'the climax of Freud's argument' occurs in this statement at the end of his eighth chapter:

> *A primary group of this kind is a number of individuals who have put one and same object in the place of their ego ideal and have consequently identified themselves with one another in their ego.*[14]

TOWARDS A SYNTHESIS OF CRITICAL PERSPECTIVES

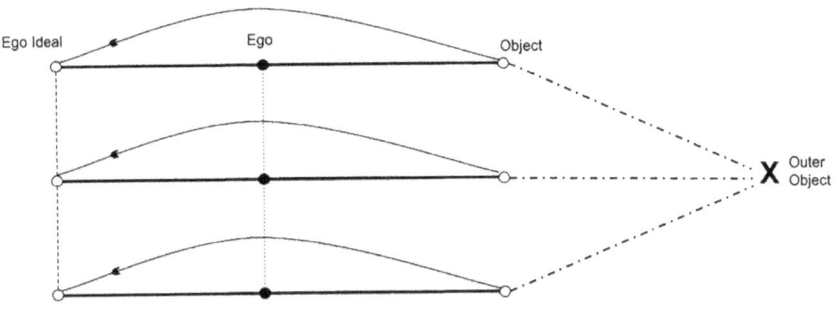

4 Freud's diagram of libidinal constitution of groups

I add here Freud's immediately following diagram of this process which, as he says, 'admits of graphic representation'.

Now, Laclau interprets this summative statement as requiring that:

> First, if we follow Freud's argument strictly at this point, identification takes place between those who are led, but not between them and the leader. So the possibility for the latter to be *primus inter pares* [first among equals] would be closed. Second, that the ground of any identification would exclusively be the common love for the leader.[15]

Much of Laclau's subsequent discussion of the Freud text seeks to disassemble both elements of this attributed 'strict' interpretation. Yet Laclau elides any reference to Freud's own preceding qualification of the above italicised statement:

> we are in a position to give a formula for the libidinal constitution of groups, or at least of such groups as we have hitherto considered – namely, *those that have a leader and have not been able by means of too much 'organization' to acquire secondarily the characteristic of an individual.*[16]

Here Freud refers to two key factors developed elsewhere in the *Group Psychology*: (i) that secondary identification with a leader-substitute such as an 'idea' is possible and (ii) that, as we saw in the discussion in Chapter 2, Freud's interest focuses on Le Bon's 'ephemeral' groups as distinct from formally constituted organizations, i.e., the distinction first drawn by McDougall. The reference to 'characteristics of an individual' above refers to Freud's critique of McDougall earlier in the *Group Psychology*. It is McDougall who introduces the example of an army as 'the type' of organization and indeed of his own conception of 'collective will'.[17] Freud too adopts the example of an army in his text. However, in his discussion of McDougall, Freud replaces the criteria McDougall derives to define an organization with the proposition that an organized group strives to attain 'those features which were characteristic of the individual and which were extinguished in him by the formation of a group'.[18]

Laclau recognizes this self-reference by Freud but replaces Freud's very evident employment of McDougall's *institutional* understanding of 'higher organized groups' with 'society' and, eventually, 'social logic'. He transforms Freud's distinction between highly organized and ephemeral groups into two modes of social aggregation which are not different types of groups but two 'social logics' which, he asserts, 'enter into the constitution of all groups' by means of, as we might expect, articulation.

Laclau's sleight of hand is undoubtedly elegant. His elisions glide from social institution to an undifferentiated 'society' to 'social logic'. Yet this is as reductive as his other hyperformalistic manoeuvres. Once again he finds a way to eliminate any role in his theory for institutional and organizational mediation. As Mouzelis pointed out in a perceptive early critique, this habitual practice of elision by Laclau misses key features of populist politics, most notably the tendency towards plebiscitarian leadership structures in populist parties which are entirely based around the figure of the leader.[19]

Indeed, it is the role of 'the leader' in Freud's analysis that Laclau's reformulation seeks to qualify. Both Laclau and Adorno cite extensively from the following paragraph in Freud's concluding chapter.[20] It relies on the schema portrayed in Figure 4:

> We have interpreted this prodigy as meaning that the individual gives up his ego ideal and substitutes for it the group ideal as embodied in the leader. And we must add by way of correction that the prodigy is not equally great in every case. In many individuals the separation between the ego and the ego ideal is not very far advanced; the two still coincide readily; the ego has often preserved its earlier self-complacency. The selection of the leader is very much facilitated by this circumstance. He need only possess the typical qualities of the individuals concerned in a particularly clearly marked and pure form, and need only give an impression of greater force and of more freedom of libido; and in that case the need for a strong chief will often meet him half-way and invest him with a predominance to which he would otherwise perhaps have had no claim. The other members of the group, whose ego ideal would not, apart from this, have become embodied in his person without some correction, are then carried away with the rest by 'suggestion', that is to say, by means of identification.[21]

Tellingly, Laclau omits the opening sentence and its use of 'prodigy' to refer to the complete surrender of the ego ideal. 'Prodigy' also here refers to its use in Freud's previous paragraph to indicate 'the complete, though only temporary, disappearance' of the individual's multiple points of identification in multiple groups in modern circumstances. As argued in Chapter 2, this use of 'prodigy' shares much with a Weberian conception of ideal or 'pure' type. For Freud, this pure form is achieved in Le Bon's 'noisy ephemeral groups, which, as it were, are superimposed' on 'stable and lasting group formations' such as 'those of his race, of his class, of his creed, of his nationality, etc'.[22]

One can see here the further problems raised by Laclau's reduction of this socio-historical complexity to his articulated dual 'social logics'. Here, however, his main purpose is to build on the implications of the proximity of ego and ego-ideal in some group members that enables 'the need for a strong chief' among the group members to 'meet him halfway'. Hence Freud's corollary, once again using the 'pure' formulation, that the leader 'need only possess the typical qualities of the individuals concerned in a particularly clearly marked and pure form'.

Like Adorno, Laclau recognizes that this means that the leader is placed in a contradictory situation. However, Adorno uses Freud's characterization to point to the capacity of modern demagogues to employ 'logically' contradictory devices – 'great little man', 'lone wolf' and so on – to exploit this liminality and to the similarly ambivalent sado-masochistic dynamic of the followers. Laclau, characteristically, uses the same passage to sideline the risk of despotism in such leadership:

> if the leader leads because he presents, in a particularly marked way, features which are common to all members of the group, he can no longer be, in all its purity, the despotic, narcissistic ruler. On the one hand, as he participates in that very substance of the community which makes identification possible, his identity is split: he is the father, but also one of the brothers. On the other hand, since his right to rule is based on the recognition by other group members of a feature of the leader which he shares, in a particularly pronounced way, with all of them, the leader is, to a considerable extent, accountable to the community. The need for leadership could still be there ... but it is a far more democratic leadership than the one involved in the notion of the narcissistic despot. We are, in fact, not far away from that peculiar combination of consensus and coercion that Gramsci called hegemony.[23]

Now, it is of course reasonable to try to expand the potential reference of Freud's model beyond despotism. However, Laclau seeks to do much more.

In a truly remarkable slippage, suddenly the 'group' has become a 'community' and the 'shared quality' necessarily entails 'accountability' and 'a far more democratic form of leadership'. Narcissism, a core feature of Freud's group psychology, has almost disappeared. It might also seem reasonable to tie the contradictory tensions within the leader's identity to the Gramscian dialectic of consent and coercion, a constitutive feature of hegemony. Yet by this point in his career (2005) Laclau's hegemony bears only a passing resemblance to Gramsci's usage and indeed his own former usage.

Laclau immediately attempts to justify this dilution of the group psychology with another long citation from the middle of Freud's book. There Freud does indeed announce, as Laclau points out, 'that much else remains to be examined and described in the morphology of groups'. Freud so outlines the prospect of 'leaderless' groups and the notion of leadership by an idea (secondary leadership). As in his earlier long citation from Freud, Laclau's reading is somewhat selective. He neglects to mention that the long citation he values so highly is followed by: 'But all these questions ... will not succeed in diverting our interest from the fundamental psychological problems that confront us in the structure of a group.' More problematically for Laclau, even within the passage he cites there is this:

> The leader or the leading idea might also, so to speak, be negative; hatred against a particular person or institution might operate in just the same unifying way, and might call up the same kind of emotional ties as positive attachment.[24]

As this passage is cited in support of his interpretation, Laclau is obliged to explain how this can be reconciled with his proto-democratic 'community'. Adorno of course could but Laclau fails to do so. He merely cites the passage and ends the section of his chapter without comment.

So this is not quite the 'inventory of other possible situations and social combinations' Laclau announces on Freud's behalf as continuing from his own revisionist perspective and then, curiously, ignores. As in the stuttering close of his book, Laclau fails to reconcile the evident need for typologization that arises from within the contradictions in his own work with his hyperformalism. His hostility to Poulantzas's 'taxonomies' casts a long shadow.

Adorno's deployment of Freud's text is very purposeful and narrower in its ambition. So it by no means outlines the full potential range of application of Freud's dynamic. Yet it makes this self-limitation transparent. Moreover, while Laclau once again elides all sociological categories, Adorno marks what he calls the points of sociological 'safe ground' Freud achieves. As we saw in Chapter 2, for Adorno, Freud's central problematic, in keeping with his avoidance of Le Bon's 'traditional contempt for the masses', is clear: 'he asks in the true spirit of enlightenment: what makes the masses into masses?'[25] Further, what is in many ways Adorno's companion piece to his 'Freudian Theory' essay, that on 'Democratic Leadership', elaborates a means of expanding Freud's psychoanalytic insights within that sociological 'safe ground'.

Here is Laclau and Adorno's closest point of contact. Each recognizes, in almost exactly the same form of words, that Freud breaks with what Laclau calls 'the denigration of the masses' and Adorno calls 'the traditional contempt for the masses'. Laclau, however, needs to distort Freud's work in order to advance what is, effectively, a variant of intellectual populism that refuses to acknowledge the possibility, *not* necessity, that Freud and Adorno both recognize: that some contingent social situations do render 'the masses into masses'.

Laclau's intellectual populism breaks through in his text's uncritical parachuting of the category of 'community' into an ostensibly rigorous discussion of psychoanalytic theory. As Raymond Williams once remarked, in a social formalist mode that Laclau might have recognized from his linguistic hyperformalism, such 'warmly persuasive' uses of 'community' are possible because it has no pejorative connotations and so 'seems never to be used unfavourably, and never to be given any positive opposing or distinguishing term'.[26] However, the more remarkable 'echo' here is of Saussure's foundational undifferentiated 'community of speakers' challenged by Vološinov.

Laclau regards his reading of Freud as the watershed of his book, so enabling its true 'starting point'. However, this is soon qualified by his invocation of Prague School Formalism (discussed in Chapter 4) as a precondition of his deployment of this reading.

In contrast to Laclau, Adorno not only maintains but seeks to elaborate further Freud's delineation of organized and ephemeral groups. He suggests that the demagogue seeking power 'has to face … not organized ones but the accidental crowds of the big city'. Drawing on the demagogy studies, he goes on:

> The loosely knit character of such motley crowds makes it imperative that discipline and coherence be stressed at the expense of the centrifugal uncanalized urge to love. Part of the agitator's task consists in making the crowd believe that it is organized like the Army or the Church. Hence the tendency towards overorganization. A fetish is made of organization as such; it becomes an end instead of a means and this tendency prevails through the agitator's speeches.[27]

Such simulation of organization offers a path to typologizing successful demagogic group leadership. This is quite distinct from Laclau's hyperformalist 'social logic' that is subject only to a blanket 'contingency' usually insusceptible to typological differentiation. Contingency for Adorno is more carefully delineated. The 'group determinants' of 'agitational' demagogic success include:

(i) a susceptible characterology of individual group members including an inability to fully develop an independent ego ideal/superego
(ii) a lack of organizational structure that renders the group in question relatively 'accidental'. This would include meetings and rallies of the kind studied by the Institute.
(iii) a mode of narcissistic leadership by the demagogue that displays little love of others, notably via the absence of a welfare-like 'positive programme'.

Nonetheless, Laclau's seizure of Freud's sole reference in his text to 'leaderless groups', and indeed secondary leadership, is not without consequence. It provides an important bridge with which to expand Adorno's delineations. As we shall see, Adorno moves some way along this path himself when he considers the role of the idea of *Volksgemeinschaft*, 'community of the people'.

(b) A Poulantzian mediation

The Gramscian line from Poulantzas to Hall offers a remarkably different prospect for critical synthesis from Laclau's near silence concerning the Institute's relevant prior work. As shown in Chapter 4, Hall's conception of authoritarian populism rested in part on a 'social formalist' reworking of the early Laclau. Not only did this provide Hall with a theoretical means of avoiding the 'formalist trap'; it enabled him to postulate that Thatcherism had mutated into a particular mode of authoritarian populist leadership 'from above'. His primary inspiration here was Poulantzas's final work, *State, Power, Socialism*, and in particular its last major chapter on 'The Decline of Democracy: Authoritarian Statism'.[28]

One feature of Poulantzas's argument here has received little comment. He repeatedly positions his book in terms adopted from the Institute's work on authority and the family as well as 'state capitalism'. While the genealogy of 'authoritarian' is never made explicit, its debt to the Institute is plain. Its work is found to be 'considerably more interesting' than others he assesses.[29] While his positionings of the Institute's work usually function as a negative foil, the problematic he pursues as 'authoritarian statism' is quite comparable to that explored within the Institute's state capitalism debates. It also foreshadows the 'illiberal' forms of state that have recently arisen in the wake of neopopulist regimes, most notably in Europe: 'intensified state-control over every sphere of socio-economic life combined with radical decline of the institutions of political democracy and the draconian and multiform curtailment of so-called "formal liberties"'.[30]

The echo of the Institute's work becomes even stronger when Poulantzas periodizes this set of developments:

> More fundamentally, therefore, authoritarian statism is bound up with the periodization of capitalism into distinct stages and phases. It seems to correspond with the current phase of imperialism and monopoly capitalism in the dominant countries, in the way the liberal State referred to the competitive stage of capitalism and the various forms of interventionist State to the previous phases of monopoly capitalism.[31]

As we have seen, the Institute worked with a similar framing of the supersession of a competitive phase of capitalism. Nonetheless, the forty years since Poulantzas's book constitute a period as long as that between its publication and that of the Institute's *Studien* in the 1930s. Notwithstanding the recent rise of a 'security state' in the wake of international terrorism, the 'intensified state control' claim superficially jars with the legacy of subsequent neoliberal privatizations of state functions. Hall's authoritarian populism, however, appears to escape such 'dating', partly because it is less fully developed and relatively silent on such specificities.[32]

It is fruitful then to turn to the recent work of Bob Jessop, a long-standing critical advocate of the ongoing relevance of Poulantzas's project. Jessop has cast the UK's Brexit crisis, for example, in classically Gramscian terms as an organic crisis of the British state. He has also extended Poulantzas's 'authoritarian statism' to the present and recent past.[33] Thus, he argues, the authoritarian statism thesis 'can be reworked for the rise of neoliberalism in a far more integrated world market and its manifold crises in the current period'.[34]

Like Poulantzas, Jessop continues to use a 'monopoly capital' framing, but here with much greater specificity. He casts the most recent phase of capitalism as 'finance-*dominated* accumulation' in the sense that while finance capital was formerly required as part of the circuit of capital movement (via production), in this phase finance capital has become dominant outside this strictly economic dimension of a social formation.

Significantly, consistent with but not explicitly recognizing Poulantzas's interest in the Institute's precedent, Jessop here draws on its research on state capitalism, notably that of Neumann. He also places this work in a more precise Weberian context than the Institute's gestures towards ideal-typical framing: Weber's own ideal typification of 'political forms of capitalism', i.e., the use of 'economically irrational' practices such as financing wars and buying favours from politicians in securing profit. Jessop later glosses these as 'predatory profit from political activities, politically guaranteed monopolies and reliance on extraordinary political favours'.[35] In a significant revitalization of this framework, Jessop argues that

> it would be mistaken to think that the political modes of securing profit belong to the past. Indeed, recognizing that they survive and may even be expanding, albeit in new as well as old forms, might lead one to different conclusions about the formal correspondence between capitalism and democracy. Indeed, one might well propose that, where political forms of profit-making are dominant, it is authoritarian rule that is the norm rather than the exception.[36]

Finance-dominated accumulation fosters such political capitalism. Jessop so recuperates the Gramscian-Poulantzas legacy at this point, recasting Gramsci's typology of modes of Bonapartism and Caesarism as varieties of 'exceptional state' that function as alternatives to liberal democracy in times of organic crisis. In effect, Gramscian organic crises are understood as conjunctures in which forms of political capitalism become ascendant. Their Weberian 'irrationality' also renders them points of contradiction and instability in the Gramscian sense. In so doing Jessop extends a typology of modes of exceptional capitalist state that Poulantzas had developed in *Fascism and Dictatorship*. Central to this argument is Poulantzas's view that fascism is the most flexible of such prior state forms.

Jessop is thus able to also elaborate Poulantzas's 'authoritarian statism' thesis into a set of distinguishing features that include: the increasing concentration of power in the executive branch of government; a correlate decline in the effective role of legal norms, the parliamentary chamber and political parties; the loosening of ties between parties and the power bloc and the increasing resort to lobbying the executive directly, so generating a 'parallel power network'. Jessop stresses that these tendencies do not constitute a 'smoothly running' social order but are fraught with contradictions such as an instability in long-term planning due to the short-term interests of finance-dominated capital. More fundamentally the rise of 'austerity' as an organizing principle in the wake of the 2008 financial crash has established the economic grounds for widespread social discontent that joins with increasing distrust in the diminished liberal democratic forms of representation.[37]

It is important to stress that Jessop in no way proposes a return to the Marxian 'inevitable capitalist collapse' scenarios that the Institute challenged via its state capitalism thesis. However, in developing this multi-faceted 'updating' of the authoritarian statism thesis, he does combine elements of Poulantzas's fascist form of exceptional state with his original version of authoritarian statism.

Significantly marginalized within this project is any systemic role for populism – or demagogy – although even Jessop's occasional references indicate its rich potential. It is immediately evident that Jessop's dialectical account of politico-economic crisis of the power bloc and decline of liberal democracy redresses a tendency in orthodox political science approaches to populism which focus on narrowly defined empirical indicators of institutional decline (especially via measurements of trust) and, discretely if at all, the impact of the 2008 recession. At best, this orthodoxy considers such linkages 'fuzzy'.[38]

Jessop's marginalization of populism reproduces its near absence in Poulantzas's work. In his laudatory 1980 obituary article, Hall's only critical observation had been that Poulantzas 'does not deal sufficiently with how this progress towards "authoritarian statism" has been secured at the base by a complementary shift in popular consent-to-authority'. He offered his 'authoritarian populism' as a solution to this lacuna.[39] Several years later Jessop challenged Hall's authoritarian populism on grounds similar to the 'instrumentalism' problem identified in Chapter 4(d).[40] Thereafter Jessop's approach has been wary of all 'discourse-theoretic' work.[41]

However, as Jessop pointed out in a different context, Poulantzas did attempt the kind of explanation Hall called for in his short 1976 essay, 'On the Popular Impact of Fascism'.[42] In an interesting anticipation of Hall's formulations, he argued:

> fascism (and this is a particular trait of its ideological functioning) was able in its ideological discourse to recapture, by corrupting them, a series of deep-seated popular aspirations, often specific to each of the classes, class fractions and social categories concerned. This was the case with the themes of self-management and workers' control of production, formulations of socialization against private property, the power of monopolies, imperialist capital, etc., advanced in the relations of fascism and the working class, and present notably amongst the national-socialist left in Germany and amongst the anarcho-syndicalist wing of Italian Fascism. It was the case with the themes of peasant unity and of the bonds of blood and soil against the exploitation of the countryside by the cities, founded on the real industry-agriculture contradiction, advanced in the relations of fascism and the popular classes of the countryside. It was, finally, equally the case for the numerous themes advanced in the fascist discourse specifically addressed to the petty bourgeoisie.[43]

While Poulantzas is here of course speaking of fascism rather than authoritarian statism/populism, this is very close to Hall's argument that Thatcher's ideological success rested on her articulation of 'the field of popular conceptions'. This formulation also shares much with the 'fusion of elements' model Laclau challenged in his critique of *Fascism and Dictatorship*. But its context is different. Poulantzas in this text challenges both 'mass society' framings of fascism based in the susceptibility of 'atomised individuals' *and* any psychoanalytic approach that might emulate Le Bon. Here the role of classes and class fractions is not so much a reductivist 'necessary class belonging' of ideological elements as an insistence on the inclusion of mediating social forms. In many ways this critique anticipates the risks in the 'anti-sociological' approach of the later Laclau. Indeed, although still framed in the Althusserian language of 'apparatuses', Poulantzas follows the above passage with a requirement to attend to mediating 'institutional structures'.

There is one further development in Poulantzas's work that aids us in redressing the apparent lacuna concerning populism in Jessop's reworking of his project for the present. As early as his first book, Poulantzas employs the category of 'people-nation', understood as state-directed means of popular unification which move in tandem with the 'disorganizing' of any counter-hegemonic alliances of the subaltern. This is allied to the Gramscian 'national-popular'. Despite the ubiquity of this term in Poulantzas's project, including in *State Power Socialism*, it remains underdeveloped by him.[44]

The rudiments of a modest synthesis of the Institute's work and the Gramscian tradition can now be elaborated.

(c) Towards a social-formalist synthesis

As I argued in Chapters 3 and 4, a major advantage in considering populism from the perspective of fascism is that it highlights the relevance of the Institute's work on 'fascist demagogues' to contemporary theorizations of populism. I further argued that a first step in such an approach was to recognize that the demagogue is a figure common to both fascist practice and populism, although its role is necessary in the former and contingent in the latter (cf. Figure 1). So the first commonality between the Institute's work and the diverse Gramscian legacy is, as we have seen, an overlapping interest in the intersections of fascism and populism.

In contrast, the fascism-populism intersection completely vexes contemporary orthodox theorization. One recent review of the orthodox literature in both populism studies and fascism studies claimed that a synthesis might emerge on the basis of their 'common ideology' yet concluded with the 'classification conundrum' problem identified in Chapter 1 now extended to both fields.[45] Here 'ideology' is understood in its political scientific sense of an informing political philosophy or 'system of ideas'. Yet attempts to discern such an ideology in fascism acknowledge that, unlike liberalism for example, even the strongest candidates for 'fascist intellectual', such as Giovanni Gentile, provide chiefly pastiches of other thinkers' work and other 'ideologies'. However, this recognition is not the same as dismissing fascist discourse as 'pure irrationality'.[46]

What emerges as Frankfurt-Gramscian common ground is the recognition that such orthodox framings are doomed to founder on 'classification conundrums'. There is no 'common ideology' but something qualitatively different, indeed 'modern', that the Laclau-Poulantzas-Hall projects recognized as, to use a distinct term, a *recombinant* process.[47] Poulantzas's 'elements' were fragments that never achieved what the Frankfurt tradition regarded as a minimal criterion to meet the definition of ideology: elaborated coherence. The Institute instead used the terms 'devices' or 'techniques' and 'themes' to characterize this process of 'fusion' of elements.

Laclau provides the most elaborated set of theoretical protocols to capture this dynamic using, primarily, formalist linguistics. These enabled key insights into what both the Russian Formalists and the Institute each recognized as 'devices'. However, he fell into the 'formalist trap' identified by Williams because he sought to present this schema as the sum total of populist practice. He was unable to delimit its role because he rejected all sociological framings of the institutional forms and agencies required to 'practise' such recombinacy. Laclau's contradictory approach to 'manipulation' – that only Leninism, not populism, might succumb to such a form of leadership – was the most notable of many elisions and self-contradictions that resulted from his elimination of such mediating forms. In so doing he ironically reproduced key features of the 'mass society' explanation of populism that he formally rejected. Poulantzas and Hall recognized different aspects of this danger. While neither was uncritical of sociology, each understood the necessity of maintaining a social-theoretical role for social institutions. Poulantzas's insistence on the class specificity of fascist 'interpellation' and the 'class *content*' of his 'elements' maintained a formal role for mediation but risked the class reductivism Laclau correctly identified. Hall explicitly recognized Laclau's excess and instead expanded the Poulantzian itinerary of 'apparatuses' to recognize a role for (news) media whereby their 'autonomy' was far more than that of an 'apparatus' of even an expanded conception of 'state'. Nonetheless, as we saw, Hall's work is prone to instrumentalism.

But it is Hall's social formalist reworking of Laclau that has the greatest 'Gramscian' potential here as it rested on a considerable depth of understanding of the structuralist project and its sources. In this sense the Poulantzas–Laclau–Hall line of theorization resulted not in a discourse-theoretic model of populism but a social formalist one which relied on the notion of recombinant fragments. Hall was fond of tracing his social formalist reworking of this model back to Gramsci's characterization of common sense as 'an infinity of traces without an inventory'.[48]

The Institute's relevant work largely predated the advent of 'Parisian structuralism'. Plainly demagogic speech did not constitute an elaborated discourse bearing a redeemable 'truth content' worthy of their use of 'ideology'. As we saw in Chapter 3, aside from the pivotal role of psychoanalysis, their framing of demagogic 'oratory' risked either class reductivism, as in Adorno's *cui bono*, or Lowenthal's social theoretical catch-all. The Institute's potential alternative here – the socio-economic framing implied in the state capitalism debates – was never sufficiently developed to redress this limitation of the demagogy studies. It is this lacuna that Jessop's reworked Poulantzian schema seems ideally suited to remedy.

Nonetheless, the demagogy studies' use of 'device'/'technique' and 'theme' was sufficiently formalist to recognize the specificity of the role of the *fragment* as the formal 'unit' of demagogic speech. This corresponds with the Poulantzas use of 'element'. Its recombinant unity is heavily dependent on the 'compositional' cultural production of the demagogic 'flight of ideas' which has a distinct psychoanalytic signature.

Is it valid to identify elements of the Institute's work with a 'social-formalist' approach? Again, using a mediating 'third party', we can bring this perspective into closer dialogue with social formalism. Lucien Goldmann's sociology of literature shared much with comparable work by Institute members, most notably Lowenthal and Adorno. His long-standing sociological critiques of Parisian structuralism – undertaken in Paris itself – resembled Williams's advocated social formalism.[49] Goldmann understood both the claims of Frankfurt ideology critique and formalist-structuralist analysis. In 1968, in what appears to be his first major contact with this mode of thinking, Adorno largely endorsed Goldmann's characterization of structuralism's chief failing: that in its conception of structure 'functional meaning disappears'.[50] Such an abandonment of 'functional meaning' was not the Institute's understanding of 'device' or 'theme'.

For Hall, Laclau's early innovations lent 'considerable sophistication' to his own 'rudimentary schemas' based on Gramsci's 'national-popular' and 'common sense'.[51] Hall was here too modest. What is perhaps most remarkable about Laclau's reworking of Gramsci is its complete inattention to the cultural elements of his 'national popular' and indeed 'historical bloc'. As we shall see in Chapter 6, the radical-democratic ruptures that Laclau sees as the European antecedents of his left-populist project were closely aligned with radical 'cultural populist' formations. Likewise, the possibility that Gramsci's background as a partisan journalist may have suggested a central role for journalism and modern means of communication in the key hegemonic phenomenon of the 'intellectual organization of consent' leaves no trace in Laclau's work.

The reason for this lacuna in the later Laclau seems clear. Poulantzas and the early Laclau explicitly employ the term 'tradition' to characterize the historical resources available for the development of the 'elements' that compose a new 'organic ideology' in the Gramscian sense. As Poulantzas puts it, 'Fascist ideology was, as it were, rooted in the tradition of the national cultures of Germany and Italy.' Likewise when Laclau reworks Poulantzas's 'elements' thesis, in his first elaborated theory of populism, he characterises his 'non-class interpellations' as filling what he sees as an absence in Marxist theory: '*the relative continuity* of popular traditions'.[52] These views are quite at odds with the 'anti-historicism' of the Althusserian project. *Its* model of interpellation is tied to a version of 'ideology in general' which echoes the abstract objectivism of the Saussurian *langue* and which Althusser later recanted. Laclau moved closer to this early Althusserian position in his later hyperformalism and so lost the historical perspective that enabled his conceptual recognition of 'tradition'. This is a problem that besets many other subsequent invocations of 'interpellation'.[53]

Poulantzas's candour at this point is telling. He appears to source the very term 'elements' to Togliatti but then stresses the significance of 'the writings of the Frankfurt School' in this context, despite 'whatever doubts one may have about them in other respects'.[54]

If we consider the Coughlin case again, we can provide a social formalist account of how the mutability of populist discourse in his demonstrated practice was achieved. As suggested, the thematics/devices examined by Lowenthal and Adorno can be considered 'fusions of elements' in the Poulantzian sense. However, the role of the specific content of these elements is pivotal. When Brinkley claimed that 'Long and Coughlin adopted the rhetoric of populist localism, but little of its substance', he referred to the same lack of a programmatic dimension that Adorno and Lowenthal regarded as a defining feature of the demagogue. However, the substance that remained, the 'content', did not have the arbitrary contingency of Laclauian signifiers. Rather, we might say, following from Hall's appropriation of Vološinov, that the *evaluative accent* of these 'elements' of populist discourse was shifted, in part by their disembedding from the detailed programmes for reform that Brinkley lists: 'marketing cooperatives, community cotton gins and flour mills, cooperative stores and credit unions'.[55] This was what Daniel Bell meant by 'a grotesque transformation of an originally progressive idea'.[56]

The early Laclau was right to stress that a process of formal semiosis was at work whereby no signifier-signified relation was guaranteed; nor was such a meaning fixable to a class-fractional location. Yet, as with the infamously asocial proposition by Saussure that the signifier-signified relation was necessarily 'arbitrary', the later Laclau failed to acknowledge that this fluidly formal 'productivity' was nonetheless socio-historically delimited. It took the form of a *tradition* that was susceptible to selective usage.

However, this disembedding does not produce only a sediment of 'mere rhetoric' as Brinkley and much political science orthodoxy would have it. Its recombinacy as demagogic practice cannot simply be brushed aside as pragmatically inconsequential.

Rather, in the cases of populism and fascism, their 'traditions' are far from discrete, depending on the 'national culture' in question. One of the most notable recent scholarly reassessments of such issues, primarily addressed to the case of Germany in the discipline of history, concerns '*Volkgemeinschaft*', usually translated as 'people's community' or 'community of the people'. This eventually became offical Nazi policy, underpinned by its antisemitic framing as an exclusionary policy. However, recent historians no longer regard the term as 'merely a propaganda buzzword'. Rather, it developed from a long politico-cultural precursor 'tradition' in Germany into an *anti-elitist* pedagogical movement in the period after the First World War.[57]

Thematic elements commonly associated with populism – such as anti-elitism – were thus intermixed with proto-fascist ones in such precursor traditions. Indeed, this is the terrain of the Gramscian national-popular, as Gramsci anticipated in his comments about the German use of *Volk*.[58]

Both Adorno and Lowenthal invoke *Volksgemeinschaft* and/or its English translation in their demagogy studies. Undoubtedly, they are influenced by its then recent legacy in Nazi propaganda but they do not dismiss it as a 'buzzword'. For Lowenthal this is a core component of demagogic mobilization of 'followers' to one of the themes, the construction of an endogamic community: 'Both the *Volksgemeinschaft* of the Nazis and the community of pure Americans proposed by the agitator are actually pseudo-*Gemeinschaften*, or pseudo-communities.'[59]

More significantly, Adorno also invokes this motif in the 'Freudian Theory' essay at a crucial point examined above, that concerning the prospect of 'negative identification' that Laclau cited from Freud but failed to discuss. As we saw in Chapter 2(b), Freud speculates that religious rejection and persecution of non-believers will not necessarily fade with the decline of religions but could be reconstituted in secular form. This comment comes shortly after the 'negative identification' passage. Without assuming a decline in religious ties per se, Adorno here inserts the demagogue-follower relationship and the relevant demagogic device whose *content* is the same (endogamic) 'community of the people' thematic identified by Lowenthal. Freud, for Adorno, has so recognized 'the libidinal function of this device'. Moreover, this libidinal dynamic provides a clearer indication of the 'narcissistic *gain*' for the *follower* that need not rely on the narcissism of the leader.[60] The modern demagogue, in effect, combines both primary and secondary leadership of the followers by the addition of libidinised devices to the 'positive attachment' to the narcissistic performance.

As with the classification conundrum in populism, then, the Institute's figure of the modern demagogue aids a clarification of the 'reach' of Freud's group psychology. The demagogue's exploitation of 'negative identification' increases the likelihood of a group identification susceptible to, as Freud puts it, 'hatred against a particular person or institution'. The follower of such a demagogue so experiences *both* positive and negative identification.

The resources for *this* modern demagogic practice draw on the available field of the national-popular as a tradition. Here scholars of nationalism would rightly insist that such traditions rely heavily on the particularity of the path to successful or unsuccesful nation-statehood and the level of reliance on primordial ethnocentrism.[61] The Gramscian framework is not incompatible with this but, as we saw, places greater emphasis on the intersection of the role of intellectuals, popular pedagogy and the bifurcations of aesthetic culture.

Given the centrality of 'anti-immigration' to many forms of contemporary populism, it is tempting to reduce the analysis of rising 'rightwing populism' to the essentialist problematic of the 'racist potential' of a fixed national culture/identity.[62] Among such an approach's failings would be inattention to the increasing economic polarization in many nation-states that has accelerated since the 2008 crash. While it is certainly true that the rise of 'neopopulism' long predates that crash, Jessop's reworking of Poulantzas's analysis for the 'finance-dominated' neoliberal order as a Gramscian 'organic crisis' provides us with a more suitable context.

Of course, neither the Gramscian nor Frankfurt traditions regard such economic dislocation as sufficient in itself to account for particular political phenomena. For Jessop, the organic crisis of the neoliberal project's quasi-clientelist 'political capitalism' renders manifest certain vulnerabilities that take the form of specific crises in political representation, legitimacy and (hegemonic) intellectual leadership.[63]

Significantly absent from Jessop's list of features of neoliberalism is what has been called 'digital capitalism', i.e., the rise and consequences of digitally and globally convergent systems of communication.[64] Likewise, it is important to add to Jessop's account Hall's pivotal recognition of mediating communications as a sociological dimension in such crisis forms. The means of social interpretation of such modes of crisis is thus also pivotal.[65]

However, it is the aesthetico-cultural dimension of the Gramscian national-popular that provides us with the fuller terrain of (popular) tradition initially sketched by Poulantzas and Laclau. While Gramsci scholars have been careful to delineate his national-popular strategy 'as radically alien to any form of populism', it is nonetheles central to a Gramscian understanding of populism, especially one that is not limited to 'political populism'.[66]

The educative dimension that informed Gramsci's understanding of a field of potential counter-hegemony so includes his interests in common sense, folklore and religion as forms of popular philosophy. Crucially, he too regarded these as fragmentary forms of knowledge embedded in modes of conduct; for him it was equally significant that, unlike the common sense of the hegemonic classes, this common sense had not been provided with an organic intellectual process of disembedding and elaboration. Such an educative intellectual project did not mean a celebration of such existent 'simple' common sense, 'but, precisely in order to construct an intellectual-moral bloc which can make politically possible the intellectual progress of the mass and not only of small intellectual groups'. This national-popular project so required redressing the gulf between intellectuals and popular forms of aesthetic culture as well as popular knowledge.[67]

It is surely no coincidence that Gramsci framed this goal of leading the masses 'to a higher conception of life' as a critique of a 'popular manual' (Bukharin's of orthodox Marxism). The Institute's attempts at popular manuals in the demagogy studies had a very different purpose but moved from a remarkably similar understanding of the forms of popular knowledge exploited by demagogues. However, this very different situation also points to the different, very 'modern', situation the Institute addressed compared to Gramsci's concern for an alliance with the southern Italian peasantry. Not only was the Institute in the midst of the 'Americanism and Fordism' that Gramsci noted from afar, but the matrix of folklore and popular culture he assumed for the 'simple' Italian situation was challenged by the complexities of the US culture industry.

As we saw in Chapter 2, the culture industry is integral to the Institute's conception of modern demagogy. Its 'montage' character was central to its mode of commodification of demagogic speech. Montages are, of course, compositions of fragments. The sense of fragment/element in the Gramscian tradition tended to be a common-sense aphorism (Gramsci), a class-ideological component of an organic ideology (Poulantzas) or an increasingly free-floating and eventually empty signifier (Laclau).

For a critical social formalist analysis of demagogic populism, we need to more fully integrate the role of the culture industry – and modern means of communication more broadly. Standing in the path of such an integration is the phenomenon of 'cultural populism'. As the next chapter details, this fraught term refers to both theoretical blockades to critical theory's influence and a deepened understanding of the links between the Gramscian national-popular and the Institute's work.

Notes

1 Chantal Mouffe, *For a Left Populism* (London: Verso, 2018). See especially her acknowledgement of unspecified potential 'negative effects' of charismatic leadership while insisting on its necessity without any indication of checks on such leadership beyond a recognition of the necessity of representative democracy – as 'highly institutionalised' societies are associated with the absence of 'populist situations'. Íñigo Errejón and Chantal Mouffe, *Podemos: In the Name of the People* (London: Lawrence & Wishart, 2016), 108–117.
2 For the definitive Althusserian critique, see: Göran Therborn, 'A Critique of the Frankfurt School', *New Left Review*, no. 1/63 (1970). Cf. Jay's contemporary critique of Therborn and his Althusserian premisses: Martin Jay, 'The Frankfurt School's Critique of Marxist Humanism', *Social Research* (1972). Poulantzas was more open to the Institute's work. Even Laclau's short essay on 'psychoanalysis and Marxism' makes no mention of the Institute: Ernesto Laclau, 'Psychoanalysis and Marxism', *Critical Inquiry* 13, no. 2 (1987). Laclau (with Zac) undertakes a brief reading of Benjamin's 'Critique of Violence' but he does not connect this with the Institute's work: Ernesto Laclau and Lilian Zac, 'Minding the Gap: The Subject of Politics', in *The Making of Political Identities*, ed. Ernesto Laclau (London: Verso, 1994).
3 Ernesto Laclau, *New Reflections on the Revolution of Our Time* (London: Verso, 1990). As Laclau indicates, the title essay refers to Laski's 1943 work of a similar name: Harold J. Laski, *Reflections on the Revolution of Our Time* (London: Allen & Unwin, 1943).
4 Laclau, *New Reflections on the Revolution of Our Time*, 51–52.
5 In the same period Laclau published a reading of Rorty's *Contingency, Irony and Solidarity* in which he simply reiterates Rorty's critique of *Dialectic of Enlightenment* without referring to the text himself. Ernesto Laclau, *Emancipation(s)* (London: Verso, 2007), 109–110; Richard Rorty, *Contingency, Irony, and Solidarity* (Cambridge: Cambridge University Press, 1989), 56–57. Rorty's critique is the familiar philosophical one that *Dialectic* does not leave any space for redemptive prospects, especially of liberalism.
6 Adorno, *The Psychological Technique of Martin Luther Thomas' Radio Addresses*, 116–117.
7 Laclau, *New Reflections on the Revolution of Our Time*, 61. Cf. Howarth's sympathetic reconstruction of the Laclauian conception of subjectivity which nonetheless points to its many problems: David Howarth, 'Hegemony, Political Subjectivity, and Radical Democracy', in *Laclau: A Critical Reader*, ed. S. Critchley and Oliver Marchant (London: Routledge, 2004).
8 One text that seeks such common ground is: Peter Ives, *Gramsci's Politics of Language: Engaging the Bakhtin Circle and the Frankfurt School* (Toronto: University of Toronto Press, 2004). He provides a succinct critique of Laclau and Mouffe in the opening pages. My use of the social formalism/hyperformalism distinction works from different premises from Ives's more philosophical framing.
9 Laclau, *Politics and Ideology in Marxist Theory: Capitalism, Fascism, Populism*, 84–86. Laclau tends to equate Fromm's work with that of Reich and asserts their affinity with Arendt's on totalitarianism.
10 Howarth, 'Hegemony, Political Subjectivity, and Radical Democracy', 264.
11 Freud makes one indirect reference to Tarde's conception of 'imitation'. Freud, *Group Psychology and the Analysis of the Ego*, 34.

12 William McDougall, *The Group Mind: A Sketch of the Principles of Collective Psychology, with Some Attempt to Apply Them to the Interpretation of National Life and Character*, 2nd edn (London: Cambridge University Press, 1927).
13 Laclau, *On Populist Reason*, 60.
14 Freud, *Group Psychology and the Analysis of the Ego*, 116 (italics in original text)
15 Laclau, *On populist Reason*, 56.
16 Freud, *Group Psychology and the Analysis of the Ego*, 116 (italicization added).
17 McDougall, *The Group Mind: A Sketch of the Principles of Collective Psychology, with Some Attempt to Apply Them to the Interpretation of National Life and Character*, 48–61.
18 Freud, *Group Psychology and the Analysis of the Ego*, 31.
19 Nicos Mouzelis, 'Ideology and Class Politics: A Critique of Ernesto Laclau', *New Left Review*, no. 1/112 (1978): 51–52.
20 I refer to the eleventh chapter, 'A Differentiating Grade in the Ego', which is followed by a postscript.
21 Freud, *Group Psychology and the Analysis of the Ego*, 102; Laclau, *On Populist Reason*, 58–59; Adorno, 'Freudian Theory and the Pattern of Fascist Propaganda', 289–290. Adorno cites the paragraph in its entirety while Laclau omits the opening and closing sentences.
22 Freud, *Group Psychology and the Analysis of the Ego*, 101–102.
23 Laclau, *On Populist Reason*, 59–60.
24 Freud, *Group Psychology and the Analysis of the Ego*, 53.
25 Adorno, 'Freudian Theory and the Pattern of Fascist Propaganda', 282.
26 Williams, *Keywords: A Vocabulary of Culture and Society*, 76. This is in part an auto-critique of Williams's own usage of the term in his early work. While this comment is confined to English language usage, his reference to the lack of a positive binary opposite for 'community' might be countered with the *gemeinschaft/gesellschaft* distinction in the German sociological tradition.
27 Adorno, 'Freudian Theory and the Pattern of Fascist Propaganda', 284n.
28 Nicos Poulantzas, *State, Power, Socialism* (London: NLB, 1978), 203–247.
29 Poulantzas, *State, Power, Socialism*, 72, 78, 205. These references are never fully sourced.
30 Poulantzas, *State, Power, Socialism*, 203–204.
31 Poulantzas, *State, Power, Socialism*, 204. Poulantzas immediately stresses that such an economic framing can only be a 'guiding thread' that is necessary but insufficient by itself.
32 Hall also 'updated' his own position modestly and schematically in his later work on neoliberalism, especially in its 'third way' form. Stuart Hall, 'The Neoliberal Revolution (2011)', in *Stuart Hall: Selected Political Writings*, ed. Sally Davison et al. (London: Lawrence & Wishart, 2016).
33 Bob Jessop, 'The Organic Crisis of the British State: Putting Brexit in Its Place', *Globalizations* 14, no. 1 (2017); Bob Jessop, 'Elective Affinity or Comprehensive Contradiction? Reflections on Capitalism and Democracy in the Time of Finance-Dominated Accumulation and Austerity States', *Berliner Journal für Soziologie* 28, no. 1 (2018).
34 Jessop, 'Elective Affinity or Comprehensive Contradiction?', 21.
35 Jessop, 'Elective Affinity or Comprehensive Contradiction?', 14–15; 27; Weber, *Economy and Society*, 164–166.
36 Jessop, 'Elective Affinity or Comprehensive Contradiction?', 15.
37 Jessop, 'Elective Affinity or Comprehensive Contradiction?', 18–24.

38 Hanspeter Kriesi and Takis Pappas, eds, *European Populism in the Shadow of the Great Recession* (Colchester: ECPR Press, 2015).
39 Stuart Hall, 'Nicos Poulantzas: State, Power, Socialism', *New Left Review* 1/119 (1980): 68.
40 Bob Jessop et al., 'Authoritarian Populism, Two Nations and Thatcherism', *New Left Review*, no. 147 (1984); Stuart Hall, 'Authoritarian Populism: A Reply', *New Left Review*, no. 151 (1985); Bob Jessop et al., 'Thatcherism and the Politics of Hegemony: A Reply to Stuart Hall', *New Left Review*, no. 153 (1985).
41 Nonetheless, Jessop does repeatedly draw on those elements of Hall's work he finds legitimate. This includes his role for the media in 'populist ventriloquism'. Jessop, 'Elective Affinity or Comprehensive Contradiction?', 22. See also the discussion of 'Semiotics for Political Economy' in: N.L. Sum and B. Jessop, *Towards a Cultural Political Economy: Putting Culture in Its Place in Political Economy* (Cheltenham: Edward Elgar, 2014).
42 Jessop, *Nicos Poulantzas: Marxist Theory and Political Strategy*, 216–217; Nicos Poulantzas, 'On the Popular Impact of Fascism (1976)', in *The Poulantzas Reader: Marxism, Law and the State*, ed. James Martin (London: Verso, 2008).
43 Poulantzas, 'On the Popular Impact of Fascism (1976)', 266.
44 Poulantzas, *Political Power and Social Classes*, 188–189.
45 Roger Eatwell, 'Populism and Fascism', in *The Oxford Handbook of Populism*, ed. Cristóbal Rovira Kaltwasser et al. (Oxford: Oxford University Press, 2017).
46 This point remains controversial. See for example, the respectively sociological and 'culturalist' assessments of Michael Mann and Zeev Sternhell: Mann, *Fascists*; Zeev Sternhell, Mario Sznajder and Maia Ashéri, *The Birth of Fascist Ideology: From Cultural Rebellion to Political Revolution*, trans. David Maisel (Princeton, NJ: Princeton University Press, 1994).
47 I here use Todd Gitlin's coinage which, while obviously borrowed from then-recent developments in biology, was influenced by Adorno and Benjamin, among others. Gitlin introduced it in his landmark analysis of prime-time television as a delineation of a particular mode of synthetic culture industry 'innovation' that was more than mere replication. It refers to a recombination of already-proven 'elements' of successful culture industry products. It thus bears a resemblance to the use of 'part-interchangeability' in the reception of Adorno in popular music studies (see Chapter 6). Gitlin was also aware of his term's proximity to Lévi-Strauss's 'bricolage': Todd Gitlin, *Inside Prime Time* (New York: Pantheon, 1985), 75–85.
48 For example, Stuart Hall, 'Gramsci's Relevance for the Study of Race and Ethnicity', *Journal of Communication Inquiry* 10, no. 2 (1986): 20. More precisely, Gramsci uses the metaphor in the context of a discussion of philosophy in his characteristically 'expanded' sense ('all men are philosophers') to include its relationship with common sense. The same passage also anticipates conceptions of fragmented subjectivity, so Hall also borrowed its phrasings to articulate such a contradictory 'ground' for successful 'articulation'. Gramsci, *Selections from the Prison Notebooks of Antonio Gramsci*, 324. Stuart Hall, *The Hard Road to Renewal: Thatcherism and the Crisis of the Left* (London Verso, 1988), 169.
49 Jones, *Raymond Williams's Sociology of Culture: A Critical Reconstruction*.
50 Lucien Goldmann and Theodor W. Adorno, 'To Describe, Understand and Explain (Jan., 1968)', in *Lucien Goldmann: Cultural Creation in Modern Society* (Saint Louis: Telos Press, 1976).
51 Hall, 'Popular Democratic vs. Authoritarian Populism: Two Ways of Taking Democracy Seriously', 176.

52 Poulantzas, *Fascism and Dictatorship*, 253; Laclau, *Politics and Ideology in Marxist Theory: Capitalism, Fascism, Populism*, 166 (italicization in original text). This is not a random use of the term 'tradition' in this text.
53 For a definition of this informing idea of 'historicism' for Althusserian high structuralism, see: B. Brewster, 'Glossary', in *Louis Althusser & Etienne Balibar: Reading Capital* (London: NLB, 1977), 314.
54 Poulantzas, *Fascism and Dictatorship*, 253n. Palmiro Togliatti, *Lectures on Fascism* (London: Lawrence and Wishart, 1976), 9–10.
55 Brinkley, *Voices of Protest*, 166.
56 See Chapter 1(b).
57 Michael Wildt, 'Volksgemeinschaft: A Modern Perspective on National Socialist Society', in *Visions of Community in Nazi Germany: Social Engineering and Private Lives*, ed. Martina Steber and Bernhard Gotto (Oxford: Oxford University Press, 2014), 49; Geoff Eley, *Nazism as Fascism: Violence, Ideology, and the Ground of Consent in Germany 1930–1945* (New York: Routledge, 2013).
58 See Chapter 4(a).
59 Lowenthal and Guterman, *Prophets of Deceit*, 106.
60 Adorno, 'Freudian Theory and the Pattern of Fascist Propaganda', 288–289, 293–295.
61 See, for example, Guy Hermet's interesting distinction between the civic form of Western European national-popular and the more primordial Eastern European paths: Guy Hermet, 'From Nation-State Populism to National-Populism', in *Revisiting Nationalism*, ed. Alain Dieckhoff and Christophe Jaffrelot (New York: Palgrave Macmillan, 2005).
62 This is, for example, the standard mode of public debate in Australia each time there is a surge in support for the 'One Nation' party.
63 Jessop, 'Elective Affinity or Comprehensive Contradiction', 28.
64 Dan Schiller, 'Power under Pressure: Digital Capitalism in Crisis', *International Journal of Communication* 5 (2011). This dimension is highlighted in Chapter 7.
65 Gender is also unaddressed here by Jessop in this analysis. The work of the feminist critical theorist Nancy Fraser is highly relevant here. Not only does her critique of 'discourse theory' share much with the social formalist position advocated in this book, but her appropriation of Gramsci to feminist theorization is also highly relevant to the analysis of populism and neoliberalism. Finally, her version of 'left populist' advocacy does not fall into the same traps as Laclau and Mouffe concerning demagogic risk. She demonstrates all this superbly in: Nancy Fraser, *The Old is Dying and the New Cannot be Born: From Progressive Neoliberalism to Trump and Beyond* (London: Verso, 2019).
66 I cite from Hoare and Nowell-Smith's editorial note: Gramsci, *Selections from the Prison Notebooks of Antonio Gramsci*, 421 n465.
67 Gramsci, *Selections from the Prison Notebooks of Antonio Gramsci*, 332–333; David Forgacs, 'National-Popular: Genealogy of a Concept', in *Formations of Nation and People*, ed. Formations Editorial Collective (London: Routledge & Kegan Paul, 1984).

Part II

Populist contradictions of the culture industry

6

Cultural populisms and culture industry

(a) From *Volk* to culture industry

Previous chapters have emphasized the utility of approaching critical theorizations of populism via their assessment of fascism. As we saw in Chapter 5, both Gramsci and the Institute linked these assessments with the domain of aesthetic culture. In both cases the relevant realm of the aesthetic was socially broadened beyond compositions identified within philosophical aesthetics: for Gramsci, the national-popular; for the Institute, the culture industry.

In more orthodox analysis, the notable parallel recognition is that between Italian fascism and aesthetic Modernism. This recognition has grown apace in recent years, and now includes leading scholars of 'political' fascism. This rethinking moves from the same rejection of earlier dismissals of fascists as 'thugs and opportunists' unworthy of detailed consideration of their informing ideas.[1]

The contrast with orthodox populism studies could not be greater. As we saw in Chapter 1, the question of populism's 'thin ideology' still haunts the dominantly inductive theorizations and the related 'classification dilemma'. Moreover, the suggestion that 'cultural populism' might have relevance for 'political populism' has been explicitly rejected.

Superficially, this difference can be easily explained. Prominent relationships between aesthetic Modernism and Italian fascism were hardly difficult to find.

Marinetti's Italian Futurists foreshadowed fascist views in their manifestos and later sought support from Mussolini's regime, though with limited success.[2] A comparable aesthetic analogue for populism does not present itself as readily. Yet if one moves beyond such 'plain sight' connections for the case of populism, then that analogue aesthetic movement would surely be found within Romanticism. More precisely, it would be that component of Romanticism that is suspicious of genteel aesthetic artifice and is drawn towards folkloric forms, if not necessarily towards the folk themselves. The historical connections between this aesthetic movement and populism are more complex than that between Italian fascism and Modernism.

Romantic folkloricism in particular shares much with the thematic motifs of populism, especially those identified by Shils in the US tradition, notably 'the virtues of uncorrupted, simple common folk' that is manifest in respect for *'authenticity'*.[3] In the British tradition, the Romantic poets Wordsworth and Coleridge adopted the folk ballad form but also laid the ground for mass/minority culture framing in Wordsworth's critical response to the first stages of the transition from a patronage- to market-based system of cultural production.[4]

The case of the late nineteenth-century Russian narodniks, discussed in Chapter 4, also demonstrates such a Romantic influence. Moreover, it prefigures a larger problem: the existence of a strain of 'intellectual populism', nowadays within the academy, that tends to 'trust the people' and/or their aesthetic judgements regarding 'popular culture', implicitly and uncritically. Bourdieu was perhaps the first to adequately articulate the problem here, in language that moves close to Adorno's. Such intellectual invocations of 'the people' and 'popular culture' can function as a means of position-taking within the modern intellectual field. However, this attempted inversion of 'the relations of symbolic force' by merely 'consecrating the dominated' in a wholesale manner is, he argues, 'still an effect of domination'.[5]

Since the consolidation of the culture industry, this intellectual phenomenon has become better known as 'cultural populism' and, as we shall see, this usually critical term has been used retrospectively in historical reconstructions of this tendency. It is important to distinguish it too from the Gramscian emphasis on the critical educational dimension of the intellectuals/national-popular relationship. While Gramsci famously made explicit his recognition of a universal intellectual capacity – 'all men are intellectuals' – he repeatedly referred to the culture of the masses as a 'simple' one that required, at the very least, considerable elaboration.

Of course, it is such cultural populism that is frequently pitted against the culture industry thesis and Adorno's work in particular. I chart the US origins of this mischaracterization in this chapter but its standard form reduces the complexity of the culture industry argument to a mere personal prejudice against 'the popular'. In keeping with the intellectually populist form of this argument, the summary charge is thus 'cultural elitism'.

But it is the German case that draws these tensions into sharpest focus for our purposes. The Nazis infamously organized public burnings of 'degenerate' works of aesthetic Modernism, 'asphalt literati'.[6] However, Herf's landmark sociological analysis also identified a 'reactionary modernism' at the core of Nazism. By this he refers to the particularity of the German fusion of anti-modern Romanticism and the embrace of modern technology. Herf's concern is principally with a broader use of the term 'modernism' to refer, in this instance, to technological 'modernization', while aesthetic Modernism plays a quite minor background role. He acknowledges the capacity of the Marxian tradition, including Poulantzas, to recognize this modern dimension of fascism. Likewise, his respect for critical theory, from Neumann to *Dialectic of Enlightenment*, is considerable. However, he makes the now familiar reduction of Adorno and Horkheimer's views to that work and the corollary claim that their analysis lacked national specificity.[7] This, of course, is quite incorrect. As the culture industry is my other focus in this chapter, I will draw on some of Adorno's related writings to redress this view.

German Romanticism was clearly connected with the rise of the *völkisch* 'ideology' that informed the Nazi appropriation of *Volkgemeinschaft* introduced in Chapter 5.[8] It forms the core of Herf's anti-modern Romanticism. As Adorno made explicit in his 1967 'resumé', 'culture industry' replaced his and Horkheimer's former use of 'mass culture' so as to avoid any possible connotation of spontaneous collective production of '*Volkskunst*', usually translated as 'popular art'.[9] Two purposes evidently lay within this strategy: the first, to avoid all association with *völkisch* thought; the second, more explicit but much overlooked by cultural populists, was to maintain a legitimate distinction between popular art and culture industry.

The first purpose is worthy of elaboration here. It is clear that Adorno was under no illusions about the links between the mystico-religious Romanticism of Richard Wagner's work and 'German supra-nationalism in its most destructive form', for example. In a 1945 (English) text composed between the two editions of *Dialectic of Enlightenment*, he brought the insights of Studies in Prejudice to bear on this relationship by identifying Wagner's son-in-law, Houston Stewart Chamberlain, as the demagogue who exploited this conjunction and articulated a fully elaborated *völkisch* antisemitism.[10] Indeed, Adorno later called for exactly the kind of historical positioning of Chamberlain that was then being published by George Mosse.[11] Chamberlain acts as a demagogic intellectual mediator, on Adorno's account, between Wagner's work and the leading Nazi ideologue,

Alfred Rosenberg, who 'borrowed most of his theses' from Chamberlain's infamous *The Foundations of the Nineteenth Century.* The 'pedigree Wagner-Chamberlain-Rosenberg', as Adorno calls it, is a demagogic one which, as established in previous chapters, only achieves fully fascist form by means of a reordering synthesis of fragments.[12] Consistent with the distinction between such phenomena and elaborated 'true' ideologies, this is the same Rosenberg whom Adorno deemed unworthy of immanent ideology critique ten years later.[13]

The *völkisch* basis of *Volksgemeinschaft* was thus not conflated by Adorno with the *Volk* or *Volkslied* (folksong). As he argued in 1965, '[t]o someone who thinks in terms of society, and who understands fascism socio-economically, the thesis that blames the German people (*Volk*) is really quite foreign'.[14] Rather, the demagogic exploitation of the legacy of the Romantic idealization of the *Volk* had met the 'decultivation' of an entire intellectual stratum and its middle class audience.

Nonetheless, alluding to the legacy of the pre-fascist *Volk* revivalist movements later incorporated by the Nazis, Adorno remained wary of any post-fascist folk revival movements that celebrated the 'calculated, synthetic nature of ... supposed folk music'.[15] Here he moves close to the critique of demagogic appeals to 'community of the people'/*Volksgemeinschaft* discussed in the previous chapter. For the other *Volk* revivalist elements Adorno rejected include what he calls 'musical collectivism' i.e. the insistence on the communal and thus proto-nationalist authorship of folk compositions. Such views have also been brought into doubt in subsequent folkloric studies and, as discussed below, in Peter Burke's historical work in this area. Béla Bartók anticipated such criticisms in his 1944 critique of 'race purity in music'. He argued the race-national interpretation of restricted traditions were qualitatively inferior musically to the result of 'impure' intermixing of formerly peasant musics.[16] Adorno wrote approvingly in 1948 of Bartok's folk-influenced compositions in similar terms: 'In contrast to the productions of Nazi blood and soil ideology, truly extra-territorial music ... has a power of alienation that associates it with the avant-garde and not with nationalist reaction'.[17]

Here Adorno uses the same terms he usually reserved for the avant-garde to recognize such hybridizing composition based in the folkloric. This makes clear that his well-known respect for the avant-garde, made explicit in the 1945 essay, is not premissed on its opposition to 'the popular' but to the culture industry and 'decultivation'. It can lead us to the second dimension of the culture industry resumé: the 'exemption' of 'popular art' from the culture industry's destruction of aesthetic autonomy. I will not pursue this at the same length here as the notion is discussed in detail in section (d). However, all such cases of 'exempted' cultural composition rest on a distinction he famously stresses in the resumé: that the 'industry' did not include aesthetic composition (aka 'production') per se. What is striking about approaching the culture industry thesis from this direction is its inverted similarity to the Gramscian national-popular. 'Decultivation' marked a reversal of the German national-popular from hegemonic leadership by a humanistic ethos (which Adorno does not explicitly endorse). The sociological precondition of this reversal was the disappearance of a stratum of non-specialist intellectuals who were active participants in aesthetico-cultural life. This culture subsequently becomes socially restricted to 'the privilege of experts and professionals', a retreat to a position structurally similar to that Gramsci lamented in the Italian case. The collapse of this humanistic aesthetico-cultural hegemony created 'a vacuum ready to absorb the arbitrarily superimposed doctrines of totalitarianism'.[18] This new socio-cultural terrain, Adorno argues, was more significant in preparing the cultural ground for fascism than any specific influence of Wagner's work.

Adorno also attributes this decultivation to a 'neutralization of culture' aided by the rise of the culture industry and its fostering of an instrumentalist mode of reception of both 'traditional works' and the newer culture industry products. Crucially, contra Herf, this thesis refers to developments specific to pre-fascist Germany throughout. The movement of this argument is strikingly similar to that regarding the shift from a 'culture-debating' to 'culture-consuming' public that Habermas developed, working primarily from the US case, in *The Structural Transformation of the Public Sphere*.[19]

This chapter proceeds by next reviewing the 'cultural populist' challenge and its failings in more detail, so raising the question of the relationship between cultural populism and 'political' populism. Moreover, it is argued that the cultural populist logic is dependent on an 'en bloc' conception of popular culture that is a variant of the 'intellectual populism' identified by Shils.

If we approach this issue from the perspective of the culture industry thesis, however, it is its capacity to act as an alternative 'crucible' of demagogues to the orthodox political sphere that becomes pivotal (cf. Figure 3). If the culture industry can generate demagogues, then contestation of 'bad populism' would assume a different shape from that usually advocated by critical analysis – the instrumentalist process of learning and emulating 'populist logics' as a counter-hegemonic practice in the Hall-Laclauian senses discussed in Chapters 4 and 5.

Accordingly, the chapter builds to a different joining of the 'popular' and the 'aesthetic', as found within the culture industry thesis and in the very earliest work of Stuart Hall – a conception of 'the popular artist' who works within specific cultural forms. Forces countering 'cultural demagogy' can then include the anti-demagogic work of certain popular artists. Chapter 7 assesses a series of examples of such practice.

(b) 'Mass culture' and the attribution of 'cultural elitism' to the culture industry thesis

It is not without good reason that Martin Jay once referred to Edward Shils as 'ever the scourge of the *Institut*'. Within a three-year period in the mid-1950s he produced both a definitive critique of *The Authoritarian Personality* and, on Jay's reckoning, was the first to accuse Institute members of joining forces with conservative critics of mass culture, so facilitating the long-term legacy of their being charged with 'cultural elitism'.[20]

'Daydreams and Nightmares: Reflections on the Critique of Mass Culture' was published by Shils in 1957 as a review article addressing both the Rosenberg and White edited collection, *Mass Culture*, and Richard Hoggart's *The Uses of Literacy*.[21] The Frankfurt School was thus not his ostensible target but the Institute played a major role in his account.

The 560-page *Mass Culture* collection included reproduced essays by Lowenthal, Kracauer and Adorno. Significantly, none of these three pieces – even Adorno's – employed the concept of culture industry. Adorno's and Horkheimer's shift in usage from mass culture to culture industry thus went unrecognized in the collection. More significantly, it included pivotal essays produced by key New York Intellectuals influenced by the Institute in their critiques of mass culture during the previous twenty years – Clement Greenberg, Dwight Macdonald and Irving Howe. Rosenberg termed these three 'radicals' who were further 'balanced' with 'arch-conservative' figures like Jose Ortega Y. Gassett as well as 'liberals' like David Riesman.[22] Only Riesman was a common member of this 'cultural' grouping and the Radical Right project. More than any other texts it is this collection, and Shils's critique, that promoted the 'mass culture' legacy of the Frankfurt School and at least implied a commonality with earlier, often avowedly 'elitist' (arch-)conservative critiques. Shils's emphasis on the Frankfurt School's influence on this collection consolidated this 'mass culture' interpretation, even though his critique also drew on further Institute texts which included key statements of the culture industry thesis.[23]

As Shils later indicated, his critique of the mass culture collection formed part of a larger set of reflections on what he regarded as the societally 'alienated' position of many intellectual formations, especially those who were a product of Weimar Germany. This perspective was a precursor to both his anti-communism and his interest in the sociology of intellectual traditions.[24] Accordingly, his argument in 'Daydreams and Nightmares' relies heavily on what now might be called the 'post-Marxist' heritage of many of the contributors, including especially Dwight Macdonald, editor of the 'little magazine', *Politics*. Shils points to another level of intellectual alienation here – the abandonment of confidence in the proletariat as a precondition of the adoption of a mass culture critique.

Macdonald, a former Trotskyist, certainly fitted this trajectory. He had initial hopes of a working-class challenge to fascism but later enthusiastically promoted a critique of mass culture from the early 1940s and for a period maintained close contact with the Institute. But his was only the most prominent instance of borrowings from the Institute by authors in *Politics* and other key little magazines such as *Dissent* (of which Rosenberg was an editor) and *Partisan Review*.[25]

A key source here for the 'radical' New York Intellectuals was the special issue of the Institute's *Zeitschrift* published in 1941 largely devoted to these themes (and the state capitalism thesis). However, another major influence was the considerable success of Fromm's *Escape from Freedom*, published the same year. His conception of a conformist path was linked to the understanding of 'mass culture' this formation adopted. Macdonald also provided the most prominent evidence that such ad hoc borrowings combined quite distinct, even opposed, positions from within the Institute's current and former membership. It was by such means that the 'popular' version of the mass culture thesis attributed to the Frankfurt School emerged: that the working class had been transformed from an oppositional to conformist force by the consumption of 'mass culture', understood primarily as popular literature and Hollywood film; its standardized rhythms achieved this by distraction; mass culture so set an inexorable path towards fascism.

It was Shils's critique, however, that cemented this conflation of the positions adopted by the 'radical' New York Intellectuals, those of the broader Frankfurt School and those employing the culture industry thesis.[26] His 'alienated intellectuals' framework reduces these distinct positions to one deriving from a common form of 'sociological romanticism' which generates 'phantasies about the qualities of the happy pre-mass culture':

> Art and the works of culture in this legendary time were vitally integrated into everyday life, the artist was aware of his function, man was in a state of peaceful self-possession. The mass of the population naturally did not have access to the works of high culture but it had its own art, namely folk art, created by itself and genuinely expressing its own relationship to the universe. Peasant society and aristocratic society had no problem of mass culture ... Men did not seek to 'escape'. If we are to believe what Professors Horkheimer and van den Haag say, pre-modern man was autonomous; he was spontaneous; his life had continuity and distinction.[27]

Of course, it is just this Romantic appeal to a lost organic community that Adorno rejected in *völkisch* thought. To be clear, Shils provides ample evidence that such views were advanced within the radical New York Intellectuals, but he has none that demonstrates that these views ventriloquize those of the Frankfurt School. On each occasion he makes this claim, there is an elision whereby figures like Rosenberg serve as substitutes. For Shils it is nonetheless the Frankfurt School that gives this (German) sociological Romanticism a more Marxian underpinning. He also adds another comment that has been oft-repeated: that this 'European' intellectual legacy was only a theoretical one until the Frankfurt School's 'traumatic' arrival in the USA. There they 'encountered the "mass" in modern society for the first time'. Their views there found 'a traumatic and seemingly ineluctable confirmation in the popular culture of the United States'.

Shils's argument was expanded four years later in an equally influential book, Bramson's *The Political Context of Sociology*.[28] It developed and elaborated Shils's alienated intellectuals framework into an historical account of the negative influence of 'European theories of the mass and mass society' on the development of American sociology. For Bramson, the intervention of European émigrés bearing this approach redirected American sociology from its former normative association with Populism and Progressivism.[29] The mass culture literature was the most significant here as it postulated a linkage between mass culture and 'totalitarianism'. For this he relies explicitly on Shils's 'composite indictment', despite reservations that Shils should have 'tempered' his critique by acknowledging the 'heroic' attempt to join Marx and Freud.[30]

Bramson effectively conflates the categories of 'mass society' and 'mass culture' which Shils had kept formally distinct.[31] By doing so Bramson is able to conflate his discussion of Hannah Arendt's work on totalitarianism with Shils's 'composite indictment' of the mass culture debate. As Jay notes, it is the Frankfurt School's insistence on the continuing existence of class antagonisms that distinguishes its work from those émigrés who adopted the mass society thesis.[32] It is this combined legacy that has tended to frame subsequent understandings of the critique of 'mass culture' – that it was a view that saw a necessary link between mass culture and totalitarianism in Arendt's 'mass society' sense.[33]

While Shils establishes many of the tropes for later dismissive critiques of the Frankfurt School, he does not go as far as the proto-nativist formulation that Bramson, seemingly inadvertently, develops. Pivotal to this is a contrast with a 'native' intellectual tradition informed by the Populist legacy. Although Shils regards his 'trauma' thesis as accounting for an explicit 'anti-American attitude' in the Frankfurt School that fails to sufficiently recognize the USA's 'thriving democracy', US Populism plays no part.[34]

The tell-tale missing element in all these 'mass culture' discussions – aside from the culture industry thesis itself – is demagogy. Demagogy is not included as a 'mass cultural practice' in any of these interpretative texts. Even when the attributed mass culture mischaracterization is directly linked to Studies in Prejudice, as Shils intimates and Bramson does explicitly, it is limited to a generic discussion of *The Authoritarian Personality*. Adorno's demagogy study had not been published at this point (1957–61) but Lowenthal's of course had. Lowenthal's extensive work on popular culture, not least his inclusion in the *Mass Culture* collection, could have played the role of intellectual bridge between even the mischaracterizing mass culture motif and the Institute's work on 'culture-industrial' demagogy.

(c) Cultural populism: deepening the concept

I noted in Chapter 1 that orthodox approaches to populism have largely dissociated themselves from – or simply ignored – 'cultural populism', however defined. That is, the domain of culture, especially aesthetic culture, is not considered of relevance to 'political' populism. In recent critical approaches to populism, only Stuart Hall's work has ventured into this territory systematically as part of his own Gramscian work and his semi-affiliation with the Laclauian project. Much the same can be said of the orthodox literature on political communication, discussed in Chapter 8, although that case is more complex due to its partial recognition of this phenomenon within discussions of tabloid journalism. Hall's influence in broader media and communication studies would again be the most consistent point of linkage.

Indeed, the dominant understanding of the term 'cultural populism' today is also closely tied to the legacy of Stuart Hall's work. 'Cultural populism' was the term McGuigan employed in his very influential 1992 book of the same name and subsequent writings. His chief target was the significant reworking of Hall's position in the 1980s within the post-Birmingham cultural studies project, not only in Britain but in the wider Anglosphere of Australia, Canada and the USA.[35] Building on a critique by James Curran, McGuigan rightly regards this as a 'revisionism' of Hall's and others' earlier, more critical work.[36]

Hall's authoritarian populism thesis moved in tandem with his more influential triple ideal-typification of modes of media 'message' reception: dominant, negotiated, resistant, where the first of these was, in Gramscian terms, a message (prototypically television news) that reproduced elements of a hegemonic ideology. Such a tripartite model of reception, as I noted in Chapter 2(c), was anticipated in *The Authoritarian Personality*. However, in the cultural populist phase of the British cultural studies project, Hall's carefully crafted typology is distorted into a speculative exaggeration of his delimited 'resistant' mode, such that any 'dominant' reception, now of 'popular culture' in general, becomes almost unimaginable.

Consistent with this, McGuigan's own core 'minimalist' definition of cultural populism, on his own later account, is the following:

> Cultural populism is the intellectual assumption, made by some students of popular culture, that the symbolic experiences and practices of ordinary people are more important analytically and politically than Culture with a Capital C.[37]

However, McGuigan warns against the correlate risk of following the practice of many other approaches that are 'silently elitist'. To this extent his book endorses a cultural populism but rejects 'an uncritical drift in the study of popular culture' and seeks to develop a perspective McGuigan calls 'critical populism': 'which can account for both ordinary people's everyday culture and its immediate experience and its material construction by powerful forces beyond the immediate comprehension and control of ordinary people'.[38]

What is most striking about McGuigan's approach in hindsight is its own uncritical orientation to the category of 'popular culture'. Notwithstanding its being productively tied by McGuigan to intellectuals, it is routinely equated with formulations like the 'ordinary tastes and pleasures' cited above. Its intellectual construction as an en bloc category is never seriously questioned. Nor, aside from the invocation of 'ordinary culture', mainly attributed to Raymond Williams, is it subjected to any form of subcategorization. Despite his accurate targeting of such uncritical cultural populism in then contemporary British cultural studies, McGuigan reads the work of the Frankfurt School in toto as '[t]he most theoretically sophisticated version of cultural elitism'.[39]

McGuigan's otherwise well-informed account of British cultural studies, his primary target, misses the fact that the culture industry, as opposed to 'mass culture', concerns of the Frankfurt School were echoed within that tradition at its outset, where these issues were formulated primarily in terms of social class. Contrary to McGuigan's account, Williams's position was never a 'populist' one. It was designed to contest what he later called the 'arrière-garde' position of T.S. Eliot's *Notes Towards a Definition of Culture* (1949) *and* the proto-populist position of Richard Hoggart's *The Uses of Literacy* (1957).[40] These two very different books each relied on an understanding of 'class culture'. Eliot's displayed a quite reactionary hostility to any social democratic challenge to a quasi-aristocratic dominant culture, especially in educational policy. Hoggart's did indeed initiate a kind of cultural-populist framework, in McGuigan's sense, in its celebration of a 'working class culture' that was a considerable legacy for the Birmingham Centre for Contemporary Cultural Studies that he founded. On Williams's reading, Hoggart too readily included all 'popular culture' within that formulation and so overlooked the existence of a culture industry responsible for this popular culture.[41]

So, rather than being an opposition between McGuigan's 'ordinary' popular culture and 'cultural elitism', the British debate in the 1950s was configured more as one concerning the reproduction of class cultures in the context of expanding educational opportunity and a related expanding culture industry, though the latter term was not used as such. Popular culture was already, in 1950s Britain, a contested concept.

These British terms of debate were established contemporaneously with the 'mass culture' debates in the USA – that is, between the early 1940s and late 1950s.[42] The class focus of the British debate partly explains why it did not employ 'mass culture' as a category systematically.[43] As McGuigan acknowledges, cultural populism hardly began with the deformation of the British cultural studies project in the 1980s. Within the intellectual tradition McGuigan examines, such a longer timeframe for cultural populism was in part recognized within E.P. Thompson's *The Making of the English Working Class* in 1963. Although it did not employ the term 'cultural populism', its portrayal of an early nineteenth-century artisanal political culture that included ballads and radical presses significantly contrasted with the less partisan rhetoric of Hoggart and (early) Williams. Its recognition of an aesthetico-cultural dimension to political self-organization provided a lasting legacy for subsequent labour and social movement studies. However, its partisanship also occluded the political ambiguity of these earlier historical phases. Nor did its 'bottom up' focus address the intra-elite dimensions of cultural populism. Both these lacunae had been addressed by Williams in *Culture and Society*.[44]

Within first-generation critical theory it was Lowenthal who provided a comparable historical depth to the Institute's work in this area, while notably preferring to characterize the debate as one concerning 'popular culture' rather than 'mass culture' in most instances. In a series of overlapping historical reconstructions, synopses and commentaries, he tracked debates about art and popular culture from the terms of an even earlier phase – the differing positions of Montaigne and Pascal concerning entertaining diversions and distractions.[45] He also provided a meticulous case study of the debates in eighteenth-century England that took place in *The Tatler*, Addison's *The Spectator* and *The Edinburgh Review* as well as the contributions of Goethe and Schelling in Germany.[46] In both cases he marks a movement from a strategy of educative improvement of the growing reading public to increasing alienation from that public by critics and authors who were, in the main, from the middle class themselves and dependent on that public's loyalty for their income. This was not an 'aristocratic' critique. Lowenthal's argument moves in striking parallel with that of Williams in *Culture and Society* concerning the Romantic avant-garde and anticipates elements of Habermas's literary public-sphere thesis. However, in his only major summation of these debates, Lowenthal laments the lack of historical research tracking positive intellectual assessments of popular culture, which are almost completely absent from his accounts.[47] Cultural populism too is largely absent. I return to his brief solution to this absence in the next section.

The author to whom McGuigan briefly turns to acknowledge the longer lineage of cultural populist debate is Peter Burke who, in 1978, had provided the very form of historical research for which Lowenthal had called.[48] Burke's work on 'the discovery of the people' traces the intellectual fascination with 'popular culture' to the collections of *Volk* materials – notably folksongs – by intellectuals like Herder and the Grimms from the late eighteenth century. He is keen to problematize the *völkisch* assumptions of the many collectors he portrays, especially their belief that the collected folksongs were communally composed and transmitted outside a process of cultural commodification. As we saw, Adorno had challenged this understanding too in 1945.

However, even Burke does not relate his historical reconstruction to the concepts of populism or cultural populism. As Lunn has observed, he ties these developments somewhat closely to the cause of nationalism among subject peoples and especially those opposing the French, understood as the bearers of the aristocratic prejudices of the Enlightenment *philosophes*. While this may seem a pedantic distinction, Lunn's point is that Burke so glosses over the radically democratic and egalitarian dimension of what he himself calls cultural populism.[49] During the period 1770–1870, the European intelligentsia – and their cultural populist positions – were fragmented. The configuration of these cultural populisms was dependent on local political and cultural traditions and not uniformly conservative-nationalistic, as Burke implies. Especially in the early nineteenth century, a 'radically democratic and pre-industrial egalitarian defence of pre-industrial culture' coexisted with the nationalist movements.

Lunn's account thus meets up with elements of Thompson's and Williams's historical work in focusing on the Romantic populist dimensions of the 'discovery of the people'. Like Burke, Lunn recognizes the formulation of organicist metaphors by the Romantic populists which established a set of famous preferences for simplicity, naivete, and archaism over the 'artifical and pseudo-elegant'. Crucially, also, the celebration of the folkloric entailed 'explicitly arguing that creativity flows from below'.[50]

Of all these observers of the debates surrounding popular culture, mass culture and cultural populism, only Lunn developed a viable meta-position that accounts for the contradictions and nuances within 'cultural populism'. This is remarkable given his project was never completed due to his untimely death. It is thus worthy of more detailed attention.

Lunn's comparative assessment of the German, French, US and British cases relies on the specificity of Romantic cultural populist intellectual stances and the available national political cultures.

Herder, who is usually regarded as the fountainhead of the very pluralization of the concept of culture, held to highly egalitarian political positions as well, including 'the self-governance of the *Volk*'. However, not only was he unable to publish these views due to Prussian censorship, but there was no radical-democratic movement with which he might have found a compatible political project. Moreover, despite his own progressive understanding of *Kultur*, Herder's legacy was principally an aesthetic conception of *Volk* practice that became vulnerable to appropriation by conservative and reactionary nationalist forces. These rearticulated the celebration of the *Volk* into that of a deferential role in a mythologized feudal order.

In France, in contrast, Michelet was able to publish historical work that borrowed from popular cultural forms in celebrations of the culture of 'le peuple' (1846) – understood more broadly than an aesthetic dimension – in the wake of the 1789 and 1830 revolutions. An educational programme that sought to reconcile Enlightenment ideals and such Romantic populism held sway in left-intellectual and political circles until the late rise of Marxist influence. It thus bears some resemblance to the subordinated 'making' culture celebrated by Thompson in England. In its advocacy of democratized education and the projection of a modern democratic polity drawing on traditional plebeian conceptions of solidarity, it also anticipates that of the early Williams.

Lunn's meta-level comparativism points to the emergence of class-based discourses as the 'progressive' historical rival to these Romantic populist efforts among intellectuals. These split the broader conception of 'the people' and laid open the prospect of the *völkisch* political mobilization on the right, most obviously in Germany. However, Lunn also points to the historical development of consumer capitalism in the twentieth century 'which was swiftly eroding the fragile working class culture of the late nineteenth century' as a major reason for the failure of Walt Whitman's 'late' intellectual Romantic populism in the USA.[51]

If we return to the USA/UK contrast developed at the opening of this section, Lunn's views are also valuable. He here takes the example of the Romantic socialist author and 'artisanal' manufacturer, William Morris – a major inspiration for both Thompson and Williams. Morris's 'mixture of craft-artisanal cultural populism and democratic radicalism' did find a stronger niche in the UK due, Lunn suggests, to the more central place of the British working class in the British polity and the existence of sympthetic figures within the British intelligentsia. His continuing influence was also aided by the late development of a consumer culture (compared with the USA's).

What emerges from these cases' end-stages for Lunn is the pivotal role played by the degree of 'integration' of the industrial working class into the respective nation-states and the role of the emergent consumer culture in this process. Likewise, a parallel dynamic exists between the fate of a peasant-artisanal culture that is dominantly represented outside urbanized areas and the growth of an urban industrial working class. It is this framework Lunn uses to assess the mass culture debates in the USA in a separate analysis whereby the Frankfurt School and 'liberal-pluralists' like Shils develop 'rival accounts of the containment of radical change, happily consuming and depoliticized publics and a functionally conservative popular culture'.[52]

It is here, however, that Lunn's analysis breaks down in my view. He certainly dismantles the charges of elitism and alienation raised by Shils and carefully distinguishes the technocratic elitism he attributes to the liberal-pluralists (such as Daniel Bell) from the Frankfurt School's critique of 'administered society'. Yet Lunn finds commonality, bizarrely, in the projects of Adorno and orthodox mass communications research, even the so-called 'hypodermic theory' of behavourist media influence. More revealingly, he appears to reject outright the Radical Right project's analysis of McCarthyism and populism in the 1950s and fails to connect this with the Institute's Studies in Prejudice project. Indeed, he apparently sees no linkage between that project and the 'mass culture' debate.[53]

Instead, if we return to Adorno's characterization of contradictory legacy of Romantic folkloricism and 'decultivation', we can see that Lunn's meta-perspective complements Adorno's focus on the 'vacuum' created by the crisis in the the role of the non-professional middle-class cultural intellectuals in the German case. As with Habermas's 1962 re-rendering of this argument as a declining literary public sphere, there is no *fully articulated* 'plebeian' dimension.[54] Lunn's reconstruction provides us with this missing plebeian complement, if only in schematic form.

What then of the culture industry and such plebeian practices? Recent cultural populists simply equate the two, and are vulnerable to Bourdieu's critique of such simplistic reversals. All sophisticated treatments of this issue have recognized the significance of what Adorno distinguished as cultural production/composition, on the one hand, and the 'distribution' focus of the culture industry, on the other.

Adorno, like Williams, initially took the view that there was no longer any folk-*compositional* process. Williams later revised his position and Adorno left open the space of 'popular art'.[55] I redress this lacuna in the final section of this chapter; in the next I address Lunn's nonetheless insightful views of the 'liberal-pluralists'. However, we now have sufficient 'depth' to the concept of cultural populism to conclude the following:

(i) Cultural populism was chiefly constituted by the legacy of Romantic aesthetic populism, a position initially associated with the Romantic avant-garde.
(ii) There was no 'necessary belonging' between this Romantic formulation and conservative-nationalist frameworks; radical-democratic and liberal-educative formulations existed too.
(iii) The consolidation of industrial capitalism bifurcated the 'bottom up' *Volk* culture celebrated by the Romantic populists, forming both an urban industrial working-class 'culture' and an alternative understanding of the people (class/proletariat), from the *Volk*, whose empirical existence was increasingly associated with rural locales.
(iv) The arrival of the culture industry complicated further the developments in (iii), while simultaneously undermining the situation of the Romantic intellectual stratum itself.
(v) The rhythm of these developments unfolded differently in each of the emergent European nation-states and the USA; the reformulations of the elements that comprised Romantic populism were subsequently heavily dependent on the intellectuals/national-popular relationship.

(d) From cultural populism to 'popular arts'

Lunn's typology of liberal-pluralist approaches to mass culture provides three categories:

(1) *Mandarin Optimists* – these include the Daniel Bell of *The End of Ideology* and Shils in their optimism that 'high culture' will continue to play a major role, despite the perceived problems of 'mass culture'.
(2) *Cultural Relativists* – the most prominent here is Herbert Gans whose advocated 'cultural democracy' is the most purely 'liberal-pluralist' approach in that it prioritizes 'taste cultures' as a 'reflection of wants' in an environment of expanded choice rather than any rejection of cultural commodification.
(3) *Aesthetic Populists* – those who discern 'selected figures and forms within mass culture' worthy of serious criticism. The pioneer here is Gilbert Seldes, although his position shifted dramatically in later life.

These are best considered ideal-types as some figures Lunn mentions would appear to sit in more than one category. Significantly, McGuigan's minimalist definition of cultural populism cited in the previous section would correspond more closely with Lunn's cultural relativists rather than his aesthetic populists.[56]

What I want to pursue here, then, is an implication of Lunn's category of aesthetic populism, as it tends to escape broader discussions of mass culture and cultural populism. For such an approach implies a potential commonality with the Institute's work via the embedded conception of aesthetic critique. Indeed, Lowenthal points to the relevance of Gilbert Seldes's work on two occasions, each prospectively. In the more extensive of these discussions Seldes plays a prominent role as one of the 'theoretical defenders of popular art'.[57]

Seldes's *The 7 Lively Arts* was first published in 1924 with a second edition in 1957, in the midst of the US and British debates discussed above. It positioned itself against a genteel tradition of cultural criticism and cultural journalism that would not concern itself at all with the 'lower' forms. Lowenthal cites Seldes's celebration of Herriman's *Krazy Kat* newspaper comic strip (which subsequently achieved considerable 'high' recognition, in part because the newspaper magnate, Randolph Hearst, Herriman's effective patron, moved it from the comics to arts section of his newspapers).

Seldes's cultural-journalistic strategy was very modest: an advocacy of consideration of certain examples of mass/popular culture *as* 'popular art' and thus *worthy of criticism*, not unmitigated 'equalizing' praise as would a cultural relativist (or cultural populist in McGuigan's sense). Indeed, in his other reference to Seldes, Lowenthal is weighing up the question of whether evaluative standards can be applied to popular culture – that is, 'what is "good" and "bad" in the arts and popular culture'.[58] Even then, hierarchicization was not absent. The passage of Seldes's praise for Herriman that Lowenthal cites reads: 'In the second order of the world's art it is superbly first rate!'[59]

Nonetheless, if followed through, the implications of Lowenthal's entertaining such a position for the Institute's conception of aesthetic critique are considerable. In Adorno's practice, the role of immanent critique for both ideologies and art are almost identical in their selection criteria for what was 'worthy' of critique.[60] That is, there needs to be a redemptive potential – 'truth content' – within the 'object' of critique. As we saw in Chapter 2, Nazi discourse fails to meet this criterion of being worthy of the category of ideology. In his discussions of popular song, most evidently, Adorno sidesteps most immanent analysis altogether by discussing instead a manual on popular song writing. As Zuidevaart has suggested, there is a tendency in Adorno's aesthetics to conflate autonomy, truth content and 'social significance'. That is, the critical potential of a work of art is conditional upon its autonomy – or as I'd rather put it, the autonomy of the conditions of composition – and the culture industry erases that possibility.[61]

Nonetheless, there are important – and revealing – counter-tendencies in no less a prominent place than the culture industry fragment of *Dialectic of Enlightenment*. One occurs quite explicitly in the discussion of Hollywood film. In one of his characteristic polemics against the corporate logic of the culture industry which privileges 'box-office success' over any respect for the audience, Adorno points to the subversive elements within what he calls 'popular art' (*volkstümliche Kunst*), *not* 'popular culture':

> The product's tendency to fall back perniciously on the pure nonsense which, as buffoonery and clowning, was *a legitimate part of popular art up to Chaplin and the Marx brothers*, emerges most strikingly in the less sophisticated genres.[62]

Much is revealed in this passage. Here culture-industrial production is found to include, in effect, the 'pernicious' use of elements of a legitimate popular art tradition which, remarkably, survives well into the cinema era. Indeed, despite the past tense in the above, as the Marx Brothers were still producing films as *Dialectic of Enlightenment* was written, this popular art would seem to be still alive for Adorno. As in his approving reference a few pages later to 'those features of the culture industry by which it resembles the circus', the implication is plain – a non-pernicious use of 'buffoonery and clowning' would be more generally possible were it not for the 'monopoly' organization of production that Adorno tends to assume. Even on this point, however, there are exceptions. Adorno recognizes that the film industry permits 'liberal deviations' from its genre formulae, such as the work of Orson Welles, if only for means of self-legitimation of its claims to artistic freedom. It may be that such positive evaluations 'within the margins' were what Horkheimer and Adorno had in mind when they committed to expanding the culture industry fragment in future with an existent draft text in which 'the positive aspects of mass culture will also be dealt with'.[63]

Yet if we return to the passage cited above, there is more than a passing resemblance to Seldes's celebration of the very same figures. Chaplin and the Marx Brothers held a quasi-canonical place in Seldes's book and he details just such a tradition of popular art. More significantly, Seldes emphasizes the conditions of Chaplin's 'autonomy': that he was soon able to self-fund his films and to write his own scripts. Chaplin so broke the Taylorized division of labour more common in the culture industry and consolidated in the Hollywood studio system.[64]

Adorno's late essays, 'Transparencies on Film' and 'Culture Industry Reconsidered' are often considered revisions to the culture industry thesis. Yet Lowenthal complained that the latter's title should have read 'Culture Industry:

A Resumé' and that it contains no 'revisions'.⁶⁵ Likewise, what is notable about the 'Transparencies' essay is the continuity with *both* the culture industry thesis *and* the 'exceptions' I have raised. Chaplin is again a leading example as Adorno focuses on the difficulties of employing the distinction between aesthetic technique and culture-industrial technology in the case of cinema. Chaplin is one of those who would meet his criteria for those who 'rebel against the colossus and thus necessarily forego the advantages of its accumulated potential'.⁶⁶ It is plain that for Adorno Chaplin's work is not following the logic of the culture industry, nor using all its accumulated capacity for 'effects'. Chaplin's work so demonstrates the dilemma of trying to apply the modernist criterion of aesthetic technical advance as a normative aesthetic criterion for cinema.

It is frequently difficult then to separate immanent critical capacity of the work and autonomy from culture industry logic in Adorno's discussions, especially those concerning artistic production that shares elements of the culture industry's enabling technologies. If working independently of the culture industry is itself to 'rebel', then it may seem superfluous to even discuss the aesthetic work so produced immanently. The 'negation' has already been found as 'society projects into film quite differently'. Hence '[t]here can be no aesthetics of the cinema, not even a purely technological one, which would not include the sociology of the cinema'.⁶⁷ Chaplin's work so demonstrates for Adorno both a continuation of a tradition of popular art and an example of cultural production empirically coexistent with the culture industry yet not reducible to it.

I stress that such a view exists at the margins of Adorno's culture industry thesis but is not incompatible with it. While it may have been formed from a background dialogue with 'liberal' sources comparable to those within the demagogy studies, it is similarly compatible with the broader theoretical project. Likewise, while the elaboration of the 'popular arts' framework in the USA continued broadly consistently with Lunn's and Rosenberg's 'liberal' characterization of it, in the UK a different trajectory developed from Seldes's innovation which had a more Marxian direction ... by none other than Stuart Hall.⁶⁸

(e) Popular arts and 'contestation'

Stuart Hall's little discussed first book, co-authored with Paddy Whannel, was published in 1964, shortly after the key 'founding' works of British cultural studies mentioned above. Like comparable works by Williams and Hoggart, it was nominally a teaching manual. However, unlike his British counterparts, Hall opened a dialogue between the British and US approaches to mass/popular culture, including especially the popular arts framework.⁶⁹

Hall's key point of US reference is Arendt's 1961 essay, 'The Crisis in Culture', an earlier version of which had appeared as a response to Shils at a 1960 *Daedalus* symposium on mass media and culture.[70] Arendt sets up a distinction between (aesthetic) culture and entertainment whereby 'culture relates to objects of the world and entertainment is a phenomenon of life'. The latter is characterized by 'functionality' while culture is not so consumed and is 'created not for men but for the world which is meant to outlast the lifespan of mortals'. More fundamentally, 'an object is cultural to the extent to which it can endure'. Her examples of such endurance tend towards 'high art' (including architectural examples like cathedrals).[71]

In what constitutes a chapter-long dialogue with this position, Hall unsettles this entertainment/culture dichotomy by deploying a Romantic conception of folk culture which, for him, 'endures' in a different way. Also avoiding the abrupt dichotomy common to conservative-Romantic historicizations of folk culture, Hall posits a phased historical transition involving mediating institutions, most notably the late nineteenth-century music hall. Thus, folk culture is regarded as including both rural and urban industrial forms: 'traditional rural songs and airs ... urban broadsides and ballads, work songs and songs of protest' as well as dances, games and craft labour practices. It was 'handed down, with slight variation, from one generation to the next'.[72] Hall carefully negotiates the consequences of regarding the rural forms of these practices as embedded in a quasi-communal 'way of life', even 'communal creators' within 'organic community'. The latter term had featured prominently in the more conservative arguments of F.R. Leavis, a significant influence, to different degrees, on Hall, Hoggart and Williams.

In contrast, Hall emphasizes the continuities between this folkloric tradition and the hybrid forms that emerged in music hall. The rapport between its productions and a stratified urban population – while recognizing the increasing individuation of performance – provided a continuity with the folkloric, despite the reduction in opportunities for participation. It is here that Hall places the emergence of 'popular art' in the performative conventions shared by performer and audience in the 'transitional' form of music hall. While the performers were now professional individuals in a commercial enterprise, these reaffirming conventions delimited the degree to which the performer is distanced from the audience.

When tracing these conventions through to the 'modern media', Hall works with a key example of a 'popular artist' in cinema, none other than Chaplin (whose career began in music hall):

> If we think of the best of Chaplin ... we begin to understand more clearly the place of popular art in the new media ... [It] ... is improvised out of the common experiences which audience and performer share, and

those experiences, known and familiar, are deepened when re-enacted. But in the modern media, that re-enactment is necessarily performed by the true popular artist who does, with the force and imprint of personal style, what 'folk poets' of an earlier period did 'instinctively' (a shorthand method of accounting for what ... was a highly complex process of making art communally). The common qualities are heightened and strengthened in performance by the use of familiar conventions and compression and stylization – Charlie's [i.e. Chaplin's] regalia or his walk, for example. And the quality of style suggests not only the way in which the popular artist makes *art* of the welter of experiences which he draws on, but the *respect* which he always holds for both his art and his audience. It is expressive of popular taste but does not exploit it.[73]

Hall contrasts this form of cultural production with a conception of 'mass culture' derived from Macdonald, Hoggart and (very briefly) Adorno and Simpson's 'On Popular Music'. Mass culture consists of 'mass art' which is produced by 'corrupting' popular art exploitatively – standardization and formulaic production turn the popular conventions and stylizations into stereotypes.

What is striking about this perspective is its curious compatibility with Adorno's, down to the example of Chaplin, while superficially also being at odds with it. Hall celebrates jazz as relentlessly as Adorno condemns it; but Hall's perspective would likely recognize the forms of jazz Adorno condemns – the big band music of the 1940s – as 'corrupted popular art' compared to that which he celebrates. His own counter-examples of culture industry logic, based on interview citations, are tellingly Adornian: Liberace's revelation of the 'tricks' of his kitsch based on a low estimation of his audience's listening capacity and a UK commercial television controller's frank statement of his estimation of his audience's 'intelligence quotient'.[74]

Indeed, Hall's mediating role for popular art was echoed soon afterwards in the emergent sociology of the 'new' popular music.[75] Although Hall initially presents a panoply of folk practices, music and comedy are the two main cultural forms he follows from music hall to popular art (including cinema) to mass art. It is popular music today that most resembles the music hall milieu Hall recognizes as transitional *and* the features he attributes to jazz and the early skiffle movement in Britain. Hall stresses that his popular artists could challenge their audiences while 'the mass artist seems to be in total subjection to this audience'.[76] Yet this is not quite an Adornian model of aesthetic autonomy due to Hall's criterion of maintaining familiarity with popular conventions. Hall's dialogical conception of convention is more subtle than popular music criticism's more polemical celebrations of 'authenticity', although the latter does have a latent presence in Hall. 'Authenticity' has frequently been used as an attempted check on the expansion of compositional and virtuoso complexity, Adorno's cultural productive forces, by popular musicians.[77]

Simon Frith, a pioneer in the sociology of rock as a popular music genre and subsequently popular music more generally, provided a critique of cultural populism that slightly predated McGuigan's. He emphasized the failure of the cultural populists in British cultural studies to recognize the difference between market success and 'popularity' as popular music fans also demonstrate evaluative judgements that do not correspond with market categories. To put this another way, the en bloc conception of popular culture frequently reveals a lack of knowledge of the conventions and genres of specific cultural forms and cultural institutions – the very elements Hall highlighted within 'popular art'. Even more bluntly, cultural populism has no capacity to distinguish between Hall's popular art and mass art. As Frith points out, this 'lack of sociological sophistication' was closely tied to the correspondingly en bloc application of (formalist) semiotic techniques of textual analysis to this 'popular culture'.[78] As in the critique of Laclau's hyperformalism, formalist methods once again find an elective affinity with a 'lack of sociological sophistication'.

The publication of *The Popular Arts* marked a 'moment' when critical theory and the nascent British cultural studies were on common ground, if not in serious dialogue. These quasi-Adornian dimensions continued into the Birmingham project as a subordinate discourse – its house journal even published the first English translation of Adorno's 'Theses on the Sociology of Art' and at least one attempt was made there to develop a 'cultural study of music' employing Adorno.[79]

Hall subsequently abandoned the popular arts perspective and adopted the en bloc conception of popular culture I have introduced. His most famous dismissive statement on 'popular culture' was introduced in Chapter 4(d) as an example of his instrumentalism. Aimed at members of a self-identifying socialist conference, he presented a straw figure mechanistic dichotomization of potential definitions of popular culture, viz.: an 'anti' one that roughly corresponds to his own former definition of 'mass art' in content to which is added the crudest assumptions of 'manipulation' of its consumers; and an entirely non-normative descriptive one based in a 'way of life' conception of culture.[80]

Against these straw figures he posits his own 'dialectical' definition: that popular culture is constituted by 'forms and activities which have their social and material roots in the social and material conditions of particular classes' and exist in a permanent tension with a dominant culture. Popular culture so becomes a dynamic field of domination and subordination that is permanently negotiated. In short, it is part of the terrain of hegemonic contestation of the Gramscian 'national-popular'. Hall so locates popular culture within his contemporaneous work on modes of political populism. He also revises/abandons the class-specific elements of his own definition and speaks of 'popular' in almost entirely Laclauian terms – the 'popular classes' who are constituted as 'the people' in moments of counter-hegemonic struggle against 'the power-bloc', the alliance of forces in holding (state-hegemonic) power.

Rather than being dialectical, this position's instrumental polarization is unrelenting: if 'we' are not constituted as part of the 'the people versus the power bloc', 'we will be constituted as its opposite force: an effective populist force, saying yes to power'. The particular example Hall proffers is highly pertinent: the contemporary political struggle in Britain to contain the rise of the National Front during the first years of Thatcherism (and, I would add, the uprisings that year against police mistreatment of minority communities in most of England's inner cities). Hall cites the considerable success of the Midlands-based 'Two-Tone Sound', though does not detail this.[81] 'Two-Tone' referred in part to the hybridity of black and white band members in each of these groups and to their popular musical innovation: a reggae and ska-dominant musical revival that spoke to this moment musically, lyrically and performatively. The Specials' 'Ghost Town' rose up the charts as youths clashed with police.[82]

It is worth noting that the Two-Tone Sound also meets Hall's earlier definition of popular art – it established a set of conventions with its audience and, like much of the emergent 'indie' forms of musical production of that period, eschewed any easy exploitation of the respect it built with that audience. Contingently, one might add that such a development was indeed vulnerable to a 'mass art' standardization, as the rise of the 'whitened' version of this sound in later years soon demonstrated. Although Hall's Gramscian perspective might recognize such a process as 'hegemonic incorporation', it does not capture the processual culture-industry dynamic of his former position.

Hall's 'Notes on Deconstructing the Popular' is perhaps most famous for the colloquial shorthand for his first definition's allegedly embedded derision for the 'manipulated' consumers of popular culture: 'cultural dopes'. The Frankfurt School is not mentioned here but strongly implied.[83] In contemporaneous essays on media research, Hall completely adopts Bramson's framework of interpretation (introduced above) and equates the Institute's work with 'mass society' and 'mass communication' approaches adopted within 'American empirical social science practice'.[84] In short, the political instrumentalization of an en bloc 'popular culture' in Hall's later position laid the ground for McGuigan's 'cultural populism'. 'Popular culture' could only be assessed as an instrumental force in the constitutive struggle between 'the people' and 'the power bloc'. As we saw in Chapter 4, this post-Laclauian framework has no capacity to recognize demagogic practices.

The collapsing of 'popular arts' into a politically instrumentalized 'popular culture' left no room for any immanent dimension to 'popular arts'. If the only value of 'popular culture' was 'constituting the people' then its role was primarily organizational in a mechanistic sense and not necessarily consistent with the Gramscian national-popular strategy. Ideology critique in the Institute's sense was certainly not required. It is true that Hall's earlier conception of popular art was too constrained by its literary-critical conception of 'evaluation' – and of course the unavailability in English of the most relevant Institute texts – to recognize this potentiality. Yet it was not inconsistent with it.

If demagogy is neglected by Hall, how can such an analysis address it? Adorno certainly identified some specific culture industry 'genre' production directly with the demagogic. These tended to be those that echoed the 'synthetic *völkisch*' characteristics he warned of in 1945. But, as we have seen, a more differentiated understanding emerges from Adorno's and Lowenthal's work on both demagogy and culture industry/popular art, especially when informed by Lunn's incomplete project on cultural populism. Following from my summation above, the Romantic cultural populist legacy can indeed be inflected towards a modern *völkisch* demagogy. But the preconditions of this include all the contingencies listed above in (c) plus the following (which continues the former numbering):

(vi) an intellectual formation lacking a socio-historical understanding of the folk and popular art traditions and socio-aesthetic conventions that are naively championed as an en bloc 'culture of the people'/popular culture
(vii) a 'vacuum' in Adorno's sense whereby a complete break has occurred in the aesthetico-political terrain of the national-popular resulting in a lack of hegemonic cultural leadership
(viii) the entry of demagogues, including 'cultural demagogues', who understand such a conjuncture as an opportunity and assemble a demagogic synthesis of elements from the cultural-popular traditions.

It follows too that such demagogues need some understanding of the aesthetico-political field and thus need not necessarily emerge from orthodox political organizations or parliamentary chambers. Indeed, as Coughlin demonstrated, they may be demagogues who emerge instead via the culture industry itself.

Fredric Jameson once argued that Raymond Williams's conception of hegemony offered a more 'modern' theory of culture than the account of the culture industry in *Dialectic of Enlightenment*. He implied the two might be complementary. Yet he omitted the fact that Williams's reworking of the Gramscian schema provided a central role for *traditions* and his own practice had often been focused on the development of 'modern' counter-traditions.[85] Adorno's own view of traditions was wary in the case of literature.[86] However, as we have seen, he assumed the existence of one in the case of 'legitimate popular art'. In Chapter 7 I present a counter-demagogic 'selective tradition' in Williams's sense that draws on the conception of 'popular art' developed above.

Notes

1 Roger Griffin, 'Fascism and Culture: A Mosse-Centric Meta-Narrative (or How Fascist Studies Reinvented the Wheel)', in *Rethinking the Nature of Fascism*, ed. António Costa Pinto (Basingstoke: Palgrave, 2011), 86. The 'thugs' characterization of early fascism studies is cited from Emilio Gentile's reconstruction of the foundational work of George L. Mosse, to which Griffin's title refers. Gentile's own work marks key turning points in this field. Curiously, Griffin also charges the Frankfurt School, Benjamin excepted, with a failure to recognize this 'cultural' connection with fascism. Cf. George L. Mosse, *The Crisis of German Ideology: Intellectual Origins of the Third Reich*, 1st ed. (New York: Grosset & Dunlap, 1964); Emilio Gentile, *The Origins of Fascist Ideology 1918–1925*, trans. Robert L. Miller (New York: Enigma Books, 2005); Emilio Gentile, *The Struggle for Modernity: Nationalism, Futurism, and Fascism*, trans. Stanley G. Payne (Westport, Conn.: Praeger, 2003).
2 Adrian Lyttelton, 'Futurism, Politics and Society', in *Italian Futurism 1909–1944: Reconstructing the Universe*, ed. Vivien Greene (New York: Guggenheim, 2014).
3 Cf. Table 1. See, for example, Bendix's account of the Romantic origins of this term in US folklore studies. Regina Bendix, *In Search of Authenticity: The Formation of Folklore Studies* (Madison, Wis.: University of Wisconsin Press, 1997).
4 Raymond Williams, *Culture and Society: 1780–1950* (London: Chatto & Windus, 1958), 30–48. Leo Lowenthal, *Literature, Popular Culture and Society* (Englewood Cliffs, NJ: Prentice-Hall, 1961), 28–29.
5 Pierre Bourdieu, 'The Uses of the "People" (1982)', in *In Other Words: Essays Towards a Reflexive Sociology* (Cambridge: Polity, 1990), 154.
6 David B. Dennis, *Inhumanities: Nazi Interpretations of Western Culture* (Cambridge: Cambridge University Press, 2012).
7 Jeffrey Herf, *Reactionary Modernism: Technology, Culture, and Politics in Weimar and the Third Reich* (Cambridge: Cambridge University Press, 1984), 9.
8 Mosse's is the classic study which in turn influenced the Italian 'cultural turn' discussed above: Mosse, *The Crisis of German Ideology*.
9 Theodor W. Adorno, 'Résumé Über Kulturindustrie', in *Ohne Leitbild: Parva Aesthetics* (Frankfurt: Suhrkamp Verlag, 1967), 60. Adorno, 'Culture Industry Reconsidered (1967)'.
10 Theodor W. Adorno, 'What National Socialism Has Done to the Arts (1945)', in *Essays on Music*, ed. Richard D. Leppert (Los Angeles: University of California Press, 2002), 374.
11 Theodor W. Adorno, 'On the Question: "What Is German?" (1965)', in *Critical Models: Interventions and Catchwords* (New York: Columbia University Press, 1998), 207. Mosse, *The Crisis of German Ideology*, 93–97.
12 Adorno, 'What National Socialism Has Done to the Arts (1945)', 374.
13 Cf. Chapter 2(b).
14 Adorno, 'On the Question: "What Is German?" (1965)', 209.
15 Adorno, 'What National Socialism Has Done to the Arts (1945)', 382.

16 Béla Bartók, 'Race Purity in Music', *Tempo*, no. 8 (1944). David Cooper, 'Béla Bartók and the Question of Race Purity in Music', in *Musical Constructions of Nationalism: Essays on the History of European Musical Culture 1800–1945*, ed. Harry White and Michael Murphy (Cork: Cork University Press, 2001).
17 Theodor W. Adorno, *Philosophy of New Music*, trans. Robert Hullot-Kentor (Minneapolis: University of Minnesota Press, 2006), n4, 176.
18 Adorno, 'What National Socialism Has Done to the Arts (1945)', 378.
19 Habermas, *The Structural Transformation of the Public Sphere*. See Chapter 8.
20 Martin Jay, 'The Frankfurt School in Exile (1972)', in *Permanent Exiles: Essays on the Intellectual Migration from Germany to America* (New York: Columbia University Press, 1986), 51; Shils, 'Authoritarianism: Right and Left.'; Edward A. Shils, 'Daydreams and Nightmares: Reflections on the Criticism of Mass Culture', *The Sewanee Review* 65, no. 4 (1957).
21 Bernard Rosenberg and David M. White, eds, *Mass Culture: The Popular Arts in America* (Glencoe, Ill.: Free Press, 1957).; Richard Hoggart, *The Uses of Literacy: Aspects of Working-Class Life, with Special Reference to Publications and Entertainments* (London: Chatto and Windus, 1957). The Hoggart book, discussed further in the next section, accounts for only a few sentences in Shils's 11-page article.
22 Bernard Rosenberg, 'Mass Culture in America', in *Mass Culture: The Popular Arts in America*, ed. Bernard Rosenberg and David M. White (Glencoe, Ill.: Free Press, 1957).
23 Shils also references: *Dialectic of Enlightenment* (then untranslated into English); Adorno's 'On Popular Music'; Adorno and Simpson, 'On Popular Music' and Horkheimer's 'Art and Mass Culture', *Zeitschrift für Sozialforschung* 9, no. 2 (1941); as well as Fromm's *Escape from Freedom*.
24 Edward A. Shils, *The Intellectuals and the Powers and Other Essays* (Chicago: University of Chicago Press, 1972).
25 I rely here considerably on Wheatland's account which in turn draws on that of Gorman. Wheatland, *The Frankfurt School in Exile*, 177–188; Paul R. Gorman, *Left Intellectuals & Popular Culture in Twentieth-Century America* (Chapel Hill: University of North Carolina Press, 1996). See also Rabinbach, 'German-Jewish Connections: The New York Intellectuals and the Frankfurt School in Exile'.
26 At a key point Shils runs together citations from Horkheimer's 'Art and Mass Culture' and Rosenberg's introduction and then footnotes: '[t]he words are Mr Rosenberg's, but the ideas are the common property of the critics'. Likewise the citations at this point from Horkheimer conflate his characterization of the Kantian 'purely aesthetic feeling' held by 'the private atomic subject' of the bourgeois family with his account of the *loss* of such privacy Shils, 'Daydreams and Nightmares: Reflections on the Criticism of Mass Culture', 597–598; Cf. Horkheimer, 'Art and Mass Culture', 290–294.
27 Shils, 'Daydreams and Nightmares: Reflections on the Criticism of Mass Culture', 598. Van der Haag was a contemporary conservative included in the *Mass Culture* collection. Gans paraphrases this entire passage, with attribution, in his *Popular Culture and High Culture: An Analysis and Evaluation of Taste (Revd Edn)*, 2nd edn (New York: Basic Books, 1999), 68–69.
28 Leon Bramson, *The Political Context of Sociology* (Princeton, NJ: Princeton University Press, 1961). Bramson's text was quite influential on the Birmingham cultural studies project (next section) where a copy held in its library was highly recommended to students (when I was a graduate student there in 1981/82). For an indicative usage

see Tony Bennett, 'Theories of the Media, Theories of Society', in *Culture, Society and the Media*, ed. M. Gurevitch et al. (London: Routledge, 1982). Storey's textbook rendering from this intellectual tradition has recommended Bramson's account of the mass culture debate as 'illuminating' through its eight traditions over twenty-five years John Storey, *Cultural Theory and Popular Culture: An Introduction*, 8th edn (London: Routledge, 2018).

29 Remarkably, Gorman approvingly cites this argument in his conclusion: Gorman, *Left Intellectuals & Popular Culture in Twentieth-Century America*, 188.
30 Bramson, *The Political Context of Sociology*, 125n, 127.
31 Shils nonetheless effectively attributes a model of a mass society of isolated individuals to Horkheimer in his misreading of the 'Art and Mass Culture' essay (Cf. note above). In two later essays which draw on elements of this critique, Shils elaborates the connections he sees between the mass society and mass culture theses but does so by reconstituting 'mass society' with his own more positive portrayal of the same transformations which he regards as redressing the imbalance in the (unnamed) mass society theorists by including neglected elements which provide evidence of the inclusion of the periphery into the 'moral consensus' of the centre. Edward A. Shils, 'Mass Society and Its Culture', in *Culture for the Millions?*, ed. Norman Jacobs (Princeton: D. Van Nostrand Co., 1961); Edward A. Shils, 'The Theory of Mass Society: Prefatory Remarks', *Diogenes* 10, no. 39 (1962).
32 Jay, 'The Frankfurt School in Exile (1972)', 51. See the parallel and more developed argument in Eugene Lunn, 'The Frankfurt School in the Development of the Mass Culture Debate', *Journal of Comparative Literature and Aesthetics* XI, nos 1–2 (1988): 12–13.
33 See, for example, the account of 'the Frankfurt School's theory of mass society' in Swingewood's *The Myth of Mass Culture*; Alan Swingewood, *The Myth of Mass Culture* (London: Macmillan, 1977), 13ff., although Swingewood employs C. Wright Mills rather than Arendt.
34 Shils, 'Daydreams and Nightmares: Reflections on the Criticism of Mass Culture', 600, 601n.
35 Jim McGuigan, *Cultural Populism* (London: Routledge, 1992); Jim McGuigan, 'Cultural Populism Revisited', in *Cultural Studies in Question*, ed. M. Ferguson and P. Golding (London: Sage, 1997); Jim McGuigan, 'Cultural Studies and the New Populism', in *Encyclopedia of Social Theory*, ed. George Ritzer (London: Sage, 2005); Jim McGuigan, 'From Cultural Populism to Cool Capitalism', *Art & the Public Sphere* 1, no. 1 (2011). I also draw here on my own somewhat differently inflected account which is related to McGuigan's later work on a 'cultural public sphere'. Paul K. Jones, 'Beyond the Semantic "Big Bang": Cultural Sociology and an Aesthetic Public Sphere', *Cultural Sociology* 1, no. 1 (2007).
36 James Curran, 'The New Revisionism in Mass Communication Research: A Reappraisal', *European Journal of Communication* 5, no. 2 (1990).
37 McGuigan, *Cultural Populism*, 4.
38 McGuigan, *Cultural Populism*, 4–5. McGuigan here partly alludes to the then-prominent divide between 'cultural studies' approaches that were cultural populist in McGuigan's sense and relied primarily on variants of semiotic analysis, on the one hand, and a British political economy of media and culture tradition, on the other.
39 McGuigan, *Cultural Populism*, 47. McGuigan relies heavily at this point on Andrew Ross's characterization of the relationship between the Frankfurt School and the US debates regarding mass culture. Andrew Ross, *No Respect: Intellectuals &*

Popular Culture (New York: Routledge, 1989). Ross conflates many different positions in his account, most notably those of Hannah Arendt and the Frankfurt School. Curran's 'revisionism' article likewise refers to 'the elitist pessimism about mass culture that was a significant strand within the radical tradition, represented by the Frankfurt school'. Curran, 'The New Revisionism in Mass Communication Research: A Reappraisal', 154.

40 T.S. Eliot, *Notes Towards the Definition of Culture* (London: Faber & Faber, 1948); Hoggart, *The Uses of Literacy*. See Jones, *Raymond Williams's Sociology of Culture: A Critical Reconstruction* for more detail.
41 Jones, *Raymond Williams's Sociology of Culture: A Critical Reconstruction*.
42 The two traditions had relatively little contact at the time. But see Dwight Macdonald's review of Williams's *The Long Revolution*. Dwight MacDonald, 'Looking Backward', *Encounter* 16, no. 6 (1961); Raymond Williams, *The Long Revolution* (London: Chatto & Windus, 1961).
43 McGuigan rightly points to Williams's overall suspicion of 'mass' in *Culture and Society* because of its rhetorical equation with 'mob' by figures like Matthew Arnold during the Chartist campaigns. However, he revised this position in later years, not least because of its mobilizing usage in the Marxist political tradition. He remained suspicious, for related but more complex reasons, of 'mass communication' and regarded the Frankfurt School's US work as tainted by its association with US sociology's 'mass society' formulations and functionalist imperatives. Nonetheless, his own work increasingly affiliated itself with the Frankfurt School tradition as he came to know it. Jones, *Raymond Williams's Sociology of Culture: A Critical Reconstruction*. See especially Raymond Williams, 'On Reading Marcuse', *Cambridge Review* 90, no. 30 (1969).
44 E.P. Thompson, *The Making of the English Working Class* (London: Victor Gollancz, 1963).
45 'Historical Perspectives of Popular Culture' (1950), The Debate over Art and Popular Culture in Eighteenth Century England' (1957, with Marjorie Fiske) and 'The Debate over Art and Popular Culture: a synopsis' (1960) were all republished and/or revised in: Lowenthal, *Literature, Popular Culture and Society*.
46 Lowenthal, *Literature, Popular Culture and Society*, 52–108, 118–125.
47 Lowenthal, *Literature, Popular Culture and Society*, 45–51.
48 McGuigan, *Cultural Populism*, 10, 17; Peter Burke, *Popular Culture in Early Modern Europe* (New York: Harper & Row, 1978). Lowenthal appears to have been unaware of this text that would also have met his requirements.
49 Eugene Lunn, 'Cultural Populism and Egalitarian Democracy', *Theory and Society* 15, no. 4 (1986): n12 511.
50 Lunn, 'Cultural Populism and Egalitarian Democracy', 482–483.
51 Other factors included the dominantly patrician high culture which isolated Whitman. But Lunn notes that Whitman's project was not appropriated by the political right as a result. Lunn, 'Cultural Populism and Egalitarian Democracy', 509–510.
52 Lunn, 'The Frankfurt School in the Development of the Mass Culture Debate', 19.
53 Here, I speculate, we reach the limits of what Lunn was able to achieve in this part of his project at a time of failing health. While this position is somewhat similar to that he asserts in his earlier *Marxism and Modernism*, it is notable that these points are made rather abruptly and without his usual careful attention to primary sources. While he goes on to provide his fruitful typology of the liberal-pluralists approaches to mass culture, discussed in the next section, there is little to no comparable attention to the culture industry thesis. A better indication of where Lunn intended

to take this critique can be found in the final fragment of his published project, a comparison of Hoggart and Riesman: 'Beyond "Mass Culture": *The Lonely Crowd, the Uses of Literacy, and the Postwar Era*', Theory and Society 19, no. 1 (1990). There he provides a subtler consideration of the then-prominent cultural studies project, chiefly in its endnotes. Sadly too, Lunn did not live to see the publication of McGuigan's book in 1992. Nor does he seem to have been aware of the cultural populist turn in British cultural studies as his discussions only cite Birmingham material up to the late 1970s.

54 See Chapter 8.
55 Jones, *Raymond Williams's Sociology of Culture: A Critical Reconstruction*.
56 This is notwithstanding McGuigan's definition's effective reversal of the high/low binary whereby popular culture is valued more highly by his cultural populists. McGuigan himself draws somewhat scattered comparisons between structural-functionalist approaches (initially associated with *both* Shils and Gans) and elements of 'uncritical' cultural populism in British cultural studies, notably in the shift from productionist to consumptionist approaches to subcultures and media decoding within and beyond the Birmingham project McGuigan, *Cultural Populism*, 48, 90, 126.
57 Lowenthal, *Literature, Popular Culture and Society*, xx–xxi, 48.
58 Lowenthal, *Literature, Popular Culture and Society*, xx–xxi.
59 Gilbert Seldes, *The 7 Lively Arts*, 2nd edn (New York: Sagamore Press, 1957), 207. Cf. Lowenthal, *Literature, Popular Culture and Society*, 48.
60 Two key texts that speak to the aesthetic application of ideology critique: Theodor W. Adorno, 'Cultural Criticism and Society', in *Prisms* (London: Neville Spearman, 1967); Theodor W. Adorno, 'On Lyric Poetry and Society (1957)', in *Notes to Literature: Volume One* (New York: Columbia University Press, 1991).
61 Lambert Zuidervaart, Adorno's Aesthetic Theory: The Redemption of Illusion (Cambridge, Mass.: MIT Press, 1991).
62 Italicization added. I follow the available translations of Adorno's 'Volk' formulations as 'popular' but am aware that 'folk' is a very likely alternative. The key point, however, is the use of 'Kunst' rather than 'Kultur'. Horkheimer and Adorno, *Dialectic of Enlightenment*, 109; Max Horkheimer and Theodor W. Adorno, *Dialektik Der Aufklärung: Philosophische Fragmente* (Frankfurt: Fischer Taschenbuch Verlag, 2006), 146.
63 That expansion never occurred and the commitment was deleted in the 1947 edition's preface. Such a text did emerge posthumously as 'The Schema of Mass Culture'. However, as Bernstein noted in introducing its first English translation, the Schema is 'the darkest and most prescient of Adorno's writings on culture'. J.M. Bernstein, 'Introduction', in *Adorno, T.W. The Culture Industry: Selected Essays on Mass Culture* ed. J.M. Bernstein (London: Routledge, 1991), 10. 'The Schema of Mass Culture' was also the name given to the entire draft from which both texts were drawn. It would seem then that the second text was never changed following the publication of *Dialectic*. Cf. G. Schmid Noerr, 'Editor's Afterword', in *Dialectic of Enlightenment: Philosophical Fragments*, ed. G. Schmid Noerr (Stanford: Stanford University Press, 2002). Peters has suggested that the draft of Adorno and Eisler's *Composing for Films* may have been another possible source for this promised 'positive view' of mass culture. Its preface (by Eisler) states: 'The art of Charles Chaplin proved to be a continuous inspiration.' John Durham Peters, 'The Subtlety of Horkheimer and Adorno: Reading "The Culture Industry"', in *Canonic Texts in Media Research: Are There Any? Should There Be? How About These?*, ed. Elihu Katz et al. (Cambridge: Polity, 2003), 65; Hanns Eisler and Theodor W. Adorno, *Composing for the Films* (London: Athlone Press, 1994), 1.

64 Seldes, *The 7 Lively Arts*.
65 Adorno, 'Culture Industry Reconsidered (1967)'; Theodor W. Adorno, 'Transparencies on Film (1966)', *New German Critique*, no. 24/25 (1981). Leo Lowenthal, 'Adorno and His Critics (1978)', in *Critical Theory and Frankfurt Theorists: Lectures, Correspondence, Conversations* (New Brunswick, NJ: Transaction, 2016).
66 Adorno, 'Transparencies on Film (1966)', 199.
67 Adorno, 'Transparencies on Film (1966)', 202.
68 A good example of a US elaboration of the popular arts framework is: Russel B. Nye, *The Unembarrassed Muse: The Popular Arts in America* (New York: Dial Press, 1970).
69 For space reasons, from hereon I refer to Hall as author of this text. Stuart Hall and Paddy Whannel, *The Popular Arts* (London: Hutchinson, 1964). Cf. Raymond Williams, *Reading and Criticism* (London: Frederick Muller, 1950).; Richard Hoggart, *Teaching Literature* (London: National Institute of Adult Education, 1963). Unlike Williams's and Hoggart's 'literature' manuals, Hall's is comparably focused on film and grew out of his and Whannel's work for the British Film Institute (BFI). Cf. Chris Rojek, *Stuart Hall* (Cambridge: Polity, 2002), 62. Thus Williams's own little-known book on cinema is the strongest influence from that tradition: Raymond Williams and Michael Orrom, *Preface to Film* (London: Film Drama Ltd, 1954). Extended discussions of *The Popular Arts* occur in Procter's and Davis's books on Hall but, like Turner's influential history of British cultural studies, tie the book solely to the British tradition and miss its uniquely transatlantic dimensions (with Davis even claiming Hall invented the term). James Procter, *Stuart Hall* (London: Routledge, 2004); Helen Davis, *Understanding Stuart Hall* (London: Sage, 2004). Turner's view that it has 'good intentions' but 'is limited by the lack of more appropriate analytical tools' is indicative of its placement in cultural studies. *British Cultural Studies: An Introduction*, 2nd ed. (London: Routledge, 1996), 68. *The Popular Arts* is omitted completely in the somewhat exhaustive overview of this literature by Hall's then Open University colleague, Tony Bennett, 'Theories of the Media, Theories of Society.' For an important corrective, see: James Curran, 'Stuart Hall Redux: His Early Work, 1964–1984', in *Stuart Hall: Conversations, Projects, and Legacies*, ed. Julian Henriques, David Morley and Vana Goblot (London: Goldsmiths Press, 2017).
70 Hannah Arendt, *Between Past and Future: Six Exercises in Political Thought* (New York: Viking, 1961), 197–226. Cf. Hannah Arendt, 'Society and Culture', in *Culture for the Millions?: Mass Media in Modern Society*, ed. Norman Jacobs (Princeton, NJ: Van Norstrand Press, 1961). and Shils, 'Mass Society and Its Culture.'.
71 Arendt, *Between Past and Future: Six Exercises in Political Thought*, 208–209.
72 Hall and Whannel, *The Popular Arts*, 52.
73 Hall and Whannel, *The Popular Arts*, 64–65.
74 Hall and Whannel, *The Popular Arts*, 70–72.
75 Laing's *The Sound of Our Time* (London: Sheed & Ward, 1969). worked with a very similar tripartite model. Hall's book, in a kind of addendum, even recognized the then-nascent capacity of The Beatles to transcend the limitations of 'mass art' *The Popular Arts*, 312.
76 Hall and Whannel, *The Popular Arts*, 70.
77 John J. Sheinbaum, 'Progressive Rock and the Inversion of Musical Values', in *Progressive Rock Reconsidered*, ed. K. Holm-Hudson (London: Routledge, 2002).
78 Simon Frith, 'The Good, the Bad, and the Indifferent: Defending Popular Culture from the Populists', *Diacritics* 21, no. 4 (1991): 104–105. Regrettably, Frith also commits all the familiar misreadings of the culture industry thesis in this essay discussed earlier in this chapter. For an excellent case study critique of intellectual

misrecognition of popular musical conventions, see Andrew Goodwin's *Dancing in the Distraction Factory: Music Television and Popular Culture* (Minneapolis: University of Minnesota Press, 1992). Goodwin dismantles formalist film theorists' attempts to interpret the emergent form of rock video in the 1980s.
79 Theodor W. Adorno, 'Theses on the Sociology of Art', *Working Papers in Cultural Studies* 2 (1972); Dick Bradley, 'The Cultural Study of Music: A Theoretical and Methodological Introduction', *Birmingham CCCS Stencilled Occasional Paper* 61 (1979). Goodwin's book cited above also started out as a Birmingham doctoral thesis.
80 Hall, 'Notes on Deconstructing "the Popular"', 117, 117n.
81 Hall, 'Notes on Deconstructing "the Popular"', 238–239.
82 For a more detailed account of this movement see Dick Hebdige, *Cut 'N' Mix: Culture, Identity and Caribbean Music*, A Comedia Book (London: Methuen, 1987), 106–117.
83 However, Hall's colleague Tony Bennett at the Open University (where both were located at this point) later 'joined the dots' to directly associate the 'cultural dopes' position with the Institute's culture industry thesis. For Bennett it was 'the paradigm case'. Tony Bennett, 'The Politics of The "Popular" and Popular Culture', in *Popular Culture and Social Relations*, ed. Tony Bennett, Colin Mercer and Janet Woollacott (Milton Keynes: Open University Press, 1986), 16–17.
84 Hall, 'Introduction to Media Studies at the Centre', 117, 117n; Stuart Hall, 'The Rediscovery of Ideology: Return of the Repressed in Media Studies', in *Culture, Society and the Media*, ed. M. Gurevitch, T. Bennett, J. Curran and J. Woollacott (London: Routledge, 1982). Hall cites Bramson explicitly in the first but does not in the second, even though his debt there is more obvious.
85 Fredric Jameson, *Late Marxism: Adorno, or, the Persistence of the Dialectic* (London: Verso, 1990), 143–144. Raymond Williams, *Marxism and Literature* (Oxford: Oxford University Press, 1977), 115–120; Paul K. Jones, 'Marxist Cultural Sociology', in *The Sage Handbook of Cultural Sociology*, ed. D. Inglis and Anna-Mari Almila (London: Sage, 2016).
86 Theodor W. Adorno, 'On Tradition (1966)', *Telos*, no. 94 (1992).

7

Counter-demagogic popular art: towards a selective tradition

> Demagoguery, because it contains a certain euphoria, a good-guy aspect, is pre-eminently American.
>
> François Truffaut.[1]

(a) *Below the Surface*

As a component of *Studies in Prejudice*, the Institute conducted advanced preparatory work on a proposed film, *Below the Surface*. This 'film experiment' was not, however, a plan for an actual Hollywood release. Rather, the film, about twenty minutes in length, was to be professionally produced and shown to selected audiences whose reactions would then be closely studied. The 'experiment' was thus both aesthetic and social psychological. In some scenarios it was to be shot in different versions to suit differently chosen audiences/subjects. The consistent motif was an ambiguous incident which resulted in injury to one character for which another was blamed. The cast included another character who practised scapegoating 'agitation' with, in some versions, his dialogue being drawn directly from Martin Luther Thomas's radio addresses. Others drew directly from the questionnaire and interview material of *The Authoritarian Personality*.

The earliest mention of the film comes in the prospectus for Studies in Prejudice published in the *Zeitschrift* in 1941. There the characters are 'boys' who are either 'Jews' or 'Gentiles' with differing configurations of 'Jewish' or 'Gentile' identifying names. Even at this early stage, two versions of the film were planned with alternative victims of aggressive action or speech.[2] By its later stages it seems very likely that the film script had been revised in the light of the findings emerging from the studies undertaken for *The Authoritarian Personality*. It will be recalled from Chapter 2 that Adorno proposed in his 'Fascist Propaganda' essay that a 'vaccine against authoritarianism' would require some mode of provoking insight among those who had succumbed to such propaganda. Adorno points to the proposed manual as the means of doing so but does not explain how this might work. The Lees' manual had relied on what Adorno regarded as the inadequate 'truth propaganda' strategy that I renamed 'liberal exposure'.

The later versions of the film script are remarkably consistent with Adorno's 'vaccine' plan. The scene of action has moved from a group of boys to a group of adults in a crowded subway car. A one-legged pedlar is bumped by a 'Jewish' character and in the commotion a female passenger falls from the car. The pedlar then initiates his antisemitic diatribe, seeking support from other passengers. Two variant endings then emerge: one in which the woman exonerates the Jew and seems to persuade the others; another in which she does not and 'the one legged man remains the accepted leader'. Variants were also sketched 'in which the Jew may be replaced by (a) a Negro (b) a German (c) an Englishman'. The film would then end with a screened caption: 'You, too, have been the eye-witness of the accident. What is your opinion?'[3]

David Jenemann, upon whose valuable detailed reconstruction of the film's planning I rely here, suggests that the variations were 'presumably because they would illustrate the range of prejudice'. He traces another planned variation to make the victim appear 'intellectual' to the Institute's work on the relationship between class and the 'essential irrationality of prejudice'.[4]

While there is no question that the film script was working with stereotypical characters as prompts to 'test' subjects' 'orientation to antisemitism', in the mode of the interviews and questionnaires for *The Authoritarian Personality*, it is also reasonable to draw parallels with the contemporaneous psychoanalytic underpinning Adorno was building in his 'Freudian Theory' and 'Democratic Leadership' essays. More than just an illustration of the *range* of prejudice, as Jenemann suggests, the character variations – and planned rescreenings – also *enact the mobility of the object of hatred*. It is this feature that Adorno thought made the strategy of provoking insight in the susceptible subject plausible. Moreover, the crowded subway car is the perfect microcosm of 'the accidental crowds of the big city' that Adorno highlights as the new 'ephemeral group' terrain of the modern demagogue.[5] In a real sense, the battle of *leadership* in the planned film plays out on a small group scale Adorno's interpretation of Freud's *Group Psychology* with more than a gesture towards his tripartite reception schema for fascist propaganda in *The Authoritarian Personality*.[6] It is little surprise then that 'the peddler ... winds up sounding like a combination of the radio demagogue and his befuddled followers' for this is precisely the contradictory form of leader-identification identified by Freud and Adorno.[7] In any case, the film was not made and its potential for disrupting false projection remained untested.

Nonetheless, the 'vaccine' metaphor Adorno later employed was already in circulation in this context. Jenemann suggests it is likely that Horkheimer believed ideas from the scenario were 'stolen' and used for the 1947 film noir, *Crossfire*, which was supported by the AJC's 'rival', the Anti-Defamation League. A script consultant for *Below the Surface*, Dore Schary, was a producer of that film.[8] The film portrayed the murder of a US soldier identified as Jewish. More significantly for the liberal exposure strategy, Horkheimer provided Schary with a sympathetic critique of his script that expressed concern that it would normalize such a form of hatred. Schary replied that: 'This film will not reform anti-Semites, but it should insulate [*sic*] people against the virus of religious or racial hate.'[9]

The Institute also actively sought collaborators for development and production among Hollywood producers, directors and scriptwriters – an environment in which both Adorno and Horkheimer moved more freely than many accounts of their time in California suggest. One of the directors approached for *Below the Surface* was Elia Kazan (in 1945) and one of the scriptwriters suggested was Budd Schulberg. This team famously produced the multi-award winning *On the Waterfront* (1954), two years after both provided names to McCarthy's Senate Committee. Kazan also directed a film about antisemitism, *Gentlemen's Agreement*, which won the Oscar for best picture in 1947.

The Studies in Prejudice project's efforts to supplant the liberal exposure model with a psychoanalytic one, if indeed that was an intent of *Below the Surface*, were thus somewhat fraught. *Prophets of Deceit*'s opening critique of the exposure strategy tied it to the attendant notion of the demagogue as 'foreign agent', one which had ignored 'domestic conditions' and 'native attitudes'.[10] If *Studies in Prejudice* did indeed shift the Hollywood consensus on antisemitism, as Jenemann speculates, it may also have had the effect of highlighting this implication of the relevance of 'domestic conditions' and 'native attitudes'. Whichever is correct, this 'native' implication would soon be more vigorously elaborated filmicly.

(b) *A Face in the Crowd:* the paradigmatic case

There is another Kazan/Schulberg project close to these themes: their 1957 release, *A Face in the Crowd* (hereafter *Face*). It receives no mention in discussions of the legacy of *Studies in Prejudice* and there is little substantive scholarly discussion of it outside film studies. Pauline Kael's summation of *Face* as 'Elia Kazan's blast at the fascist potential in American mass culture' is indicative of its mainstream critical placement.[11] Although contemporary film critics were divided in their qualitative assessment, subsequent critical revisitations have remained focused on the accuracy of the film's prediction of changing relations between the media, especially television, and political institutions. These anticipations are usually considered to be remarkably insightful.[12]

One of Kazan's own placements of the film might be seen as a corrective to Kael's:

> We were always talking about and looking out for native, grass-roots fascism. One thing that people overlooked is that Fascism always had attractive elements of populism in it.[13]

Kazan and Schulberg's extensive pre-production research deliberately sought out these 'attractive elements' within the USA as well as the emergent culture industry: 'We went to Madison Avenue like explorers going into a strange country.'[14] They also went to Nashville, the home of country music. As Kael's and Kazan's comments imply, *Face* does not address antisemitism, although its wise intellectual scriptwriting character, Mel Miller, is effectively identified as a Jewish intellectual, the kind of bespectacled figure planned for *Below the Surface*. The film's charismatic demagogue is no longer the antisemitic US proto-fascist who emulates European fascism, like Coughlin or Thomas. Unlike such agitators, Lonesome Rhodes has no established position of institutional leadership within the state or even religion. He is almost entirely a creation of the culture industry. Instead of hectoring or preaching, he initially cracks jokes and sings as he mocks all authority. Although eventually reliant on a team of scriptwriters, he remains to the end capable of improvising an entire programme. This is what Kazan called a 'hayseed fascism' but one very much in dialogue with the emergent television-centred culture industry. As Kazan also put it, 'Well, it's 1957 and television is now the "industry".'[15]

Face is based on a short story by Schulberg, 'Your Arkansas Traveller' (Schulberg, 1954).[16] The film presents an account of the rise of a folk-singing radio host to national television prominence and, eventually, candidate for Minister for Information in a plotted right-wing ascendancy. The core narrative changes in one major element from Schulberg's story to its reworking as the screenplay: Lonesome does not die accidentally but instead is 'figuratively' killed by his creator.[17] Significantly, however, the narratorial devices are very differently gendered. In the short story the narrator is the worldwise and astute radio producer, Marcia Jeffries, who discovers Lonesome Rhodes and develops his popular base only to discover she has created the proverbial monster. In the film there is no omniscient narrator but Marcia's role (Patricia Neal) is split between two characters. As a result, much of the reflective critical wisecracks go to Walter Matthau's Mel Miller, frequently reducing Marcia to the conventional tortured woman prone to hysteria – as she displays in the climactic 'exposure' scene of Lonesome's 'figurative' death. There she unmasks Lonesome's 'true self' to his public by broadcasting the usually silenced audio signal from a studio microphone during his programme's rolling of its final credits. Lonesome (Andy Griffith) is seen and heard describing his audience to the floor crew as 'morons', a 'cage full of guinea pigs' and 'trained seals':

> 'Shucks, I sell them chicken fertilizer as caviar. I can make them eat dog food and think it's steak ...You know what the public's like? A cage full of guinea pigs. Goodnight, you stupid idiots. Goodnight, you miserable slobs. They're a lot of trained seals. I toss them a dead fish and they'll flap their flippers.'[18]

His previously enthralled audience is then revisited in cutaway shots, 'awakening' to this revelation in disgust. It is Mel who persuades Marcia to tell Lonesome she was the one responsible for his demise. This, Mel explains, is the necessary stake through the heart. The film ends with Lonesome alone on his penthouse balcony, repeatedly playing his applause machine, shouting from the rooftop.

To this 'surface' extent *A Face in the Crowd* can be placed firmly within the tradition of liberal exposure which the Mel character in the film explicitly represents. He leaves Lonesome's employ to write an exposé, *Demagogue in Denim*:

> The publishers are pretty high on it. They think the time is just right to pull the mask off him... to let the public know what a fraud he really is.[19]

Mel is even given the last lines in the film, in a statement that simultaneously consoles both Marcia and the viewer:

> You were taken in. The way we were all taken in. But we get wise to 'em. That's our strength. We get wise to 'em.[20]

This alone was a highly charged theme for Kazan as testimony and exposure had themselves become core concerns in the wake of his and Schulberg's cooperative 1952 testimony to McCarthy's hearings. In this context *On The Waterfront* is often read as Kazan's defence of the brave whistleblowing witness who provides such testimony, rather than the 'stool pigeon'. As Kazan exposed the excesses of the Stalinism he saw in the US Communist Party, *Waterfront*'s protagonist, Terry Malone, exposes a corrupt waterfront union administration. In contrast, *A Face in the Crowd* so becomes Kazan's apologia to liberal intellectuals, an implicit acknowledgement of McCarthyism's demagogic potential.[21]

Consistent with his exploration of nativist populist attractions, Kazan's own later reading of the film stresses the ambivalence he sought in all the characterizations and plot developments. The contrast with his film on antisemitism ten years before, *Gentlemen's Agreement*, could not be greater. In 1999 Kazan considered the latter 'agit prop on a middle-class level' that performed a worthy task for its time but made no sense to those who had experienced later periods of antisemitism. Exposure there had aimed to do no more than provoke a guilty liberal WASP conscience. In contrast, *Face* has usually been regarded as prescient politically as well, including by Kazan himself.[22]

If *Face* has a filmic precursor it is Frank Capra's 1941 *Meet John Doe*.[23] That film too is centred on the exposure of a 'fake' populist figure who arises from below. In this case, however, the fakery is clear from the start and the populist leader is the opposite of a narcissistic demagogue. A circulation-boosting opportunistic publicity stunt is launched by a journalist, Ann Mitchell (Barbara Stanwyck), to save her job when her newspaper is taken over by a ruthless magnate, D.B. Norton (Edward Arnold), who has ambitions for the presidency. The fakery takes the form of a fraudulent letter from a 'John Doe' who plans a public suicide on Christmas Eve as a political protest. John Willoughby (Gary Cooper) is 'cast' as the pseudo-suicidal John Doe by Mitchell, and her editor and Norton soon see the potential. Mitchell scripts Doe's newspaper columns, radio addresses and speeches, all underwritten by Norton. Doe preaches neighbourly trust and 'John Doe clubs' arise, initially spontaneously, with their crucial exclusion of 'politicians' from membership. Norton subsidizes their expansion and organizes a giant national convention. Here Doe is scheduled to declare his support for Norton's bid for the presidency, so reversing the clubs' abstention from formal politics and completing Norton's takeover. Doe/Willoughby is warned by Mitchell's editor that Norton is a 'fifth columnist', and plans to expose Norton at the convention. Instead, Norton 'exposes' him as a fraud. John Doe's followers turn against him.

Capra's film plainly owes much to the example of Coughlin's and Huey Long's demagogic populism. Indeed ,it was released in the same period as the Lees' work on Coughlin and while Coughlin was still broadcasting at his most explicitly fascistic. The John Doe clubs in particular are highly reminiscent of the similarly structured movements Coughlin and Long established, largely on the basis of their radio broadcasts: Coughlin's National Union for Social Justice and Long's Share Our Wealth Society.[24] Dickstein's recent re-reading of this body of Capra's work is surely correct in regarding the film as 'populism against itself' in that *John Doe* abandons Capra's former 'populist' confidence in 'the ultimate benevolence of ordinary humanity to resolve all deep conflicts'.[25] Accordingly, much scholarship on Capra links his work with accounts of the US populist tradition, with some even drawing on the orthodox historians' criticisms of Hofstadter and employing Shils's definition of populism positively (devoid of his role for demagogy).[26]

Capra goes to considerable lengths to demonstrate that the appeal to a 'neighbourly' ethic is the source of Doe's populist success and the inspirational basis of the spontaneous formation of the clubs – a celebration of a rediscovered benevolence based in mutual trust. Yet, crucially, Doe's denigration by the John Doe Club Convention members marks this trust as fickle and dangerous. Likewise, it is implied, a cooperative if not socialistic populism was equally likely to have been inflected into Norton's proto-fascism had Doe followed the prepared script. Famously, Capra was unable to find a narrative resolution to the film that fully satisfied himself or his critics.[27]

Nonetheless, the populism Capra critically dramatizes in *Doe* is primarily that which is instigated within a quasi-political sphere, even in its 'anti-politician' moments. The populist agitation is undertaken with some level of bad faith and is always rewarded. In contrast, the 'authentic' hobo world from which John Willoughby emerges remains relatively unscathed. Each time Willoughby tries to flee from his role as Doe and return to his hobo life, the moment of transition is signified as he and his companion play their mouth harps and dance a jig. As we have seen, Kazan's *Face* is more thoroughgoing in its critical distancing from populism in seeing such 'nativist' cultural traditions as just as vulnerable to proto-fascist populist inflection. Although *Doe* places considerable emphasis on a rapaciously circulation-driven press baron who also owns radio stations, Norton's own political ambitions are paramount and 'the media' are instrumental to this. Capra's narrative so remains faithful to the 'people vs elite' dichotomy that typically informs his narrative populism.

In this sense Capra's aesthetic dilemma with *Doe* reproduces the conceptual dilemma of orthodox populism studies. Like that field, he is unable to successfully narrativize the distinction between populist movement and demagogic capture.

In contrast, *Face* successfully narrativizes both demagogy and culture industry. There is a more evident culture industry 'logic' at work and a key component is the cynical exploitation and commodification of folkloric music and folkways, most notably in Lonesome's own use of music and *The Cracker Barrel Hour* TV programme. In a reversal of the power relation between Norton and Doe, *Face*'s proto-fascist figure, Senator Fuller, needs to be taught such folkish ways by Lonesome. Lonesome's own first act of manipulative deceit, we later realize, is to trade his freedom from jail for a blues-like song 'instantly' composed and played into Marcia's tape recorder, 'Free Man in the Morning'. His 'discovery' by Marcia in a jail is a significantly 'whitened' echo of the prison-focused folksong collecting practice of the Lomaxes who 'discovered' figures like Leadbelly and contributed to the Smithsonian audio archive on which later folk revivals, including the British skiffle movement, relied.[28] By the time we reach Lonesome's hyperbolic 'performance' of the extraordinary 'Vitachex' advertising jingle, the transformative culture industry logic is self-evident. The entire score for the film, including the songs, was composed by Tom Glazer, whose folkish ballads were recorded by leading figures in the US folk revival of the 1950s and, later, Bob Dylan; he also parodied the form himself in a hit single of the early 1960s, 'On Top of Spaghetti'. Glazer's abilities to cross over between 'authentic' and 'synthetic' folk music and popular song fulfilled perfectly Kazan and Schulberg's fascination with 'synthetic folksiness'.[29]

Indeed, the enactment of the synthetic was also a claimed deliberate strategy by Kazan. He sought to present Lonesome Rhodes as a 'synthetic personality'. Significantly, in Andy Griffith he cast as Lonesome Rhodes a stand-up comedian with no acting experience but considerable capacity to improvise. As we have seen, such improvisational ability was identified as a core feature in the Institute's demagogy studies.

In short, *A Face in the Crowd*'s prescience renders it more than merely 'illustrative' of some Institute themes: it effectively *elaborates* certain components of the Institute's work that were relatively underdeveloped. This capacity could be cast in terms of Habermas's *proto-political* literary public sphere argument. However, that schema turns on the pivotal but subsequent role of aesthetic criticism and debate of the aesthetic work. *Face* instead fulfils Raymond Williams's portrayal of certain art as proto-theoretical in that it anticipates, via aesthetic practices such as enactment, matters that are only subsequently recognized theoretically.[30] In this instance, a work of 'popular art' provides a bridge between a body of theoretical work and its potential elaboration. *A Face in the Crowd* could thus be read as a work of critical theory.

As we have seen, Kazan was at least aware of the Institute's plans for *Below the Surface* and perhaps the broader context of Studies in Prejudice. Yet his criticism of his own *Gentleman's Agreement* indicates that he moved beyond the terrain of the 'Hollywood films about antisemitism' to broader critical theoretical concerns. The most likely influence here is Erich Fromm's

Escape from Freedom, a book Kazan praised in a letter to Tennessee Williams in November, 1949 as 'one of the best books I've read in the last ten years' and 'one that had a great influence on me'.[31] It may be that Kazan (or Schulberg) was also aware of the reworking of Fromm's argument and the 1941 special issue of the *Zeitschrift* into the variants of left mass culture critique in the little magazines examined in Chapter 6. The title of the film also echoes Riesman's hugely popular Fromm-influenced work of 1950, *The Lonely Crowd*, and is almost identical to that of its successor 1952 volume, *Faces in the Crowd*.[32] The followers of Lonesome Rhodes could easily be understood as following Fromm's 'conformist path' of submission to external authority.[33]

More pointedly, the film's chief 'elaboration' concerns the mode by which the culture industry could produce a 'demagogue in denim'. It employs the same conjunction of advertising and demagogic devices that Adorno identified and likewise the susceptibility of Romantic *Volk*-revival practice to demagogic distortion. While Adorno implies the potential of the culture industry as a new crucible for demagogues, distinct from the political chamber but influential upon it, this is never quite made explicit. *A Face in the Crowd*'s enactment of this dynamic is perhaps its supreme 'theoretical' achievement.

We can see these elements all indicated in a Hitchcock-like critical theoretical cameo. In one scene Marcia visits the writers' room of Lonesome's television programme (Figures 5 and 6). She inadvertently stands next to a dartboard

5 First still from writers' room scene, *A Face in the Crowd*

6 Second still from writers' room scene, *A Face in the Crowd*

formed from an image of Lonesome's face with 'Escape from Freedom' beneath it in block letters. On her other side is a piece of demagogic kitsch, a toy in Lonesome's image with a guitar.[34]

The French *nouvelle vague* film director François Truffaut enthusiastically reviewed *Face* on its release. Truffaut recognized the film's unmasking of demagogy and regarded it as superior to *On the Waterfront*, a film he felt had succumbed to demagogy itself due to external pressures outside Kazan and Schulberg's control.[35] His praise for *Face* builds on the claim that the film is 'as inexorable as a "Mythology" of Roland Barthes'.[36] Barthes's *Mythologies* had been published the same year (1957), so the comment could be read as merely a contemporary allusion for the Parisian readership of *Cahiers du Cinema*. However, its insight was considerable, and certainly prophetic.

At the theoretical core of Barthes's conception of mythology is a proposed 'second order semiological system' whereby the Saussurean signifier/signified division of the linguistic sign is reiterated. Thus, an established sign becomes a signifier once again and a supraordinate new sign within a 'metalanguage' is so produced – in effect a realm of metaphor.[37] It was by this means that Barthes developed a semiology of images. At this point in his career Barthes's approach defers to a distinctly sociological dimension; it is not so susceptible to the Vološinovian social formalist critique of Saussure. Indeed, the *Mythologies* framework is ostensibly Marxian and the myths Barthes tracks – the face of

Garbo, the brain of Einstein, the great family of man, and so on – are seen to have a broadly legitimating ideological function, traced to the French 'political alliance of the bourgeoisie and the petite-bourgeoisie'.[38] The myths so perform the 'naturalizing' function of legitimating ideologies.

Truffaut's proposition of an 'anti-demagogic' mythology is thus a qualitative advance on Barthes, suggesting a quasi-Gramscian dimension. The mythological status of *Face* for Truffaut is tied to its 'inexorable' capacities and it is in this sense that his view is prophetic. The film can be made to stand in a selective tradition of anti-demagogic popular art, as I have proposed. However, it has also had an ongoing resonance, itself becoming subject to what Eco, drawing on Russian technicist and social formalists calls 'intertextual collage', the use of film-fragments, usually called motifs, that are 'unhinged' from their source.[39] *Face*, or rather motifs within it, so became a template and resource for subsequent anti-demagogic references. On my analysis, it is precisely because the film works *both* aesthetically and 'theoretically' that it remains such a recurrent point of departure and citation.

Tim Robbins's 1992 film, *Bob Roberts*, is the most complete recombinant reworking of the Kazan/Schulberg thesis. It portrays a folk-singing conservative presidential candidate. Rather than use an entirely synthetic folk repertoire, *Bob Roberts* employs a more obvious device of 'reversal' of that of Bob Dylan e.g. 'The Times They are a-Changin' Back' etc. (Dylan's career commenced a few years after *Face*.) While *Face*'s narrative form is usually considered melodramatic, *Bob Roberts* parodies British current affairs/documentary reportage of US politics in a more hyperbolic form.

More bizarrely, and in keeping with contemporary motif borrowings, Glenn Beck, a key figure in the surge in US aggressive talk radio that was pivotal to the establishment of a conservative 'echo chamber' in the 1990s, was identified as the modern re-embodiment of Lonesome Rhodes. He was even sent a DVD of the film by George Soros.[40] Such citations of 'Lonesome' have continued through to the comparisons between Rhodes and Trump that emerged, from both liberal and conservative sources, soon after his candidacy was announced.[41] Here the motif of liberal exposure in popular art provides a warrant for journalistic exposure, albeit indicative rather than investigative.

But such journalistic focus on 'prediction' is at best a minimal motif borrowing. It misses, or inadvertently reproduces, something more fundamental that Kazan and Schulberg also grasp about culture industry logic: that Lonesome himself becomes a template. As his fall is tracked at the end of *Face*, we see his erstwhile manager (no longer the Marcia character) already promoting 'the next Lonesome Rhodes'. Demagogic performance so becomes another example of 'part interchangeability' in its 'remarkable stereotypy'.

(c) Left-demagogy and counter-demagogic popular art

Of course, the Capra/Kazan cinematic mode of counter-demagogic popular art is also consistent with the 'liberal deviations' that Adorno considered possible in Hollywood cinema. They form the most prominent examples of the populist contradictions of the source culture industry, that of the USA. As child migrants to the USA, Capra and Kazan also shared with the Institute émigrés the perspective of 'outsiders' who were able to distinguish within the USA's populism its nativist elements.[42]

As I argued above, *Face* can be interpreted as a cinematic elaboration of the some of the Institute's concerns while also being a good example of 'liberal exposure' in its narrative strategy towards its audience. To this extent its focus is the familiar affinity between the culture industry and the proto-fascist form of demagogy.

As we saw in Chapter 1, the historical orthodoxy in the USA challenged by Hofstadter was one that attributed a necessarily progressive character to its populist movements. This model strongly informed conceptions of subsequent social movements as inheritors of this legacy.[43] Coughlin's and Long's movements started as ostensibly progressive critiques of the New Deal but, by the time of the Institute's research, only Coughlin's increasingly fascistic demagogy survived. This left the Institute's work open to the superficial charge by Shils that it was unable to address 'left authoritarians'.[44]

The social movements of the 1960s also became the basis of subsequent theorizations of 'new social movements'. However, with the notable exception of Marcuse, the student movements became a matter of fraught tension for many of the critical theorists, especially those who had returned to (West) Germany.[45]

Retrospectively, key figures in these movements have identified contingent forms of demagogy that arose within them, including within some African-American post-civil-rights movements, echoing Du Bois's earlier warnings.[46] While in Germany the role of the culture industry towards the new movements chiefly took the form of the hostile partisanship of the Springer Press, in the USA and Britain the balance of forces was more complex. The US civil rights movement actively developed the use of folk music as a 'resource' but also found an echo in contemporary soul music. Key figures who had emerged in popular music so became participants to some degree.[47]

In the US student movements, in Todd Gitlin's accounts, modes of leadership were constantly debated but never resolved. Key figures 'abdicated' rather than assume such attributed power.[48] Active attempts were made to avoid individuals' being cast as the 'spokespeople' required by television news reporters.[49] Thus 'suspicion of verticality' prevailed 'as the reigning spirit of left-wing protest movements of the last half century' from 'a kind of anarchism of direct participation' with roots in Quaker practice through to the 'horizontalism' of Occupy.[50] Gitlin characterizes each of his thick descriptions of these developments as a dilemma of movement organization in the face of the culture industry (though the latter is not his preferred term).[51] He warns of the risks of disorganization or, in the case of the fate of the 1960s movements he traces, intervention by opportunists who exploit this intersection of a leadership quasi-vacuum and culture industry practice.

The leading examples of this tendency for Gitlin are the Yippie figures, Jerry Rubin and Abbie Hoffman. They reversed the New Left wariness towards culture industry practices and relied on them to foster their own mode of televisual publicity and recruitment, devoid of traditional forms of political organization. The staging of newsworthy spectacle became an end in itself, with the violation of cultural taboos – nudity, threats of violence – a common device. For Rubin the task 'was to grab the imagination of the world and play on appropriate paranoias'. For Hoffman, 'once you get the image right the details aren't important'.[52]

Rubin's explicit reference to paranoia is only the most obvious parallel with the Institute's analysis of demagogues. Gitlin's emphasis on its contrast with political organizational forms indicates the attendant lack of mediating organizational layers: the leader/follower dynamic so relied on a comparable 'organized flight of ideas' but its imagistic quality also invokes Freud's secondary leadership. Finally, the leadership vacuum within a mobilized popular movement is analogous to, but of course completely different in scale from, the crisis/vacuum of aesthetico-cultural leadership Adorno identified in pre-Nazi Germany. But this is more than the kind of missing left-demagogy case study Shils's critique had demanded; its integration with the culture industry is as complete as that of Lonesome Rhodes. Gitlin wryly footnotes that Rubin and Hoffman received job offers from three advertising agencies.[53]

Hoffman's approach led him to advocate increasingly adventurist forms of action, always geared to a large audience. Perhaps it was inevitable then that the Woodstock Music and Arts Festival in August 1969 drew his attention as an exploitable opportunity. Even if its scale was far greater than any had anticipated, it constituted a new field of Yippie recruitment, a new intersection of counter-culture and culture industry. The number of attendees exceeded by a factor of one hundred that of the demonstrators at the Chicago Democratic Convention the year before. Those protests were the site of the Yippies' most famous actions which led to the subsequent trial of the 'Chicago Seven', including Hoffman.[54] While the provocation of 'institutional violence' was also a standard Yippie strategy, at Woodstock Hoffman met his culture industry nemesis, Pete Townshend of the British rock group, The Who.

Hoffman had negotiated with the Woodstock promoters a role in providing 'survival information' as part of a political space, 'Movement City'. During negotiations he threatened to disrupt the festival. One of the agreed ground rules was that political activity would have no place on the main performing stage.[55] However, frustrated and in an agitated state, he interrupted The Who's performance by seizing the microphone and began a speech about the activist John Sinclair's 10-year imprisonment for marijuana possession. He managed to say 'I think all this is shit while John Sinclair rots in prison' when Townshend interrupted him, shouting: 'Fuck off! Fuck off my fucking stage!'

Accounts of this event, including those from both participants' subsequent memories, differ on exactly what means Townshend employed in simultaneously removing Hoffman from 'his' stage; whether by striking him with the neck of his guitar or a kick in the pants. No visual record exists.[56] Both were likely affected by the backstage drinking water that had been laced with LSD. Few disagree that it was an ignominious end to Hoffman's intervention. While Townshend had a history of taking such action towards apparent trespassers on 'his' stage, violence was also an inherent part of his performative style. However, this usually took a form of *auto*-destruction, famously involving the destruction of his guitar, usually after its use to produce forms of abrasive feedback. He had been influenced by Gustav Metzger's auto-destructive aesthetics while at Ealing Art College and later funded Metzger's first major UK exhibition.[57]

Most commentators simply note this Woodstock 'incident' rather than seek to interpret it contextually or immanently, or indeed follow through on its possible connection with the participants' subsequent aesthetico-political work, notably Townshend's 'anti-political' anthem, 'Won't Get Fooled Again', and Hoffman's *Woodstock Nation*. Peterson's early assessment that it 'accomplished little, except to demonstrate the gulf between rock music and politics' appears to have gone unchallenged.[58] Yet each participant, whether drug-addled or not, was in a heightened affective state enabling improvisational performance. Each regarded some degree of transgressive 'symbolic violence' as integral to their own understanding of aestheticized action. This was a face-to-face collision of two different self-understandings of such symbolic violence.

At the point Hoffman intervened in The Who's performance, they were midway through *Tommy*, their first 'rock opera'. So, what Hoffman interrupted was not the typically variable rock group setlist, but a self-styled integrated work. *Tommy* was among the first of the rock operas and is usually considered the defining moment of the genre.[59] Composed almost entirely by Townshend, it employs multiple characters, maintains a continuous narrative through twenty-four songs and instrumental pieces and employs distinct musical and lyrical motifs. Shortly after the Woodstock performance, it set precedents by being performed, and well-received, in European opera houses and the New York Metropolitan Opera House. It is difficult to imagine a stronger claimant to the category of 'popular art'. The Who's co-manager and Townshend's mentor, Kit Lambert, was the son of composer Constant Lambert and a strong advocate of the aesthetic legitimacy of popular music.[60]

Moreover, while Townshend has given many versions of its intended meaning, it is plausible to immanently analyse *Tommy* as a counter-demagogic work. Like much comparable popular music composition of this period, it is strongly informed by 'eastern' religious thematics of self-realization. The character of Tommy is rendered mute, deaf and blind by a childhood trauma (and is subsequently repeatedly abused). However, his remaining senses become heightened, enabling him to become a 'pinball wizard' with a large following of fans. He achieves a miracle cure and his relationship with his followers changes to that of charismatic preacher and leader. However, when he tells his followers that their path to enlightenment requires an individually conformist simulation of his own sensory-deprivation journey, they rebel and renounce him. Tommy then retreats into his former state.

At the very least, *Tommy* is an allegorical rendering of the risks of the modes of charismatic leader/follower relationship that were emerging within popular music at that time. Perhaps because of its religious grounding, it is also remarkably consistent with the Weberian configuration of charismatic leader and demagogue. Psychoanalytically, Tommy's narcissism is also highly visible but the links between it and his rejection by the followers is immanent. There is no external 'liberal hero' who exposes him to his followers. It is Tommy's demand for yet more ego-identification that triggers a break in the charismatic-identificatory bond.[61] The key moment, on such a reading, is the climactic, 'We're Not Gonna Take It', which enacts Tommy's demand for conformism and its rejection by the followers. Townshend retrospectively referred to this as 'a song I'd had knocking about on the cards for ages about fascism'.[62]

Woodstock Nation: A Talk-Rock Album was published by Hoffman later in 1969, most of it written in the 'five days after Woodstock' as he was nursing his wounds from his encounter with Townshend and his 'bad trip'.[63] Marshall McLuhan is cited within the opening pages and the 'talk-rock album' format is remarkably similar to the montage presentation of McLuhan's *The Medium is the Massage* published two years prior. McLuhan's montage was also intended as an aesthetico-political provocation that shared much with advertising. McLuhan's formalist prioritization of the medium over the message/massage was famously indifferent to meaningful 'content' and especially to the institutional forms of 'the media'.[64] Hoffman's montage is as well-suited to his demagogy as was the fragmentary 'flights of ideas' to the radio demagogues of the 1930s and 1940s.

Unusually for the hit-and-run style of his cultural provocations, a section of Hoffman's book is devoted to a retort to Townshend. He does this by reproducing, apparently with permission, the lyrics of 'We're Not Gonna Take It' and provides a series of graffiti-like 'comments' pasted alongside. Crucially, he removes all signification of the dialogical form of the lyric by character identification (i.e. 'Tommy' and 'followers'). His comments are thus directed to 'Peter', as if the lyrics were those of a freestanding confessional song, notably when Tommy moves into his most demagogic demand of his followers. There could not be a more explicit contrast between demagogic speech and autonomous aesthetic composition.[65]

Ironically, as an observer of US popular movements more removed than Capra or Kazan, Townshend was as critical of Woodstock as Hoffman was in *Woodstock Nation*. At the time he was actively resisting calls for the politicization of his music, 'to use The Who for a political message', in stark contrast to John Lennon's contemporaneous *agit prop* phase in which he and Yoko Ono briefly moved into an alliance with Hoffman and Rubin's Yippie strategy.[66] In another song Townshend planned as a rock operatic climax, 'Won't Get Fooled Again', his resistance to such instrumentalization is given forceful utterance. A revolutionary scenario is portrayed but the narrator speaks in a voice not unlike that of Mel in *A Face in the Crowd*. He *prays* that 'we don't get fooled again' as the revolution appears only to have installed a 'new boss'. Detached from its role in a planned narrative as complex as *Tommy* that was never completed, the text of the song is sufficiently open to have even been placed at the very top of 'The 50 Greatest Conservative Rock Songs' by *The National Review*.

As with the Hoffman incident, Townshend shifted in his own views on the 'politics' of this song. In what appears his last word on this matter, he wrote in 2006: 'The song was meant to let politicians and revolutionaries alike know that what lay in the centre of my life was not for sale, and could not be co-opted into any obvious cause.'[67]

This is clearly consistent with the 1969 defence of the autonomy of 'his' stage. Townshend seemingly does not regard commercial licensing of his songs as such a violation. Here we see the culture-industrial limits of the 'popular art' framework. While Townshend's songs are at least compositionally autonomous and not easily reducible to the part-interchangeable template of Adorno, their specific commodity form leaves them susceptible to a contingent 'technical merger' with advertising or other forms of popular art. Nonetheless, in the case of *Tommy*, Townshend's autonomous avant-gardism enabled the composition of a work that not only identified the risks of charismatic demagogy but managed to 'trap' Hoffman into what might be called auto-identification as a demagogue.

Hoffman also anticipates elements of more recent demagogic practice. His provocations are remarkably similar to Umberto Eco's characterization of those of Silvio Berlusconi as a 'bomb effect' whereby outrageous statements – such as his assertion that a German member of the European Parliament 'would have made a good concentration camp guard' – dominate the news cycle for days. Of course, the specifics of Hoffman's and Berlusconi's provocations need not correspond. Rather, it is their quasi-McLuhanist disregard for the consequences of their 'content' that constitutes the resemblance. Eco notes the inadequacy of McLuhan's own suggested 'press blackout' to curb publicity for terrorists, yet he is unable to offer any alternative beyond the employment of similar 'bomb' techniques in response.[68] This echoes the problem identified in Stuart Hall's work on authoritarian populism: the instrumentalization of the understanding of the field of the national-popular. But the Townshend-Hoffman interaction suggests another option: the provocation of demagogic self-incrimination.

The transatlantic dimensions of the Townshend-Hoffman exchange and their echo in Berlusconi also highlight the degree to which demagogic dimensions of US populism and its culture industry are no longer confined to the US national-popular. Berlusconi's success was contingent on his related role in 'Americanizing' the Italian media system.[69] However, it is important to return to the US 'tradition' of counter-demagogic popular art to develop further my point regarding demagogic self-incrimination.

(d) Successful liberal exposure: Murrow's 'slaying' of the McCarthyist dragon and its aesthetic legacy

In 1956, the year before *The 7 Lively Arts*, Gilbert Seldes published *The Public Arts*. Among his case studies was a careful analysis of the famous 1954 exchange between Edward R. Murrow's *See It Now* and Joseph McCarthy.[70] I do not stretch my definition of 'popular art' to include journalism per se but Seldes's interest in this episode is significant as it foreshadows the near-mythical status the encounter subsequently attained. One element is common to the two fields, the issue of autonomous composition/production within the culture industry. Murrow, it must be noted, enjoyed an unusual degree of such autonomy although, as Seldes notes, the decision to challenge McCarthy likely undermined the future of his programme. My discussion here outlines the specificity of the Murrow-McCarthy exchange and then tracks its recent 'reincarnations' within the popular arts of cinema and television drama.

Murrow is widely lauded as perhaps the most significant innovator in the translation of 'in depth' news techniques to broadcasting, initially in radio and later in television. As one 2004 tribute put it: 'Techniques he introduced on both are still in use today, from the multipoint radio roundup to the split-screen TV interview.'[71] Another assessment in 2011 argued Murrow's CBS television programme, *See it Now* 'established a format for the serious news magazine that has continued to this day'.[72] He is equally lauded as a paragon of 'moral excellence' in journalism in any medium.[73] Even the US State Department has run an Edward R. Murrow Program for Journalists and issued an illustrative pamphlet documenting his achievements.[74]

It is his challenging and wounding of McCarthy, however, that is usually regarded as the high point of his career and the key instance warranting heroicization. More than this, Murrow has become, with considerable justification, the very embodiment of the liberal exposure strategy for challenging demagogues. However, just how Murrow achieved this is not a matter of widespread agreement among those who hold this view.

Murrow's now legendary *See It Now* programme on McCarthy was broadcast on what became known, in homage, as 'Good Tuesday' (9 March 1954). The 'slaying the dragon' metaphor is usually sourced to a drawing by Ben Shahn, who had provided graphic sketches for the programme's publicity and sent his drawing to Murrow as a tribute.[75]

It is true that Murrow's was hardly the first journalistic challenge to McCarthy. Yet, as if in response to such doubts, 'A Report on Senator Joseph R. McCarthy' was celebrated in the trade magazine *Billboard* as the moment when broadcast journalism, and especially television journalism, challenged the leadership role of newspapers. Even here the 'lance' metaphor was in play:

> Where the strongest conservative newspapers such as *The New York Times* and *New York Herald Tribune* had failed to arouse any mass public indignation over the Senator's methods of investigation, a single 30-minute TV show may well go down as the lance that pricked and completely deflated the McCarthy balloon.[76]

Most accounts of the conflict with McCarthy tend to be Murrow-centric in the sense that Murrow's undoubted courage in openly challenging blacklisting and similar features of Cold War 'McCarthyism' are at the fore. Murrow emerges, in the title of one biographer, as the embodiment of 'heroic truth'.[77] Such heroicization of Murrow the courageous individual, however, must also be seen as a substitute for grasping the complex specificity of his strategy towards

McCarthy. McCarthy's own use of television, in part by exploiting 'right of reply' rules in its regulation, left him especially vulnerable to an exposé conducted with screen-based evidence.

One problem with the dragon slayer metaphor is that Murrow and McCarthy had no onscreen direct confrontation. Murrow did not interview McCarthy adversarially. Rather, as *See it Now* planned its programme, all at CBS agreed with Murrow's view that an offer of *reply* should be included.[78] This offer formed part of Murrow's introduction and McCarthy subsequently accepted. This reply agreement is especially significant for the most celebrated technique of Murrow's exposé, the use of McCarthy's own words and statements to 'convict himself'. The programme consisted primarily of recordings of McCarthy's speeches 'called to account' by Murrow's 'fact checking' of McCarthy's accusations using verified evidence. McCarthy was left in the peculiar position of replying to a programme mainly composed of footage of himself in action. It created a situation where McCarthy to some degree needed to 'reply to himself'.

However, Murrow's critique of McCarthy went beyond such orthodox journalistic techniques, even by the standards of his own programme and the critical newspaper journalism that preceded it. Yet this does have a clear precursor from the Coughlin case, not in journalism as such but in the Lees' analysis of Coughlin's devices. Like the Lees, Murrow focused on the repetitive use of certain specific demagogic devices, most famously McCarthy's insinuation of guilt by association and similar innuendo. *See It Now* was able to employ relatively new recording and especially editing techniques to demonstrate audio-visually the devices common to multiple instances of McCarthy's demagogy, across a range of different victims.

This critical montage practice, albeit refined, remains a mainstay of contemporary television satire, including those that in recent years are considered to have replaced television news itself in terms of trust. Thus *The New York Times*'s reportage of the 2015 retirement of the leading figure in this genre, Jon Stewart, included the following:

> In becoming the nation's satirist-in-chief, Mr Stewart imbued the program with a personal sense of justice, even indignation. For a segment of the audience that had lost faith in broadcast and print news outlets or never regarded them as sacrosanct in the first place, Mr Stewart emerged as a figure as trusted as Walter Cronkite or Edward R. Murrow.[79]

In effect, Murrow's audience members were trained as critical citizens in the Good Tuesday programme by familiarization with the techniques of a visual rhetorical analysis as effectively as any student of Propaganda Recognition

101. They were thus likely well-prepared for every 'personal attack' trick that McCarthy employed in his reply. McCarthy attempted to demonstrate that Murrow too was part of the communist conspiracy and so revealed exactly the same techniques as those that Murrow had already called to account in his programme.[80] Here was the moment of 'self-incrimination'. If Murrow was indeed a dragon slayer, he had, like Townshend, first employed his skills to identify demagogy as such. He drew the demagogic dragon out of its lair and demonstrated publicly that it did indeed breathe fire.

Four years later Murrow made his much-quoted 'wires and lights in a box' address decrying the wastage of (US) television as a communicative space where advertising and ratings ruled over autonomous informational content.[81] In this sense Murrow's critical perspective enabled both a practical critique of demagogy *and* a critique of the consolidation of a drift to dominance of commodification, so sharing important elements with Kazan and Schulberg. Unlike the latter, however, Murrow did not address the commodification of demagogy as such.

Nonetheless, it is Murrow's apparent legacy that has been the stronger influence, especially as mobilized during the most recent populist surges. George Clooney's 2005 cinematic reconstruction of the Murrow/McCarthy encounter, *Goodnight and Good Luck*, bookends the film with extracts from the 'lights in a box' speech. Clooney's film was designed in part to prick the conscience of contemporary commercial television journalism, most notably in the wake of widespread criticism that investigative challenges had not been brought to bear on the George W. Bush administration's case for war against Iraq. Clooney's film largely escaped the charge of hagiography and was also praised for the accuracy of its depiction of journalistic procedures.[82]

In stark contrast, Aaron Sorkin's 2012–14 commercially successful HBO television series, *The Newsroom*, was largely castigated on release, even though its strategy worked from a similar conscience-pricking premiss.[83] The narrative of its first series targeted the same commercial imperatives that Murrow had identified and the resultant failure to challenge the rising Tea Party movement. Murrow's image appears in the opening titles and his name is repeatedly invoked as the news programme's anchor undergoes a crisis of conscience, abandoning his former pursuit of ratings and issuing a public apology for news media coverage in recent years. His forté, however, is not an emulation of Murrow's strategy towards McCarthy, but rapid-fire adversarial interviewing coupled with appropriately labelled editorials. In anticipation of the likely backlash, the transformed anchor announces with pride, 'we are the élite'.[84]

Such 'reanimation' of Murrow is flawed not only because it fails to recognize what Murrow actually did. Its advocacy of adversarial interviewing as the appropriate form of counter-demagogy is itself problematic. The Australian demagogic populist, Pauline Hanson, was one of the early figures to emerge in the current populist wave. Shortly after she gained national prominence in 1996, she was interviewed by the Australian version of CBS's *60 Minutes*, a popular (if not populist) current affairs programme format. Now it is true, as Mazzoleni et al. argued in 2003, that within the 'rules' of this adversarial interview genre (even today), 'Hanson has usually performed badly, due largely to her lack of facility with words and her unskilled methods of debate'.[85] However, this 'lack of facility with words' takes the form of Adorno's improvisational 'flight of ideas', often delivered in a quavering, seemingly vulnerable, voice. The affect communicated is qualitatively different from 'being caught out' and so Adorno's warning against 'truth propaganda' comes into play. Hanson was widely credited with having 'won' the pivotal *60 Minutes* confrontation precisely because the interviewer, also female, appeared to set out to humiliate her. Even their different modes of dress appeared to signify that the interviewer was part of the elite and Hanson was the 'battler' underdog. The much-cited centrepiece of the exchange was the following:

Tracy Curro (interviewer): Are you xenophobic?

Hanson: ... (long pause) Please explain?[86]

The enactment of counter-demagogy within popular art is thus very closely aligned with 'actual' counter-demagogy, successful and unsuccessful. Mazzoleni et al.'s underestimation of Hanson is indicative of the under-preparedness of the field of political communication studies for the current populist insurgency. I address this problem in my final major chapter.

Notes

1 François Truffaut, 'A Face in the Crowd (1957)', in *The Films in My Life* (New York: Da Capo Press, 1994).
2 Max Horkheimer, 'Research Project on Anti Semitism' *Zeitschrift für Sozialforschung* 9, no.1 (1941), 142–143.
3 [Horkheimer and Adorno] 'Project of a Test Film', March 1945, Max Horkheimer-Archiv, IX, 150, 1 1a. Cited in Jenemann, *Adorno in America*, 136–137.
4 Jenemann, *Adorno in America*, 138.
5 Adorno, 'Freudian Theory and the Pattern of Fascist Propaganda', 284n. Cf. discussion in Chapter 5(a).
6 Cf. Chapter 2(c).
7 Jenemann, *Adorno in America*, 139. Cf. discussion in Chapter 5(a).
8 Jenemann, *Adorno in America*, 145ff.

9. Cited in Jennifer E. Langdon, *Caught in the Crossfire: Adrian Scott and the Politics of Americanism in 1940s Hollywood* (New York: Columbia University Press, 2008), chapter 7.
10. Lowenthal and Guterman, *Prophets of Deceit*, xv.
11. Pauline Kael, *5001 Nights at the Movies* (New York: Arena, 1987), 177.
12. J. Hoberman, 'The Long Road of Lonesome Rhodes: Reconsidering *A Face in the Crowd*', *The Virginia Quarterly Review* 84, no. 4 (2008); R. Ecksell, 'Fascism, American Style: Revisiting Kazan and Schulberg's *A Face in the Crowd*', *Bright Lights Film Journal* no. 61 (2008).
13. Elia Kazan and Jeff Young, *Kazan: The Master Director Discusses His Films: Interviews with Elia Kazan* (New York: Newmarket Press, 1999), 235.
14. Elia Kazan, 'Introduction', in Budd Schulberg, *A Face in the Crowd: A Play for the Screen* (New York: Random House, 1957), xvii.
15. Kazan and Young, *Kazan: The Master Director Discusses His Films*, 238; Kazan, 'Introduction', xiii.
16. Budd Schulberg, 'Your Arkansas Traveler', in *Some Faces in the Crowd* (New York: Random House, 1953). The title alludes to a mythical Arkansas figure celebrated in folklore and a folksong of the same name. Archie Green, 'The Visual Arkansas Traveler', *JEMF Quarterly* 21, nos 75–76 (1985).
17. This is Kazan's later characterization of his death. Elia Kazan, *Elia Kazan: A Life* (Boston: De Capo, 1997), 586.
18. I cite here a transcription from the film itself as the language of this scene is even more direct than that in the published screenplay.
19. Budd Schulberg, *A Face in the Crowd: A Play for the Screen* (New York: Random House, 1957), 136.
20. Schulberg, *A Face in the Crowd*, 172.
21. Ecksell's reading is indicative of the 'liberal apologia' interpretation. In contrast, Litvak's 'stoolpigeon' [sic] reading argues for an anti-communism in *Face* as well, so missing the significance of fascist demagogy (despite his book's use of 'Elements of Anti-Semitism' elsewhere). Ecksell, 'Fascism, American Style: Revisiting Kazan and Schulberg's *A Face in the Crowd*'; Joseph Litvak, *The Un-Americans: Jews, the Blacklist, and Stoolpigeon Culture* (Durham, NC: Duke University Press, 2009). In his autobiography Kazan reproduces a review of *Face* from the Communist Party's *People's World* which repeats the stool pigeon characterization of Kazan and Schulberg but praises the film. Kazan, *Elia Kazan: A Life*, 566.
22. Kazan and Young, *Kazan: The Master Director Discusses His Films*, 48. For Kazan on *Face*'s prescience, which he attributes to Schulberg: Kazan, *Elia Kazan: A Life*, 566.
23. Other possible precursors include the 1946 *All the King's Men* developed from Robert Penn Warren's novel of the same name that is usually assumed to be based on Huey Long.
24. Charles Wolfe, 'Authors, Audiences and Endings', in *Meet John Doe: Frank Capra, Director*, ed. Charles Wolfe (New Brunswick: Rutgers University Press, 1989), 6–7. Wolfe details the entry of this material into the development of Robert Riskin's script.
25. Morris Dickstein, *Dancing in the Dark: A Cultural History of the Great Depression* (New York: W.W. Norton & Company, 2009), 479. Dickstein's draws this definition from: Richard Griffith, *Frank Capra* (London: BFI, 1949).
26. Respectively, Brian Neve, *Film and Politics in America: A Social Tradition* (New York: Routledge, 1992), 28–54; Wes D. Gehring, *Populism and the Capra Legacy* (Westport, Conn.: Greenwood Press, 1995).

27 Joseph McBride, *Frank Capra: The Catastrophe of Success* (New York: Simon & Schuster, 1992), 434ff. Wolfe, 'Authors, Audiences and Endings'.
28 John F. Szwed, *The Man Who Recorded the World: A Biography of Alan Lomax* (New York: Arrow, 2011).
29 Kazan, 'Introduction', xvii.
30 Jones, *Raymond Williams's Sociology of Culture: A Critical Reconstruction*.
31 Elia Kazan, *The Selected Letters of Elia Kazan* (New York: Knopf Doubleday, 2014), 139. Kazan also praises its sequel, *Man For Himself*.
32 Riesman, Glazer and Denney, *The Lonely Crowd: A Study in the Changing American Character*. David Riesman and Nathan Glazer, *Faces in the Crowd* (New Haven: Yale University Press, 1952).
33 Perhaps inevitably then, there are cultural populist critiques of the film: John Yates, 'Smart Man's Burden: Nashville, A Face in the Crowd, and Popular Culture', *Journal of Popular Film* 5, no. 1 (1976). Courtney Maloney, 'The Faces in Lonesome's Crowd: Imaging the Mass Audience in "A Face in the Crowd"', *Journal of Narrative Theory* 29, no. 3 (1999).
34 Litvak also reproduces stills from this scene but does not comment on the Fromm connection. Litvak, *The Un-Americans: Jews, the Blacklist, and Stoolpigeon Culture*, 145.
35 Truffaut, 'A Face in the Crowd (1957)', 113. Litvak's attempt to 'equate' the two films is, in effect, a chapter-length retort to Truffaut's assessment. Litvak, *The Un-Americans: Jews, the Blacklist, and Stoolpigeon Culture*, 105ff.
36 Truffaut, 'A Face in the Crowd (1957)', 115.
37 Roland Barthes, *Mythologies* (New York: Noonday Press, 1972), 113–114.
38 Barthes, *Mythologies*, 140. Barthes's Marxian framework chiefly relies on *The German Ideology* and, briefly, *The Eighteenth Brumaire*.
39 Umberto Eco, '"Casablanca": Cult Movies and Intertextual Collage', *SubStance* 14, no. 2 (1985). However, Eco appears to regard the possibility that such works constitute an artform an impossibility.
40 Eric Randall, 'How Andy Griffith Predicted Glenn Beck', *The Atlantic* (2012).
41 Cal Thomas, 'Trump Is "Lonesome Rhodes"', *The Washington Times* (2015); Marc Fisher, 'The Movie That Foretold the Rise of Donald Trump', *The Washington Post* (2016).
42 Yves Carlet, 'Frank Capra and Elia Kazan, American Outsiders', *European Journal of American Studies* 5, no. 5–4 (2010).
43 Kazin is the most obvious example here but see also Grattan for a more recent illustration: Kazin, *The Populist Persuasion: An American History (Revised)*; Laura Grattan, *Populism's Power: Radical Grassroots Democracy in America* (New York: Oxford University Press, 2016).
44 Shils, 'Authoritarianism: Right and Left'.
45 Habermas's 'left fascism' comment in one meeting with student activists is the most famous. Wiggershaus provides a detailed account of this and the wider debates. Wiggershaus, *The Frankfurt School: Its History, Theories, and Political Significance*, 609–636.
46 For example, Tariq Ali, *Street Fighting Years: An Autobiography of the Sixties* (London: Verso, 2005). Garry Bertholf, 'Black Sophists: A Critique of Demagoguery' (University of Pennsylvania, 2013).
47 William G. Roy, *Reds, Whites, and Blues: Social Movements, Folk Music, and Race in the United States* (Princeton: Princeton University Press, 2013).
48 Todd Gitlin, *The Whole World Is Watching: Mass Media in the Making and Unmaking of the New Left* (Berkeley: University of California Press, 1980), 176–178.

49 Gitlin, *The Whole World Is Watching*. Todd Gitlin, *The Sixties: Years of Hope, Days of Rage*, rev. trade edn (New York: Bantam Books, 1993).
50 Todd Gitlin, *Occupy Nation: The Roots, the Spirit, and the Promise of Occupy Wall Street* (New York: HarperCollins, 2012), 80ff. Gitlin cites in support the early feminist essay: Jo Freeman, 'The Tyranny of Structurelessness', *Berkeley Journal of Sociology* (1972).
51 Gitlin's initial critique is grounded more in C. Wright Mills's *The Power Elite*, on which Habermas drew in similar ways in his critique of the culture industry in *Structural Transformation*. Gitlin, *The Whole World Is Watching*, 145–149; Habermas, *The Structural Transformation of the Public Sphere*, 249.
52 Each cited in Gitlin, *The Sixties: Years of Hope, Days of Rage*, 234, 236 respectively.
53 Gitlin, *The Sixties: Years of Hope, Days of Rage*, 236n.
54 M. Jezer, *Abbie Hoffman: American Rebel* (New Brunswick: Rutgers University Press, 1993), 189.
55 M. Lang, *The Road to Woodstock* (New York: HarperCollins, 2009). For Hoffman's version of these negotiations: Abbie Hoffman, *Woodstock Nation: A Talk-Rock Album* (New York: Random House, 1969), 126–133.
56 Although Woodstock produced a famously successful film, only certain sections of the many performances were filmed and this was not one of them. The audio track was released by The Who in 1994: The Who, 'Abbie Hoffman Incident', in *Thirty Years Of Maximum R & B* (London: Polydor, 1994).
57 Peter Stanfield, 'The Who and Pop Art: The Simple Things You See Are All Complicated', *Journal of Popular Music Studies* 29, no. 1 (2017); Pete Townshend, *Who I Am: A Memoir* (New York: Harper, 2012), 64, 464. The aesthetics of Metzger, an orphaned Polish Jewish Kindertransport evacuee, have been linked recently to Adorno's: Anna-Verena Nosthoff, 'Art after Auschwitz: Responding to an Infinite Demand: Gustav Metzger's Works as Responses to Theodor W. Adorno's "New Categorical Imperative"', *Cultural Politics* 10, no. 3 (2014). Metzger spent some childhood years near Nuremburg and witnessed many Nazi Nuremburg rallies. He later suggested in interviews that his hostility towards those 'mechanical' performances was a possible source for his auto-destructive aesthetics: Jonathan Jones, 'Interview, Gustav Metzger: The Liquid Crystal Revolutionary', *The Guardian* 28 September (2009); Stuart Jeffries, 'Interview, Gustav Metzger: 'Destroy, and You Create', *The Guardian*, 26 November (2012).
58 Richard A. Peterson, 'The Unnatural History of Rock Festivals: An Instance of Media Facilitation', *Popular Music & Society* 2, no. 2 (1973): 107.
59 For example, Martina Elicker, 'Rock Opera – Opera on the Rocks?', *Word & Music Studies* 4, no. 1 (2002).
60 Andrew Motion, *The Lamberts: George, Constant & Kit* (New York: Farrar, Straus & Giroux, 1987), 336–340.
61 For a comparable psychotherapeutic, if not quite psychoanalytic, reading of *Tommy* (the film version), see: David Ingle, 'Tommy', *BMJ* 344, no. 7845 (2012). Cf. also: Paul Williams and Brian Edgar, 'Tommy, Primal Therapy, and the Countercultural Critique of "Sick Society" and "Cripple Psychology"', *Journal of Literary & Cultural Disability Studies* 9, no. 2 (2015).
62 Richard Barnes and Pete Townshend, *The Story of Tommy* (London: Eel Pie Publishing, 1977), 114.
63 Hoffman, *Woodstock Nation: A Talk-Rock Album*.
64 Marshall McLuhan and Quentin Fiore, *The Medium Is the Massage* (New York: Random House, 1967). Williams's critique remains the most pertinent. Cf. Paul K. Jones, 'The Technology Is Not the Cultural Form?: Raymond Williams's Sociological

Critique of Marshall Mcluhan', *Canadian Journal of Communication* 23, no. 4 (1998).
65 Hoffman, *Woodstock Nation: A Talk-Rock Album*, 122–124.
66 Richie Unterberger, *Won't Get Fooled Again: The Who from Lifehouse to Quadrophenia* (London: Jawbone Press, 2011), 76. Jon Wiener, *Come Together: John Lennon in His Time* (New York: Random House, 1984), 174ff. Wiener draws attention to the contrast with Townshend himself.
67 Pete Townshend, 'Won't Get Judged Again', *Pete's Diaries* (27 May 2006), https://web.archive.org/web/20061205225327/http://www.petetownshend.co.uk/diary/display.cfm?id=285&zone=diary.
68 Umberto Eco, *Turning Back the Clock: Hot Wars and Media Populism*, trans. Alastair McEwen (Orlando: Harcourt, 2007), 135–141.
69 See Chapter 8.
70 Gilbert Seldes, *The Public Arts* (New York: Simon & Schuster, 1956).
71 Bob Edwards, *Edward R. Murrow and the Birth of Broadcast Journalism* (Hoboken, NJ: John Wiley & Sons, 2004), 107.
72 R.N. Jacobs and E. Townsley, *The Space of Opinion: Media Intellectuals and the Public Sphere* (New York: Oxford University Press, 2011), 38.
73 E.H. Spence et al., *Media, Markets, and Morals* (Chichester: Wiley, 2011), 208.
74 See Bureau of Educational and Cultural Affairs: http://eca.state.gov/highlight/edward-r-murrow-program-journalists.
75 Thomas Doherty, *Cold War, Cool Medium: Television, McCarthyism, and American Culture* (New York: Columbia University Press, 2003), 161. Frances K. Pohl, *Ben Shahn: New Deal Artist in a Cold War Climate, 1947–1954* (Austin: University of Texas Press, 1989), 148–149.
76 *Billboard*, 20 March 1954 (p. 2) cited in: Doherty, *Cold War, Cool Medium: Television, McCarthyism, and American Culture*, 178.
77 Norman H. Finkelstein, *With Heroic Truth: The Life of Edward R. Murrow* (Lincoln, NE: iUniverse, 2005).
78 Fred W. Friendly, *The Good Guys, the Bad Guys, and the First Amendment: Free Speech vs. Fairness in Broadcasting* (New York: Random House, 1976).
79 Itzkoff, Dave, 2005. 'John Stewart Will Leave *The Daily Show* on a Career High Note.' *The New York Times* (February 10).
80 Instead, comparative discussion of the two programmes has tended to focus on their relative 'professionalism' and whether McCarthy was thus at a disadvantage: Thomas Rosteck, *See It Now Confronts McCarthyism: Television Documentary and the Politics of Representation* (Tuscaloosa: University of Alabama Press, 1994). Seldes, *The Public Arts*, 218–228.
81 The speech can be found at: http://www.rtdna.org/content/edward_r_murrow_s_1958_wires_lights_in_a_box_speech
82 Lawrence N. Strout, 'The Edward R. Murrow of Docudramas and Documentary', *Media History Monographs* 12, no. 1 (2010).
83 Michael Koliska and Stine Eckert, 'Lost in a House of Mirrors: Journalists Come to Terms with Myth and Reality in the Newsroom', *Journalism* 16, no. 6 (2015).
84 Aaron Sorkin and Scott Rudin, *The Newsroom: The Complete First Season* (Burbank, CA: Home Box Office: Warner Home Video,, 2013), videorecording.
85 Mazzoleni, Stewart and Horsfield, *The Media and Neo-Populism: A Contemporary Comparative Analysis*, 229–230.
86 For a more detailed reading, on which I have relied at points in this paragraph, see: Meaghan Morris, '"Please Explain?" Ignorance, Poverty and the Past', *Inter-Asia Cultural Studies* 1, no. 2 (2000).

Excursus: an outline of Trumpian psychotechnics

It is hardly surprising that Donald Trump's rise to political power has been interpreted in terms of his demagogy and what many believe is his self-evidently narcissistic conduct. The latter charge, however, has mainly been applied in its common sense meaning of conspicuously craven vanity.[1] With rare exceptions, the invocations of 'demagogue' follow the 'journalistic' usage that Kazin claimed was the root source of all subsequent critical intellectual invocations.[2] This is not to underestimate the significance of the calling out of Trump as a demagogue early in his campaigning by key institutions of US high journalism. *The New York Times* notably placed him in a 'tradition' of US demagogues in a leader editorial. This was liberal exposure at its most eloquent.[3]

Much of the evidence of his excesses in analyses to date is derived from his use of Twitter.[4] The tweets often display signs of direct borrowings from, or reactions to, content on the Fox news channel, widely reported to be one of Trump's chief sources of information. His retweeting of others might be considered one form of demagogic recombinacy. Less commented on but still well-documented is the role of the culture industry format of reality television in his rise.[5]

So, Trump can definitely be seen as a product of the culture industry. In that sense, the early headline that 'The Frankfurt School Knew Trump Was Coming' is correct.[6] However, he did not quite follow the Lonesome Rhodes trajectory, despite the inevitable association of the two in critical commentary.[7]

EXCURSUS: AN OUTLINE OF TRUMPIAN PSYCHOTECHNICS

Trump can hardly claim, as Rhodes frequently did, to be 'just a country boy'. No matter how dubious its mode of accumulation, Trump had access to considerable capital all his adult life. Lonesome-like hucksterism, however, is consistent with his characteristic mode of interaction, that of the highly speculative property developer with its attendant forms of clientelism. The television format that launched him into the political public sphere was tailor-made to enact, and legitimate, this huckstering hyperbolic self-promotion. Trump reportedly functioned as a de facto co-producer of the programme in its later stages, though here too his hyperbole is in play.[8] Nor, of course, did he come to prominence via an aesthetico-folkloric 'discovery' like Rhodes's. Instead, he was cast as the discoverer of business acumen. Indeed, there is little that is musically folkloric about Trump, aside from his repeated unapproved use of anthemic rock songs.[9] His demagogic career does not demonstrate Kazan's enactment of the development of an increasingly synthetic personality. It appears always to have been so.

Hochschild was surely correct in pointing to the Tea Party movement as the social movement-like groundswell that Trump was able to exploit.[10] Yet, given Trump is unable to draw on any aspect of his background as fitting the cultural populist criterion of authenticity, his 'demagogic labour' needs to be all the more intense in order to establish points of identification. There is what might be called the Trumpian device of 'my success can be yours too', a hollowly aspirational motif that has also been associated with Berlusconi.[11] Allied to this is the projective name-calling pitched at immediate rivals, with the more aggressive forms notably aimed at female political leaders. Indeed, like Berlusconi, Trump's claimed 'success' is articulated with a form of nostalgia for an imagined masculinist normality, deriving from an equally longstanding motif of attempted 'buddying up' by male employers with male workers. Here Trump can present himself as embodying 'politically incorrect' masculine norms. But this is a high-risk strategy, as Berlusconi discovered. Yet to date, even the liberal exposure of evidence of Trump's boasting of sexual assaults has foundered, consistent with Adorno's warning that 'truth propaganda' may be insufficient to break the identificatory bond.

Indeed, in the wake of that story and other sexual misconduct allegations during the 2016 campaign, Trump addressed a rally in North Carolina, flanked by a line of women wearing red 'Women for Trump' T-shirts. Speaking without any reference to notes, he demonstrated Adorno's 'great little man' and 'lone wolf' devices to perfection:

> I am a victim of one of the great political smear campaigns in the history of our country. They are coming after me to try and destroy what is considered, even by them, the greatest movement in the history of our

country. There's never been anything like it. Bill O'Reilly and others have said it's the single greatest political phenomena [sic] in his [sic] lifetime. And others have said the same thing. The political establishment is trying to stop us because they know we are a threat to their totally corrupt controls. It's true [sotto voce]. These allegations are 100% false, as everybody, I think you know. I, I think you get it. I think you get it. They're made up. They never happened.[12]

The speech pattern is the familiar semi-incoherence of modern demagogy that is at its most effective – and affective – in the use of the repeated 'I think you get it', a form of audience-monitoring which leads to a pause from which Trump moves on to the 'full denial' of all allegations and (later) an attack on investigative journalistic reliance on anonymous sources, a foreshadowing of the 'enemy of the people' charge that was launched against journalists present within his audience a few months later . The monitoring dynamic is very similar to the 1940s demagogues' use of humour to monitor audiences (which Trump also practises).

It is surprising then that the least discussed aspect of Trump's presidency is his ongoing programme of rallies. There had been sixty-four of these by August 2019, averaging more than one per month.[13] It may be that the very stereotype Adorno identified in such rallies makes them less newsworthy and so less prominent for analysis. They are routinely regarded by journalists and political scientists as 'ensuring the base' as if their primary function is consumptive. Yet it is here, I would argue, that Trump develops and/or elaborates his major demagogic *production*. Here too the lessons Adorno drew from Freud's *Group Psychology* can be applied, as well as the catalogued demagogic devices. We can legitimately refer to Trump's performances as fostering the 'disinhibited hysteria' Adorno identified.

The rallies' relative under-reportage grants them a similar 'closed' status to that of the rallies by demagogues in the 1940s. The 'insider/public' distinction that the Institute identified – where the former is more 'explicit' than the latter – is thus reproduced in a more complex form. This is why it is characteristic for Trump to 'walk back' his comments after a rally when challenged by journalists, only to resume them at the next. Although they are recorded and streamed, their face-to-face character so provides a 'purer' form of his demagogy than even that enabled by Twitter's socio-technical configuration of leader/follower. Indeed, the tweets provide no option for Trump to comparably monitor his audience and so often achieve a kind of 'uncalibrated' excess. They have so become a point of complaint by even his ardent followers.

There was a brief moment when Trump's posture appeared to be to the left of the Obama legacy, with the promise of unspecified infrastructure spending, along with returning manufacturing jobs to the rustbelt. It was as if, just for that moment, he was adopting the Long left-populist agenda. The reduction of that infrastructure promise to 'the wall' and the manufacturing jobs to a tariff war and climate-change denial is perhaps the strongest evidence that such 'policies' are demagogic in that they follow the form of a 'flight of ideas' rather than any orthodox, or radical, model of policymaking. Moreover, that 'flight' has a remarkably consistent social psychological signature.

For, although Trump lacks a folkloricism, he is consistently *völkisch* in his invocations of V*olksgemeinschaft* motifs which are almost always configured as projective conspiracies against an Other. Indeed, it was the first major such instance in the 2016 campaign – the false charge that people of Arabic descent in New York had cheered the fall of the Twin Towers – that drew *The New York Times* to label him a demagogue.[14] Likewise, the only 'aesthetic' dimension of Trump's demagogy is his improvisational use of humour. Again, this is not used to demonstrate a quasi-folkloric authenticity, except perhaps in its deployment of 'amusing' name-calling. Rather, it not only replicates the audience-monitoring humour documented by the Institute, but also Adorno's insight that such figures are taken seriously because they 'risk making fools of themselves', so fostering the disinhibited hysteria.[15] This is manifest in the crowd chants (famously, 'lock her up') that fulfil the 'wave motion' crescendo portrayed in Figure 2. Such are clearly the core of his demagogy.

Trump so represents an extreme case of the contradictory leader location Adorno identified. The combination of paranoia and projection, both highly evident in the rally extract, also leads to a kind of overproduction of conspiracy discourses; and an apparent personal susceptibility to them, if his 'retweets' are taken as a guide here – or the role of the Ukraine conspiracy theory in his impeachment. In short, Trumpian psychotechnics has evident 'new' features but their dynamic uncannily resembles that identified by the Institute.

Notes

1 For a critique of such approaches that emphasises his attraction as a point of narcissistic identification, broadly consistent with Freud's *Group Psychology*: Elizabeth Lunbeck, 'The Allure of Trump's Narcissism', *Los Angeles Review of Books* (2017).
2 See Chapter 1.
3 The New York Times Editorial Board, 'Mr. Trump's Applause Lies', *The New York Times*, 24 November (2015). Cf. Paul K. Jones, 'Demagogic Populism and US Culture Industries: A Long Tradition', *Australasian Journal of American Studies* 35, no. 1 (2016).
4 Brian L. Ott, 'The Age of Twitter: Donald J. Trump and the Politics of Debasement', *Critical Studies in Media Communication* 34, no. 1 (2017); Ramona Kreis, 'The "Tweet Politics" of President Trump', *Journal of Language & Politics* 16, no. 4 (2017).

5. James Poniewozik, 'Trump's Campaign Classroom: Reality TV', *The New York Times*, 10 October (2015); Emily Nussbaum, 'The TV That Created Donald Trump', *The New Yorker*, 31 July (2017).
6. Alex Ross, 'The Frankfurt School Knew Trump Was Coming', *The New Yorker* no. 16 December (2016).
7. Thomas, 'Trump Is "Lonesome Rhodes"'.
8. P.R. Keefe, 'How Mark Burnett Resurrected Donald Trump as an Icon of American Success', *The New Yorker*, 7 January (2019).
9. Nick Deriso, 'Classic Rock vs. Donald Trump: Musicians Who Already Can't Stand Our New President', *Ultimate Classic Rock* (2017).
10. Hochschild, 'The Ecstatic Edge of Politics: Sociology and Donald Trump'.
11. Paolo Mancini, *Between Commodification and Lifestyle Politics: Does Silvio Berlusconi Provide a New Model of Politics for the Twenty-First Century?* (Oxford: Reuters Institute for the Study of Journalism, University of Oxford, 2011).
12. Transcribed from: Associated Press, 'Trump: I Am the Victim of a Great Smear', YouTube.
13. Dan Zak, 'Fear and Gloating in Cincinnati', *The Washington Post*, 2 August (2019). One of the few academic studies that focus on the rallies to date regrettably moves from a Kazin-like hostility to social psychological framings: Stephen Reicher and S. Alexander Haslam, 'The Politics of Hope: Donald Trump as an Entrepreneur of Identity', in *Why Irrational Politics Appeals: Understanding the Allure of Trump*, ed. Mari Fitzduff (Santa Barbara, Calif.: Praeger, 2017). In contrast, Kellner's early, and subsequently updated, 'Frommian Analysis' highlighted the rallies: Douglas Kellner, 'Donald Trump as Authoritarian Populist: A Frommian Analysis', *Logos: A Journal of Modern Society & Culture* 15, nos 2–3 (2016).
14. Editorial Board, 'Mr. Trump's Applause Lies'.
15. See Chapter 2(c).

8

Structural transformations of demagogic populism

(a) Towards a conclusion: mediated physiognomics and demagogic populism

The introductory sections of this book stated that its remit was delimited to 'demagogic populism' rather than populism in its broader usage. Nonetheless, the identification of demagogic populism can certainly inform that wider conception by specifying the role of the demagogic within populist practice. As argued throughout, it is the Institute's work within the Studies in Prejudice project that provides us with a core understanding of 'modern demagogy' and its distinctiveness. Necessarily, this has meant that the primary case under discussion has been the USA, notwithstanding the commonly overestimated but real role European fascism played in the Institute's work. This US focus is not merely a matter of happenstance resulting from the Institute's exile; the USA's role was pivotal to the development of 'modern demagogy'. It so stands in contrast to other paradigmatic historical instances put forward in recent scholarship, notably Argentina's proposed role as a crucible of 'modern populism' discussed in Chapter 3.

It is this dynamic that informs my concluding framework of 'structural transformations of demagogic populism'. My aim is not to provide an authoritative account of the Habermasian conception of the public sphere. Rather it is to recoup the structural transformation thesis as a 'bridge', albeit schematic, from the demagogy studies towards the present by immanently developing the role of populism and demagogy within it. Habermas's initial structural transformation thesis regarding the public sphere owes much to the first-generation critical theorists, visible in his use of ideal-typification and the centring of relevant 'social structures' in the contradictory situation of the bourgeois family.[1] In so doing its framework has the potential to redress a tendency in most existing treatments of 'mediated populism': to treat mediation as an 'externality' to populism, primarily as a phenomenon of journalistic reportage of populist parties. Such instrumentally party-dependent conceptions of mediated populism fail to recognize the *integral* relationship between modern means of communication and demagogic populism. We can here specify features of this relationship:

- First, Chapter 5's achieved social formalist position outlined the intersection between the montage form within culture industrial production – paradigmatically the broadcast advertisement – and the recombinant form of demagogic speech.
- Second, it will be recalled that Shils and Worsley identified the 'desirability of an unmediated relationship between people and leadership' as a core 'populist principle'.[2] The Adornian physiognomics of broadcasting introduced in Chapter 2 speaks directly to this unfulfilled desire. 'Time coincidence' and 'space ubiquity' each enable a mediated 'fulfilment' of this populist desire by establishing a form of what Thompson conceptualized as 'mediated quasi-interaction', the 'extended availability' of those communicative elements borne by modern technological means of communication.[3] The proliferation of the signifier 'mediation' in parsing this problem is indicative of the phenomenon's capacity to conflate different orders of social organization. In effect, the populist desire to bypass modern 'mediating' institutions is fulfilled by the mediation of modern 'media' of communication.
- Third, while such mediated quasi-interaction is of course distinctively different from face-to-face interaction, it is particularly effective in the monologue-dominant mode preferred by demagogues. Weber recognized this problem in principle in his critique of the abuse of the lectern for charismatic demagogy. Shils's warnings about this affinity are pertinent too.[4] As we have seen, demagogues tend to be 'early adopters' of such means of communication: from Long's use of loudspeakers to Trump's use of Twitter.

While contemporary so-called social media are often celebrated for their 'horizontality' (as opposed to the verticality of broadcast 'mass media'), their capacity for demagogic communication is equally potent. Indeed, to some extent the dynamic between populist movement and demagogic capture is digitally reproduceable. Moreover, in both their 'vertical' and 'horizontal' forms, they enable accelerated digital production and circulation of culture industry montage-practices.

If we consider this integral role of mediation within populism historically, it becomes clearer why the USA is such a pivotal case. As we saw in Chapter 1, the complementary work of the New York Intellectuals developed a more detailed historical frame for the USA's distinct capacity to generate populist movements and charismatic modes of leadership, including demagogues. To this dynamic we can add the role of the US culture industry in transforming key elements of this historical legacy. To put this thesis more dialectically: US populism was a key component in the development of the US culture industry; that culture industry in turn significantly transformed that legacy by increasing the likelihood of capture of populist insurgencies 'from below' by 'modern' demagogues and for demagogy 'from above' to foster a populist constituency. Today, however, that dynamic, or significant parts of it, has been 'globalized' as key elements of the contemporary culture industry, while US-based, have a global constituency of user-participants.

The structural transformation thesis enables us to configure this relationship immanently and dialectically. What I have termed 'the dialectic of commercialization' in the discussion (section 8(d)) can be understood as a microanalytic revision of the liberal vs organized/monopoly/state capitalism dichotomy that informs much of the first generation's writings. That is, at least for the case of the 'media' institutions of the public sphere, *each wave* of 'technological innovation' has its own 'liberal' moment whereby a balance of forces exists that enables key features of a viable public sphere. However, these waves are then subject to a tendency towards commercialization that undoes this iteration of a liberal public sphere. The next section opens with a recent observation by Habermas that there has been, in effect, no 'liberal phase' in the most recent wave. However, since the early twentieth century, decommodifying 'communications policy' has emerged as another counterforce.

(b) A disintegrating public sphere?

> the classical configuration of the liberal public sphere ... depends on implausible social and cultural assumptions, mainly the existence of alert journalism, with newspapers of reference and mass media capable of directing the interest of the majority toward topics that are relevant to the formation of political opinion; and also the existence of a reading population that is interested in politics, educated, accustomed to the

conflictive process of forming opinions, and which takes the time to read quality, independent press.

Nowadays, this infrastructure is no longer intact, although as far as I know it still exists in countries such as Spain, France and Germany. But even there, the splintering effect of internet has changed the role of traditional media, particularly for the younger generations. Even before the centrifugal and atomic tendencies of the new media came into force, *the commercialization of public attention had already triggered the disintegration of the public sphere.* An example is the US and its exclusive use of private TV channels. Now, new means of communication have a much more insidious model of commercialization in which the goal is not explicitly the consumer's attention, but the economic exploitation of the user's private profile. They rob customers' personal data without their knowledge in order to manipulate them more effectively, at times even with perverse political ends, as in the recent Facebook scandal.

…

… it's the first media revolution in the history of mankind to first and foremost serve economic as opposed to cultural ends.
                                                (Jürgen Habermas, 2018, emphasis added)[5]

This remarkable interview excerpt from Habermas rearticulates core elements of his influential immanent ideology critique of the 'bourgeois category' of the public sphere and applies them to present circumstances. What most renders this passage remarkable is his reintroduction of the theme of *disintegration*, which was central to his 1962 work, *The Structural Transformation of the Public Sphere*.[6]

In this final chapter I wish to use the structural transformation/disintegration framework to draw together some of the motifs of this book. Its appeal lies partly in the effective, yet not quite systematic, contrast Habermas relied on in 1962 between US developments and European ones. The argument he advanced was never simply one of encroaching 'Americanization'. Rather, the US and European public spheres were seen to follow trajectories that sometimes converged and at other times were quite disarticulated. As Habermas makes evident above, a key factor in the disintegration thesis is the degree of *commercialization* of public attention made possible by the institutional configuration of each wave of 'new media'.

While 'disintegration' was never formally abandoned as such by Habermas, his subsequent self-distancings and revisions to the scenario of his first book, especially its pessimistic final sections, had placed such a framework in considerable doubt. Central to this self-distancing was his association of its 'pessimism' with the 'strong influence of Adorno's theory of mass culture'.[7] As we saw in Chapter 3, by 1982 Habermas had formulated a swingeing critique of the culture industry thesis and its alleged foreclosure of any prospect of recognizing a public sphere. His systematic usage of 'disintegration' in reference to recent developments such as the Facebook scandal(s), strongly implies a revision of his mid-period doubts about such an approach, while not necessarily embracing the culture industry thesis in toto.

The culture industry writings had certainly been largely silent on one of its core commodities: the journalistic production of news. Noting this absence in 1985, four years before the English translation of *Structural Transformation* was published, the US critical political communication scholar Daniel Hallin remarked that: '[O]ne might think that by now ... critical theory might have produced a substantial body of research on the institutions of political communication'.[8] This of course is an overstatement, but it is an interesting one.

Structural Transformation had already redressed the apparent lacuna Hallin saw because it shared Hallin's prioritization of journalism. More accurately, 'the press' for Habermas, is 'the public sphere's pre-eminent institution'.[9] Studies in Prejudice had of course addressed a different mode of 'political communication' – modern demagogy – which is absent from Habermas's schema.

One task of this chapter then is to bring these two bodies of work into fuller dialogue. This requires mapping the structural transformation of Habermas's political-communicative 'institutions of the public sphere' *while including* modern demagogy. Also facilitating such dialogue is the critical perspective both Adorno and the early Habermas take towards 'opinion research', which itself becomes a 'player' in its facilitation of the entry of public relations and marketing into the public sphere.

In keeping with the contextualist approach towards Institute texts adopted in this book, relevant developments in the period between the Studies in Prejudice research and *Structural Transformation* become highly significant. However, it is useful initially to follow Habermas's account of structural transformation, focused on his proclaimed central institution, the press.

(c) Structural transformation of 'social structures' and institutions of the public sphere

Habermas's attention to histories of journalism is one of the more striking features of *Structural Transformation*. Britain is his paradigmatic case of an emergent public sphere, in part because overt censorship is reduced there as early as 1695; but he draws on histories of journalism in Germany, France and the USA as well. Significantly, he tends to embed his discussions of early journalism within the role of aesthetic culture, especially the English novel, in enabling the formation of a proto-political literary public sphere. Literary-critical debate forms a prototype of political discussion. Like Lowenthal, Habermas places great emphasis on the educative dimension of British publications of the early eighteenth century such as *The Tatler* and *The Spectator*.[10]

These are also his leading examples of publications circulating in his now-famous key 'social structure' of the emergent public sphere, the London coffee houses. These houses permitted inter-class deliberation between aristocracy and bourgeoise that was impossible in the royal court; but this participation, Habermas stresses, explicitly excluded women. The German 'private reading societies' instituted democratic procedures and proto-parliamentary debate but also excluded women. While the French salons had famously operated on different criteria of gendered access, they did not permit comparable cross-class interaction and later emulations of the English gentlemen's clubs even reversed such tendencies. Habermas's explicitness on the implications of this point is worth noting: 'Women and dependants were factually and legally excluded from the political public sphere, whereas female readers as well as apprentices and servants often took a more active part in the literary public sphere than the owners of private property and family heads themselves.' In this sense, consistent with emancipatory ideology critique, Habermas argues that 'what the public itself believed to be and to be doing was ideology and simultaneously more than ideology'. This leads to his pivotal formulation that the identification of bourgeois property owners and 'human beings pure and simple' equips the bourgeois category of the public sphere with a redeemable emancipatory potential.[11]

The multiple feminist critiques of *Structural Transformation* that followed upon its English translation have been well documented, as has Habermas's agreement that the analysis just outlined insufficiently recognized the *constitutive* character of this gendered division of emergent modes of publicness.[12] However, most of these critiques tend to attribute to *Structural Transformation* a simple 'liberal' private vs public divide, often in the now-familiar decontextualizing mode of philosophers.[13] Instead, Habermas's pinpointing of the tension between female participation in the literary public sphere and the masculinized political public sphere derives from his complex account of the relationship between bourgeois intimacy, 'publicly oriented privateness' and the public sphere. The intimacy of the bourgeois family is regarded as qualitatively new, as is the related development of the intimate letter-writing that provides the foundational form of publicly oriented privateness. The latter is enabled by the development of the modern postal system, Habermas's first acknowledgement of a 'new technology' of communication that post-dates handicraft printing. Such letter-writing, predominantly practised by women, is foundational for the emergence of the epistolary novel. The bourgeois novel so provides a key means of exploring the contradictions inherent in the presumption that bourgeois intimacy had no relationship with its role in social reproduction. Thus: 'the subjectivity originating in the interiority of the conjugal family, by communicating with itself, attained clarity about itself'.[14] In this sense bourgeois intimacy renders the bourgeois family a site of (dominantly female) aesthetico-cultural *production*.

Here too lies the relevance of the later Habermas's insistence that his adoption of these feminist correctives did not alter the standing of emancipatory ideology critique per se (despite his own views of its limits). While he acknowledged that his book had 'moved totally within the circle of a classical Marxian critique of ideology, at least as it was understood in the Frankfurt environment', he also insisted that 'the universalistic discourses of the bourgeois public sphere ... did not remain unaffected by criticisms from within because they differ from Foucaultian discourses by virtue of their capacity for self-transformation'.[15] Few of Habermas's critics have grasped this most basic principle: that the liberal ideal of the public sphere could function as a legitimating ideology *and* 'lay a claim to truth inasmuch as it transcends the status quo in a utopian fashion'; similarly, '[b]ourgeois culture was not mere ideology'.[16]

As we shall see, Habermas's defence of these aspects of ideology critique becomes even more pronounced in his response to critics of the role of journalism in *Structural Transformation*. That account focuses on the transition from a *first phase*, based on the handicraft single-person profit-making publishing enterprise which collated, printed and sold only 'news'. A *second phase* marks the arrival of the literary journalism of the literary public sphere, initially as a rival to news publishers. The handicraft news-producers then became dealers in 'opinion' themselves and share the pedagogical practices of the literary public sphere. Crucially, '[a]t this point the commercial purpose of such enterprises receded almost entirely into the background', so 'violating all the rules of profitability'.[17]

The need for financial support leads to a later division of labour between (financier) publishers and editors (the former handicraft publishers). This *third phase* initially enables a continuance of editorial autonomy (around the turn of the nineteenth century). Editors, not yet positioned as employees, continued to enjoy 'the kind of freedom that in general characterized the communication of private people functioning as a public' while publishers 'procured for the press a commercial basis without commercializing it as such'.[18]

Now, it is by such socio-historically informed dialectical conceptualizations that Habermas draws out a key contradiction within the role of the culture industry in the public sphere. He identifies the possibility of autonomous production being maintained under ostensibly capitalist relations of production. Certainly, we are still at this point in Habermas's analysis dealing with subsidized, rather than fully capitalized, handicraft production (dependent primarily on hand-powered presses) rather than a culture industry per se. Yet even in the advanced culture industry of the twentieth century, Adorno regarded its compositional labour to be primarily of a handicraft form, still permitting autonomous 'popular art'. Alternately, as shown in Chapter 6, we could hold to a stricter sense of culture industry and only apply it to those circumstances where such compositional autonomy is completely replaced by standardizing logics. The following sections of this chapter demonstrate that this becomes quite complicated in the case of broadcasting and later socio-technical configurations of means of communication.

Habermas's dialectical formulation of 'commercialization' is pivotal to his analysis of the *disintegration* of the political public sphere under culture industry pressure. The press becomes fully capitalized and industrialized with the use of steam presses. In what is effectively *a fourth phase*, editors lose the kind of autonomy enjoyed in earlier phases. The accelerated manufacture of news becomes the priority and the editorial section becomes increasingly dependent on advertising. 'Publicity' shifts from autonomous publicization of political news and opinion to 'public relations' which, on the model of highly organized advertising, addresses the public as consumers rather than citizens. It is this mode of pseudo-public display that Habermas labels 'refeudalization'.

Habermas draws together the fate of the literary public sphere and political public sphere, including their 'social structures'. These too undergo a *reversal* in the dialectic of commercialization from the mid-nineteenth century. Bourgeois intimacy, together with its publicly oriented privateness, retreats from its role as a site of socio-aesthetic production; the dominantly female and subaltern reading public likewise is cut off from the exploratory dialectic of the new bourgeois self. Both are supplanted by the rise of a consumptionist culture industry. There is a shift from a 'culture-debating to culture-consuming public'.

Habermas so goes 'beyond Adorno' in his portrait of domination by the culture industry. Unlike Adorno's role for popular art, 'liberal deviations' and a disempowered self-awareness of advertising's propagandism, there is little evidence of a dialectical counterforce left in the logic of commercialization by the end of *Structural Transformation*. His later autocritique of this as 'unilinear' and too simplistic' is quite accurate: 'At the time, I could not imagine any other vehicle of critical publicity than internally democratized interest associations and parties.'[19] With such self-criticism, it seemed, the disintegration thesis was buried. Its 2018 resurrection would seem to be driven by Habermas's analysis of the recent revolution in means of communication in the long citation above, i.e., that it produced a new media system that had no initial 'liberal' phases enabling autonomy.

The later Habermas did, of course, find a counterforce to his early 'pessimism' in the new social movements. The subsequent theorization of counter-publics has tended to emphasize social movements as the incubators of new forms of self-identity; these so play a role comparable to that of the emergent bourgeois intimate sphere but are rarely theorized as such.[20] The role of the literary public sphere has not received comparable attention from the later Habermas. Indeed, one of the ironies here is that in his autocritique of this aspect of his work he embraced Stuart Hall's framework of 'decoding' media messages as an improvement on 'the older explanatory models still assuming linear causal processes'.[21] However, by this point (1989), the legacy of Hall's work had been transformed into the cultural populism detailed in Chapter 6. Habermas displays no awareness that an almost identical reception model had been proposed in *The Authoritarian Personality* (see Chapter 2).

However, Habermas did maintain a role for, and public intellectual advocacy of, 'the press' as 'the backbone of the public sphere', including within the long passage cited above.[22] In the case of the press we can find another, albeit incompletely theorized, dialectic at work in *Structural Transformation*.

(d) The dialectic of contradictory institutionalization and demagogic populism

In his elaboration of the early development of the political public sphere, Habermas pursues his ideology-critical approach through to the 'contradictory institutionalization of the public sphere in the bourgeois constitutional state'. The self-understanding of a 'formless humanity' developed within the intimate sphere of the patriarchal conjugal bourgeois family is rendered more concrete within a key ideological claim: that legitimate formation of laws by parliaments – grounded in constitutional documents including guarantees of basic human rights – should lead to a mode of rule in which domination was 'dissolved'. The guarantor of this dissolution of domination was public opinion which, in Schmitt's phrase, ensured the transformation of *voluntas* (will) into *ratio* (reason).[23]

The reversal of the dynamic of commercialization exposes the unacknowledged dominative dimension of this constitutionality: that both the intimate and private sphere were constituted via a market system that was anything but the felicitous fiction of classical economics. The 'civic privatism' underpinning the model of human rights so comes into conflict with its claims to publicness based on reason rather than interests. Habermas thus makes plain both the fictive dimension of this legitimative schema and its 'approximation' of reality:

> these conditions were by no means fulfilled even in the first half of the nineteenth century. Nevertheless, the liberal model sufficiently approximated reality so that the interest of the bourgeois class could be identified with the general interest and the third estate could be set up as the nation – during that phase of capitalism, the public sphere as the organizational principle of the bourgeois constitutional state had credibility.[24]

Habermas's use of the archaic conception of estate here is not accidental. He distinguishes states like Great Britain, where the constitutional state emerged 'as a fact out of the older formation of a state structured by estates', from those that had fully articulated constitutional provision for all basic rights. There is a corresponding tendency for Habermas at this level of argument to regard 'the *institutions* and *instruments* of the public sphere', most notably 'the press', as having been secured by such bills or rights.[25] Yet Great Britain, Habermas's paradigmatic case, falls into the first category of constitutional state. Moreover, it is this case that generates the highly ambiguous metaphor of 'the fourth estate' to designate the institutional place of 'the press' in the consolidating democratic order. Indeed, Habermas uses the term to designate the very first 'coffee house' phase of political journalism in the early eighteenth century. Here he seems to abandon his usual *Begriffsgeschichte* historical semantic care with 'bourgeois' categories. For 'fourth estate' does not consolidate as a term of reference until the very mid-nineteenth century moment that Habermas marks as the point of reversal of the dialectic of commercialization. Indeed, it is tied to the achievement of hegemony by the 'respectable press', and *The Times* in particular, over all other newspapers in Britain, most especially the defeated Chartist presses.[26]

The tension between these placements of 'the press' are never fully resolved in Habermas. While he is highly attentive to the contradictory institutionalization of the public sphere, he is not so attentive to the contradictory institutionalization of this key 'instrument' of the public sphere. In *Between Facts and Norms*, where he undertook his major revision of the public sphere thesis, 'fourth branch of government' is used somewhat ironically while his preferred term is 'power of the media', alluding to both a quasi-constitutional power and the gatekeeping capacity of news media (in 1992) to set the agenda for public debate.[27]

Now, Habermas's relevant critics tend not to recognize this conceptual problem in their haste to cast *Structural Transformation* as a work of nostalgia and Whig journalism history.[28] Yet one figure who did briefly 'fill' this conceptual lacuna was Adorno. Adorno's laudatory reference to *Structural Transformation* in his 1964 essay on opinion and publicness draws out a lesson from Habermas's analysis that seems to have escaped its author:

> Once previously objective societal institutions like the press monopolized the democratic title to public opinion, public opinion became centralized and therefore moved in opposition to the idea of living subjects, whose diverse opinion it should record.[29]

This short essay does not offer any historical detail, but Adorno's comment suggests a very different way of approaching the mid-nineteenth-century 'commercializing' structural transformation. For the centralization Adorno critically identifies assumed a legitimate form which consolidated as liberal historical orthodoxy: that the fourth estate, as embodied most notably in *The Times*, represented public opinion itself, or even the voice of 'the people'. One of the most famous statements of *The Times*'s claim to constitute the fourth estate as such came in 1855 from one of its former leader writers who nonetheless felt obliged to warn of this concentrated representation of 'opinion'.[30] By 1886, W.T. Stead, a pioneer of popular investigative journalism, could claim of this chamber 'in perpetual session':

> The Press is at once the eye and the ear and the tongue of the people. It is the visible speech if not the voice of the democracy.[31]

If we understand Adorno's 'centralization of opinion' in this way, we are well-positioned to place demagogic populism within the framework of structural transformation. For, as Habermas noted, the 'central article stating that all power came from the people' was the key fault line whereby 'the constitutional establishment of a public sphere in the political realm' betrayed 'its character as an order of domination'.[32]

This fiction so constituted a potential politico-cultural vacuum as well. The claim to fulfil this fiction/promise was open to the fourth estate, radical-popular movements and, eventually, modern demagogic populists. Indeed, a similar framing informs Urbinati's emphasis on the role of populism within constitutional democracies and, most relevantly, the shifting balance between popular 'will' and 'opinion'.[33] In short, Habermas's imprecision concerning the status of 'the press' as claiming to represent 'opinion' indicates a deeper point of under-theorization: that the contradictory institutionalization of the political public sphere *simultaneously establishes the potential for populist invocations* of 'the people', including especially those delivered via 'media'.

In contrast with his response to his feminist critics, the later Habermas argued that his setting aside of the formation of a 'plebeian public sphere' in *Structural Transformation* was defensible given that most of the historical research that supported such a sphere post-dated his book. However, it was hardly the case that he had dismissed these presses as 'an ideological pollutant', as one critic claimed. Rather, Habermas contrasts the situation of *all* presses in advocating the liberty of the press as such, as in times of revolution, with that following the establishment of 'the bourgeois constitutional state and the legalization of a political public sphere'. Only then, could the press 'abandon its polemical stance and concentrate on the profit opportunities of a commercial business'. It is this point (the 1830s) that marks the beginning of his de facto fourth phase of development where 'commercialization' begins to become a priority.[34]

So, the commencement of Habermas's 'disintegration' coincides with the advent of Adorno's monopolization 'of the democratic title to public opinion'. It also marks the advent of a commercial counterforce to the radical-popular cultural populism discussed in Chapter 6. Indeed, critics of the Whig histories of the British case emphasize a similar trajectory whereby the radical presses were overtaken by the fully capitalized industrial presses that newspapers like *The Times* pioneered. By the last decade of the nineteenth century, Habermas and his critics would agree, the development of the tabloid newspaper, usually marked by the foundation of the *Daily Mail* and *Daily Express* in Britain, constitutes a culminating moment of these tendencies. Here journalism and the nascent popular culture of the music hall era are intermixed on a fully commercialized basis.[35]

The 'media' preconditions of 'modern demagogy' were thus also in place by this point. The disintegration tendencies Habermas tracked in this phase did not, however, include demagogy. Here, Habermas's initial account of disintegration suffers from its lack of a developed comparative dimension. While the paradigmatic instance of an emergent public sphere is Britain, the instance of near-complete disintegration is the USA. Yet, as Habermas makes explicit, the US case does not compare well with his mapping of the emergent public spheres in Western Europe.[36] Adorno's work revealed considerable familiarity with relevant US circumstances in the 1930s and 1940s; but it also lacked such historical depth. As we saw in Chapter 1, the Radical Right project had located US demagogy within an articulated historical narrative from the USA's constitutional foundation.

It is not insignificant then that among the strongest critics of *Structural Transformation* are those who would defend the full 'commercialization' of US journalism. On such accounts, Habermas's mid-nineteenth century watershed instead marks the point where US journalism distinguished itself from partisan affiliation, so achieving a neo-Durkheimian differentiated autonomy as part of civil society. The chief weakness of such work for this discussion is the somewhat straw figure characterization of the public sphere thesis that informs it. It also struggles to make this alternative historicization speak to the broadcasting era in which modern demagogy emerged, most prominently in the USA.[37]

In contrast, the First Amendment and media-regulation scholar, C. Edwin Baker, developed a position in his final writings that constituted a well-informed dialogue with the public sphere thesis. Baker placed an emphasis comparable to Habermas's on the unusual vulnerability of the US media system to advertising, both as 'subsidy', potential 'censor' and even 'subversion' of, especially, the democratic role of the press.[38] Most significantly, he also developed an entire 'democratic safeguard' model of democracy to address what he called 'the Berlusconi effect' and its risk of 'demagogic power'. He saw definite risks for US democracy – indeed all democracies – in the precedent set by that European case.[39]

Yet Baker's model of demagogic media power is a somewhat limited one, even if it does account for real threats. It relies on another figure who emerged from the late nineteenth-century commercialization of journalism: the 'politically minded press owner', i.e., a proprietor-publisher 'press baron' who subordinates journalistic professionalism and editorial autonomy to the use of publications for personally preferred *political* goals.[40] Berlusconi can be seen as such a figure to some degree but he benefited from the late introduction of the economic preconditions of a 'tabloid culture' in Italy. He was also unusual in that he sought political office for himself rather than exercising influence from the sidelines.

Baker's sketch of 'demagogic power' is nonetheless an important corrective to Habermas's poorly theorized 'media power'.[41] A historical case could certainly be advanced that the rise of the press baron saw a 'distributed' form of demagogic power in play, whereby the tabloid format's 'populist' idiom was inflected to demagogic purposes, most notably in times surrounding war. However, this 'British' form of demagogic tabloidism had few contemporary parallels.[42] While his work had an unusually critical and international focus for a First Amendment scholar, Baker died in 2009 without elucidating what a 'globally' exercised demagogic power might look like. As I argue in the next section, the US equation of freedom of speech with 'free markets' is pivotal to the emergence of such a phenomenon.

(e) The return of the repressed?

The significance Adorno attaches to the institutional concentration of 'opinion' also speaks to the fact that figures like Coughlin had been permitted to purchase airtime at the advent of US broadcasting via a policy that literally equated 'diversity of opinion' and a 'marketplace of ideas'.[43] The dynamic between US populism and modern demagogy outlined in the opening of this chapter was highly visible in the period from the institution of Adorno's key feature of the culture industry, advertising-funded broadcasting, in the 1920s until the defeat of McCarthy in 1954. Yet modern demagogy became less noticeable for the following forty years. Certainly, prominent demagogues arose within orthodox political institutions, most notably the campaigns by Alabama Governor George Wallace in the 1960s, but the dialectic with the culture industry was not as critical. Such figures did not rely on *commodified* demagogic speech.

What had changed? In the wake of the Coughlin period, moves were made in the USA to restrict the opportunities for broadcast demagogic speech, initially by self-regulation of 'religious' broadcasting. Eventually, and most remarkably, the US Federal Radio/Communications Commission resorted to overt content regulation known as The Fairness Doctrine. One key feature was a right of reply requirement, triggered by complaint, that Murrow pre-emptively employed in his challenge to McCarthy (see Chapter 7). In so doing, the USA finally began to match the standard European practice of requiring broadcast opinion to be mediated by journalists.[44]

Such regulatory constraints upon the 'pure' culture-industrial facilitation of demagogues decreased the prominence of modern demagogy in the USA for two generations. Key elements of the culture industry of course remained – most notably, advertising continued its expansion in a broadcasting system uniquely overdependent on it as a source of revenue.

Intellectual recognition of these developments outside critical theory were marginal and, even then, often tellingly instrumental. The US field of communication(s) studies still echoes with the tension between 'critical' and 'administrative' research. This labelling arose from Paul Lazarsfeld's essay written in the wake of his fraught relationship with Adorno, first published in the *Zeitschrift* in 1941.[45] The publication of Adorno's 'On Popular Music' adjacent to Lazarsfeld's *Zeitschrift* essay contributed to the impression that the sole ground of this disagreement concerned the research on (popular) music within which Adorno had been employed in the Princeton Radio Research Project.[46] Yet Adorno's later references to this tension equally referred to 'opinion research'.[47] By this term he unmistakeably alludes to the 'voting studies', published between 1944 and 1955, for which Lazarsfeld became most famous.

Adorno's critiques of this emergent US field of political communication studies were not based on an outright rejection of comparable empirical research. Upon its return to Germany, the Institute undertook the *Gruppenexperiment*, a large-scale focus group project. It was designed to challenge the officially conducted opinion survey practices commissioned by the Allied occupation forces which claimed to have verified the success of de-Nazification.[48]

Rather, as we can see in his 1964 endorsement of Habermas's *Structural Transformation*, Adorno's target is principally the same as that which Habermas termed the 'manufactured public sphere of the election campaign'. Indeed, Habermas develops this position from a critique of Lazarsfeld's first voting study.[49]

While Lazarsfeld's studies were by no means the only pioneering 'opinion' research undertaken in that period, they normalized key components of modern 'political communication' and its 'administration'. In part this was because they systematized the previously ad hoc development of polling techniques. These components included: the near-total prioritization of the election campaign period as the sole moment of informing citizens, so becoming the primary focus of political communication research; the legitimacy of the equation of candidate selection by voters and product selection by consumers; the instrumental use of survey polling and 'panel' focus groups for both academic analysis and party strategy; the dual role of political journalism and party advertising, via newspapers and broadcasting, as the primary legitimate sources of information. While the 'propaganda' research undertaken during the Second World War was generically acknowledged and the term 'propaganda' employed routinely to refer to partisan information, the prominent role of the radio demagogues from the 1920s to 1940s, played no role. In a post-hoc methodological preface to the second edition of the first voting study, the 'dynamic research' of a discrete period was explicitly advocated as both 'a new method' and as an alternative to the allegedly over-ambitious goals of sociological theory.[50] From this point, orthodox political communication studies, and much political science, regarded the voting studies' components as constituting political communication *as such*.

It was the continuing instrumentalization of this political communication orthodoxy – within market research, much journalism and especially political party practice – that is largely responsible for the 'inauthentic' performance of professional politicians as 'spin'. This performativity became, in effect, another culture industry template, most noticeably during the 'manufactured public sphere'. To this extent, Adorno and Habermas identified a root source of later 'populist' discontent.[51]

This orthodox understanding of political communication has now entered a kind of existential crisis. Its journalism-centrism faces the harsh reality that the 'agenda-setting' role of journalism has declined dramatically and the institutional resources sustaining political journalism have shrunk, primarily due to a shift in advertising revenue away from commercial news-producing organizations.[52] As we saw in Chapter 7, this orthodoxy struggled to recognize the significance of the rise of demagogic figures in the 1990s. 'Mediated populism' had become defined from the early 2000s by the increasing prominence of 'tabloid' forms of journalism beyond their printed origins and their possible 'complicity' in the rise of populist parties.⁵³

What might be called *critical* political communication studies, however, had pointed to a growing 'crisis in public communication' from the 1980s. Significantly, such research focused on what has since become known as 'media systems', i.e., the specific configuration of (orthodox) political communication, news-producing institutions, regulatory frameworks and means of mediated communication.⁵⁴

However, while some references to 'populism' occurred within these forebodings, likewise linked to growing 'tabloidization', demagogy did not. This is somewhat ironic as an implicit and often explicit theme of this dominantly European literature was the question of encroaching Americanization. Europe's regulatory insulation of broadcasting from the US culture industry was a key factor. The chief instrument of this protection was the institution of public service broadcasting across Western Europe.⁵⁵

A looming institutional reorganization based on satellite technology's challenge to these primarily nation-state regulatory orders was increasingly acknowledged, mostly as an anticipated struggle between 'public service' and 'market' models of media systems, due to emergent Thatcherist neoliberalism.⁵⁶ Nicholas Garnham's landmark defence of the UK regulatory system directly tied the British understanding of public service, centred on but not confined to the BBC, to the promotion of Habermas's work on the public sphere. *Structural Transformation* had only briefly mentioned this institutional form, but Habermas later endorsed the UK practice of what he termed 'regulated pluralism' as his preferred media system configuration. The ground was so laid for the widespread adoption of the public sphere thesis in media and communications studies including critical political communication studies.⁵⁷

In the USA the re-emergence of demagogic practices within 'mainstream' media followed quickly upon the deregulation of the Fairness Doctrine from 1987 by the Reagan administration. These developments were empirically tracked by US political communication scholars, both orthodox and critical. However, 'demagogy' was not an ordering concept. The first cultural form to manifest these renewed demagogic tendencies within 'the mainstream' became known as 'aggressive talk radio'. It underwent a 250 per cent expansion in the USA between 1990 and 2006, frequently replacing orthodox radio news services.⁵⁸ The 'format' of a day-long rota of such figures owed much to developments in the 1960s by the mainly 'underground' demagogic producers and unlicensed radio stations which had initially evaded the Fairness Doctrine.⁵⁹

It was here that the Coughlin legacy was revived and transformed from a sermon-like presentation into a variant of the established form of talk radio, the quasi-dialogue of selected listeners calling in combined with the more dominant monologue of the 'host'. Coughlin's business strategy of forming his own networks by selling programmes to syndicated stations was also emulated to varying degrees but now 'orthodox' advertising was introduced as well. The structural significance of this development for the culture industry lay not in its dependence on the 'old' means of communication of radio but in its challenge to journalism as the central means of political communication and as, in effect, a rival informational product/commodity. Moreover, broadcasting proved the most lucrative means of economic survival, but not necessarily political influence, for those who sought to practise modern demagogy as a career. Those 'ultras', as they became known, who did not adopt broadcasting tended to decline.[60]

Rupert Murdoch's Fox News cable television channel was established in 1996, within a decade of the deregulation of the Fairness Doctrine. It emulated the aggressive talk radio practice of directly challenging the legitimacy of mainstream news media, charging it with the bias of 'liberal elites'. It became best known for its 'opinion' programmes anchored by a single figure who emulated aggressive talk radio. Murdoch's Australian television interests had been insulated from most forms of modern media regulation owing to that nation's remarkable policy laxity in this area. It was via the importation of Australian 'tabloid' television formats that the British understanding of tabloid news finally reached the USA in its purest form.[61]

By the turn of the century, the term 'echo chamber', usually attributed to the public intellectual writings of Cass Sunstein, was in wide circulation in the USA. For Sunstein, the term referred to the 'balkanization' of the public into polarized groupings with little exposure to alternative viewpoints. His main focus was the emergent hyperlinking tendencies of political internet sites, including those of a panoply of antisemitic agitators already prominent. He also addressed the rise of aggressive talk radio in the wake of the deregulation of the Fairness Doctrine.[62] The first major empirical examination of 'the conservative echo chamber', published in 2008, placed the aggressive talk radio figure, Rush Limbaugh, at its core with Murdoch's Fox News and his *Wall Street Journal*'s opinion pages providing the other pillars.[63] By 2014 the ultimate irony was reached whereby (critical) political communication scholars identified the intensification of the commodification of such practices as 'the outrage industry', without any connection being made to the Adornian culture industry thesis.[64]

Moves towards reviving the Fairness Doctrine by congressional Democrat leaders were not supported by the incoming Obama administration.[65] Sunstein was appointed by Obama as Administrator of the White House Office of Information and Regulatory Affairs. Indeed, his primary expertise concerned the intersection of constitutional law and regulation, notably focused on first amendment principles of freedom of expression.[66] He became strongly associated with the notion of 'nudging', an extremely modest mode of regulation tied to the work of his co-author, Richard Thaler, in 'behavioural economics'.[67] Sunstein's proposed policy remedies to echo chambers were similarly pitched at the kind of 'indirect suggestion' later advocated as nudging: modest redesigns of websites, for example, analogous to consumer information labelling. Even 'voluntary self-regulation' was regarded by Sunstein as a 'more aggressive' stance.[68]

This detail is significant because it exemplifies what has since been criticized as the neoliberal re-framing of this field by *all* US administrations since Reagan. It has thus been recently argued that rising 'populism' can be regarded as facilitated by 'media policy failure'. Policy failure here refers to the absence of implemented policies of a fundamental 'structural' form to redress the phenomena Sunstein identified, such as cross-ownership regulation provisions that might have delimited the consolidation of the Limbaugh/Murdoch echo chamber. While making some such linkage is pivotal, there is a risk here of not only the familiar conflation of an over-stretched 'populism' but of conflating 'liberal' and 'neoliberal' policy. Such conflations effectively erase the possibility of discerning the role of modern demagogy in contemporary media systems.[69] Rather, the neoliberal deregulation of the Fairness Doctrine by the Reagan administration re-enabled 'legitimate' commodification of modern demagogy rather than populism.

The rejection of the revival of the Fairness Doctrine was based primarily on First Amendment principles. Its placement of a 'burden on speech' had always been anomalous from this perspective. Its exceptional status had been justified, in part, by the communicative limits of analogue broadcasting, its so-called 'spectrum scarcity' that limited the possible number of channels and so rendered the airwaves a de facto public resource. The development of digital multi-channelling, especially for 'free to air' television (as distinct from subscription-based cable) undermined this rationale. As with the advent of satellite broadcasting in Europe, the claim that these were 'technologies of freedom' enabled neoliberal deregulatory logics to take hold among policymakers. This was, in effect a return to the domestic US policy logic that had enabled the radio demagogues in the 1920s and 1930s.[70]

However, a feature of the latest round of technical innovations in means of communication intensified Adorno's 'time coincidence' and 'space ubiquity': key features here are instantaneous digital transmission across national boundaries and the potentiality of progressive 'convergence' of previously discrete 'media' into a common digital infrastructure. Habermas's 2018 renewal of his disintegration thesis cited above goes further to suggest that the current phase of technical innovation is unique not only because of such intensified capacities but also because of the lack of any liberal phase prior to full commercialization. This stands in stark contrast to the first phase of the internet, in which Habermas's conception of the public sphere was invoked to advance utopian claims of its potential based in its *apparent* independence from commercialization and even its supposed recreation of the circumstances of eighteenth-century private individuals forming a public.[71]

The detailed work of Dan Schiller on the most recent consequences of 'digital capitalism', developed before the Facebook data scandals, supports Habermas's role for 'social media': that the current 'geopolitics of information' has resulted from 'a new cycle of commodification' entailing 'a bottomless commercialization of cultural interaction and private life, via smartphones, search engines, social networks, ecommerce, and 24/7 surveillance'.[72] Although neither Schiller nor Habermas elaborates this thesis further, it would follow that the publicly oriented privateness enabled by social media – via the composition of user profiles and similar 'sharing' practices – has also lacked a liberal phase, even if there was a brief apparent one comparable to that of the early internet.

This new cycle of commodification is also pivotal to the revitalization of terms such as 'propaganda' in the wake of the 'fake news' phenomenon – that is, the production and circulation (whether algorithmic or not) of online materials that simulate orthodox journalism. While the actors involved may be domestic or international state actors, the transmission mechanism is chiefly one of commodification.[73]

Underpinning this new geopolitics of information is the fate of the 'global culture industry'. In contrast with the dominance of the USA in the period following the Second World War, it was possible by the 1990s to regard the global exchange of many culture industry commodities as increasingly decentred. However, a key feature of the neoliberal order of world trade agreements negotiated in that decade was the emergence of the economic preconditions of 'a US-centric extraterritorial Internet'. Here the USA achieved a bargaining advantage comparable to its more aggressive defeat of the UNESCO proposal for a New World Information Order, which had challenged the hegemony of Western news agencies, such as Reuters, in the 1980s.[74] In both instances, freedom of expression and freedom of exchange were equated, this time on a global scale. Crucially, it was by such means that an ethos developed whereby the domination of what became 'Silicon Valley' was legitimated as a benign 'global connectedness', as in Facebook's (now abandoned) corporate motto: 'Making the world more open and connected'.[75]

It is appropriate then to re-employ here the Habermasian thesis of contradictory institutionalization, this time embedded in a set of global trade agreements rather than a 'constitutional state'. Yet the same dialectic is evident: a domination self-interpreted as a freedom that is benignly universalized to all humanity. More pragmatically, this also meant that *the US communications policy laxity of the 1920s was repeated for the US-centric Internet and, most notably, so-called 'social media'*. In the former, 'marketplace of ideas' had been literally translated as the retailing of unregulated content to all purchasers, so granting demagogues the opportunity to commodify their propaganda; in the latter, the notion of social media as a 'neutral platform' of free expression functioned almost identically to facilitate the commodification of demagogic speech, 'modern demagogy'. However, this time the policy failure had *global* rather than domestic implications.

It is important to reiterate that this contradictory institutionalization is not a unilinear explanatory device, neither for Habermas in 1962 nor in the account above. The distinctly different 'disintegration thesis' is derived from the dialectic of commercialization which is certainly a process that has become more systemic with each wave of innovation in the means of communication.

Yet if we move to the phenomenon which replaced the literary public sphere – and corrected the early 'pessimism' – in Habermas's work, that of social movements, another level of contradiction becomes evident. Zeynep Tufekci's work, for example, eloquently demonstrates the mobilizing capacity of the 'horizontal' form of contemporary 'social' media. However, while this has meant rapid organization of discrete protest campaigns, most notably during the Arab Spring, it has reversed the more typical historical momentum of social movements from 'thick' organization to protest action, from strategy to tactics. Moreover, the tactical advantage of this online capacity is vulnerable to counteractions by state actors. This problem of 'shallow' organizational form is also one that haunted Coughlin's and Long's broadcasting-based movements.[76] For demagogic populism, then, this likely means that the risk of demagogic capture of populist surges – a major theme of this book – remains (including that by existent state actors).

Habermas's revisitation of the disintegration thesis thus enables the elucidation of the intensity of contemporary commercialization and the related decline of the 'infrastructure' of 'the classical liberal public sphere'. Its reworking also helps us locate the current infrastructure of modern demagogy and to sketch the balance of forces in contemporary social movement practices. Moreover, Habermas's initial account of 'disintegration' was more pessimistic than Adorno's and his later writings supported the policy development of 'regulated pluralism' and the maintenance of an independent press, including by state subsidy. This necessary liberal dimension of the public sphere remains a valid, if considerably weakened, counterforce. As I have indicated in this chapter, conflating it with the neoliberalism that undermined those liberal institutions is potentially disastrous, especially if the key distinction between populism and demagogy also remains unrecognized. This means that communications policy intervention is also a viable counter-demagogic force.[77]

As we saw in Chapter 3, Habermas's 1982 reading of the culture industry thesis was one-dimensional because it neglected the context of the demagogy studies. Accordingly, he maintained no ongoing theoretical role for the complex dynamic Adorno identified: the tendency for the 'montage character' of the culture industry to facilitate the 'technical merger' between demagogic speech and advertising *and* the counterforces of popular art and the contradictory role of 'liberal deviations' within some sectors of the culture industry. As we saw in Chapter 7, all these forces, especially the counterforces, are still in play, although of course highly accelerated.

In short, demagogic populism's dependence on modern demagogy in all its forms is beset by contradictions as well. It would seem, however, that the global reach of commodified modern demagogy has yet to be met by a global counter-demagogic tradition, whether aesthetically or social movement-based. However, these and the other contradictions just indicated are certainly ongoing.

Notes

1. Habermas, *The Structural Transformation of the Public Sphere*.
2. Chapter 1(b); Table 1.
3. Thompson, *The Media and Modernity: A Social Theory of the Media*, 86–87. John B. Thompson, 'Mediated Interaction in the Digital Age', *Theory, Culture & Society* (2020).
4. See Chapter 4(c).
5. Jürgen Habermas, 'Jürgen Habermas: "For God's Sake, Spare Us Governing Philosophers!"', *El País Semanal In English*, 25 May (2018). The Facebook scandal to which Habermas alludes is that of the Cambridge Analytica 'data harvesting'. For an account: Jim Isaak and Mina J. Hanna, 'User Data Privacy: Facebook, Cambridge Analytica, and Privacy Protection', *Computer* 51, no. 8 (2018).
6. Habermas, *The Structural Transformation of the Public Sphere*.
7. Jürgen Habermas, 'Further Reflections on the Public Sphere (1989)', in *Habermas and the Public Sphere*, ed. Craig J. Calhoun (Cambridge, Mass.: MIT Press, 1992), 438.
8. Daniel C. Hallin, 'The American News Media: A Critical Theory Perspective', in *Critical Theory and Public Life*, ed. John Forester (Cambridge, Mass.: MIT Press, 1985). Hallin makes good use of the available Habermas translations but seems unaware of *Structural Transformation*, the English translation of which was published four years later.
9. Habermas, *The Structural Transformation of the Public Sphere*, 181.
10. Habermas, *The Structural Transformation of the Public Sphere*, 42–44. Cf. my discussion of Lowenthal in Chapter 6.
11. Habermas, *The Structural Transformation of the Public Sphere*, 88.

12 See, for example: Johanna Meehan, ed., *Feminists Read Habermas: Gendering the Subject of Discourse* (New York: Routledge, 1995). For critical overviews of these debates: Johnson, *Habermas: Rescuing the Public Sphere*, 33–36; Jean L. Cohen, 'Critical Social Theory and Feminist Critiques: The Debate with Jürgen Habermas', in *Feminists Read Habermas*, ed. Johanna Meehan (New York: Routledge, 1995). For Habermas's initial response to his feminist critics: Habermas, 'Further Reflections on the Public Sphere (1989)'.
13 It is striking that none of the contributors to the Meehan collection in previous endnote, for example, are sociologists. Almost all are philosophers and political scientists/philosophers.
14 Habermas, *The Structural Transformation of the Public Sphere*, 51.
15 Habermas, 'Concluding Remarks', 463. Habermas, 'Further Reflections on the Public Sphere (1989)', 429. See pp. 442–443 of same text for his summation of the limits of ideology critique.
16 Habermas, *The Structural Transformation of the Public Sphere*, 88, 160.
17 Habermas, *The Structural Transformation of the Public Sphere*, 182.
18 Habermas, *The Structural Transformation of the Public Sphere*, 183.
19 Habermas, 'Further Reflections on the Public Sphere (1989)', 440.
20 Nancy Fraser's work here is the most influential: Nancy Fraser, 'Rethinking the Public Sphere: A Contribution to the Critique of Actually Existing Democracy', *Social Text*, no. 25/26 (1990).
21 Habermas, 'Further Reflections on the Public Sphere (1989)', 439.
22 Jürgen Habermas, 'Media, Markets and Consumers: The Quality of Press as Backbone of the Public Sphere', in *Europe: The Faltering Project* (Oxford: Polity, 2009).
23 Habermas, *The Structural Transformation of the Public Sphere*, 81. The later Habermas distanced himself from his usage of Schmitt's *Constitutional Theory*: but his citation here is hardly essential to his argument: Jürgen Habermas, *Between Facts and Norms: Contributions to a Discourse Theory of Law and Democracy*, trans. W. Rehg (Cambridge, Mass.: MIT Press, 1996), n75, 563.
24 Habermas, *The Structural Transformation of the Public Sphere*, 87. Habermas later saw the legitimative support of this schema by classical economics in the nineteenth century being replaced by elitist theories of democracy and technocratic discourses. Jürgen Habermas, *Legitimation Crisis* (Boston: Beacon Press, 1975), 37.
25 Habermas, *The Structural Transformation of the Public Sphere*, 83.
26 The provenance of 'fourth estate' in this context is hardly a matter of consensus. It is usually credited to Thomas Carlyle who in 1841 attributed it, in an unsourced reference, to Edmund Burke. According to Carlyle, Burke referred to the parliamentary Reporters' Gallery as the Fourth Estate. Carlyle extends it to declare that all published speech had become 'a Power' due to the printing press. Thomas Carlyle, *On Heroes, Hero-Worship, and the Heroic in History* (New Haven: Yale University Press, 2013), 139. However, Macaulay published a similar statement in 1828: Thomas Macaulay, 'The Constitutional History of England, from the Accession of Henry VII. To the Death of George II. By Henry Hallam', *The Edinburgh Review* 48, no. 95 (1828): 165. For the definitive critical account emphasising the role of *The Times* and the defeat of the radical presses (which also guided me to many historical sources) see: George Boyce, 'The Fourth Estate: The Reappraisal of a Concept', in *Newspaper History: From the Seventeenth Century to the Present Day*, ed. George Boyce, James Curran and Pauline Wingate (London: Constable, 1978).
27 Habermas, *Between Facts and Norms: Contributions to a Discourse Theory of Law and Democracy*.

28 For example, John Keane, *The Media and Democracy* (Cambridge: Polity, 1991).
29 Adorno, 'Opinion Research and Publicness (Meinungsforschung Und Öffentlichkeit 1964)', 183.
30 Henry Reeve, 'The Newspaper Press', *The Edinburgh Review* 102, no. 208 (1855). On the liberal media-historical orthodoxy in the UK: James Curran, 'Narratives of Media History Revisited', in *Media and Democracy* (London: Routledge, 2011).
31 W.T. Stead, 'Government by Journalism', *The Contemporary Review* 49, no. 1 (1886), 656.
32 Habermas, *The Structural Transformation of the Public Sphere*, 84.
33 Urbinati, *Democracy Disfigured*.
34 Habermas, *The Structural Transformation of the Public Sphere*, 184. For the 'pollutant' charge: James Curran, 'Rethinking the Media as a Public Sphere', in *Communication and Citizenship*, ed. Peter Dahlgren and Colin Sparks (London Routledge, 1991), 40. For Habermas's later response to his historian critics: Habermas, 'Further Reflections on the Public Sphere (1989)', 425–427.
35 For example, Martin Conboy, *Journalism: A Critical History* (London: Sage, 2004), 210ff.
36 Habermas, *The Structural Transformation of the Public Sphere*, n65, 267.
37 Schudson's work on US journalism has strongly informed that of Jeffrey C. Alexander, from some of his earliest neo-Durkheimian framings of journalism to his most recent which locate it within his 'civil sphere' theory. Schudson's critique of *Structural Transformation* was explicitly rejected by Habermas due to its mistaking of ideology critique for a 'golden age' nostalgism while Alexander has most recently equated Habermas's work with Arendt's in supposedly relying on the model of the ancient agora. Despite the tendency of both authors towards insistent optimism, the civil sphere framework nonetheless has considerable potential to recognize the 'dark side' of Durkheimian solidarization. Michael Schudson, 'Was There Ever a Public Sphere? If So, When? Reflections on the American Case', in *Habermas and the Public Sphere*, ed. Craig J. Calhoun (Cambridge, Mass.: MIT Press, 1992). Habermas, 'Concluding Remarks', 463. Jeffrey C. Alexander, 'The Crisis of Journalism Reconsidered: Cultural Power', *Fudan Journal of the Humanities and Social Sciences* 8, no. 1 (2015): 18; Alexander, *The Dark Side of Modernity*.
38 C. Edwin Baker, *Advertising and a Democratic Press* (Princeton: Princeton University Press, 1995).
39 C. Edwin Baker, *Media Concentration and Democracy: Why Ownership Matters* (Cambridge: Cambridge University Press, 2007); C. Edwin Baker, 'Viewpoint Diversity and Media Ownership', *Federal Communications Law Journal* 61 (2008); C. Edwin Baker, 'Press Performance, Human Rights, and Private Power as a Threat', *Law & Ethics of Human Rights* 5, no. 2 (2011); C. Edwin Baker, 'Media Concentration: Giving up on Democracy', *Florida Law Review* 54 (2002): 906ff.
40 Jean K. Chalaby, 'No Ordinary Press Owners: Press Barons as a Weberian Ideal Type', *Media, Culture & Society* 19, no. 4 (1997).
41 I regard 'media power' as a discretely separate category from the conception of communicative power that strongly informs *Between Facts and Norms*. While Habermas also engages with First Amendment scholarship in that work, including Sunstein's, unfortunately he does not discuss Baker's.
42 This is confusing territory as the term 'tabloid' has covered a range of newspaper (and later television) formats that are actually quite distinct across different national-popular cultures. See: Daniel C. Hallin and Paolo Mancini, *Comparing Media Systems: Three Models of Media and Politics* (Cambridge: Cambridge University

Press, 2004), 158–159. On the complex interaction between early British and US developments of the tabloid form: M. Conboy, *Tabloid Britain: Constructing a Community through Language* (London: Routledge, 2006). Chalaby's work is the most compatible with the Habermasian disintegration thesis and has the further advantage of analysing the 'populist idiom' of the British tabloid press from a perspective comparable to the 'social formalist' one I have advocated in this book: Jean K. Chalaby, *The Invention of Journalism* (Houndmills, Basingstoke: Macmillan, 1998).

43 Michele Hilmes, *Only Connect: A Cultural History of Broadcasting in the United States*, 4th edn (Boston: Wadsworth Cengage, 2014). Jones, 'Demagogic Populism and US Culture Industries: A Long Tradition'.

44 Louise Margaret Benjamin, *Freedom of the Air and the Public Interest: First Amendment Rights in Broadcasting to 1935* (Carbondale: Southern Illinois University Press, 2001); Stewart M. Hoover and Douglas K. Wagner, 'History and Policy in American Broadcast Treatment of Religion', *Media, Culture & Society* 19, no. 1 (1997); Hilmes, *Only Connect: A Cultural History of Broadcasting in the United States*.

45 Paul F. Lazarsfeld, 'Remarks on Administrative and Critical Communications Research', *Zeitschrift für Sozialforschung* 9, no. 1 (1941). On the continuing resonance of this distinction in communication studies, cf.: Sonia Livingstone, 'Elihu Katz's Commitments, Disciplinarity and Legacy: Or, "Triangular Thinking"', *International Journal of Communication* 8 (2014).

46 Adorno and Simpson, 'On Popular Music'.

47 Andrew J. Perrin and Lars Jarkko, 'Introduction to T.W. Adorno, 'Opinion Research and Publicness (Meinungsforschung Und Öffentlichkeit 1964)'', *Sociological Theory* 23, no. 1 (2005). Adorno, 'Scientific Experiences of a European Scholar in America (1968)'.

48 Friedrich Pollock et al., *Group Experiment and Other Writings: The Frankfurt School on Public Opinion in Postwar Germany* (Cambridge, Mass.: Harvard University Press, 2011).

49 Adorno, 'Opinion Research and Publicness (Meinungsforschung Und Öffentlichkeit 1964)'; Habermas, *The Structural Transformation of the Public Sphere*, 213–214.

50 Paul F. Lazarsfeld, Bernard Berelson and Hazel Gaudet, 'Preface to the Second Edition', in *The People's Choice: How the Voter Makes up His Mind in a Presidential Campaign* (New York: Columbia University Press, 1948).

51 For parallel critical theoretical accounts in dialogue with Habermas's work: Leon H. Mayhew, *The New Public: Professional Communication and the Means of Social Influence* (Cambridge: Cambridge University Press, 1997); Thomas Meyer, *Media Democracy: How the Media Colonize Politics* (Cambridge: Polity, 2002).

52 For recent critical overviews: W. Lance Bennett and Steven Livingston, 'The Disinformation Order: Disruptive Communication and the Decline of Democratic Institutions', *European Journal of Communication* 33, no. 2 (2018); W. Lance Bennett and Barbara Pfetsch, 'Rethinking Political Communication in a Time of Disrupted Public Spheres', *Journal of Communication* 68, no. 2 (2018).

53 Gianpietro Mazzoleni, 'Mediated Populism', in *The International Encyclopedia of Communication*, ed. Wolfgang Donsbach (London: Blackwell Publishing, 2008). Gianpietro Mazzoleni, 'Populism and the Media', in *Twenty-First Century Populism*, ed. D. Albertazzi and D McDonnell (Houndmills, Basingstoke: Palgrave, 2008).

54 Jay G. Blumler and Michael Gurevitch, *The Crisis of Public Communication* (London: Routledge, 1995); Hallin and Mancini, *Comparing Media Systems: Three Models of Media and Politics*.

55 The best overview of these European systems from this period is: Peter Humphreys, *Mass Media and Media Policy in Western Europe* (Manchester: Manchester University Press 1996).
56 For one of the earliest and most prescient: Nicholas Garnham, 'Public Service Versus the Market', *Screen* 24, no. 1 (1983).
57 Garnham, 'The Media and the Public Sphere'; Habermas, *The Structural Transformation of the Public Sphere*, 188; Habermas, *Between Facts and Norms: Contributions to a Discourse Theory of Law and Democracy*, 378; n370, 557.
58 Berry and Sobieraj mark another wave of content deregulation from 2000 which has heightened this tendency. Heather Hendershot, *What's Fair on the Air?: Cold War Right-Wing Broadcasting and the Public Interest* (Chicago: The University of Chicago Press, 2011); Jeffrey M. Berry and Sarah Sobieraj, *The Outrage Industry: Political Opinion Media and the New Incivility* (New York: Oxford University Press, 2014), 79. The 250 per cent figure is derived from: Project for Excellence in Journalism., 'The State of the News Media 2007, Talk Radio', Project for Excellence in Journalism, http://stateofthemedia.org/2007/radio-intro/talk-radio/.
59 Hendershot, *What's Fair on the Air?: Cold War Right-Wing Broadcasting and the Public Interest*; Jones, 'Demagogic Populism and US Culture Industries: A Long Tradition'.
60 All the primary information in this paragraph is drawn from: Hendershot, *What's Fair on the Air?: Cold War Right-Wing Broadcasting and the Public Interest*. However, I have placed it in the interpretative 'culture industry/modern demagogy' framework. Hendershot underestimates Coughlin's example and while she productively employs the Radical Right project and related work, she does not connect this to the Institute's research.
61 Paul K. Jones and Michael Pusey, 'Political Communication and "Media System": The Australian Canary', *Media, Culture & Society* 32, no. 3 (2010); Reece Peck, *Fox Populism: Branding Conservatism as Working Class* (Cambridge: Cambridge University Press, 2019).
62 Cass R. Sunstein, *Republic.Com* (Princeton: Princeton University Press, 2001); Cass R. Sunstein, *Echo Chambers: Bush V. Gore, Impeachment, and Beyond* (Princeton: Princeton University Press 2001).
63 Kathleen Hall Jamieson and Joseph N. Cappella, *Echo Chamber: Rush Limbaugh and the Conservative Media Establishment* (New York: Oxford University Press, 2008).
64 Berry and Sobieraj, *The Outrage Industry: Political Opinion Media and the New Incivility*.
65 R. Trevor Hall and James C. Phillips, 'The Fairness Doctrine in Light of Hostile Media Perception', *CommLaw Conspectus* 19 (2010).
66 Cass R. Sunstein, *Democracy and the Problem of Free Speech* (New York: Free Press, 1993).
67 Richard H. Thaler and Cass R. Sunstein, *Nudge: Improving Decisions About Health, Wealth, and Happiness* (New Haven: Yale University Press, 2008).
68 Sunstein, *Republic.Com*, 177.
69 Freedman's otherwise pertinent analysis falls into this trap, reproducing the perspective of Michael Kazin discussed in Chapter 1: Des Freedman, 'Populism and Media Policy Failure', *European Journal of Communication* 33, no. 6 (2018).
70 Respectively, the key US and UK advocacy texts here were: Ithiel de Sola Pool, *Technologies of Freedom* (Cambridge, Mass.: Belknap Press, 1983); Richard Collins and Cristina Murroni, *New Media, New Policies: Media and Communications Strategies for the Future* (Cambridge: Polity, 1996).

71 The most utopian of the internet as public sphere advocacies was: Howard Rheingold, *The Virtual Community: Homesteading on the Electronic Frontier* (Reading, Mass.: Addison-Wesley Pub. Co., 1993).

72 Dan Schiller, 'Geopolitics and Economic Power in Today's Digital Capitalism', in *Presentation to the Hans Crescent Seminar* (London, 13 December 2015). Dan Schiller, *Digital Capitalism: Networking the Global Market System* (Cambridge, Mass.: MIT Press, 1999).

73 Martin Hirst, 'Towards a Political Economy of Fake News', *The Political Economy of Communication* 5, no. 2 (2017); Damian Tambini, 'How Advertising Fuels Fake News', *LSE Media Policy Blog*, 20 June (2017).

74 Dan Schiller, 'Digital Capitalism: A Status Report on the Corporate Commonwealth of Information', in *A Companion to Media Studies*, ed. Angharad N. Valdivia (New York: Wiley, 2007); Schiller, 'Geopolitics and Economic Power in Today's Digital Capitalism'.

75 Anna Lauren Hoffmann, Nicholas Proferes and Michael Zimmer, '"Making the World More Open and Connected": Mark Zuckerberg and the Discursive Construction of Facebook and Its Users', *New Media & Society* 20, no. 1 (2018).

76 Zeynep Tufekci, *Twitter and Tear Gas: The Power and Fragility of Networked Protest* (New Haven: Yale University Press, 2017); Zeynep Tufekci, 'A Response to Johanne Kübler's a Review of *Twitter and Tear Gas: The Power and Fragility of Networked Protest*', *International Journal of Politics, Culture, and Society* (2019); Zeynep Tufekci, 'How Social Media Took Us from Tahrir Square to Donald Trump', *MIT Technology Review* (2018). Brinkley, *Voices of Protest*.

77 In practice, this is of course more complex. As advertising is pivotal to all these developments in culture industry commercialization, including the undermining of the viability of orthodox journalism, proposals to tax advertising itself and create a subsidy scheme emerge as the most pertinent. Subsidy proposals have emerged from figures as diverse as Michael Schudson in the USA and the Corbyn-led British Labour Party. Strategies to decommodify demagogic speech itself would of course be the ideal goal. On that, the remarkably bipartisan UK parliamentary inquiry into fake news continues the UK's history of best practice in this field. Leonard Downie and Michael Schudson, 'The Reconstruction of American Journalism', *Columbia Journalism Review* 19 (2009); Jim Waterson, 'Corbyn Proposes "Public Facebook" as Part of Media Overhaul', *The Guardian*, 23 August (2018). House of Commons Digital Culture Media and Sport Committee, 'Disinformation and 'Fake News': Final Report' (London: House of Commons, 2019). The US First Amendment tradition remains a central point of contention in such policymaking: Philip M. Napoli, 'What If More Speech Is No Longer the Solution? First Amendment Theory Meets Fake News and the Filter Bubble', *Federal Communications Law Journal* 70, no. 1 (2018).

Appendix

Adorno, Theodor W. 'Introduction to *Prophets of Deceit*' (1949, previously unpublished)

(Draft) Introduction to Leo Lowenthal and Norbert Guterman, *Prophets of Deceit: A Study of the Techniques of the American Agitator* (Harper & Brothers 1949) © Theodor W. Adorno-Estate. Reprinted with the friendly permission of Suhrkamp Verlag Berlin. Reproduced from: Leo Lowenthal Archive; MS Ger 185 (153), Houghton Library, Harvard University.

The following is a draft of an introduction to Lowenthal and Guterman's *Prophets of Deceit*, dated 20 June 1949. It is presented as a photographic reproduction of the typescript and as a transcription. The latter sets aside the crossouts but otherwise aims to respect the minor corrections.

I came across the document while checking the Lowenthal archive at Harvard Houghton Library (online). Although 'TWA' is clearly indicated in the header, the published introduction to the book was attributed to Horkheimer. I consulted Jack Jacobs at CUNY regarding its provenance (to whom I express my thanks). Adorno and Horkheimer's correspondence at the time makes it evident that they were exchanging draft versions of the introduction texts with Adorno drafting and Horkheimer editing. So the most likely scenario would be that this is a draft Adorno prepared and sent to Horkheimer for comment and that the edits are by Horkheimer. Also, as I argue in Chapter 3, the discussion of physiognomy is consistent with Adorno's usage elsewhere. As Jacobs points out in his *The Frankfurt School, Jewish Lives and Antisemitism*, both Adorno and Horkheimer were strongly sympathetic towards *Prophets*. Lowenthal had, after all, contributed to 'Elements of Anti-Semitism' a few years before. So it is perhaps appropriate that this is the only one of the Studies in Prejudice series – besides *The Authoritarian Personality*, of which Adorno was lead author – to which either Adorno or Horkheimer wrote a dedicated introduction.

My thanks to: the Adorno Estate for granting permission to reproduce this text; the librarians at Harvard Houghton for their assistance with the document; Lisa-Marie Fleck at Suhrkamp for organizing permission from the Adorno Estate; Alun Richards for organizing the transcription.

PKJ

The Prophets of Deceit   6.20.49. TWA (2)

INTRODUCTION

The present book has grown out of studies undertaken by the INSTITUTE OF SOCIAL RESEARCH during the past two decades. A large part of them was devoted to the scrutiny of ideologies, to what was later on recognised – under the name of "content analysis" – as an important part of social research. However, the tradition on which our previous studies in this field (dealing with philosophers, poets, novelists, popular literature and music) were based, differed insofar from today's content analysis as it employed only incidentally quantitative methods. Its main concern were ideologies as meaningful structural units. We felt that they had to be "understood" rather than measured in order to provide us with productive insights into the substantial and yet in so many respects evasive entity which some philosophers and social scientists of the nineteenth century called spirit. Consequently, the book by Drs. Lowenthal and Guterman is confined to objective qualitative analysis. It is not concerned with the frequency of ideas, formula and devices in agitational material (as was, e.g. the study on Gerald K. Smith by   in   ), but concentrates entirely on its meaning which is interpreted through social and psychological categories.[1]

None of the "devices" or techniques of agitation have to be evaluated in isolation. Each one of them may equally occur in an entirely different political and social context. Their specific significance as means of fascist mass manipulation is obtained only within the structural unity of meaning evolved by the authors, and emphasis should be laid on this unity rather than on any particular manifestation of demagoguery.

The guiding conception is that consumption is largely determined by production. Under conditions of modern, highly industrialised and centralised society, this applies also to ideologies in the broadest sense, ranging from public opinion to attitudes and behaviors. They are largely "manufactured" and cannot be traced back naively and exclusively to the dispositions and urges of the people. The latter do not "choose" them freely but accept them, yielding to the pressure of actual or pretended power. Thus, the mere study of the people themselves does not suffice. In a social field in which stimuli no less than reactions have definite meanings of their own, it seems appropriate to devote at least some attention to their nature so as to understand mass phenomena in their proper proportion, Otherwise one might attribute to an underlying public frame of mind what may actually be due to the impact of calculated techniques of communication.

Inasmuch as the main emphasis is placed on the meaning of the phenomena, the latter should be viewed in the light of their potential implications within the totality of present-day society and its dynamics, rather than their immediate effectiveness. Even when the direct impact of fascist agitation is at an ebb, the nature of its content and technique remains important as an example of modern mass manipulation in its purest and most sinister form.

The study employs mostly psychological concepts. However, this does not necessarily imply a "psychological" bias on the part of the authors. Their explanations pertain to the technique of the agitator who reckons with certain psychological dispositions upon which to play with psychological means. These, on the other hand, he puts into the service of definite though not always fully conscious political aims. In this sphere, psychology is not an end but a means.

The agitator may be defined as the expert propagandist who assumes the role of the leader. The most important Nazis were agitators by profession and it seems to be an intrinsic characteristic of the modern demagogue that he earns his living through his performance. Due to his skill agitation assumes the aspect of a secondary reality. The more it becomes a means for a hidden end, the more does it pretend to be the end itself. The performance offers the audience vicarious gratifications, substituting just that social change from which their minds are deflected. The confusion between means and ends is part and parcel of a whole system of manufactured irrationality.

Historically, demagoguery makes its appearance regularly at times when democratic societies tend to tilt over into dictatorships. Demagoguery has always been the means to guide masses, with whose potential impact one has to reckon, towards ends which run counter to their own true interests. This contradiction, inherent in all agitation, is the objective reason of its irrationality, in the last analysis of the role which it applies to psychological techniques.

The agitator who incessantly plays up his own subjectivity is actually a mere function of objective social forces. It is not accidental that he pretends to be the leader as well as the common man, as is pointed out in Chapter IX of the book. Only through the display of his defectiveness does he allow for those identifications as the agent of which he functions. He has to present himself in such a way that those who worship him are not even reminded of the potentialities of independent thinking and autonomous decisions. He sets the pattern, as it were, for the ego-less, incoherent and, therefore, malleable characters into whom fascism intends to transform the nations. He manipulates his own weakness for the sake of the power he intends to wield.

The relative accidentalness and emptiness of the content of agitation, its complete subordination to manipulative purposes, is obvious. There are profound reasons for this conspicuous lack of content, above all the absence of a tradition of autochthonous and aggressive imperialist nationalism in America. Thus,

American patterns of non-political manipulation – and especially certain marginal phenomena – had to be fused artificially with fascist notions of the Italian and German brand. One has to think of the barker who puts such high pressure behind advertising that it approaches violence. Much has also been borrowed from fanatic religious revivalism, promoting an ecstasy which is relished as such and unrelated to any concrete content, while rigid, dogmatic stereotypes, as e.g. the distinction between the damned and the saved ones, are ruthlessly plugged. The modern American agitator shrewdly feeds on these old-fashioned methods. He warms them up for psychotechnical reasons and handles them quite consciously – as a political "human relations expert". Methods derived from industry and standardized mass culture are presented under a backward, obsolete "character mask" and thus transferred to politics.

The mixture of the obsolescent and the streamlined is characteristic of the whole sphere of agitation. Its novel feature is the idea of a totalitarian transformation of men into potential objects. However, the anachronistic element remains indispensable. It is as intrinsically connected with the function of agitation as is the cheap entertainment of the country fair booth with the monster productions of modern film palaces. The eternal nucleus of agitation is its subjective and objective affinity to what is contemptuously called "rabble". Demagoguery is addressed to certain social groups which so to speak form a kind of social refuse throughout history at the margin of society. The frightening eternity of these phenomena reflects but the unchanged continuity of social pressure itself. Contact with this sphere, and the apocryphal nature of the agitators themselves function in the interest of the abolition of formal democratic processes and legal guaranties. The toughness, unruliness and lawlessness of the *Lumpenproletariat* is seized by powerful groups for the purpose of establishing their own usurpatory, unchecked rule. A-social individuals and groups are the agents of a widespread social tendency to dominate through crude violence. However, the survival of these marginal groups is not an accident which merely disturbs the "normal" life of society, but is concomitant with the ultimate reference to violence by which this society is being held together. Accordingly, agitation, a marginal phenomenon whose ultimate meaning is violence, never disappears entirely. Society is not supposed to ever come to rest – it is continuously reminded of the naked physical force on which it is based.

It would be naive to assume that all or most of the marginal figures who sell hatred are bought or have a mandate from really powerful groups. In this country they have failed so far to build up a unified organization, and they have equally failed to win large-scale financial backing although there are certain indications that this might change sooner than is generally anticipated. Fascism is the *ultima ratio* of repression and it is chosen by the real powers that be only if social conflicts increase to such an extent that control cannot be maintained by any other means. The very fear of the ruling strata of their prospective henchmen, however, is indicative of the potential seriousness of the danger, no matter how insignificant the agitators may appear to be. The concept of marginal figures is not an absolute. Social dynamics may well transfer to the center what today still leads a disreputable life at the border of the social and political field.

This book is not so much devoted to the agitators' social physiognomies as to the psychological contents of their standard devices, that is to say, to the elucidation of those inner and largely unconscious mechanisms at which agitation is directed. However, the psychological emphasis of the technique itself has to be understood sociologically. Since fascism's aim is not an essentially new society but the perpetuation of the old one in congealed, hierarchically rigid forms, it is set against any critique, reflection and self-awareness which is dubbed "destructive". Everything is subordinated to the confirmation of the *status quo*. The individual, instead of being induced to think, is held at bay through the manipulation of his own unconscious and ego-alien mechanisms which are to stay unconscious; he is prevented from gaining insight into his real social interests. Even the technique's rigid stereotypy, monotony and repetitiveness have their social significance. As pointed out in other books of this series, these aspects correspond to certain specific character traits of the personalities susceptible to prejudice, while, socially, they mean standardization of consciousness and adaptation of the individual to the prevailing mode of mass production. The psyche of men themselves is formed in a mould, as it were, and ultimately "expropriated" by those social agencies as whose mouthpiece the agitators style themselves. Here, as in many other aspects, fascism achieves suddenly, with one stroke – "*schlagartig*" was a favorite Nazi term – and seemingly from outside, what is brought about more inconspicuously and slowly through anonymous inner developmental tendencies of society itself.

Such sociological trends provide the proper perspective for the psychological constructs of the book. It does not pretend to give a photographic picture of today's political reality, and it does not overrate the immediate and literal importance of contemporary American demagoguery. Rather, it takes certain phenomena, which appear *prima facie* as negligible, under a microscope in order to gain pertinent diagnostic insights into the latent threat against democracy through the enlargement of its most extreme and apparently unrealistic manifestations. It is hoped that the microscopic diagnosis of remote and inconsiderable social deformations, undertaken free from the pressure of any immediate political or economic crisis, will contribute to the evolution of well-planned and effective long-term defense measures against the danger of terror that has survived Hitler's defeat.

The Prophets of Deceit   6.20.49. TWA (2)

INTRODUCTION

The present book has grown out of studies undertaken by the INSTITUTE OF SOCIAL RESEARCH during the past two decades. A large part of them was devoted to the scrutiny of ideologies, to what was later on recognized -- under the name of "content analysis" -- as an important part of social research. However, the tradition on which our previous studies in this field (dealing with philosophers, poets, novelists, popular literature and music) were based, differed insofar from today's content analysis as it employed only insidentally quantitative methods. Its main concern were ideologies as meaningful structural units. We felt that they had to be "understood" rather than measured in order to provide us with productive insights into the substantial and yet in so many respects evasive entity which the objective philosophers and social scientists of the nineteenth century called spirit. Consequently, the book by Drs. Lowenthal and Guterman is confined to qualitative analysis. It is not concerned with the frequency of ideas, formulas and devices in agitational material (as was, e.g. the study on Gerald K. Smith by   in   ), but concentrates entirely on its meaning which is interpreted through social and psychological categories.

None of the "devices" or techniques of agitation have to be evaluated in isolation. Each one of them may equally occur in an entirely different political and social context. Their specific significance as means of fascist mass manipulation is obtained only within the structural unity of

2

meaning evolved by the authors, and emphasis should be laid on this unity rather than on any particular manifestation of demagoguery.

The guiding conception is that consumption is largely determined by production. Under conditions of modern, highly industrialized and centralized society, this applies also to ideologies in the broadest sense, ranging from public opinion to attitudes and behaviors. They are largely "manufactured" and cannot be traced back naively and exclusively to the dispositions and urges of the people. The latter do not "choose" them freely but accept them, yielding to the pressure of actual or pretended power. Thus, the mere study of the people themselves does not suffice. In a social field in which stimuli no less than reactions have definite meanings of their own, it seems appropriate to devote at least some attention to their nature so as to understand mass phenomena in their proper proportion. Otherwise one might attribute to an underlying public frame of mind what may actually be due to the impact of calculated techniques of communication.

Inasmuch as the main emphasis is placed on the meaning of the phenomena, the latter should be viewed in the light of their potential implications within the totality of present-day society and its dynamics, rather than their immediate effectiveness. Even when the direct impact of fascist agitation is at an ebb, the nature of its content and technique remains important as an example of modern mass manipulation in its purest and most sinister form.

The study employs mostly psychological concepts. However, this does not necessarily imply a "psychological" bias on the part of the authors. Their explanations pertain to the technique of the agitator who reckons with certain psychological dispositions upon which to play with psychological means. These, on the other hand, he puts into the service of definite though not always fully conscious political aims. In this sphere, psychology is not an end but a means.

3

The agitator may be defined as the expert propagandist who assumes the role of the leader. The most important Nazis were agitators by profession and it seems to be an intrinsic characteristic of the modern demagogue that he earns his living through his performance. Due to his skill agitation assumes the aspect of a secondary reality. The more it becomes a means for a hidden end, the more does it pretend to be the end itself. The performance offers the audience vicarious gratifications, substituting just that social change from which their minds are deflected. The confusion between means and ends is part and parcel of a whole system of manufactured irrationality.

Historically, demagoguery makes its appearance regularly at times when democratic societies tend to tilt over into dictatorships. Demagoguery has always been the means to guide masses, with whose potential impact one has to reckon, towards ends which run counter to their own true interests. This contradiction, inherent in all agitation, is the objective reason of its irrationality, in the last analysis of the role which it applies to psychological techniques.

The agitator who incessantly plays up his own subjectivity, is actually a mere function of objective social forces. It is not accidental that he pretends to be the leader as well as the common man, as is pointed out in Chapter IX of the book. Only through the display of his defectiveness does he allow for those identifications as the agent of which he functions. He has to present himself in such a way that those who worship him are not even reminded of the potentialities of independent thinking and autonomous decisions. He sets the pattern, as it were, for the ego-less, incoherent and, therefore, malleable characters into whom fascism intends to transform the nations. He manipulates his own weakness for the sake of the power he intends to wield.

4

The relative accidentalness and emptiness of the content of agitation, its complete subordination to manipulative purposes, is obvious. There are profound reasons for this conspicuous lack of content, above all the absence of a tradition of autochthonous and aggressive imperialist nationalism in America. Thus, American patterns of non-political manipulation -- and especially certain marginal phenomena -- had to be fused artificially with fascist notions of the Italian and German brand. One has to think of the barker who puts such high pressure behind advertising that it approaches violence. Much has also been borrowed from fanatic religious revivalism, promoting an ecstasy which is relished as such and unrelated to any concrete content, while rigid, dogmatic stereotypes, as e.g. the distinction between the damned and the saved ones, are ruthlessly plugged. The modern American agitator shrewdly feeds on these old-fashioned methods. He warms them up for psychotechnical reasons and handles them quite consciously -- as a political "human relations expert". Methods derived from industry and standardized mass culture are presented under a backward, obsolete "character mask" and thus transferred to politics.

The mixture of the obsolescent and the streamlined is characteristic of the whole sphere of agitation. Its novel feature is the idea of a totalitarian transformation of men into potential objects. However, the anachronistic element remains indispensable. It is as intrinsically connected with the function of agitation as is the cheap entertainment of the country fair booth with the monster productions of modern film palaces. The eternal nucleus of agitation is its subjective and objective affinity to what is contemptuously called "rabble". Demagoguery is addressed to certain social groups which so to speak form a kind of social refuse throughout history at the margin of society. The frightening eternity of these phenomena reflects but the unchanged continuity of social pressure itself. Contact with this sphere, and the apocryphal nature of the agitators themselves function in the interest of the abolition of formal democratic processes and legal guaranties. The toughness, unruliness and lawlessness of the *lumpenproletariat* is seized by powerful groups for the purpose of establishing their own usurpatory, unchecked rule. A-social individuals and groups are the agents of a widespread social tendency to dominate through crude violence. However, the survival of these marginal groups is not an accident which merely disturbs the "normal" life of society, but is concomitant with the ultimate reference to violence by which this society is being held together. Accordingly, agitation, a marginal phenomenon whose ultimate meaning is violence, never disappears entirely. Society is not supposed to ever come to rest -- it is continuously reminded of the naked physical force on which it is based.

It would be naive to assume that all or most of the marginal figures who sell hatred are bought or have a mandate from really powerful groups. In this country they have failed so far to build up a unified organization, and they have equally failed to win large-scale financial backing although there are certain indications that this might change sooner than is generally anticipated. Fascism is the *ultima ratio* of repression and it is chosen by the real powers that be only if social conflicts increase to such an extent that control cannot be maintained by any other means. The very fear of the ruling strata of their prospective henchmen, however, is indicative of the potential seriousness of the danger, no matter how insignificant the agitators may appear to be. The concept of marginal figures is not an absolute. Social dynamics may well transfer to the center what today still leads a disreputable life at the borders of the social and political field.

6

This book is not so much devoted to the agitators' social physiognomics as to the psychological contents of their standard devices, that is to say, to the elucidation of those inner and largely unconscious mechanisms at which agitation is directed. However, the psychological emphasis of the technique itself has to be understood sociologically. Since Fascism's aim is not an essentially new society but the perpetuation of the old one in congealed, hierarchically rigid forms, it is set against any critique, reflection and self-awareness which is dubbed "destructive". Everything is subordinated to the confirmation of the *status quo*. The individual, instead of being induced to think, is held at bay through the manipulation of his own unconscious and ego-alien mechanisms which are to stay unconscious; he is prevented from gaining insight into his real social interests. Even the technique's rigid stereotypy, monotony and repetitiveness have their social significance. As pointed out in other books of this series, these apply correspond to certain specific character traits of the personalities susceptible to prejudice, while, socially, they means standardization of consciousness and adaptation of the individual to the prevailing mode of mass production. The psyche of men themselves is formed in a mould, as it were, and ultimately "expropriated" by those social agencies as whose mouthpiece the agitators style themselves. Here, as in many other aspects, fascism achieves suddenly, with one stroke -- "schlagartig" was a favorite Nazi term -- and seemingly from outside, what is brought about more inconspicuously and slowly through anonymous inner developmental tendencies of society itself.

Such sociological trends provide the proper perspective for the psychological constructs of the book. It does not pretend to give a photographic picture of today's political reality, and it does not overrate the immediate and literal importance of contemporary American demagoguery. Rather, it takes

7

certain phenomena, which appear prima facie as negligible, under a microscope in order to gain pertinent diagnostic insights into the latent threat against democracy through the enlargement of its most extreme and apparently unrealistic manifestations. It is hoped that the microscopic diagnosis of remote and inconsiderable social deformation, undertaken free from the pressure of any immediate political or economic crisis, will contribute to the evolution of well planned and effective long-term defense measures against the danger of terror that has survived Hitler's defeat.

— — — — — — —

Note

1 Adorno likely refers here to an article by Morris Janowitz, co-author with Bruno Bettelheim of one of the volumes in the Harper series. That article does indeed pursue a far more quantitative content analysis than the demagogy monographs. The figure of Gerald K. Smith is introduced in Chapter 2(b): Morris Janowitz, 'The Technique of Propaganda for Reaction: Gerald L.K. Smith's Radio Speeches', *The Public Opinion Quarterly* 8, no. 1 (1944).

Bibliography

Aalberg, Toril, Frank Esser, Carsten Reinemann, Jesper Stromback and Claes De Vreese, eds. *Populist Political Communication in Europe*. London: Routledge, 2016.
Ackerman, Nathan W., and Marie Jahoda. *Anti-Semitism and Emotional Disorder: A Psychoanalytic Interpretation*. New York: Harper, 1950.
Adair-Toteff, Christopher. 'Max Weber's Charisma'. *Journal of Classical Sociology* 5, no. 2 (2005): 189–204.
Adamson, Walter L. 'Gramsci's Interpretation of Fascism'. *Journal of the History of Ideas* 41, no. 4 (1980): 615–633.
Adorno, Theodor W. 'The Actuality of Philosophy'. *Telos* no. 31 (1977): 120–133.
Adorno, Theodor W. 'Anti-Semitism and Fascist Propaganda'. In *Anti-Semitism: A Social Disease*, edited by Ernst Simmel, 125–137. Madison, Wis.: International Universities Press, 1946.
Adorno, Theodor W. 'Cultural Criticism and Society'. Translated by S. Weber. In *Prisms* 19–34. London: Neville Spearman, 1967.
Adorno, Theodor W. 'Culture Industry Reconsidered (1967)'. *New German Critique*, no. 6 (1975): 12–19.
Adorno, Theodor W. 'Democratic Leadership and Mass Manipulation'. In *Studies in Leadership: Leadership and Democratic Action*, edited by Alvin W. Gouldner, 418–438. New York: Harper & Row, 1950.
Adorno, Theodor W. 'Freudian Theory and the Pattern of Fascist Propaganda'. *Psychoanalysis and the Social Sciences* 3 (1951): 279–300.
Adorno, Theodor W. 'How to Look at Television'. *The Quarterly of Film Radio and Television* 8, no. 3 (1954): 213–235.
Adorno, Theodor W. '(Draft) Introduction to *Prophets of Deceit*'. Leo Lowenthal Archive; MS Ger 185 (153), Houghton Library, Harvard University, 1949. (Published for first time as an appendix to this book).
Adorno, Theodor W. *Introduction to Sociology*. Translated by E.F.N. Jephcott. Stanford: Stanford University Press, 2000.
Adorno, Theodor W. *Introduction to the Sociology of Music*. Translated by E.B. Ashton. New York: Continuum, 1976. 1962.
Adorno, Theodor W. *Mahler: A Musical Physiognomy*. Translated by Edmund Jephcott. Chicago: University of Chicago Press, 1992. 1960.
Adorno, Theodor W. *Negative Dialectics*. Translated by E.B. Ashton. London, RKP, 1973. 1966.
Adorno, Theodor W. 'On Lyric Poetry and Society (1957)'. In *Notes to Literature: Volume One*, 37–54. New York: Columbia University Press, 1991.
Adorno, Theodor W. 'On the Question: 'What Is German?' (1965)'. Translated by Henry W. Pickford. In *Critical Models: Interventions and Catchwords*, 205–214. New York: Columbia University Press, 1998.
Adorno, Theodor W. 'On Tradition (1966)'. *Telos*, no. 94 (1992): 75–82.
Adorno, Theodor W. 'Opinion Research and Publicness (Meinungsforschung Und Öffentlichkeit 1964)'. In *Group Experiment and Other Writings: The Frankfurt School*

on *Public Opinion in Postwar Germany*, edited by Andrew J. Perrin and Lars Jarkko. Cambridge, Mass.: Harvard University Press, 2011.
Adorno, Theodor W. *Philosophy of New Music*. Translated by Robert Hullot-Kentor. Minneapolis: University of Minnesota Press, 2006. 1949.
Adorno, Theodor W. *The Psychological Technique of Martin Luther Thomas' Radio Addresses*. Stanford: Stanford University Press, 2000. 1975.
Adorno, Theodor W. 'Radio Physiognomics'. In *Current of Music: Elements of a Radio Theory*, edited by Robert Hullot-Kentor, 41–132. Cambridge: Polity, 2009.
Adorno, Theodor W. 'Résumé Über Kulturindustrie'. In *Ohne Leitbild: Parva Aesthetics*, 60–70. Frankfurt: Suhrkamp Verlag, 1967.
Adorno, Theodor W. 'Scientific Experiences of a European Scholar in America (1968)'. Translated by Henry W. Pickford. In *Critical Models: Interventions and Catchwords*, 215–244. New York: Columbia University Press, 1998.
Adorno, Theodor W. 'Theses on the Sociology of Art'. *Working Papers in Cultural Studies* 2 (1972): 121–128.
Adorno, Theodor W. 'Transparencies on Film (1966)'. *New German Critique*, no. 24/25 (1981): 199–205.
Adorno, Theodor W. 'Veblen's Attack on Culture: Remarks Occasioned by the *Theory of the Leisure Class*'. *Zeitschrift für Sozialforschung* 9, no. 3 (1941): 389–413.
Adorno, Theodor W. 'What National Socialism Has Done to the Arts (1945)'. In *Essays on Music*, edited by Richard D. Leppert, 373–390. Los Angeles: University of California Press, 2002.
Adorno, Theodor W., and George Simpson. 'On Popular Music'. *Zeitschrift für Sozialforschung* 9, no. 1 (1941): 17–48.
Adorno, Theodor W., Else Frenkel-Brunswik, Daniel J. Levinson and R. Nevitt Sanford. *The Authoritarian Personality*. New York: Harper & Row, 1950.
Albertazzi, Daniele, and Duncan McDonnell, eds. *Twenty-First Century Populism: The Spectre of Western European Democracy*. Basingstoke, UK: Palgrave Macmillan, 2008.
Alexander, Jeffrey C. 'The Crisis of Journalism Reconsidered: Cultural Power'. *Fudan Journal of the Humanities and Social Sciences* 8, no. 1 (2015): 9–31.
Alexander, Jeffrey C. *The Dark Side of Modernity*. Cambridge: Polity, 2013.
Ali, Tariq. *Street Fighting Years: An Autobiography of the Sixties*. London: Verso, 2005.
Altemeyer, Bob. *The Authoritarian Specter*. Cambridge, Mass.: Harvard University Press, 1996.
Altemeyer, Bob. *Right-Wing Authoritarianism*. Winnipeg: University of Manitoba Press, 1981.
Althusser, Louis. 'Contradiction and Overdetermination (1962)'. Translated by Ben Brewster. In *For Marx*, 87–128. London: NLB, 1977.
Althusser, Louis. 'Elements of Self-Criticism (1974)'. Translated by G. Lock. In *Essays in Self-Criticism*, 101–161. London: NLB 1976.
Althusser, Louis. 'Ideology and Ideological State Apparatuses (Notes Towards an Investigation) (1969–1970)'. Translated by B. Brewster. In *Lenin and Philosophy and Other Essays*, 121–173. London: NLB, 1977.
Althusser, Louis, and Etienne Balibar. *Reading Capital*. Translated by B. Brewster. London: NLB, 1970. 1968.
Anderson, Perry. *Considerations on Western Marxism*. London: NLB, 1976.
Anderson, Perry. *The H-Word: The Peripeteia of Hegemony*. London: Verso, 2017.
Apostolidis, Paul. *Stations of the Cross: Adorno and Christian Right Radio*. Durham, NC: Duke University Press, 2000.
Arditi, Benjamin. 'Populism as a Spectre of Democracy: A Response to Canovan'. *Political Studies* 52, no. 1 (2004): 135–143.

BIBLIOGRAPHY

Arendt, Hannah. *Between Past and Future: Six Exercises in Political Thought*. New York: Viking, 1961.
Arendt, Hannah. 'Society and Culture'. In *Culture for the Millions?: Mass Media in Modern Society*, edited by Norman Jacobs, 43–52. Princeton, NJ: Van Norstrand Press, 1961.
Associated Press. 'Trump: I Am the Victim of a Great Smear'. YouTube.
Baker, C. Edwin. 'Advertising and a Democratic Press'. *University of Pennsylvania Law Review* (1992): 2097–2243.
Baker, C. Edwin. *Advertising and a Democratic Press*. Princeton: Princeton University Press, 1995.
Baker, C. Edwin. 'Media Concentration: Giving up on Democracy'. *Florida Law Review* 54 (2002): 839.
Baker, C. Edwin. *Media Concentration and Democracy: Why Ownership Matters*. Cambridge: Cambridge University Press, 2007.
Baker, C. Edwin. 'Press Performance, Human Rights, and Private Power as a Threat'. *Law & Ethics of Human Rights* 5, no. 2 (2011): 219–256.
Baker, C. Edwin. 'Viewpoint Diversity and Media Ownership'. *Federal Communications Law Journal* 61 (2008): 651.
Bakhtin, M.M., and P.N. Medvedev. *The Formal Method in Literary Scholarship: A Critical Introduction to Sociological Poetics*. Translated by A.J. Wehrle. Baltimore: Johns Hopkins University Press, 1978. 1928.
Barnes, Richard, and Pete Townshend. *The Story of Tommy*. London: Eel Pie Publishing, 1977.
Barthes, Roland. *Mythologies*. Translated by Annette Lavers. New York: Noonday Press, 1972. 1957.
Bartók, Béla. 'Race Purity in Music'. *Tempo*, no. 8 (1944): 132–133.
Beechey, Veronica, and James Donald. 'Introduction'. In *Subjectivity and Social Relations: A Reader*, ix–xviii. Milton Keynes: Open University Press, 1985.
Bell, Daniel. 'Afterword: 1996'. In *The Cultural Contradictions of Capitalism: 20th Anniversary Edn.*, 283–339. New York: Basic Books, 1996.
Bell, Daniel. 'The Face of Tomorrow'. *Jewish Frontier* 11 (1944): 15–20.
Bell, Daniel. 'Interpretations of American Politics'. In *The New American Right*, edited by Daniel Bell, 3–32. New York: Criterion Books, 1955.
Bell, Daniel ed. *The New American Right*. New York: Criterion Books, 1955.
Bell, Daniel. 'Preface'. In *The Radical Right*, edited by Daniel Bell, xi–xiii. New York: Anchor, 1964.
Bell, Daniel, ed. *The Radical Right*. 3rd edn. New Brunswick: Transaction Publishers, 2002.
Bell, Daniel, ed. *The Radical Right: The New American Right Expanded and Updated*. Garden City, New York: Doubleday, 1963.
Bendix, Regina. *In Search of Authenticity: The Formation of Folklore Studies*. Madison, Wis.: University of Wisconsin Press, 1997.
Benjamin, Louise Margaret. *Freedom of the Air and the Public Interest: First Amendment Rights in Broadcasting to 1935*. Carbondale: Southern Illinois University Press, 2001.
Bennett, David H. *Demagogues in the Depression: American Radicals and the Union Party, 1932–1936*. New Brunswick, NJ: Rutgers University Press, 1969.
Bennett, David H. *The Party of Fear: From Nativist Movements to the New Right in American History*. Chapel Hill: UNC Press, 1988.
Bennett, Tony. 'The Politics of The "Popular" and Popular Culture'. In *Popular Culture and Social Relations*, edited by Tony Bennett, Colin Mercer and Janet Woollacott, 6–21. Milton Keynes: Open University Press, 1986.

Bennett, Tony. 'Theories of the Media, Theories of Society'. In *Culture, Society and the Media*, edited by M. Gurevitch, T. Bennett, J. Curran and J. Woollacott, 30–55. London: Routledge, 1982.

Bennett, W. Lance, and Steven Livingston. 'The Disinformation Order: Disruptive Communication and the Decline of Democratic Institutions'. *European Journal of Communication* 33, no. 2 (2018): 122–139.

Bennett, W. Lance, and Barbara Pfetsch. 'Rethinking Political Communication in a Time of Disrupted Public Spheres'. *Journal of Communication* 68, no. 2 (2018): 243–253.

Berezin, Mabel. *Illiberal Politics in Neoliberal Times*. Cambridge: Cambridge University Press, 2009.

Bernstein, J.M. 'Introduction'. In *Adorno, T.W. The Culture Industry: Selected Essays on Mass Culture* edited by J.M. Bernstein 1–25. London: Routledge, 1991.

Berry, Jeffrey M., and Sarah Sobieraj. *The Outrage Industry: Political Opinion Media and the New Incivility*. New York: Oxford University Press, 2014.

Bertholf, Garry. 'Black Sophists: A Critique of Demagoguery'. PhD dissertation, University of Pennsylvania, 2013.

Bettelheim, Bruno, and Morris Janowitz. *Dynamics of Prejudice: A Psychological and Sociological Study of Veterans*. New York: Harper, 1950.

Bettelheim, Bruno, and Morris Janowitz. 'Reactions to Fascist Propaganda: A Pilot Study'. *Public Opinion Quarterly* 14, no. 1 (1950): 53–60.

Betz, Hans-Georg. 'Political Conflict in the Postmodern Age: Radical Right-Wing Populist Parties in Europe'. *Current Politics and Economics of Europe* 1 (1990): 11–27.

Betz, Hans-Georg. *Postmodern Politics in Germany: The Politics of Resentment*. Houndmills, Basingstoke: Macmillan, 1991.

Betz, Hans-Georg. 'The Radical Right and Populism'. In *The Oxford Handbook of the Radical Right*, edited by Jens Rydgren, 86–104. Oxford: Oxford University Press, 2018.

Betz, Hans-Georg. *Radical Right-Wing Populism in Western Europe*. New York: St Martins Press, 1994.

Betz, Hans-Georg. 'The Two Faces of Radical Right-Wing Populism in Western Europe'. *The Review of Politics* 55, no. 4 (1993): 663–686.

Betz, Hans-Georg, and Stefan Immerfall, eds. *The New Politics of the Right: Neo-Populist Parties and Movements in Established Democracies*. New York: St Martin's Press, 1998.

Billig, Michael. *Fascists: A Social Psychological View of the National Front*. London: Academic Press, 1978.

Blatter, Jeremy. 'Screening the Psychological Laboratory: Hugo Münsterberg, Psychotechnics, and the Cinema, 1892–1916'. *Science in Context* 28, no. 1 (2015): 53–76.

Blumler, Jay G., and Michael Gurevitch. *The Crisis of Public Communication*. London: Routledge, 1995.

Bourdieu, Pierre. 'The Uses of the "People" (1982)'. Translated by Matthew Adamson. In *In Other Words: Essays Towards a Reflexive Sociology*, 150–155. Cambridge: Polity, 1990.

Boyce, George. 'The Fourth Estate: The Reappraisal of a Concept'. In *Newspaper History: From the Seventeenth Century to the Present Day*, edited by George Boyce, James Curran and Pauline Wingate, 19–40. London: Constable, 1978.

Bradley, Dick. 'The Cultural Study of Music: A Theoretical and Methodological Introduction'. *Birmingham CCCS Stencilled Occasional Paper* 61 (1979).

Bramson, Leon. *The Political Context of Sociology*. Princeton, NJ: Princeton University Press, 1961.

Brewster, B. 'Glossary'. In *Louis Althusser & Etienne Balibar: Reading Capital*, 309–324. London: NLB, 1977.

Brewster, B. 'Glossary'. In *Louis Althusser: For Marx*, 249–258. London: NLB, 1977.
Brinkley, Alan. *Voices of Protest: Huey Long, Father Coughlin, and the Great Depression*. New York: Knopf, 1982.
Brown, David S. *Richard Hofstadter: An Intellectual Biography*. Chicago: University of Chicago Press, 2008.
Buck-Morss, Susan. *The Origin of Negative Dialectics: Theodor W. Adorno, Walter Benjamin and the Frankfurt Institute*. New York: Free Press, 1977.
Burke, Peter. *Popular Culture in Early Modern Europe*. New York: Harper & Row, 1978.
Burns, Ken. *Huey Long*. Alexandria, Va.: PBS Video, 2010. videorecording.
Canovan, Margaret. *Populism*. New York: Harcourt Brace Jovanovich, 1981.
Canovan, Margaret. 'Trust the People! Populism and the Two Faces of Democracy'. *Political Studies* 47, no. 1 (1999): 2–16.
Carlet, Yves. 'Frank Capra and Elia Kazan, American Outsiders'. *European Journal of American Studies* 5, no. 5–4 (2010).
Carlyle, Thomas. *On Heroes, Hero-Worship, and the Heroic in History*. New Haven: Yale University Press, 2013. 1841.
Cavalletto, George. *Crossing the Psycho-Social Divide: Freud, Weber, Adorno and Elias*. Burlington, Vt.: Ashgate, 2007.
Chalaby, Jean K. 'No Ordinary Press Owners: Press Barons as a Weberian Ideal Type'. *Media, Culture & Society* 19, no. 4 (1997): 621–641.
Chalaby, Jean K. *The Invention of Journalism*. Houndmills, Basingstoke: Macmillan, 1998.
Claudin, Fernando. *Eurocommunism and Socialism*. London: NLB, 1978.
Cohen, Jean L, and Andrew Arato. *Civil Society and Political Theory*. Cambridge, Mass.: MIT Press, 1994.
Cohen, Jean L. 'Critical Social Theory and Feminist Critiques: The Debate with Jürgen Habermas'. In *Feminists Read Habermas*, edited by Johanna Meehan, 73–106. New York: Routledge, 1995.
Collins, Richard, and Cristina Murroni. *New Media, New Policies: Media and Communications Strategies for the Future*. Cambridge: Polity, 1996.
Conboy, Martin. *Journalism: A Critical History*. London: Sage, 2004.
Conboy, Martin. *Tabloid Britain: Constructing a Community through Language*. London: Routledge, 2006.
Cook, Deborah. 'Adorno on Late Capitalism'. *Radical Philosophy* 89 (1998): 16–26.
Cooper, David. 'Béla Bartók and the Question of Race Purity in Music'. In *Musical Constructions of Nationalism: Essays on the History of European Musical Culture 1800–1945*, edited by Harry White and Michael Murphy, 16–32. Cork: Cork University Press, 2001.
Cortner, Richard C. *The Kingfish and the Constitution: Huey Long, the First Amendment, and the Emergence of Modern Press Freedom in America*. Westport, Conn.: Greenwood Publishing Group, 1996.
Coughlin, Charles E. *Father Coughlin's Radio Discourses 1931–1932*. Royal Oak, Mich.: The Radio League of the Little Flower/Wildside Press, undated.
Crook, Stephen. 'Introduction: Adorno and Authoritarian Irrationalism'. In *Theodor W. Adorno: The Stars Down to Earth and Other Essays on the Irrational in Culture*, edited by Stephen Crook, 1–45. London: Routledge, 1994.
Curran, James. 'Narratives of Media History Revisited'. In *Media and Democracy*, 123–139. London: Routledge, 2011.
Curran, James. 'The New Revisionism in Mass Communication Research: A Reappraisal'. *European Journal of Communication* 5, no. 2 (1990): 135–164.

Curran, James. 'Rethinking the Media as a Public Sphere'. In *Communication and Citizenship*, edited by Peter Dahlgren and Colin Sparks, 27–57. London: Routledge, 1991.
Curran, James. 'Stuart Hall Redux: His Early Work, 1964–1984'. In *Stuart Hall: Conversations, Projects, and Legacies*, edited by Julian Henriques, David Morley and Vana Goblot, 38–46. London: Goldsmiths Press, 2017.
Dahms, Harry F. 'Critical Theory as Radical Comparative–Historical Research'. In *The Palgrave Handbook of Critical Theory*, 165–184. New York: Springer, 2017.
Dahms, Harry F. 'The Early Frankfurt School Critique of Capitalism: Critical Theory between Pollock's 'State Capitalism' and the Critique of Instrumental Reason'. In *The Theory of Capitalism in the German Economic Tradition*, edited by Peter Koslowski, 309–367. New York: Springer, 2000.
Davis, Helen. *Understanding Stuart Hall*. London: Sage, 2004.
Dennis, David B. *Inhumanities: Nazi Interpretations of Western Culture*. Cambridge: Cambridge University Press, 2012.
Deriso, Nick. 'Classic Rock Vs. Donald Trump: Musicians Who Already Can't Stand Our New President'. *Ultimate Classic Rock* (20 January 2017).
Dickstein, Morris. *Dancing in the Dark: A Cultural History of the Great Depression*. New York: W.W. Norton & Company, 2009.
Doherty, Thomas. *Cold War, Cool Medium: Television, McCarthyism, and American Culture*. New York: Columbia University Press, 2003.
Downie, Leonard, and Michael Schudson. 'The Reconstruction of American Journalism'. *Columbia Journalism Review* 19 (2009): 2009.
Du Bois, W.E. *The Philadelphia Negro*. New York: Schocken Books, 1971.
Eatwell, Roger. 'Charisma and the Radical Right'. In *The Oxford Handbook of the Radical Right*, edited by Jens Rydgren, 366–388. Oxford: Oxford University Press, 2018.
Eatwell, Roger. 'Populism and Fascism'. In *The Oxford Handbook of Populism*, edited by Cristóbal Rovira Kaltwasser, Paul Taggart, Paulina Ochoa Espejo and Pierre Ostiguy, 363–383. Oxford: Oxford University Press, 2017.
Ecksell, R. 'Fascism, American Style: Revisiting Kazan and Schulberg's *A Face in the Crowd*'. *Bright Lights Film Journal* no. 61 (31 July 2008).
Eco, Umberto. '"Casablanca": Cult Movies and Intertextual Collage'. *SubStance* 14, no. 2 (1985): 3–12.
Eco, Umberto. *Turning Back the Clock: Hot Wars and Media Populism*. Translated by Alastair McEwen. Orlando, Fla.: Harcourt, 2007.
Editorial Board, The New York Times. 'Mr. Trump's Applause Lies'. *The New York Times*, 24 November (2015), A26.
Edwards, Bob. *Edward R. Murrow and the Birth of Broadcast Journalism*. Hoboken, NJ: John Wiley & Sons, 2004.
Eisler, Hanns, and Theodor W. Adorno. *Composing for the Films*. London: Athlone Press, 1994.
Eley, Geoff. *Nazism as Fascism: Violence, Ideology, and the Ground of Consent in Germany 1930–1945*. New York: Routledge, 2013.
Elicker, Martina. 'Rock Opera – Opera on the Rocks?' *Word & Music Studies* 4, no. 1 (2002): 299–314.
Eliot, T.S. *Notes Towards the Definition of Culture*. London: Faber & Faber, 1948.
Errejón, Íñigo, and Chantal Mouffe. *Podemos: In the Name of the People*. London: Lawrence & Wishart, 2016.
Feenberg, Andrew. *The Philosophy of Praxis: Marx, Lukács, and the Frankfurt School*. London: Verso, 2014.

Finchelstein, Federico. *From Fascism to Populism in History*. Oakland: University of California Press, 2017.
Finchelstein, Federico. *Transatlantic Fascism: Ideology, Violence, and the Sacred in Argentina and Italy, 1919–1945*. Durham: Duke University Press, 2010.
Finchelstein, Federico, and Nadia Urbinati. 'On Populism and Democracy'. *Populism* 1 (2018): 15–37.
Finkelstein, Norman H. *With Heroic Truth: The Life of Edward R. Murrow*. Lincoln, NE: iUniverse, 2005.
Fisher, Marc. 'The Movie That Foretold the Rise of Donald Trump'. *The Washington Post*, 8 February (2016).
Forgacs, David. 'Gramsci's Notion of the "Popular" in Italy and Britain: A Tale of Two Cultures'. In *Performing National Identity*, edited by M. Pfister and R. Hertel, 179–195. Amsterdam: Rodopi, 2008.
Forgacs, David. 'The Left and Fascism: Problems of Definition and Strategy'. In *Rethinking Italian Fascism: Capitalism, Populism and Culture*, edited by David Forgacs, 21–51. London: Lawrence & Wishart, 1986.
Forgacs, David. 'National-Popular: Genealogy of a Concept'. In *Formations of Nation and People*, edited by Formations Editorial Collective, 83–98. London: Routledge & Kegan Paul, 1984.
Frankfurt Institute for Social Research. *Aspects of Sociology*. Translated by John Viertel. Boston: Beacon, 1972. 1956.
Fraser, Nancy. *The Old is Dying and the New Cannot be Born: From Progressive Neoliberalism to Trump and Beyond*. London: Verso, 2019.
Fraser, Nancy. 'Rethinking the Public Sphere: A Contribution to the Critique of Actually Existing Democracy'. *Social Text*, no. 25/26 (1990): 56–80.
Freedman, Des. 'Populism and Media Policy Failure'. *European Journal of Communication* 33, no. 6 (2018): 604–618.
Freeman, Jo. 'The Tyranny of Structurelessness'. *Berkeley Journal of Sociology* (1972): 151–164.
Frenkel-Brunswick, Else. 'Further Explorations by a Contributor to "The Authoritarian Personality"'. In *Studies in the Scope and Method of 'The Authoritarian Personality'*, edited by Richard Christie and Marie Jahoda, 226–275. Glencoe, Ill.: Free Press, 1954.
Frenkel-Brunswik, Else, and R. Nevitt Sanford. 'The Anti-Semitic Personality: A Research Report'. In *Anti-Semitism: A Social Disease*, edited by Ernst Simmel, 33–78. New York: International Universities Press, 1946.
Freud, Sigmund. *Group Psychology and the Analysis of the Ego*. Translated by James Strachey. London: The International Psychoanalytical Press, 1922.
Freud, Sigmund. *The Interpretation of Dreams*. Translated by A.A. Brill. London: Macmillan, 1915 [1899].
Freud, Sigmund. *Massenpsychologie Und Ich-Analyse*. Leipzig: Internationaler Psychoanalytischer Verlag GMBH., 1921.
Friendly, Fred W. *The Good Guys, the Bad Guys, and the First Amendment: Free Speech Vs. Fairness in Broadcasting*. New York: Random House, 1976.
Frith, Simon. 'The Good, the Bad, and the Indifferent: Defending Popular Culture from the Populists'. *Diacritics* 21, no. 4 (1991): 102–115.
Fromm, Erich. *Escape from Freedom*. New York: Farrar & Rinehart, 1941.
Fromm, Erich. *The Fear of Freedom*. London: Routledge & Kegan Paul, 1942.
Fromm, Erich. 'The Method and Function of an Analytic Social Psychology: Notes on Psychoanalysis and Historical Materialism (1932)'. In *The Crisis of Psychoanalysis*, 137–162. New York: Holt, Rinehart & Winston, 1976.

Fromm, Erich. 'Psychoanalytic Characterology and Its Application to the Understanding of Culture'. In *Culture and Personality*, edited by S.S. Sargent and M.W. Smith. New York: Viking, 1949.

Fromm, Erich. 'Psychoanalytic Characterology and Its Relevance for Social Psychology (1932)'. In *The Crisis of Psychoanalysis*, 163–189. New York: Holt, Rinehart & Winston, 1976.

Fromm, Erich. *The Working Class in Weimar Germany: A Psychological and Sociological Study*. Leamington Spa: Berg, 1984.

Gangl, Manfred. 'The Controversy over Friedrich Pollock's State Capitalism'. *History of the Human Sciences* 29, no. 2 (2016): 23–41.

Gans, Herbert J. *Popular Culture and High Culture: An Analysis and Evaluation of Taste (Revd Edn)* 2nd edn. New York: Basic Books, 1999.

Garnham, Nicholas. 'The Media and the Public Sphere'. In *Communicating Politics: Mass Communications and the Political Process*, edited by P. Golding, G. Murdock and P. Schlesinger, 37–54. Leicester: Leicester University Press, 1986.

Garnham, Nicholas. 'Public Service Versus the Market'. *Screen* 24, no. 1 (1983): 6–27.

Gehring, Wes D. *Populism and the Capra Legacy*. Westport, Conn.: Greenwood Press, 1995.

Gentile, Emilio. *The Origins of Fascist Ideology 1918–1925*. Translated by Robert L. Miller. New York: Enigma Books, 2005. 1974.

Gentile, Emilio. *The Struggle for Modernity: Nationalism, Futurism, and Fascism*. Translated by Stanley G. Payne. Westport, Conn.: Praeger, 2003.

Geras, Norman. 'Ex-Marxism without Substance: Being a Real Reply to Laclau and Mouffe'. *New Left Review*, no. 169 (1988): 34–61.

Geras, Norman. 'Post-Marxism?'. *New Left Review*, no. 163 (1987): 40–82.

Gitlin, Todd. *Inside Prime Time*. New York: Pantheon, 1985 [1983].

Gitlin, Todd. *Occupy Nation: The Roots, the Spirit, and the Promise of Occupy Wall Street*. New York: HarperCollins, 2012.

Gitlin, Todd. 'Occupy's Predicament: The Moment and the Prospects for the Movement'. *The British Journal of Sociology* 64, no. 1 (2013): 3–25.

Gitlin, Todd. *The Sixties: Years of Hope, Days of Rage*. Rev. trade edn. New York: Bantam Books, 1993.

Gitlin, Todd. *The Whole World Is Watching: Mass Media in the Making and Unmaking of the New Left*. Berkeley: University of California Press, 1980.

Goldmann, Lucien, and Theodor W. Adorno. 'To Describe, Understand and Explain (Jan., 1968)'. In *Lucien Goldmann: Cultural Creation in Modern Society*, 131–147. Saint Louis: Telos Press, 1976.

Goodman, David. *Radio's Civic Ambition: American Broadcasting and Democracy in the 1930s*. New York: Oxford University Press, 2011.

Goodwin, Andrew. *Dancing in the Distraction Factory: Music Television and Popular Culture*. Minneapolis: University of Minnesota Press, 1992.

Gorman, Paul R. *Left Intellectuals and Popular Culture in Twentieth-Century America*. Chapel Hill: University of North Carolina Press, 1996.

Gramsci, Antonio. *Selections from Cultural Writings*. London: Lawrence & Wishart, 1985.

Gramsci, Antonio. *Selections from the Prison Notebooks of Antonio Gramsci*. Translated by Quintin Hoare and Geoffrey Nowell-Smith. London: Lawrence & Wishart, 1971.

Gramsci, Antonio. 'Some Aspects of the Southern Question (1926)'. Translated by Quintin Hoare. In *Selections from Political Writings 1921–1926*, 441–462. London: Lawrence & Wishart, 1978.

BIBLIOGRAPHY

Grattan, Laura. *Populism's Power: Radical Grassroots Democracy in America*. New York: Oxford University Press, 2016.
Green, Archie. 'The Visual Arkansas Traveler'. *JEMF Quarterly* 21, nos 75–76 (1985): 31–46.
Griffin, Roger. 'Fascism and Culture: A Mosse-Centric Meta-Narrative (or How Fascist Studies Reinvented the Wheel)'. In *Rethinking the Nature of Fascism*, edited by António Costa Pinto, 85–116: Basingstoke: Palgrave, 2011.
Griffith, Richard. *Frank Capra*. London: BFI, 1949.
Habermas, Jürgen. *Between Facts and Norms: Contributions to a Discourse Theory of Law and Democracy*. Translated by W. Rehg. Cambridge, Mass.: MIT Press, 1996. 1992.
Habermas, Jürgen. 'Concluding Remarks'. In *Habermas and the Public Sphere*, edited by Craig J. Calhoun, 462–479. Cambridge, Mass.: MIT Press, 1992.
Habermas, Jürgen. 'Further Reflections on the Public Sphere (1989)'. In *Habermas and the Public Sphere*, edited by Craig J. Calhoun, 421–461. Cambridge, Mass.: MIT Press, 1992.
Habermas, Jürgen. 'Jürgen Habermas: "For God's Sake, Spare Us Governing Philosophers!"'. *El País Semanal In English*, 25 May (2018).
Habermas, Jürgen. *Legitimation Crisis*. Boston: Beacon Press, 1975 [1973].
Habermas, Jürgen. 'Media, Markets and Consumers: The Quality of Press as Backbone of the Public Sphere'. In *Europe: The Faltering Project*, 131–137. Oxford: Polity, 2009.
Habermas, Jürgen. 'Modernity: An Unfinished Project'. In *Habermas and the Unfinished Project of Modernity: Critical Essays on the Philosophical Discourse of Modernity*, edited by Maurizio Passerin d'Entrèves and Seyla Benhabib, 38–55. Boston, Mass.: MIT Press, 1997.
Habermas, Jürgen. 'Notes on the Developmental History of Horkheimer's Work'. *Theory, Culture & Society* 10, no. 2 (1993): 61–77.
Habermas, Jürgen. 'Political Communication in Media Society: Does Democracy Still Enjoy an Epistemic Dimension? The Impact of Normative Theory on Empirical Research'. *Communication Theory* 16, no. 4 (2006): 411–426.
Habermas, Jürgen. *The Structural Transformation of the Public Sphere: An Inquiry into a Category of Bourgeois Society*. Translated by T. Burger. Cambridge, Mass.: MIT Press, 1989. 1962.
Habermas, Jürgen. *The Theory of Communicative Action Volume One*. Translated by Thomas McCarthy. Boston: Beacon Press, 1981. 1984.
Habermas, Jürgen. *The Theory of Communicative Action Volume Two*. Translated by Thomas McCarthy. Boston: Beacon Press, 1981. 1987.
Hall, R. Trevor, and James C. Phillips. 'The Fairness Doctrine in Light of Hostile Media Perception'. *CommLaw Conspectus* 19 (2010): 395–422.
Hall, Stuart. 'Authoritarian Populism: A Reply'. *New Left Review*, no. 151 (1985): 115–124.
Hall, Stuart. 'Culture, the Media and the "Ideological Effect"'. In *Mass Communication and Society*, edited by James Curran, Michael Gurevitch and Janet Woollacott, 315–348. London: Arnold, 1977.
Hall, Stuart. 'Encoding and Decoding in the Television Discourse'. *CCCS Stencilled Occasional Paper* 7 (1973).
Hall, Stuart. 'Gramsci's Relevance for the Study of Race and Ethnicity'. *Journal of Communication Inquiry* 10, no. 2 (1986): 5–27.
Hall, Stuart. *The Hard Road to Renewal: Thatcherism and the Crisis of the Left*. London: Verso, 1988.
Hall, Stuart. 'Introduction to Media Studies at the Centre'. In *Culture, Media, Language*, edited by S. Hall, H. Hobson, A. Lowe and P. Willias, 117–121. London: Hutchinson, 1980.

Hall, Stuart. 'The Neoliberal Revolution (2011)'. In *Stuart Hall: Selected Political Writings*, edited by Sally Davison, David Featherstone, Michael Rustin and Bill Schwarz, 283–300. London: Lawrence & Wishart, 2016.

Hall, Stuart. 'Nicos Poulantzas: State, Power, Socialism'. *New Left Review*, 1/119 (1980): 60–69.

Hall, Stuart. 'Notes on Deconstructing "the Popular"'. In *People's History and Socialist Theory* edited by Raphael Samuel, 227–241. London: Routledge & Kegan Paul, 1981.

Hall, Stuart. 'On Postmodernism and Articulation: An Interview with Stuart Hall'. *Journal of Communication Inquiry* 10, no. 2 (1986): 45–60.

Hall, Stuart. 'Popular Culture and the State'. In *Popular Culture and Social Relations*, edited by T. Bennett, C. Mercer and J. Woollacott, 22–49. Milton Keynes: Open University Press, 1986.

Hall, Stuart. 'Popular Democratic Vs. Authoritarian Populism: Two Ways of Taking Democracy Seriously'. In *Marxism and Democracy*, edited by Alan Hunt, 157–185. London: Lawrence & Wishart, 1980.

Hall, Stuart. 'The Rediscovery of Ideology: Return of the Repressed in Media Studies'. In *Culture, Society and the Media*, edited by M. Gurevitch, T. Bennett, J. Curran and J. Woollacott, 56–90. London: Routledge, 1982.

Hall, Stuart. 'Signification, Representation, Ideology: Althusser and the Post-Structuralist Debates'. *Critical Studies in Mass Communication* 2, no. 2 (1985): 91–114.

Hall, Stuart. 'Some Problems with the Ideology/Subject Couplet'. *Ideology and Consciousness* 3 (1978): 115–125.

Hall, Stuart. 'The Toad in the Garden: Thatcherism Among the Theorists'. In *Marxism and the Interpretation of Culture*, edited by C. Nelson and L. Grossberg, 35–73. Urbana: University of Illinois Press, 1988.

Hall, Stuart, Ian Connell, and Lidia Curti. 'The "Unity" of Current Affairs Television'. *Working Papers In Cultural Studies* 9 (1976): 51–94.

Hall, Stuart, and Paddy Whannel. *The Popular Arts*. London: Hutchinson, 1964.

Halle, R. *Queer Social Philosophy: Critical Readings from Kant to Adorno*. Urbana: University of Illinois Press, 2004.

Hallin, Daniel C. 'The American News Media: A Critical Theory Perspective'. In *Critical Theory and Public Life*, edited by John Forester, 121–146. Cambridge, Mass.: MIT Press, 1985.

Hallin, Daniel C., and Paolo Mancini. *Comparing Media Systems: Three Models of Media and Politics*. Cambridge: Cambridge University Press, 2004.

Hebdige, Dick. *Cut 'N' Mix: Culture, Identity and Caribbean Music*. A Comedia Book. London: Methuen, 1987.

Held, David. *Introduction to Critical Theory: Horkheimer to Habermas*. Berkeley: University of California Press, 1980.

Hendershot, Heather. *What's Fair on the Air?: Cold War Right-Wing Broadcasting and the Public Interest*. Chicago: The University of Chicago Press, 2011.

Herf, Jeffrey. *Reactionary Modernism: Technology, Culture, and Politics in Weimar and the Third Reich*. Cambridge: Cambridge University Press, 1984.

Hermet, Guy. 'From Nation-State Populism to National-Populism'. In *Revisiting Nationalism*, edited by Alain Dieckhoff and Christophe Jaffrelot, 191–201. New York: Palgrave Macmillan, 2005.

Hilmes, Michele. *Only Connect: A Cultural History of Broadcasting in the United States*. 4th edn. Boston: Wadsworth Cengage, 2014.

Hirst, Martin. 'Towards a Political Economy of Fake News'. *The Political Economy of Communication* 5, no. 2 (2017).

Hixson, William B. *Search for the American Right Wing: An Analysis of the Social Science Record, 1955–1987*. Princeton: Princeton University Press, 1992.
Hoberman, J. 'The Long Road of Lonesome Rhodes: Reconsidering *A Face in the Crowd*'. *The Virginia Quarterly Review* 84, no. 4 (2008): 116–127.
Hochschild, Arlie Russell. 'The Ecstatic Edge of Politics: Sociology and Donald Trump'. *Contemporary Sociology* 45, no. 6 (2016): 683–689.
Hoffman, Abbie. *Woodstock Nation: A Talk-Rock Album*. New York: Random House, 1969.
Hoffmann, Anna Lauren, Nicholas Proferes, and Michael Zimmer. '"Making the World More Open and Connected": Mark Zuckerberg and the Discursive Construction of Facebook and Its Users'. *New Media & Society* 20, no. 1 (2018): 199–218.
Hofstadter, Richard. *The Age of Reform: From Bryan to FDR*. New York: Knopf, 1955.
Hofstadter, Richard. *Anti-Intellectualism in American Life*. New York: Vintage, 1963.
Hofstadter, Richard. 'Pseudo-Conservatism Revisited: A Postscript (1962)'. In *The Radical Right*, edited by Daniel Bell, 81–86. Garden City, New York: Doubleday, 1963.
Hofstadter, Richard. 'The Pseudo-Conservative Revolt'. In *The New American Right*, edited by Daniel Bell, 33–55. New York: Criterion Books, 1955.
Hoggart, Richard. *Teaching Literature*. London: National Institute of Adult Education, 1963.
Hoggart, Richard. *The Uses of Literacy: Aspects of Working-Class Life, with Special Reference to Publications and Entertainments*. London: Chatto & Windus, 1957.
Honneth, Axel. 'Communication and Reconciliation: Habermas' Critique of Adorno'. *Telos*, no. 39 (1979): 45–61.
Honneth, Axel. *The Critique of Power: Reflective Stages in a Critical Social Theory*. Translated by Kenneth Baynes. Cambridge, Mass: MIT Press, 1991.
Honneth, Axel. *The Fragmented World of the Social: Essays in Social and Political Philosophy*. Translated by Charles W. Wright. Albany: State University of New York Press, 1995.
Honneth, Axel. *Pathologies of Reason: On the Legacy of Critical Theory*. Translated by James Ingram. New York: Columbia University Press, 2009. 2007.
Honneth, Axel, Judith Butler, Raymond Geuss, Jonathan Lear and Martin Jay. *Reification: A New Look at an Old Idea*. Oxford: Oxford University Press, 2008.
Hoover, Stewart M., and Douglas K. Wagner. 'History and Policy in American Broadcast Treatment of Religion'. *Media, Culture & Society* 19, no. 1 (1997): 7–27.
Horkheimer, Max. 'Art and Mass Culture'. *Zeitschrift für Sozialforschung* 9, no. 2 (1941): 290–304.
Horkheimer, Max. 'Authority and the Family (1936)'. In *Critical Theory: Selected Essays*, 47–128. New York: Continuum, 1972.
Horkheimer, Max. *Briefwechsel 1941–1948 (Correspondence 1941–1948)*. Gesammelte Schriften (Complete Writings), Vol. 17. Frankfurt am Main: S. Fischer, 1996.
Horkheimer, Max. *Eclipse of Reason*. New York: Oxford University Press, 1947.
Horkheimer, Max 'Notes on Institute Activities'. *Zeitschrift für Sozialforschung* 9, no. 1 (1941): 121–123.
Horkheimer, Max. 'Preface'. *Zeitschrift für Sozialforschung* 9, no. 2 (1941): 195–199.
Horkheimer, Max. 'Research Project on Anti-Semitism'. *Zeitschrift für Sozialforschung* 9, no. 2 (1941): 124–133.
Horkheimer, Max, ed. *Studien Über Autorität Und Familie*, Schriften Des Instituts Für Sozialforschung. Paris: Felix Alcan, 1936.
Horkheimer, Max, and Theodor W. Adorno. *Dialektik Der Aufklärung: Philosophische Fragmente*. Frankfurt: Fischer Taschenbuch Verlag, 2006. 1944.

Horkheimer, Max, and Theodor W. Adorno. *Dialectic of Enlightenment: Philosophical Fragments*. Translated by Edmund Jephcott. Stanford: Stanford University Press, 2002. 1944/1947.

House of Commons Digital Culture Media and Sport Committee. 'Disinformation and "Fake News": Final Report'. London: House of Commons, 2019.

Howarth, David. 'Hegemony, Political Subjectivity, and Radical Democracy'. In *Laclau: A Critical Reader*, edited by S. Critchley and Oliver Marchant, 256–276. London: Routledge, 2004.

Howarth, David, and Yannis Stavrakakis. 'Introducing Discourse Theory and Political Analysis'. In *Discourse Theory and Political Analysis*, edited by David Howarth, Aletta Norval and Yannis Stavrakakis, 1–23. Manchester: Manchester University Press, 2000.

Hullot-Kentor, Robert. 'Editor's Introduction'. In *Adorno, Theodor W. Current of Music: Elements of a Radio Theory*, edited by Robert Hullot-Kentor, 1–40. Cambridge: Polity, 2009.

Humphreys, Peter. *Mass Media and Media Policy in Western Europe*. Manchester: Manchester University Press, 1996.

Huyssen, Andreas. 'Breitbart News and the Frankfurt School: A Strange Meeting of Minds'. *Public Seminar* (2017). Published electronically 28 September. https://publicseminar.org/2017/09/breitbart-bannon-trump-and-the-frankfurt-school/.

Ingle, David. 'Tommy'. *BMJ* 344, no. 7845 (2012): 34–34.

Ionescu, Ghita, and Ernest Gellner, eds. *Populism: Its Meanings and National Characteristics*. London: Weidenfeld & Nicolson, 1969.

Isaak, Jim, and Mina J. Hanna. 'User Data Privacy: Facebook, Cambridge Analytica, and Privacy Protection'. *Computer* 51, no. 8 (2018): 56–59.

Itzkoff, Dave. '*Jon Stewart Will Leave The Daily Show on a Career High Note*.' *The New York Times*, February 10 2015.

Ives, Peter. *Gramsci's Politics of Language: Engaging the Bakhtin Circle and the Frankfurt School*. Toronto: University of Toronto Press, 2004.

Jacobs, Jack. 'Antisemitism, Islamophobia, and Racism in the Era of Donald Trump: The Relevance of Critical Theory'. *Berlin Journal of Critical Theory* 3, no. 1 (2019): 5–18.

Jacobs, Jack. *The Frankfurt School, Jewish Lives, and Antisemitism*. New York: Cambridge University Press, 2015.

Jacobs, R.N., and E. Townsley. *The Space of Opinion: Media Intellectuals and the Public Sphere*. New York: Oxford University Press, 2011.

Jakobson, R. 'The Dominant (1935)'. In *Readings in Russian Poetics: Formalist and Structuralist Views* edited by Ladislav Matejka and Krystyna Pomorska, 82–87. Cambridge, Mass.: MIT Press, 1971.

Jakobson, R., and J. Tynyanov. 'Problems of Literary and Linguistic Studies (1928)'. *New Left Review*, no. 1/37 (1966): 58–61.

Jameson, Fredric. *Late Marxism: Adorno, or, the Persistence of the Dialectic*. London: Verso, 1990.

Jameson, Fredric. *The Prison-House of Language: A Critical Account of Structuralism and Russian Formalism*. Princeton, NJ: Princeton University Press, 1972.

Jamieson, Kathleen Hall, and Joseph N. Cappella. *Echo Chamber: Rush Limbaugh and the Conservative Media Establishment*. New York: Oxford University Press, 2008.

Janowitz, Morris. 'The Technique of Propaganda for Reaction: Gerald L.K. Smith's Radio Speeches'. *The Public Opinion Quarterly*, no. 1 (1994): 84–93.

Jansen, Robert S. 'Populist Mobilization: A New Theoretical Approach to Populism'. *Sociological Theory* 29, no. 2 (2011): 75–96.

Jay, Martin. *Adorno*. London: Fontana, 1984.

Jay, Martin. 'Adorno in America'. *New German Critique* 31 (1984): 157–182.
Jay, Martin. 'Dialectic of Counter-Enlightenment: The Frankfurt School as Scapegoat of the Lunatic Fringe'. *Salmagundi* no. 168/9, no. Fall/Winter (2011): 30–40.
Jay, Martin. *The Dialectical Imagination: A History of the Frankfurt School and the Institute of Social Research, 1923–1950*. London: Heinemann, 1973.
Jay, Martin. 'The Frankfurt School's Critique of Marxist Humanism'. *Social Research* (1972): 285–305.
Jay, Martin. 'The Frankfurt School in Exile (1972)'. In *Permanent Exiles: Essays on the Intellectual Migration from Germany to America*, 28–61. New York: Columbia University Press, 1986.
Jay, Martin. 'The Jews and the Frankfurt School: Critical Theory's Analysis of Anti-Semitism'. *New German Critique*, no. 19 (1980): 137–149.
Jeffries, Stuart. 'Interview, Gustav Metzger: "Destroy, and You Create"'. *The Guardian*, 26 November (2012).
Jenemann, David. *Adorno in America*. Minneapolis: University of Minnesota Press, 2007.
Jessop, Bob. *The Capitalist State*. New York: New York University Press, 1982.
Jessop, Bob. 'Elective Affinity or Comprehensive Contradiction? Reflections on Capitalism and Democracy in the Time of Finance-Dominated Accumulation and Austerity States'. *Berliner Journal für Soziologie* 28, no. 1 (2018): 9–37.
Jessop, Bob. 'The Future of Capitalism'. In *Classic Disputes in Sociology*, edited by R.J. Anderson, J.A. Hughes and W.W. Sharrock, 36–66. London: Allen & Unwin, 1987.
Jessop, Bob. *Nicos Poulantzas: Marxist Theory and Political Strategy*. London: Macmillan, 1985.
Jessop, Bob. 'The Organic Crisis of the British State: Putting Brexit in Its Place'. *Globalizations* 14, no. 1 (2017): 133–141.
Jessop, Bob, Kevin Bonnett, Simon Bromley and Tom Ling. 'Authoritarian Populism, Two Nations and Thatcherism'. *New Left Review*, no. 147 (1984): 32.
Jessop, Bob, Kevin Bonnett, Simon Bromley, and Tom Ling. 'Thatcherism and the Politics of Hegemony: A Reply to Stuart Hall'. *New Left Review*, no. 153 (1985): 87.
Jezer, M. *Abbie Hoffman: American Rebel*. New Brunswick: Rutgers University Press, 1993.
Johnson, Pauline. *Habermas: Rescuing the Public Sphere*. London: Routledge, 2006.
Jones, Jonathon. 'Interview, Gustav Metzger: The Liquid Crystal Revolutionary'. *The Guardian*, 28 September (2009).
Jones, Paul K. 'Beyond the Semantic 'Big Bang': Cultural Sociology and an Aesthetic Public Sphere'. *Cultural Sociology* 1, no. 1 (2007): 73–95.
Jones, Paul K. 'Demagogic Populism and US Culture Industries: A Long Tradition'. *Australasian Journal of American Studies* 35, no. 1 (2016): 11–28.
Jones, Paul K. 'Insights from the Infamous: Recovering the Social-Theoretical First Phase of Populism Studies'. *European Journal of Social Theory* 22, no. 4 (2019): 458–476.
Jones, Paul K. 'Márkus and the Retrieval of the Sociological Adorno'. *Thesis Eleven* (2021).
Jones, Paul K. 'Marxist Cultural Sociology'. In *The Sage Handbook of Cultural Sociology*, edited by D. Inglis and Anna-Mari Almila, 11–25. London: Sage, 2016.
Jones, Paul K. *Raymond Williams's Sociology of Culture: A Critical Reconstruction*. Basingstoke: Palgrave Macmillan, 2004.
Jones, Paul K. 'The Technology Is Not the Cultural Form?': Raymond Williams's Sociological Critique of Marshall Mcluhan'. *Canadian Journal of Communication* 23, no. 4 (1998): 423–454.
Jones, Paul K., and David Holmes. *Key Concepts in Media and Communications*. London: Sage, 2011.

Jones, Paul K., and Michael Pusey. 'Political Communication and "Media System": The Australian Canary'. *Media, Culture & Society* 32, no. 3 (2010): 451–471.
Jowett, Garth, and Victoria O'Donnell. *Propaganda & Persuasion*. Sixth edn. Thousand Oaks, Calif.: Sage, 2015.
Kael, Pauline. *5001 Nights at the Movies*. New York: Arena, 1987.
Kalberg, Stephen. 'Max Weber's Types of Rationality: Cornerstones for the Analysis of Rationalization Processes in History'. *American Journal of Sociology* 85, no. 5 (1980): 1145–1179.
Kazan, Elia. *Elia Kazan: A Life*. Boston: De Capo, 1997.
Kazan, Elia. 'Introduction'. In *Bud Schulberg: A Face in the Crowd: A Play for the Screen*, viii–xxiv. New York: Random House, 1957.
Kazan, Elia. *The Selected Letters of Elia Kazan*. New York: Knopf Doubleday, 2014.
Kazan, Elia, and Jeff Young. *Kazan: The Master Director Discusses His Films: Interviews with Elia Kazan*. New York: Newmarket Press, 1999.
Kazin, Michael. 'How Can Donald Trump and Bernie Sanders Both Be "Populist"?'. *The New York Times Sunday Magazine* (27 March 2016): MM13.
Kazin, Michael. *The Populist Persuasion: An American History (Revised)*, 2nd edn. Ithaca, NY: Cornell University Press, 1998.
Keane, John. *The Media and Democracy*. Cambridge: Polity, 1991.
Keefe, P.R. 'How Mark Burnett Resurrected Donald Trump as an Icon of American Success'. *The New Yorker*, 7 January (2019).
Kellner, Douglas. 'Donald Trump as Authoritarian Populist: A Frommian Analysis'. *Logos: A Journal of Modern Society & Culture* 15, nos 2–3 (2016).
Killen, Andreas. 'Weimar Psychotechnics between Americanism and Fascism'. *Osiris* 22, no. 1 (2007): 48–71.
Koliska, Michael, and Stine Eckert. 'Lost in a House of Mirrors: Journalists Come to Terms with Myth and Reality in *The Newsroom*'. *Journalism* 16, no. 6 (2015): 750–767.
Kreis, Ramona. 'The "Tweet Politics" of President Trump'. *Journal of Language & Politics* 16, no. 4 (2017): 607–618.
Kriesi, Hanspeter, and Takis Pappas, eds. *European Populism in the Shadow of the Great Recession*. Colchester: ECPR Press, 2015.
Laclau, Ernesto. *Emancipation(s)*. London: Verso, 2007. 1996.
Laclau, Ernesto. 'Feudalism and Capitalism in Latin America'. *New Left Review*, no. 1/67 (1971): 19–38.
Laclau, Ernesto. *New Reflections on the Revolution of Our Time*. London: Verso, 1990.
Laclau, Ernesto. *On Populist Reason*. London: Verso, 2005.
Laclau, Ernesto. *Politics and Ideology in Marxist Theory: Capitalism, Fascism, Populism*. London: NLB, 1977.
Laclau, Ernesto. 'Populism: What's in a Name?'. In *Populism and the Mirror of Democracy*, edited by Francisco Panizza, 32–49. London: Verso, 2005.
Laclau, Ernesto. 'Psychoanalysis and Marxism'. *Critical Inquiry* 13, no. 2 (1987): 330–333.
Laclau, Ernesto, and Chantal Mouffe. *Hegemony and Socialist Strategy: Towards a Radical Democratic Politics*. London: Verso, 1985.
Laclau, Ernesto, and Chantal Mouffe. 'Post-Marxism without Apologies'. *New Left Review* 1/166, no. 11–12 (1987): 79–106.
Laclau, Ernesto, and Lilian Zac. 'Minding the Gap: The Subject of Politics'. In *The Making of Political Identities*, edited by Ernesto Laclau, 11–39. London: Verso, 1994.
Laing, Dave. *The Sound of Our Time*. London: Sheed & Ward, 1969.
Lane, Melissa. 'The Origins of the Statesman–Demagogue Distinction in and after Ancient Athens'. *Journal of the History of Ideas* 73, no. 2 (2012): 179–200.

Lang, M. *The Road to Woodstock*. New York: HarperCollins, 2009.
Langdon, Jennifer E. *Caught in the Crossfire: Adrian Scott and the Politics of Americanism in 1940s Hollywood*. New York: Columbia University Press, 2008.
Laski, Harold J. *Reflections on the Revolution of Our Time*. London: Allen & Unwin, 1943.
Lazarsfeld, Paul F. 'Remarks on Administrative and Critical Communications Research'. *Zeitschrift für Sozialforschung* 9, no. 1 (1941): 2–16.
Lazarsfeld, Paul F., Bernard Berelson and Hazel Gaudet. *The People's Choice: How the Voter Makes up His Mind in a Presidential Campaign*, 2nd edn. New York: Columbia University Press, 1948.
Lazarsfeld, Paul F., Bernard Berelson and Hazel Gaudet. 'Preface to the Second Edition'. In *The People's Choice: How the Voter Makes up His Mind in a Presidential Campaign*, vii–xxviii. New York: Columbia University Press, 1948.
Lee, Alfred McClung. 'Prophets of Deceit: A Study of the Techniques of the American Agitator (Book Review)'. *Public Opinion Quarterly* 14 (1950): 347–348.
Lee, Alfred McClung, and Elizabeth Briant Lee. *The Fine Art of Propaganda: A Study of Father Coughlin's Speeches*. New York: Harcourt Brace and Company, 1939.
Lee, Alfred McClung, and Elizabeth Briant Lee. 'Introduction to the Octagon Edition'. In *The Fine Art of Propaganda*. New York: Octagon Press, 1972.
Lévi-Strauss, Claude. *The Savage Mind*. London: Weidenfeld & Nicolson, 1966. 1962.
Lévi-Strauss, Claude. *Structural Anthropology*. New York: Basic Books, 1963. 1958.
Ligensa, Annemone, Klaus Kreimeier, and Järg Schweinitz. 'The Aesthetic Idealist as Efficiency Engineer: Hugo Münsterberg's Theories of Perception, Psychotechnics and Cinema'. In *Film 1900: Technology, Perception, Culture*, edited by Annemone Ligensa and Klaus Kreimeier, 77–86. New Barnet, UK: John Libbey, 2009.
Lipset, Seymour Martin. 'The Sources of the Radical Right'. In *The New American Right* edited by Daniel Bell, 166–233. New York: Criterion, 1955.
Lipset, Seymour Martin. 'Three Decades of the Radical Right: Coughlinites, McCarthyites, and Birchers'. In *The Radical Right: The New American Right Expanded and Updated*, edited by Daniel Bell, 373–446. Garden City, New York: Anchor, 1964.
Litvak, Joseph. *The Un-Americans: Jews, the Blacklist, and Stoolpigeon Culture*. Durham, NC: Duke University Press, 2009.
Livingstone, Sonia. 'Elihu Katz's Commitments, Disciplinarity and Legacy: Or, "Triangular Thinking"'. *International Journal of Communication* 8 (2014): 2178–2185.
Lowenthal, Leo. 'Adorno and His Critics (1978)'. In *Critical Theory and Frankfurt Theorists: Lectures, Correspondence, Conversations*, 59–72. New Brunswick, NJ: Transaction, 2016.
Lowenthal, Leo. 'Biographies in Popular Magazines'. In *Radio Research 1942–1943*, edited by Paul Lazarsfeld and Frank Stanton, 507–548. New York: Duell, Sloan and Pearce, 1944.
Lowenthal, Leo. *Literature, Popular Culture and Society*. Englewood Cliffs, NJ: Prentice-Hall, 1961.
Lowenthal, Leo. 'Scholarly Biography: A Conversation with Helmut Dubiel, 1979'. In *An Unmastered Past: The Autobiographical Reflections of Leo Lowenthal*, edited by Martin Jay, 111–138. Berkeley: University of California Press, 1987.
Lowenthal, Leo. *An Unmastered Past: The Autobiographical Reflections of Leo Lowenthal*. Berkeley: University of California Press, 1987.
Lowenthal, Leo, and Norbert Guterman. 'Portrait of the American Agitator'. *Public Opinion Quarterly* 12, no. 3 (1948): 417–429.
Lowenthal, Leo, and Norbert Guterman. *Prophets of Deceit: A Study of the Techniques of the American Agitator*. New York: Harper, 1949.

Löwy, Michael. 'Figures of Weberian Marxism'. *Theory and Society* 25, no. 3 (1996): 431–446.
Lukács, György. *History and Class Consciousness: Studies in Marxist Dialectics.* Translated by Rodney Livingstone. London: Merlin Press, 1971. 1923.
Lukács, György. 'The Intellectual Physiognomy of Literary Characters (1936)'. In *Radical Perspectives in the Arts*, edited by Lee Baxandall, 89–141. Harmondsworth: Penguin, 1972.
Lunbeck, Elizabeth 'The Allure of Trump's Narcissism'. *Los Angeles Review of Books* (1 August 2017).
Lunn, Eugene. 'Beyond "Mass Culture": The Lonely Crowd, the Uses of Literacy, and the Postwar Era'. *Theory and Society* 19, no. 1 (1990): 63–86.
Lunn, Eugene. 'Cultural Populism and Egalitarian Democracy'. *Theory and Society* 15, no. 4 (1986): 479–517.
Lunn, Eugene. 'The Frankfurt School in the Development of the Mass Culture Debate'. *Journal of Comparative Literature and Aesthetics* XI, no. 1–2 (1988): 1–37.
Lunn, Eugene. *Marxism and Modernism: An Historical Study of Lukács, Brecht, Benjamin, and Adorno*. Berkeley: University of California Press, 1982.
Luthin, Reinhard H. *American Demagogues: Twentieth Century*. Boston: Beacon Press, 1954.
Lyttelton, Adrian. 'Futurism, Politics and Society'. In *Italian Futurism 1909–1944: Reconstructing the Universe*, edited by Vivien Greene, 58–76. New York: Guggenheim, 2014.
Macaulay, Thomas. 'The Constitutional History of England, from the Accession of Henry VII. To the Death of George II. By Henry Hallam'. *The Edinburgh Review* 48, no. 95 (1828): 96–169.
MacDonald, Dwight. 'Looking Backward'. *Encounter* 16, no. 6 (1961): 79–84.
Maloney, Courtney. 'The Faces in Lonesome's Crowd: Imaging the Mass Audience in "A Face in the Crowd"'. *Journal of Narrative Theory* 29, no. 3 (1999): 251–277.
Mancini, Paolo. *Between Commodification and Lifestyle Politics: Does Silvio Berlusconi Provide a New Model of Politics for the Twenty-First Century?* Oxford: Reuters Institute for the Study of Journalism, University of Oxford, 2011.
Mann, Michael. *Fascists*. Cambridge: Cambridge University Press, 2004.
Márkus, György. *Culture, Science, Society: The Constitution of Cultural Modernity*. Leiden: Brill, 2011.
Marx, Karl. '*The Eighteenth Brumaire of Louis Bonaparte* (1852)'. Translated by Terrell Carver. In *Marx: Later Political Writings*, edited by Terrell Carver, 31–127. Cambridge: Cambridge University Press, 2009.
Marx, Karl. '"Preface" to *A Contribution to the Critique of Political Economy* (1859)'. Translated by Terrell Carver. In *Marx: Later Political Writings*, edited by Terrell Carver, 158–162. Cambridge: Cambridge University Press, 2009.
Massing, Paul W. *Rehearsal for Destruction: A Study of Political Anti-Semitism in Imperial Germany*. New York: Harper, 1949.
Mayhew, Leon H. *The New Public: Professional Communication and the Means of Social Influence*. Cambridge: Cambridge University Press, 1997.
Mazzoleni, Gianpietro. 'Mediated Populism'. In *The International Encyclopedia of Communication*, edited by Wolfgang Donsbach, 3031–3033. London: Blackwell Publishing, 2008.
Mazzoleni, Gianpietro. 'Populism and the Media'. In *Twenty-First Century Populism*, edited by D. Albertazzi and D. McDonnell, 49–64. Houndsmills, Basingstoke: Palgrave, 2008.
Mazzoleni, Gianpietro, J. Stewart and B. Horsfield, eds. *The Media and Neo-Populism: A Contemporary Comparative Analysis*. Westport, Conn.: Praeger, 2003.

McBride, Joseph. *Frank Capra: The Catastrophe of Success*. New York: Simon & Schuster, 1992.
McDougall, William. *The Group Mind: A Sketch of the Principles of Collective Psychology, with Some Attempt to Apply Them to the Interpretation of National Life and Character*, 2nd edn. London: Cambridge University Press, 1927 [1920].
McGuigan, Jim. *Cultural Populism*. London: Routledge, 1992.
McGuigan, Jim. 'Cultural Populism Revisited'. In *Cultural Studies in Question*, edited by M. Ferguson and P. Golding, 138–154. London: Sage, 1997.
McGuigan, Jim. 'Cultural Studies and the New Populism'. In *Encyclopedia of Social Theory*, edited by George Ritzer, 178–181. London: Sage, 2005.
McGuigan, Jim. 'From Cultural Populism to Cool Capitalism'. *Art & the Public Sphere* 1, no. 1 (2011): 7–18.
McLaughlin, Neil. 'Critical Theory Meets America: Riesman, Fromm, and *The Lonely Crowd*'. *The American Sociologist* 32, no. 1 (2001): 5–26.
McLaughlin, Neil. 'Nazism, Nationalism, and the Sociology of Emotions: *Escape from Freedom* Revisited'. *Sociological Theory* (1996): 241–261.
McLaughlin, Neil. 'Origin Myths in the Social Sciences: Fromm, the Frankfurt School and the Emergence of Critical Theory'. *Canadian Journal of Sociology* (1999): 109–139.
McLuhan, Marshall, and Quentin Fiore. *The Medium Is the Massage*. New York: Random House, 1967.
Meehan, Johanna, ed. *Feminists Read Habermas: Gendering the Subject of Discourse*. New York: Routledge, 1995.
Mény, Yves, and Yves Surel, eds. *Democracies and the Populist Challenge*. New York: Palgrave, 2002.
Merleau-Ponty, Maurice. *Adventures of the Dialectic*. Evanston, Ill.: Northwestern University Press, 1973. 1955.
Meyer, Thomas. *Media Democracy: How the Media Colonize Politics*. Cambridge: Polity, 2002.
Moffitt, Benjamin, and Simon Tormey. 'Rethinking Populism: Politics, Mediatisation and Political Style'. *Political Studies* 62, no. 2 (2014): 381–397.
Morelock, Jeremiah, ed. *Critical Theory and Authoritarian Populism*. London: University of Westminster Press, 2018.
Morris, Meaghan. '"Please Explain?" Ignorance, Poverty and the Past'. *Inter-Asia Cultural Studies* 1, no. 2 (2000): 219–232.
Mosse, George L. *The Crisis of German Ideology: Intellectual Origins of the Third Reich*, 1st edn. New York: Grosset & Dunlap, 1964.
Motion, Andrew. *The Lamberts: George, Constant & Kit*. New York: Farrar, Straus, Giroux, 1987.
Mouffe, Chantal. *For a Left Populism*. London: Verso, 2018.
Mouzelis, Nicos. 'Ideology and Class Politics: A Critique of Ernesto Laclau'. *New Left Review*, no. 1/112 (1978): 45.
Mudde, Cas. *On Extremism and Democracy in Europe*. London: Routledge, 2016.
Mudde, Cas. *Populist Radical Right Parties in Europe*. Cambridge: Cambridge University Press, 2007.
Mudde, Cas. 'The Populist Radical Right: A Pathological Normalcy'. *West European Politics* 33, no. 6 (2010): 1167–1186.
Mudde, Cas, ed. *The Populist Radical Right: A Reader*. London: Routledge, 2017.
Mudde, Cas. 'The Populist Zeitgeist'. *Government and Opposition* 39, no. 4 (2004): 542–563.

Mudde, Cas, and Cristobal Rovira Kaltwasser. *Populism: A Very Short Introduction.* Oxford: Oxford University Press, 2017.

Mudde, Cas, and Cristóbal Rovira Kaltwasser. 'Populism and (Liberal) Democracy: A Framework for Analysis'. In *Populism in Europe and the Americas: Threat or Corrective for Democracy?*, edited by Cas Mudde and Cristóbal Rovira Kaltwasser, 1–26, Cambridge: Cambridge University Press, 2012.

Mudde, Cas, and Cristóbal Rovira Kaltwasser, eds. *Populism in Europe and the Americas: Threat or Corrective for Democracy?* Cambridge: Cambridge University Press, 2012.

Muirhead, Russell, and Nancy L. Rosenblum. *A Lot of People Are Saying: The New Conspiracism and the Assault on Democracy.* Princeton, NJ: Princeton University Press, 2019.

Mukařovský, Jan. *Aesthetic Function, Norm and Value as Social Facts.* Translated by Mark E. Suino. Ann Arbor: Department of Slavic Languages and Literature, University of Michigan, 1970.

Münsterberg, Hugo. *The Photoplay: A Psychological Study.* New York: Appleton, 1916.

Napoli, Philip M. 'What If More Speech Is No Longer the Solution? First Amendment Theory Meets Fake News and the Filter Bubble'. *Federal Communications Law Journal* 70, no. 1 (2018): 55–104.

Neumann, Franz L. *Behemoth: The Structure and Practice of National Socialism.* London: V. Gollancz, 1942.

Neve, Brian. *Film and Politics in America: A Social Tradition.* New York: Routledge, 1992.

Noerr, G. Schmid. 'Editor's Afterword'. In *Dialectic of Enlightenment: Philosophical Fragments*, edited by G. Schmid Noerr, 217–247. Stanford: Stanford University Press, 2002.

Nosthoff, Anna-Verena. 'Art after Auschwitz: Responding to an Infinite Demand: Gustav Metzger's Works as Responses to Theodor W. Adorno's "New Categorical Imperative"'. *Cultural Politics* 10, no. 3 (2014): 300–319.

Nussbaum, Emily. 'The TV That Created Donald Trump'. *The New Yorker*, 31 July (2017).

Nye, Russel B. *The Unembarrassed Muse: The Popular Arts in America.* New York: Dial Press, 1970.

Offe, Claus. *Reflections on America: Tocqueville, Weber and Adorno in the United States.* Cambridge: Polity, 2005.

Ott, Brian L. 'The Age of Twitter: Donald J. Trump and the Politics of Debasement'. *Critical Studies in Media Communication* 34, no. 1 (2017): 59–68.

Pappas, Takis S. 'Are Populist Leaders "Charismatic"? The Evidence from Europe'. *Constellations* 23, no. 3 (2016): 378–390.

Pappas, Takis S. 'Modern Populism: Research Advances, Conceptual and Methodological Pitfalls, and the Minimal Definition'. In *Oxford Research Encyclopedia of Politics*, edited by William M. Thompson. Oxford: Oxford University Press, 2016.

Peck, Reece. *Fox Populism: Branding Conservatism as Working Class.* Cambridge: Cambridge University Press, 2019.

Perrin, Andrew J., and Lars Jarkko. 'Introduction to T.W. Adorno, "Opinion Research and Publicness (Meinungsforschung Und Öffentlichkeit 1964)"'. *Sociological Theory* 23, no. 1 (2005): 116–120.

Peters, John Durham. 'The Subtlety of Horkheimer and Adorno: Reading "The Culture Industry"'. In *Canonic Texts in Media Research: Are There Any? Should There Be? How About These?* edited by Elihu Katz, John Durham Peters, Tamar Liebes and Avril Orloff, 58–73. Cambridge: Polity, 2003.

Peterson, Richard A. 'The Unnatural History of Rock Festivals: An Instance of Media Facilitation'. *Popular Music & Society* 2, no. 2 (1973): 97–123.

Plotke, David. 'Introduction to the Transaction Edition'. In *The Radical Right, 3rd Edition*, edited by Daniel Bell, xi–lxxvi. New Brunswick, NJ: Transaction Publishers, 2002.
Pohl, Frances K. *Ben Shahn: New Deal Artist in a Cold War Climate, 1947–1954*. Austin: University of Texas Press, 1989.
Pollock, Frederick. 'Is National Socialism a New Order?'. *Zeitschrift für Sozialforschung* 9, no. 3 (1941): 440–455.
Pollock, Frederick. 'State Capitalism: Its Possibilities and Limitations'. *Zeitschrift für Sozialforschung* 9, no. 2 (1941): 200–225.
Pollock, Friedrich, Theodor W. Adorno, Andrew J. Perrin, Jeffrey K. Olick and Institut für Sozialforschung. *Group Experiment and Other Writings: The Frankfurt School on Public Opinion in Postwar Germany*. Cambridge, Mass.: Harvard University Press, 2011.
Poniewozik, James. 'Trump's Campaign Classroom: Reality TV'. *The New York Times*, 10 October (2015), C1.
Postone, Moishe, and Barbara Brick. 'Critical Theory and Political Economy'. In *On Max Horkheimer: New Perspectives*, edited by Seyla Benhabib, Wolfgang Bonss and John McCole, 215–256. Cambridge, Mass.: MIT Press, 1993.
Poulantzas, Nicos. *Fascism and Dictatorship: The Third International and the Problem of Fascism*. Translated by Judith White. London: NLB, 1974. 1970.
Poulantzas, Nicos. 'On the Popular Impact of Fascism (1976)'. In *The Poulantzas Reader: Marxism, Law and the State*, edited by James Martin, 258–269. London: Verso, 2008.
Poulantzas, Nicos. *Political Power and Social Classes*. Translated by Timothy O'Hagan. London: NLB, 1975. 1968.
Poulantzas, Nicos. 'Preliminaries to the Study of Hegemony in the State (1965)'. In *The Poulantzas Reader*, edited by James Martin, 74–119. London: Verso, 2008.
Poulantzas, Nicos. *State, Power, Socialism*. London: NLB, 1978.
Procter, James. *Stuart Hall*. London: Routledge, 2004.
Project for Excellence in Journalism. 'The State of the News Media 2007, Talk Radio'. Project for Excellence in Journalism, http://stateofthemedia.org/2007/radio-intro/talk-radio/.
Pye, Lucian W., ed. *Communications and Political Development*. New Jersey: Princeton University Press, 1963.
Rabinbach, Anson. 'German-Jewish Connections: The New York Intellectuals and the Frankfurt School in Exile'. *German Politics & Society* 13, no. 3 (36) (1995): 108–129.
Rabinbach, Anson. *The Human Motor: Energy, Fatigue, and the Origins of Modernity*. Berkeley: University of California Press, 1990.
Randall, Eric. 'How Andy Griffith Predicted Glenn Beck'. *The Atlantic* (3 July 2012).
Reeve, Henry. 'The Newspaper Press'. *The Edinburgh Review* 102, no. 208 (1855): 470–498.
Reicher, Stephen, and S. Alexander Haslam. 'The Politics of Hope: Donald Trump as an Entrepreneur of Identity'. In *Why Irrational Politics Appeals: Understanding the Allure of Trump*, edited by Mari Fitzduff, 25–40. Santa Barbara: Praeger, 2017.
Reid, Donald. 'Inciting Readings and Reading Cites: Visits to Marx's *The Eighteenth Brumaire of Louis Bonaparte*'. *Modern Intellectual History* 4, no. 3 (2007): 545–570.
Rensmann, Lars. 'The Noisy Counter-Revolution: Understanding the Cultural Conditions and Dynamics of Populist Politics in Europe in the Digital Age'. *Politics and Governance* 5, no. 4 (2017): 123–135.
Rensmann, Lars. *The Politics of Unreason: The Frankfurt School and the Origins of Modern Antisemitism*. Albany: SUNY Press, 2017.
Rheingold, Howard. *The Virtual Community: Homesteading on the Electronic Frontier*. Reading, Mass.: Addison-Wesley Pub. Co., 1993.

Rice-Oxley, Mark, and Ammar Kalia. 'How to Spot a Populist'. *The Guardian*, 3 December (2018).
Ricœur, Paul. 'Structure and Hermeneutics (1963)'. In *The Conflict of Interpretations: Essays in Hermeneutics*, 27–61. Evanston: Northwestern University Press, 1974.
Riesman, David, and Nathan Glazer. *Faces in the Crowd*. New Haven: Yale University Press, 1952.
Riesman, David, Nathan Glazer and Reuel Denney. *The Lonely Crowd: A Study in the Changing American Character*. New Haven: Yale University Press, 1950.
Rogin, Michael Paul. *The Intellectuals and McCarthy: The Radical Specter*. Cambridge, Mass.: MIT Press, 1967.
Roiser, Martin, and Carla Willig. 'The Strange Death of the Authoritarian Personality: 50 Years of Psychological and Political Debate'. *History of the Human Sciences* 15, no. 4 (2002): 71–96.
Rojek, Chris. *Stuart Hall*. Cambridge: Polity, 2002.
Rorty, Richard. *Contingency, Irony, and Solidarity*. Cambridge: Cambridge University Press, 1989.
Rosenberg, Bernard. 'Mass Culture in America'. In *Mass Culture: The Popular Arts in America*, edited by Bernard Rosenberg and David M. White, 3–12. Glencoe, Ill.: Free Press, 1957.
Rosenberg, Bernard, and David M. White, eds. *Mass Culture: The Popular Arts in America*. Glencoe, Ill.: Free Press, 1957.
Ross, Alex. 'The Frankfurt School Knew Trump Was Coming'. *The New Yorker*, 16 December (2016).
Ross, Andrew. *No Respect: Intellectuals & Popular Culture*. New York: Routledge, 1989.
Rosteck, Thomas. *See It Now Confronts McCarthyism: Television Documentary and the Politics of Representation*. Tuscaloosa: University of Alabama Press, 1994.
Roy, William G. *Reds, Whites, and Blues: Social Movements, Folk Music, and Race in the United States*. Princeton: Princeton University Press, 2013.
Rydgren, Jens. 'The Sociology of the Radical Right'. *Annu. Rev. Sociol.* 33 (2007): 241–262.
Saloutos, Theodore, ed. *Populism: Reaction or Reform?* New York: Holt Rinehart & Winston, 1978.
Sanford, Nevitt. 'Authoritarian Personality in Contemporary Perspective'. *Handbook of Political Psychology* (1973): 139–170.
Sartori, Giovanni. 'Concept Misformation in Comparative Politics'. *The American Political Science Review* 64, no. 4 (1970): 1033–1053.
Sartori, Giovanni. *Parties and Party Systems: A Framework for Analysis*. Cambridge: Cambridge University Press, 1976.
Saussure, Ferdinand de. *Course in General Linguistics*. Translated by Wade Baskin. New York: Philosophical Library, 1959 [1915].
Schecter, Darrow. *Critical Theory and Sociological Theory: On Late Modernity and Social Statehood*. Manchester: Manchester University Press, 2019.
Schiller, Dan. *Digital Capitalism: Networking the Global Market System*. Cambridge, Mass.: MIT Press, 1999.
Schiller, Dan. 'Digital Capitalism: A Status Report on the Corporate Commonwealth of Information'. In *A Companion to Media Studies*, edited by Angharad N. Valdivia, 137–156. New York: Wiley, 2007.
Schiller, Dan. 'Geopolitics and Economic Power in Today's Digital Capitalism'. In *Presentation to the Hans Crescent Seminar*. London, 2015.
Schiller, Dan. 'Power under Pressure: Digital Capitalism in Crisis'. *International Journal of Communication* 5 (2011): 18.

Schmidt, James. '"Racket", "Monopoly", and the *Dialectic of Enlightenment*'. *Nonsite. org*, (January 2016).
Schudson, Michael. 'Was There Ever a Public Sphere? If So, When? Reflections on the American Case'. In *Habermas and the Public Sphere*, edited by Craig J. Calhoun, 143–163. Cambridge, Mass.: MIT Press, 1992.
Schulberg, Budd. *A Face in the Crowd: A Play for the Screen*. New York: Random House, 1957.
Schulberg, Budd. 'Your Arkansas Traveler'. In *Some Faces in the Crowd*, 3–44. New York: Random House, 1953.
Seldes, Gilbert. *The 7 Lively Arts*, 2nd edn. New York: Sagamore Press, 1957.
Seldes, Gilbert. *The Public Arts*. New York: Simon & Schuster, 1956.
Sheinbaum, John J. 'Progressive Rock and the Inversion of Musical Values'. In *Progressive Rock Reconsidered*, edited by K. Holm-Hudson, 21–42. London: Routledge, 2002.
Shils, Edward. *Tradition*. London: Faber & Faber, 1981.
Shils, Edward A. 'Authoritarianism: Right and Left'. In *Studies in the Scope and Method of 'The Authoritarian Personality'*, edited by Richard Christie and Marie Jahoda, 24–49. New York: Free Press., 1954.
Shils, Edward A. 'Charisma, Order, and Status'. *American Sociological Review* 30, no. 2 (1965): 199–213.
Shils, Edward A. 'Daydreams and Nightmares: Reflections on the Criticism of Mass Culture'. *The Sewanee Review* 65, no. 4 (1957): 587–608.
Shils, Edward A. 'Demagogues and Cadres in the Political Development of the New States'. In *Communications and Political Development*, edited by Lucian W. Pye, 64–77. Princeton, NJ: Princeton University Press, 1963.
Shils, Edward A. *The Intellectuals and the Powers and Other Essays*. Chicago: University of Chicago Press, 1972.
Shils, Edward A. 'Mass Society and Its Culture'. In *Culture for the Millions?*, edited by Norman Jacobs, 1–27. Princeton: D. Van Nostrand Co., 1961.
Shils, Edward A. 'The Theory of Mass Society: Prefatory Remarks'. *Diogenes* 10, no. 39 (1962): 45–66.
Shils, Edward A. *The Torment of Secrecy: The Background and Consequences of American Security Policies*. London: Heinemann, 1956.
Sola Pool, Ithiel de. *Technologies of Freedom*. Cambridge, Mass.: Belknap Press, 1983.
Sorkin, Aaron, and Scott Rudin. *The Newsroom: The Complete First Season*. Burbank, CA: Home Box Office: Warner Home Video, 2013. Video recording.
Spence, E.H., A. Alexandra, A. Quinn and A. Dunn. *Media, Markets, and Morals*. Chichester: Wiley, 2011.
Sproule, J. Michael. 'Progressive Propaganda Critics and the Magic Bullet Myth'. *Critical Studies in Media Communication* 6, no. 3 (1989): 225–246.
Sproule, J. Michael. *Propaganda and Democracy: The American Experience of Media and Mass Persuasion*. Cambridge: Cambridge University Press, 1997.
Stanfield, Peter. 'The Who and Pop Art: The Simple Things You See Are All Complicated'. *Journal of Popular Music Studies* 29, no. 1 (2017): e12203.
Stavrakakis, Yannis. 'Antinomies of Formalism: Laclau's Theory of Populism and the Lessons from Religious Populism in Greece'. *Journal of Political Ideologies* 9, no. 3 (2004): 253–267.
Stavrakakis, Yannis, and Anton Jäger. 'Accomplishments and Limitations of the "New" Mainstream in Contemporary Populism Studies'. *European Journal of Social Theory* 21, no. 4 (2018): 547–565.

Stead, W.T. 'Government by Journalism'. *The Contemporary Review* 49, no. 1 (1886): 653–674.
Stenner, K. *The Authoritarian Dynamic*. Cambridge: Cambridge University Press, 2005.
Sternhell, Zeev, Mario Sznajder and Maia Ashéri. *The Birth of Fascist Ideology: From Cultural Rebellion to Political Revolution*. Translated by David Maisel. Princeton, N.J.: Princeton University Press, 1994. 1989.
Storey, John. *Cultural Theory and Popular Culture: An Introduction*, 8th edn. London: Routledge, 2018.
Strout, Lawrence N. 'The Edward R. Murrow of Docudramas and Documentary'. *Media History Monographs* 12, no. 1 (2010).
Sum, N.L., and B. Jessop. *Towards a Cultural Political Economy: Putting Culture in Its Place in Political Economy*. Cheltenham: Edward Elgar, 2014.
Sunstein, Cass R. *Democracy and the Problem of Free Speech*. New York: Free Press, 1993.
Sunstein, Cass R. *Echo Chambers: Bush V. Gore, Impeachment, and Beyond*. Princeton: Princeton University Press, 2001.
Sunstein, Cass R. *Republic.Com*. Princeton: Princeton University Press, 2001.
Swedberg, Richard. 'How to Use Max Weber's Ideal Type in Sociological Analysis'. *Journal of Classical Sociology* 18, no. 3 (2018): 181–196.
Swingewood, Alan. *The Myth of Mass Culture*. London: Macmillan, 1977.
Symonds, Michael J. *Max Weber's Theory of Modernity: The Endless Pursuit of Meaning*. Farnham, Surrey: Ashgate, 2015.
Szwed, John F. *The Man Who Recorded the World: A Biography of Alan Lomax*. New York: Arrow, 2011.
Taggart, Paul A. *Populism*. Milton Keynes: Open University Press, 2000.
Tambini, Damian. 'How Advertising Fuels Fake News'. *LSE Media Policy Blog* (20 June 2017).
Thaler, Richard H., and Cass R. Sunstein. *Nudge: Improving Decisions About Health, Wealth, and Happiness*. New Haven: Yale University Press, 2008.
Therborn, Göran. 'A Critique of the Frankfurt School'. *New Left Review*, no. 1/63 (1970): 65–96.
Thomas, Cal. 'Trump Is "Lonesome Rhodes"'. *The Washington Times* (14 September 2015).
Thompson, E.P. *The Making of the English Working Class*. London: Victor Gollancz, 1963.
Thompson, John B. *The Media and Modernity: A Social Theory of the Media*. Stanford: Stanford University Press, 1995.
Thompson, John B. 'Mediated Interaction in the Digital Age'. *Theory, Culture & Society* 37, no. 1 (2020): 3–28.
Togliatti, Palmiro. *Lectures on Fascism*. London: Lawrence & Wishart, 1976.
Townshend, Pete. *Who I Am: A Memoir*. New York: Harper, 2012.
Townshend, Pete. 'Won't Get Judged Again', *Pete's Diaries*, 27 May (2006). https://web.archive.org/web/20061205225327/http://www.petetownshend.co.uk/diary/display.cfm?id=285&zone=diary.
Truffaut, François. 'A Face in the Crowd (1957)'. In *The Films in My Life*, 113–115. New York: Da Capo Press, 1994.
Tufekci, Zeynep. 'How Social Media Took Us from Tahrir Square to Donald Trump'. *MIT Technology Review* (14 August 2018).
Tufekci, Zeynep. 'A Response to Johanne Kübler's A Review of *Twitter and Tear Gas: The Power and Fragility of Networked Protest*'. *International Journal of Politics, Culture, and Society* 32 (2019): 365–369.

Tufekci, Zeynep. *Twitter and Tear Gas: The Power and Fragility of Networked Protest*. New Haven: Yale University Press, 2017.
Turner, Graeme. *British Cultural Studies: An Introduction*, 2nd edn. London: Routledge, 1996.
Turner, Stephen. 'Charisma Reconsidered'. *Journal of Classical Sociology* 3, no. 1 (2003): 5–26.
Umrath, Barbara. 'A Feminist Reading of the Frankfurt School's Studies on Authoritarianism and Its Relevance for Understanding Authoritarian Tendencies in Germany Today'. *South Atlantic Quarterly* 117, no. 4 (2018): 861–878.
Unterberger, Richie. *Won't Get Fooled Again: The Who from Lifehouse to Quadrophenia*. London: Jawbone Press, 2011.
Urbinati, Nadia. 'Democracy and Populism'. *Constellations* 5, no. 1 (1998): 110–124.
Urbinati, Nadia. *Democracy Disfigured: Opinion, Truth, and the People*. Cambridge, Mass.: Harvard University Press, 2014.
Van Reijen, Willem, and Jan Bransen. 'The Disappearance of Class History in "Dialectic of Enlightenment": A Commentary on the Textual Variants (1947 and 1944)'. In *Dialectic of Enlightenment*, 248–252. Stanford: Stanford University Press, 2002.
Vološinov, Valentin N. *Marxism and the Philosophy of Language*. Translated by Ladislav Matejka and I.R. Titunik. New York: Seminar Press, 1973. 1930.
Walicki, Andrzej. 'Russia'. In *Populism: Its Meaning and National Characteristics*, edited by Ghiţa Ionescu and Ernest Gellner, 62–96. London: Weidenfeld & Nicolson, 1969.
Warren, Donald I. *Radio Priest: Charles Coughlin, the Father of Hate Radio*. New York: Free Press, 1996.
Waterson, Jim. 'Corbyn Proposes "Public Facebook" as Part of Media Overhaul'. *The Guardian*, 23 August (2018).
Waugh, Linda R. 'The Poetic Function in the Theory of Roman Jakobson'. *Poetics Today* 2, no. 1a (1980): 57–82.
Weber, Max. *Economy and Society*. Berkeley: University of California Press, 1978.
Weber, Max. '"Objectivity" in Social Science and Social Policy'. Translated by Edward Shils and Henry A. Finch. In *On the Methodology of the Social Sciences*, 50–112. New York: Free Press, 1949.
Weber, Max. *On Charisma and Institution Building: Selected Papers*, edited by S.N. Eisenstadt. Chicago: University of Chicago Press, 1968.
Weber, Max. 'The Profession and Vocation of Politics'. Translated by Ronald Speirs. In *Weber: Political Writings*, edited by Peter Lassman and Ronald Speirs, 309–369. Cambridge: Cambridge University Press, 1994.
Weber, Max. *The Protestant Ethic and the Spirit of Capitalism*. Translated by Talcott Parsons. London: Allen & Unwin, 1930. 1904.
Weber, Max. 'Science as a Vocation'. Translated by Rodney Livingstone. In *The Vocation Lectures/Max Weber*, edited by David S. Owen and Tracy B. Strong. Indianapolis: Hackett Publishing, 2004.
Wheatland, Thomas. *The Frankfurt School in Exile*. Minneapolis: University of Minnesota Press, 2009.
Who, The. '"Abbie Hoffman Incident"'. In *Thirty Years Of Maximum R&B*. Audio recording. London: Polydor, 1994.
Wiener, Jon. *Come Together: John Lennon in His Time*. New York: Random House, 1984.
Wiggershaus, Rolf. *The Frankfurt School: Its History, Theories, and Political Significance*. Translated by Michael Robertson. Cambridge, Mass.: MIT Press, 1995. 1986.

Wildt, Michael. 'Volksgemeinschaft: A Modern Perspective on National Socialist Society'. In *Visions of Community in Nazi Germany: Social Engineering and Private Lives*, edited by Martina Steber and Bernhard Gotto, 43–59. Oxford: Oxford University Press, 2014.

Williams, Paul, and Brian Edgar. 'Tommy, Primal Therapy, and the Countercultural Critique of "Sick Society" and "Cripple Psychology"'. *Journal of Literary & Cultural Disability Studies* 9, no. 2 (2015): 207–238.

Williams, Raymond. 'Base and Superstructure in Marxist Cultural Theory'. *New Left Review*, no. 82 (1973): 3–16.

Williams, Raymond. *Culture and Society: 1780–1950*. London: Chatto & Windus, 1958.

Williams, Raymond. *Keywords: A Vocabulary of Culture and Society*, 2nd edn. London: Fontana, 1983.

Williams, Raymond. *The Long Revolution*. London: Chatto & Windus, 1961.

Williams, Raymond. *Marxism and Literature*. Oxford: Oxford University Press, 1977.

Williams, Raymond. 'On Reading Marcuse'. *Cambridge Review* 90, no. 30 (1969): 366–368.

Williams, Raymond. 'The Paths and Pitfalls of Ideology as an Ideology'. *Times Higher Education Supplement*, (10 June 1977): 13.

Williams, Raymond. *The Politics of Modernism: Against the New Conformists*. London: Verso, 1989.

Williams, Raymond. *Reading and Criticism*. London: Frederick Muller, 1950.

Williams, Raymond, and Michael Orrom. *Preface to Film*. London: Film Drama Ltd, 1954.

Wodak, Ruth. *The Politics of Fear: What Right-Wing Populist Discourses Mean*. London: Sage, 2015.

Wolfe, Charles. 'Authors, Audiences and Endings'. In *Meet John Doe: Frank Capra, Director*, edited by Charles Wolfe. New Brunswick: Rutgers University Press, 1989.

Worsley, Peter. 'The Concept of Populism'. In *Populism: Its Meanings and National Characteristics*, edited by Ghita Ionescu and Ernest Gellner, 212–250. London: Weidenfeld & Nicholson, 1969.

Worsley, Peter. *The Third World*. Chicago: University of Chicago Press, 1964.

Yates, John. 'Smart Man's Burden: *Nashville, A Face in the Crowd*, and Popular Culture'. *Journal of Popular Film* 5, no. 1 (1976): 19–28.

Zak, Dan. 'Fear and Gloating in Cincinnati'. *The Washington Post*, 2 August (2019).

Zakaria, Fareed. 'The Rise of Illiberal Democracy'. *Foreign Affairs* 76, no. 6 (1997): 22–43.

Ziege, Eva-Maria. *Antisemitismus Und Gesellschaftstheorie: Die Frankfurter Schule Im Amerikanischen Exil*. Frankfurt am Main: Suhrkamp, 2009.

Ziege, Eva-Marie. 'The Irrationality of the Rational: The Frankfurt School and Its Theory of Society in the 1940s'. In *Antisemitism and the Constitution of Sociology*, edited by Marcel Stoetzler, 274–295. Lincoln: University of Nebraska Press, 2014.

Ziege, Eva-Maria. 'Patterns within Prejudice: Antisemitism in the United States in the 1940s'. *Patterns of Prejudice* 46, no. 2 (2012): 93–127.

Žižek, Slavoj. 'Against the Populist Temptation'. *Critical Inquiry* 32, no. 3 (2006): 551–574.

Zuidervaart, Lambert. *Adorno's Aesthetic Theory: The Redemption of Illusion*. Cambridge, Mass.: MIT Press, 1991.

Index

Note: Page numbers in italics are figures.

The 7 Lively Arts (Seldes) 160
60 Minutes 195

'The Actuality of Philosophy' (Adorno) 73
Adamson, Walter L. 94
Adorno, Theodor W.
  and 'The Actuality of Philosophy' 73
  and *The Authoritarian Personality* 16, 26, 29
  and *Below the Surface* 176, 177
  on big band music of the 1940s 164
  compared with Laclau 120, 121–122, 125, 126–128
  on the culture industry 66, 147, 148–149, 160–162, 172n, 183, 212, 225
  and demagogue-follower relationship 42–43
  on demagogic devices 201–202
  on 'disinhibited hysteria' 202, 203
  and 'Elements of Anti-Semitism' 67–69
  and fascist stimuli 44
  and ideal-typification 77
  and influence of the Lees 36, 37–38, 39
  '(Draft) Introduction to *Prophets of Deceit*' 25, 47–48, 68, 79, 80, 231–243
  and 'lone wolf' 45
  and music 165
  and Offe 84, 85
  on opinion 217–219
  and Pollock 76
  and psychoanalysis 40–41
  and psychotechnics 47–50
  and 'Radio Physiognomics' 78
  on reification 70–71
  and religious devices 46
  and Romantic folkloricism 158
  on structuralism 134
  on *Structural Transformation* 215
  and time coincidence and space ubiquity 222
  and traditions 167–168
  and 'truth propaganda' 33
  and *Volksgemeinschaft* 136
  and Weber 32, 81–83
adversarial interviewing 194–195
advertising 50, 212, 217, 218, 221, 230n
the aesthetic 106, 107, 145–146, 182, 203
aesthetic culture 153, 210
aesthetic Modernism 145–146, 147
aesthetico-cultural production 211
aesthetic populism 159, 160
The Age of Reform: Bryan to FDR (Hofstadter) 7, 16
agitators (aka demagogues) 13, 30, 33, 46–48, 177, 221
  and Adorno 49, 69, 79, 80, 127
  and Lowenthal 50, 66, 136
agit prop phase 190

INDEX

alienated intellectuals framework (Shils) 151, 152
alienation 70, 148, 151, 155, 158
Althusser, Louis 98, 99, 135
Americanization 208, 220
American Jewish Committee (AJC) 25, 29, 36
analogue broadcasting 222
antidemocratic propaganda 30, 51
anti-immigration 137
antisemitism 8, 9, 26, 36, 40, 68–69, 113
  and *Below the Surface* 176
  and *Gentlemen's Agreement* 177, 180
  and Horkheimer 39
  and ideal-typification 77
  and Jay 67
  and Rosenberg 147–148
Apostolidis, Paul 57n
Arditi, Benjamin 22n
Arendt, Hannah 152, 163
Argentina 63
Aristotle 31
articulation 100, 101, 104, 109, 110, 111
Aspects of Sociology (Frankfurt Institute for Social Research) 37
audience-monitoring 49, 202, 203
austerity 130
Australia 142n, 221
authenticity 146, 164–165, 201
authoritarianism 26, 27, 28, 62, 64, 97, 103
  and Adorno's 'vaccine' 71, 79, 176
The Authoritarian Personality (Adorno et al.) 16, 26, 29–30, 64–65, 67, 176
  and *Below the Surface* 175, 177
  and critical social theoretical account 68–69
  and *cui bono* 83
  and demagogic propaganda 50, 51
  and Offe 84
authoritarian populism 92, 109, 111, 112, 128, 129, 153
  and Jessop 131
  and national-popular 191
authoritarians 29, 186
authoritarian statism 128–129, 130, 131
authority, social 28
'Authority and the Family' (Horkheimer) 28
auto-destructive aesthetics 188
auto-identification 191
automaton conformity 28
autonomy 160, 161, 212, 213
the avant-garde 148, 156, 190–191

Baker, C. Edwin 217
Bakhtin, M.M. 109
Barthes, Roland 184–185
Bartók, Béla 148
BBC 111
The Beatles 173n
Beck, Glenn 185
Begriffsgeschichte 31
Behemoth (Neumann) 74
Bell, Daniel 8, 9–11, 12, 13, 135, 159
Below the Surface 175–177
Bennett, Tony 174n
Berlusconi, Silvio 191, 201, 217
Bernstein, Richard 172n
Between Facts and Norms (Habermas) 214, 226n, 227n
Betz, Hans-Georg 5, 6, 20n
Billboard 192
Billig, Michael 29, 64, 65, 79
bloc 95
  historical 94, 98, 134
  power 98, 100, 101–102, 110, 130, 131

INDEX

Bob Roberts 185
Le Bon, Gustave 40, 41, 122, 123, 125, 127, 132
Bonapartism 95, 98, 130
Bourdieu, Pierre 146
bourgeois family 27, 28, 206, 210–211, 213
bourgeoisie 98, 102
bourgeois intimacy 210, 211, 212, 213
bourgeois novel 211
Bramson, Leon 152, 166, 169n, 174n
Brensen, Jan 74
bricolage 98
Brinkley, Alan 135, 136
Britain
  and class cultures 155
  and cultural populism 157–158
  and public sphere 209–210
  Thatcherism 109, 110–111, 128, 131, 166
broadcasting 15, 48–49, 78, 103, 206, 220, 222
  and Coughlin 76–77, 181
  and The Fairness Doctrine 217–218
  and Murrow 192
  and Shils 103
Bryan, William Jennings 11
Buck-Morss, Susan 70
Burke, Peter 156

Caesarism 95, 98, 101, 112, 130
Canovan, Margaret 7, 13
Cantril, Hadley 56n
capitalism
  consumer 94, 157
  digital 137, 223
  industrial 159
  and Jessop 129–130
  and Laclau 119–120
  monopoly 74, 101
Capra, Frank 180–181, 186

Cavalletto, George 57n
Chamberlain, Houston Stewart 147
Chaplin, Charlie 161, 162, 163–164, 172n
characterology 27–28
charisma 13, 80, 82–83, 85
charismatic authority 82, 83
charismatic demagogy 190–191
charismatic individual 101
charismatic leadership 13, 15, 31, 32, 83, 112, 189
Chicago Democratic Convention 187
'Chicago Seven' 187
civic privatism 213–214
civil rights movement, US 186
civil sphere 103
class 133, 154–155, 157, 158
classical liberal public sphere 224
'classification dilemma' (re populism) 3, 4, 18, 98, 132, 133, 145
  and Laclau 104, 105
  and Mudde 5
class interpellations 101
Cleon 31
clientelism 102
Clooney, George 194
coercion 95, 125, 126
coffee houses 210
Coleridge, Samuel Taylor 146
comedy 164
commercialization 208, 212, 213, 216, 217, 223, 224
commodification 49, 120, 182, 194, 221, 222, 223, 224
  broadcast 15
  cultural 156, 159
  culture-industrial 50, 64
  and montage 138
common sense 110, 134, 138
communications policy 207, 224, 225, 230n

communicative monopoly 32
comparativist typology 85–86
concept-construction 82
'The Concept of Populism' (Worsley) 122
conceptual stretching 4
condensation 100–101
conformity 28
consent, organization of 94
conspiracy narrative 7, 40, 44–45, 194, 203
    'cultural Marxist' 17, 23n
consumer capitalism 94, 157
consumer culture 158
Cook, Deborah 89n
Coughlin, Father Charles 8, 9, 15, 43, 45–46, 47, 221, 229n
    and Brinkley 135
    and the Lees 36, 37
    and *Meet John Doe* 180–181
    on New Deal 76–77, 186
counterculture 187
counter-demagogic popular art 186–191
counter-demagogy 195
counter-publics 213
crises 95, 98, 101, 130, 137
'The Crisis in Culture' (Arendt) 163
critical political communication studies 220
'critical populism' 154
The Critique of Power (Honneth) 72
The Critique of Pure Reason (Kant) 39
Crook, Stephen 38, 57n
Crossfire 177
The Crowd: A Study of the Popular Mind (Le Bon) 40, 122
cui bono 68–69, 81, 83
cultural capital 33
cultural democracy 159
'cultural dopes' (Hall) 166, 174n

cultural elitism 18, 147, 150, 154, 155
cultural politics 10, 11
cultural populism 138, 146, 149, 153–159, 160, 165, 166, 167, 197n
cultural production 50, 75, 134, 146, 158, 162, 164, 211
cultural relativists 159, 160
Culture and Society (Williams) 155, 156
culture industry 51, 85–86, 120, 138, 154, 159, 225
    and Adorno 48, 49–50, 66, 84, 147, 148–149, 160–162
    and advertising 218
    and class cultures 155
    and *A Face in the Crowd* 181–182, 183
    global 223
    and Lowenthal 53
    and New Left 187–188
    and the public sphere 211–212
    and reality television 200
    and social media 207
    and van Reijen and Brensen 74–75
    see also 'montage character'
'Culture Industry Reconsidered' (Adorno) 161–162
Curran, James 153, 171n, 174n, 227n

'Daydreams and Nightmares: Reflections on the Critique of Mass Culture' (Shils) 150–151, 169n, 170n
decultivaiton 148, 149, 158
demagogic devices 41, 42–43, 45–46, 80, 120, 133, 134
    and *cui bono* 68–69
    and Freud 125
    'great little man' device 42, 125, 200–201
    and the Lees 37, 38–39, 52–53

INDEX

'lone wolf' device 45, 125, 201–202
   and McCarthy 193
   and paranoia and pseudo-knowledge 40
   and Trump 201–202
demagogic power (Baker) 217
demagogic self-incrimination 191
demagogic 'techniques' 48, 68, 76, 79, 95, 133, 134
demagogic thematics 12, 44, 46, 51, 52, 64, 79, 135
   see also demagogic devices
demagogue-follower relationship 41, 42–43, 136–137
demagogues see agitators
'Democratic Leadership and Mass Manipulation' (Adorno) 32, 127
devices, see demagogic devices
Dialectic of Enlightenment (Horkheimer and Adorno) 25, 39, 45, 63, 64, 67, 70–75, 74, 80, 84, 139n, 147, 161, 167, 169n, 172n
Dickstein, Morris 181
digital capitalism 137, 223
disenchantment 5, 67, 71
disinhibited hysteria 45, 202, 203
dislocation 120, 137
displacement 39, 100, 177
dominant ideology 104, 107
Du Bois, W.E. 11, 186

echo chamber 221, 222
Eco, Umberto 185, 191
Economy and Society (Weber) 71, 82
editors 211, 212
ego-ideal 41–42, 125
ego-identification 189
The Eighteenth Brumaire of Louis Bonaparte (Marx) 94, 101
Eisler, Hanns 172n
election campaigns 219

'elements' (in formalist/structuralist analysis)
   and Althusser 99
   and Gramscian tradition 138
   and Laclau 98, 106, 133
   and Lévi-Strauss 98-99
   and organic ideology 100, 135
   and Poulantzas 98, 132, 133, 134, 135
   signifying 106–107
   see also recombinant
'Elements of Anti-Semitism' (Adorno and Horkheimer) 39, 40, 45, 67–68
'Elements of Self-Criticism' (Althusser) 99
Eliot, T.S. 154
elitism 18, 136, 147, 150, 154, 155, 158, 171n
emulation 100, 111, 194, 210
The End of Ideology (Bell) 159
Enlightenment 35, 39, 71
Escape from Freedom (Fromm) 27, 28, 64, 151, 183
estate 214, 215
European populisms 6, 30, 62–63
evangelicism 10, 11
exceptional state 98, 130
extremism 6

Facebook 223
A Face in the Crowd 178–180, 181–182, 183–184, 185, 186
Faces in the Crowd (Riesman and Glazer) 183
Fairness Doctrine 218, 220, 221
'fake news' 223
'false projection' 40
family 27, 28–29, 206
fascism 44, 62–63, 64, 67, 132–133, 145–146
   and Gramsci 95
   and Laclau and Mouffe 104

and Poulantzas 97–98, 100, 131
and Žižek 113
Fascism and Dictatorship (Poulantzas) 99, 100, 130
fascists 29, 30, 47, 64, 95, 145
Fear of Freedom (Fromm) 121
  see also *Escape From Freedom* (Fromm)
film industry 161
financial crash, 2008 137
Finchelstein, Federico 63, 85
The Fine Art of Propaganda (The Lees) 36–37
First Amendment 222, 230n
'flight of ideas' 38, 134, 187, 190, 195, 203
folk ballad 146
folk culture 163
folklore 138
folkloricism 146, 158
folk music 182, 186
folksongs 156
followers 29, 30, 42–43, 45, 122, 136–137
  and *Tommy* 189
  and Twitter 202
Forgacs, David 96
formalism 99, 107, 108–109, 110
  see also social formalism
formalist linguistics 133
The Foundations of the Nineteenth Century (Chamberlain) 147
fourth estate 214, 215, 226n
Fox News 200, 221
fragment 133, 134, 138, 148
France 157
Frankel-Brunswick, Else 64–65
The Frankfurt School, Jewish Lives and Antisemitism (Jacobs) 231
Fraser, Nancy 142n, 226n
'freezing' 49, 50

French salons 210
Freud, Sigmund 27, 40, 41–42, 43, 121–128, 136, 137, 177
'Freudian Theory and the Pattern of Fascist Propaganda' (Adorno) 40, 49, 136, 176
Frith, Simon 165, 173n
Fromm, Erich 27–28, 29, 64, 121, 151, 182–183
F-scale 29, 52
functional meaning 134
Futurists 146

Gans, Herbert 159, 169n
Garnham, Nicholas 220
Gassett, Jose Ortega Y. 150
gender 28, 54n, 55n, 57n, 60n, 86n, 142n, 179, 195, 201, 210-211, 226n
Gentlemen's Agreement 177, 180, 182
Germany 102, 135, 147, 149, 157, 186, 187, 210
  Nazi period 74, 131, 136
  Weimar 48
'Ghost Town' 166
Gitlin, Todd 141n, 186–187, 198n
Gladstone, William 32
Glazer, Tom 182
global culture industry 223
Goldmann, Lucien 134
Goodnight and Good Luck 194
Goodwin, Andrew 174n
Gramsci, Antonio 93–96, 98, 101, 102, 104, 111–112, 114n,115n, 116n, 141n, 142n
  and common sense 110, 134
  on culture 146
  and Jessop 130
  and Laclau 134–135
  and national-popular 119, 132, 137–138, 149
  on use of *Volk* 136

INDEX

Greenberg, Clement 150
grievances 8, 44
Griffin, Roger 168n
in-group 43
The Group Mind (McDougall) 122
Group Psychology and the Analysis of the Ego (Freud) 40, 121–128, 177
Gruppenexperiment 218
Guterman, Norbert 26, 43, 45, 46–47

Habermas, Jürgen 72, 83–84, 111, 149, 156, 197n 205–206, 208–217
 on culture industry 225
 and disintegration thesis 222–223, 224
Haider, Jörg 19n
Hall, Stuart 52, 92, 99–100, 109–112, 128, 129, 162–167
 and crisis 137
 and Habermas 213
 on Laclau 134
 and media 'message' reception 153–154
 on national-popular 191
 on popular art 161–164
 on popular culture 111, 165–167
 and social formalism 133–134
 and Thatcherism 131
Halle, Randall 58n
Hallin, Daniel 209, 225n
handicraft publishers 211
Hanson, Pauline 195
hegemony 94, 95, 98, 104, 111, 167
 and Laclau 97, 100, 112, 126
Hegemony and Socialist Strategy (Laclau and Mouffe) 97, 120
Held, David 76
Hendershot, Heather 228n
Herder, Johann Gottfried 157
Herf, Jeffrey 147
Hermet, Guy 142n
high art 163

high culture 151, 159
historical bloc 94, 95, 98, 134
History and Class Consciousness (Lukács) 70
Hochschild, Arlie Russell 201
Hoffman, Abbie 187, 189–190, 191
Hofstadter, Richard 8, 9, 10, 11, 16, 26
Hoggart, Richard 154–155
homophobia 58n
Honneth, Axel 72–73, 77–78, 79
horizontality 206, 207
Horkheimer, Max 28–29, 55n, 56n, 71, 72, 79, 81, 89n, 90n, 169n, 170n, 231, 232
 on antisemitic demagogy 39
 and *Below the Surface* 177
 and ideal-typification 75–76
 on paranoia 40
Howe, Irving 61n, 150
humour 49, 202, 203
hyperformalism 109, 110, 111, 112, 120, 121, 126
 and Althusser 135
 definition 107
hysteria, disinhibited 45, 202, 203

ideal-typification 73, 75–76, 80, 105, 106, 159, 206
 and Adorno 77, 78, 82, 85
identification 123, 136, 137, 177, 189, 190, 191, 201
 ego-ideal 41, 42, 122, 124, 125
identificatory bond 122, 189, 201
ideological state apparatuses 99
ideology 34, 99, 102, 213
 dominant 104, 107
 organic 94, 98, 100, 135, 138
 in political scientific sense 132–133
 thin 6, 12, 145
 see also immanent (ideology) critique

immanent (ideology) critique 37,
    81–83, 134, 148, 160, 167, 208,
    210, 211, 226n, 227n
  and Adorno 37, 82–83, 148, 160
  and Goldmann 134
  and Habermas 83, 208, 210, 211,
    226n, 227n
  and Horkheimer 81
industrial capitalism 159
industrial working class 158
'insider/public' distinction 202
The Institute for Propaganda Analysis
    36, 175–177
The Institute for Social Research 25,
    119, 120, 128–129, 133, 134, 166,
    218
  and New York Intellectuals 16
institutional violence 187–188
instrumentalism 131, 133, 165
instrumentalization 5, 6, 34, 37, 166,
    190, 191, 219
  and Hall 111, 166
intellectual populism 146, 149, 157
internal frontier 120
interpellation 99–100, 101, 102, 116n,
    135
  popular-democratic 101, 102
  religious 100–101
interviewing, adversarial 194–195
intimacy, bourgeois 21, 210, 211,
    212
'Introduction to Prophets of Deceit'
    (Adorno) 25, 47–48, 68, 79, 80,
    231–243
Introduction to the Sociology of Music
    (Adorno) 69
Italy 95–96, 102, 145–146, 191
Ives, Peter 139n

Jacobinism 102
Jacobs, Jack 56n, 231

Jakobson, Roman 98, 106, 107, 116n
Jameson, Fredric 167
Jay, Martin 17, 39, 53n, 57n, 66,
    67- 68, 71, 139n, 150, 152
jazz 164
Jenemann, David 176
Jessop, Bob 99, 115n, 129–131, 134,
    137, 141n
journalism 110, 111, 118n, 134,
    209–210, 216–217, 219, 221

Kael, Pauline 178
Kant, Immanuel 39
Kazan, Elia 177, 178, 180, 181,
    182–183, 186, 196n, 201
Kazin, Michael 7–8, 9, 13, 200
Kellner, Douglas 204n
Ku Klux Klan 15, 43

Laclau, Ernesto 15, 92, 97–98,
    100–101, 102–103, 113, 114n,
    115n, 116n, 117n, 118n, 135–136,
    138, 139n, 140n
  and Caesarism 112
  compared with Adorno 120–122,
    124–126, 127–128
  on *Fascism and Dictatorship* 99, 132
  and formalist linguistics 133
  and Hall 109
  *Politics and Ideology in Marxist
    Theory* 110
  On Populist Reason 104, 105
  preconditions of populism 108
Laing, Dave 173n
Lambert, Kit 189
Lane, Melissa 31, 32, 33, 34
langue 100, 109, 135
Latin America 63
Lazarsfeld, Paul 218, 219
Le Bon, Gustave 40, 41, 51, 58n, 122,
    123, 125, 127, 132

INDEX

Le Pen, Jean-Marie 19n
leader–group bonding 48
leaders 30, 49, 122, 125, 136–137
leadership 126, 186–187, 189, 202
   charismatic 15, 31, 32, 112
Leavis, F.R. 163
Lee, Alfred 36–37, 38–39, 52–53, 56n, 176, 181
Lee, Elizabeth 36–37, 38–39, 52–53, 176, 181
left authoritarians 29, 186
left populism 9, 19, 119, 134, 203
left-wing protest movements 187
Legitimation Crisis (Habermas) 226n
Leninism 133
Lennon, John 190
letter-writing 210–211
Lévi-Strauss, Claude 98–99, 106
liberal exposure 33, 38–39, 176, 177
liberal-pluralists 159–160
liberal public sphere 224
Limbaugh, Rush 221
linguistics 98, 105, 106, 109, 133
literary public sphere 210, 211, 212, 213
Litvak, Joseph 196n, 197n
London coffee houses 210
The Lonely Crowd: A Study in the Changing American Character (Riesman, Glazer and Denney) 183
Long, Huey 8–9, 43, 84, 180, 181, 186, 206
loudspeakers 206
Lowenthal, Leo 26, 43, 44, 45, 46–47, 50, 56n, 57n, 59n, 61n, 65, 87n, 134-136, 150, 153, 155-156, 160, 167, 171n, 210
   on culture industry 53, 161–162
   on popular culture 153, 155–156
   and Seldes 160

   on social malaise 66–67
   and *Volksgemeinschaft* 136
Löwy, Michael 71
Lukács, György 70, 119
Lunn, Eugene 89n, 156–160, 167, 170n 171n

Macdonald, Dwight 150, 151
The Making of the English Working Class (Thompson) 155
mandarin optimists 159
manipulation 34–35, 104, 120, 133
Mann, Michael 86
manufactured public sphere 219
Márkus, György 57n
Marx, Karl 70, 94, 98, 101
Marx Brothers 161
Marxism and The Philosophy of Language (Vološinov) 109
mass art 164, 166
mass communication 166
mass culture 51, 66, 147, 152, 154, 155, 158, 172n
   and Hall 164
   and Shils 150–151, 153, 170n
Mass Culture (Rosenberg and White) 150
mass media 102, 103, 104, 120, 207
mass society 66, 133, 152, 166, 170n
Mazzoleni, Gianpietro 195
McCarthy, Joseph 7, 11, 12, 65, 79, 191–194, 218
McCarthyism 10, 65, 158, 180
McDougall, William 122, 123, 124
McGuigan, Jim 153, 154, 155, 159–160, 166, 170n, 171n, 172n
McLuhan, Marshall 189, 191
media 102, 103, 104, 110, 111, 133, 207, 208
   and Adorno 120
'message' reception 153

policy failure 222, 224
power 217
systems 220
see also broadcasting; social media
mediated populism 206, 219–220
mediated quasi-interaction 206
mediations 68, 69, 85
The Medium is the Massage (McLuhan) 189
medium theory 78
Medvedev, P.N. 109
Meet John Doe 180–181
Merleau-Ponty, Maurice 71
'message' reception 153
Metzger, Gustav 188, 198n
Michelet, Jules 157
middle class 28, 158
mobility of object of hatred 52, 60n, 176
mode of production 67, 94, 101, 104
Modernism 145–146, 147
modern populism 63, 64, 85, 205
monopoly capital 98, 102
monopoly capitalism 74, 101
'montage character' (of culture industry and demagogy) 50, 61n, 138, 189–190, 206, 207, 225
see also recombinant
moralism 10, 11, 13, 103
morality 72, 111, 112
Morris, Meaghan 199
Morris, William 157
Mosley, Oswald 33
motifs 146, 175, 185, 189, 201, 203
and Adorno 70, 80, 83, 136
and Lowenthal 66, 153
Mouffe, Chantal 97, 104–108, 119, 139n
'Movement City' 188
Mudde, Cas 5–7
Münsterberg, Hugo 48

Murdoch, Rupert 221
Murrow, Edward R. 191–194, 218
music 69, 148, 165, 186, 201
popular 50, 164, 166, 188–189, 218
music hall 163, 216
Mythologies (Barthes) 184–185
myths 98

narcissism 40, 42, 122, 126, 136, 189, 200
narodniks 96, 114n, 146
National Front 166
national-popular 95, 96, 112, 119, 132, 134, 191
German 149
as tradition 137–138
use of *Volk* 136
Nazism 28, 32, 33, 73, 77, 102, 147
and Neumann 74
and Poulantzas 131
and *Volksgemeinschaft* 136
Negative Dialectics (Adorno) 82
negative identification 136, 137
neoliberalism 129, 137, 220, 222, 223, 224–225
neopopulism 137
Neumann, Franz 74, 75–76, 129, 147
The New American Right 7, 9, 10
New Deal 46, 76–77, 186
New Left 93, 187
new media 208, 213
The Newsroom 194
New York Intellectuals 7, 11, 12, 28, 65, 150, 152, 207
and Institute for Social Research 16
and *Zeitschrift* 151
The New York Times 193, 200, 203
'normal pathology' thesis 6
nostalgia 201, 214–215
'Notes on Deconstructing the Popular' (Hall) 166

Notes Towards a Definition of Culture (Eliot) 154
novels 210, 211
nudging 222

'"Objectivity" in Social Science and Social Policy' (Weber) 73
Occupy 187
Offe, Claus 84–85, 91n
Ono, Yoko 190
operas 188–189
operationalization 5
opinion 217–219
ordinary culture 154
organic community 152, 163
organic crisis 95, 98, 101, 130, 137
organic ideology 94, 98, 100, 135, 138
organization of consent 94, 134
out-group 43

paramilitary activity 86
paranoia 11, 39, 40, 45, 52, 187, 203
parole 109
'part-interchangeability' 50, 190
party-centrism 5
pathological normalcy 6
patriarchal family 27, 28, 66
people-nation 132
Pericles 31
Peronism 63
pessimism 64, 71, 76, 83, 120
  and Habermas 208, 209, 213, 224
Peters, John Durham 172n
Peterson, Richard A. 188
petty bourgeoisie 98, 102
physiognomics 17, 78, 80, 206
physiognomy 77, 78–79, 80, 85, 231–232
plebeian public sphere 216

policy failure, media 222, 224
political capitalism 129–130, 137
political communication 15, 219, 220, 221
The Political Context of Sociology (Bramson) 152, 169n, 174n
'politically incorrect' masculine norms 201
political populism 138, 149, 153
political public sphere 210, 212, 213
Politics and Ideology in Marxist Theory (Laclau) 110
polling techniques 219
Pollock, Frederick 73–76, 77
popular art 147, 161, 163, 164, 165, 167, 172n, 186–191
  and Chaplin 162
  and Two-Tone Sound 166
The Popular Arts (Hall and Whannel) 165, 173n
popular culture 153, 155, 156, 160, 165–166, 167
popular-democratic interpellation 101, 102
'On the Popular Impact of Fascism' (Poulantzas) 131
popular morality 111
popular music 50, 164, 165, 166, 186, 188–189, 218
'On Popular Music' (Adorno and Simpson) 50, 218
popular songs 160, 182
'Populism: What's in a Name' (Laclau) 105
The Populist Persuasion: An American History (Kazin) 8, 197n
populist radical right 5, 6
On Populist Reason (Laclau) 104, 106, 112, 122
positive identification 137
post-structuralism 107

Poulantzas, Nicos 97, 98, 99, 100, 106, 119, 128–132, 134, 139n, 140n, 141n
  and social institutions 133
  and tradition 135
Powell, Enoch 33
power, demagogic 217
power bloc 98, 100, 101–102, 110, 130, 131, 166
the press 209, 212, 213, 214, 215, 216, 217
press baron 217
private reading societies 210
prodigy 41, 124, 125
production
  cultural 50, 75, 134, 146, 158, 162, 164, 211
  mode of 67, 94, 101, 104
profit 129–130
projection 16, 39, 40, 43, 44–45, 52, 203
proletariat 101–102
propaganda 33, 34, 36, 50, 52, 219, 224
  antidemocratic 30, 51
  and 'fake news' 223
  and Freud 122, 177
  and the Lees 36, 37, 39, 176
  and *Volksgemeinschaft* 136
Prophets of Deceit: A Study of the Techniques of the American Agitator (Lowenthal and Guterman) 16, 26, 36, 43, 44–45, 50, 59n, 79
  and Adorno 80
  and exposure strategy 177
  (Draft) Introduction to (Adorno) 25, 47–48, 68, 79, 80, 231–243
The Protestant Ethic and The Spirit of Capitalism (Weber) 71, 82
pseudo-conservatism 10, 16

pseudo-participation 14, 15
The Psychological Technique of Martin Luther Thomas' Radio Addresses (Adorno) 26, 36, 48, 55n, 56n, 58n, 59n, 60n, 139n, 175
psychic projection 40
psychoanalysis 35, 39, 40–41, 53
The Psychological Technique of Martin Luther Thomas' Radio Addresses (Adorno) 26, 36, 48, 56n, 57n, 175
The Public Arts (Seldes) 191
public relations 209, 212
public service broadcasting 220
public sphere 83, 207–213, 222–223, 224
  contradictory institutionalization of 213, 214, 215
  disintegration of 83, 84, 208–209, 212–213, 216, 222–223, 224
  literary 156, 158, 182, 210–213, 224
  manufactured 219
  plebeian 158, 216
  political 201, 210, 212, 213, 215, 216
public sphere thesis 72, 111, 156, 205–206, 214, 217, 220
  feminist critiques of 210–211
publishers 211
'pure type' 80

quasi-demagogic leadership 119

The Radical Right (Bell) 7, 11
the Radical Right project 7–16, 17, 62, 65, 158, 216
radical right/radical right-wing 5, 6, 7
radio 78, 80, 181, 185, 192, 220–221
  demagogues 9, 36, 37, 175, 190, 222
'Radio Physiognomics' (Adorno) 78

INDEX

radio physiognomy 78
rallies 48, 202
rationalization 71–72
Reading Capital (Althusser and Balibar) 99
reading societies 210
recombinant 133, 135, 185, 206
  see also 'montage character'
reality television 200
reductivism 97–98
refeudalization 212
reflective insight 71
reification 70–71, 83
religion 40, 43, 46, 136, 138
religious interpellation 100–101
'A Report on Senator Joseph R. McCarthy' (*See It Now*) 192
Riesman, David 28, 150, 172n, 183
right of reply 218
right-wing populism 5, 137
Robbins, Tim 185
rock operas 188–189
rock songs 201
Romantic avant-garde 156, 159
Romantic cultural populism 156, 167
Romanticism 146, 147, 151–152, 158
Romantic populism 157, 159
Romantic populists 156, 157
Rorty, Richard 139n
Rosenberg, Alfred 37, 147–148
Rosenberg, Bernard 150
Ross, Andrew 170n
Rubin, Jerry 187, 190

sado-masochism 28, 43, 125
salons (literary) 210
Sartori, Giovanni 4
Saussure, Ferdinand de 99, 105, 110, 127, 135–136
The Savage Mind (Lévi-Strauss) 98
Schary, Dore 177

'The Schema of Mass Culture' (Adorno) 172n
Schiller, Dan 223
Schmidt, James 74
Schmitt, Carl 213
Schulberg, Budd 177, 178, 180
See It Now 191, 192, 193
Seldes, Gilbert 159, 160, 161, 191
self-incrimination, demagogic 191, 194
Shahn, Ben 192
Shils, Edward 12, 13, 14, 16, 29, 103–104, 106, 153
  'Daydreams and Nightmares: Reflections on the Critique of Mass Culture' 150–151, 169n, 170n
  and folkloricism 146
  and intellectual populism 149
  on left authoritarians 186
  as mandarin optimist 159
  and mediated populism 206
  and 'sociological Romanticism' 152
Schudson, Michael 227n, 230n
signifiers 92, 99, 104, 105, 107, 135, 206
  and conceptual stretching 4
  and Laclau 108, 138
signifier/signified 109, 135–136, 184
Silicon Valley 223
Sinclair, John 188
Smith, Gerald L.K. 21n, 43, 47
social authority 28
social character typology 27–28
social formalism 109, 133–134
social formation 101, 102, 129
social logics 107–108, 125
social malaise 66
social media 206–207, 223, 224
social movements 213, 224
social reality 77, 78
social theory 68, 81, 110

INDEX

sociological poetics 109
sociological Romanticism 151, 152
songs 156, 160, 182, 201
Sorkin, Aaron 194
soul music 186
space ubiquity 78, 206, 222
The Specials 166
Springer Press 186
State, Power, Socialism (Poulantzas) 128–132
state capitalism thesis 73–76, 77, 120, 128, 129, 134
statesman 31, 32, 33, 34, 35, 39, 40
status politics 10, 11
Stead, W.T. 215
Stewart, Jon 193
Structural Anthropology (Lévi-Strauss) 98–99
structuralism 98, 99, 107, 110, 134
structural transformation 209–213
The Structural Transformation of the Public Sphere (Habermas) 149, 208–209, 211, 212, 216, 220
  and Adorno 83, 214–215, 219
structural transformation thesis 206, 207
student movements 186–187
Studien über Autorität und Familie 26–27, 28
Studies in Prejudice 16, 17, 25, 26, 29, 36, 37, 65–66
  and *Below the Surface* 175–177
  and four protocols 81
  and Lunn 158
Sunstein, Cass 221–222
Symonds, Michael 90n
synthetic personality 182, 201

tabloid journalism 216, 217, 219–220, 221, 227n

talk radio 220–221
Tea Party 194, 201
Thaler, Richard 222
Thatcher, Margaret 110–111, 131
Thatcherism 109, 128, 166, 220
The Theory of Communicative Action (Habermas) 83
'Theses on the Sociology of Art' (Adorno) 165
'thin ideology' 6, 12, 145
Thompson, E.P. 155
Thompson, John B. 206
time coincidence 78, 206, 222
The Times 214, 215, 216
Tommy 188–189, 190
The Torment of Secrecy (Shils) 12
totalitarianism 149, 152
Townshend, Pete 188, 189, 190–191
tradition
  and Adorno 167
  and Laclau 135, 136
  and national-popular 137
transformism 102
'Transparencies on Film' (Adorno) 161–162
Truffaut, François 175, 184, 185
Trump, Donald 185, 200–203, 206
Trump presidency 63
'truth propaganda' 33, 34, 39, 176, 195, 201
Tufekci, Zeynep 224
Twitter 200, 202, 206
Two-Tone Sound 166

UK
  cultural populism 157–158
  and public service broadcasting 220
  see also Britain
Urbinati, Nadia 6, 21n, 30–31, 33, 62–64, 85, 112, 113, 215

INDEX

USA
  civil rights and student movements 186
  communications policy laxity 223–224
  and culture industry 207
  and development of 'modern demagogy' 205
  and Fairness Doctrine 220, 221–222
  and intellectual Romantic populism 157
  and journalism 216–217
  and mass culture 155, 158
  and populism 6–12, 13–14, 46–47, 63–64
The Uses of Literacy (Hoggart) 154–155

'vaccine' metaphor 71, 79, 176, 177
vanity 200
van Reijen, Willem 74
verticality 206, 207
violence 47, 187–188, 235
Volk 136, 148, 156, 157, 159, 172n
völkisch demagogy 167, 203
Volksgemeinschaft 136, 147, 148, 203
Volkskunst 147, 172n
  see also popular art
Volkslied 148
Vološinov, Valentin 109, 127
voting studies 219

Wagner, Richard 147
Wall Street Journal 221
On the Waterfront 177, 180, 184
Weber, Max 13–14, 31–32, 71–72, 73, 75, 80, 206
  and demagogy 13–14, 31–33, 35, 80, 189, 205

and ideal-typification 76, 77, 82–83
  see also charisma, charismatic authority, charismatic leadership
'Weberian Marxism' 71
Weltschmerz 66
'We're Not Gonna Take It' 189, 190
Whitman, Walt 157
The Who 188–189, 190
Williams, Raymond 109, 118n, 127, 133, 140n, 154, 155, 156, 158, 173n, 198n
  and Frankfurt School 171n
  and hegemony 167
Wodak, Ruth 86n
'Won't Get Fooled Again' 188, 190
Woodstock Music and Arts Festival 187, 188, 190
Woodstock Nation: A Talk-Rock Album 188, 189, 190
Wordsworth, William 146
working class 154–155, 157, 158
Worsley, Peter 3–4, 12, 14–15, 104–106, 122, 206
writers' room scene
  first still, *A Face in the Crowd* 183
  second still, *A Face in the Crowd* 184

Yippie figures 187–188, 190
'Your Arkansas Traveller' (Schulberg) 178, 196n

Zeitschrift, special issue, 1941 151, 183
zero-sum game 111
Žižek, Slavoj 112–113
Zuidevaart, Lambert 160

EU authorised representative for GPSR:
Easy Access System Europe, Mustamäe tee 50,
10621 Tallinn, Estonia
gpsr.requests@easproject.com

www.ingramcontent.com/pod-product-compliance
Lightning Source LLC
Chambersburg PA
CBHW071404300426
44114CB00016B/2173